Ronald Taylor is Professor of German at the University of Sussex. He has been Visiting Professor at the University of Chicago, at Northwestern University and at the University of British Columbia, and has lectured widely on literary and musical topics at universities in Britain, Germany, the United States and Canada. Among his other books are *The Romantic Tradition in Germany*, *The Art of the Minnesinger* and *Robert Schumann: His Life and Work*. He has contributed articles on music to various cultural journals, is a well-known translator of German literature, and has played piano music on BBC and German radio.

By the same author

E. T. A. Hoffmann
The Art of the Minnesinger
The Romantic Tradition in Germany
The Intellectual Tradition of Modern Germany
Literature and Society in Germany 1918–1945
Robert Schumann: His Life and Work

RONALD TAYLOR

Richard Wagner

His Life, Art and Thought

PANTHER
Granada Publishing

Panther Books
Granada Publishing Ltd
8 Grafton Street, London W1X 3LA

Published by Panther Books 1983

First published in Great Britain by
Paul Elek Ltd 1979

Copyright © Ronald Taylor 1979

ISBN 0-586-06061-8

Printed and bound in Great Britain by
Collins, Glasgow

Set in Times

For Brigitte

Contents

Illustrations

Acknowledgements

Passages from copyright sources are reprinted in the Postscript by permission as follows:

Eduard Hanslick, 'Richard Wagner's Stage Festival in Bayreuth' (1876), taken from Eduard Hanslick, *Vienna's Golden Years of Music 1850-1900*, trans. Henry Pleasants III, Copyright © 1950 by Henry Pleasants III; reprinted by permission of Simon & Schuster, a Division of Gulf & Western Corporation, and by John Farquharson Ltd.

Leo Tolstoy, 'What Is Art?' (1898), taken from Leo Tolstoy, *What Is Art? and Essays on Art*, trans. Aylmer Maude (World's Classics edition, 1930); by permission of Oxford University Press.

George Bernard Shaw, 'Preliminary Encouragements' from *The Perfect Wagnerite* (1898); by permission of The Society of Authors on behalf of the Bernard Shaw Estate.

Romain Rolland, 'Wagner: A Note on *Siegfried* and *Tristan*', taken from Romain Rolland, *Essays on Music*, ed. D. Ewen (1959); by permission of Dover Publications, Inc.

Ernest Newman, *Wagner as Man and Artist* (1914); by permission of J.M. Dent & Sons Ltd and Alfred A. Knopf, Inc.

Thomas Mann, 'Sufferings and Greatness of Richard Wagner' (1933), taken from Thomas Mann, *Essays of Three Decades*, trans. H. T. Lowe-Porter; by permission of Martin Secker & Warburg Ltd and Alfred A. Knopf, Inc. Copyright 1933 by Alfred A. Knopf, Inc.

Virgil Thomson, 'Dissent from Wagner', first published in the *New York Herald Tribune*, 7 March 1943; by permission of the author.

Bruno Walter, _Theme and Variations_ (1947); by permission of Alfred A. Knopf, Inc.

Igor Stravinsky, 'Wagner's Prose' (1965), taken from Igor Stravinsky and Robert Craft, _Themes and Episodes_; by permission of Alfred A. Knopf, Inc. and of Faber & Faber Ltd (who publish under the title _Themes and Conclusions_).

Igor Stravinsky, _Poetics of Music_ (1947); by permission of Harvard University Press. Copyright © 1942, 1947, 1970 by the President and Fellows of Harvard College; renewed 1970, 1975 by the President and Fellows of Harvard College.

Theodor W. Adorno, _Versuch über Wagner_ (1952), Copyright © 1952 Theodor W. Adorno; by permission of Suhrkamp Verlag.

Pierre Boulez, Preface to _Wagner – A Documentary Study_, compiled and edited by Herbert Barth, Dietrich Mack and Egon Voss (1975), © 1975 Universal Edition AG, Vienna, English translation © 1975 Thames & Hudson Ltd, London; by permission of Universal Edition A.G., Thames & Hudson Ltd, and Oxford University Press, New York.

Preface

To write a book on Wagner – trying to turn a deaf ear to the muttered incredulity of '*Another* book on Wagner?' – means giving even more than the usual thought to deciding whom one is writing for, and therefore what to leave out. When a life is so agitated, so fascinatingly bound up with the events of his time as was Wagner's; when the literary *oeuvre* that faces us ranges from philosophical and political essays to studies in the history, theory and practice of music; and when the works of art before us are among the most magnificent, most defiant achievements in the whole of Western culture, works which polarized opinion in their day and have done so ever since: then the burden, and with it the frustration, of choice becomes overwhelming.

So let me say at once that the modest aim of this book has been to offer a modern, integrated account of Wagner's life and work for the benefit of those interested to read about the personality, the career and the intellectual and spiritual development of the composer of the Overture to *Tannhäuser*, the Prelude to *Tristan und Isolde*, the Prize Song from *Die Meistersinger* or whatever individual piece of music may have captured their imagination.

The restless existence that Wagner led from his schooldays to the end of his life, his love affairs, his revolutionary activity, his pursuit of luxury, his perpetual debts, the famous men and women around him, the building of his personal temple, the Festival Theatre in Bayreuth: all this is the stuff of entertaining biography. It is fully documented in scholarly standard works, in many cases with a wealth of detail on Wagner the man that only the

devotee and the scholar will need. There are also countless detailed studies of Wagner the artist – investigations
into the structure and meaning of his operas, his dramatic
libretti, his musical language, Wagner and mythology,
Wagner and German nationalism, the productions and
personalities of the Bayreuth Festival over the past hundred years, and scores of other specific topics. At the
other extreme, brief studies of both Wagner's life and
work are readily available.

The present book has been written for the reader in the
middle ground between these two extremes. There is
plenty of dispute over what we are pleased to call the
'facts' of Wagner's life, and still more over their interpretation; further documentary evidence – letters, contemporary memoirs – may well still come to light. We cannot
even say for certain who his father was. Nor, it seems,
could Wagner himself. With a figure who achieved so
much, who said and wrote so much, who aroused, and
arouses, so much passionate devotion and so much violent
hostility, the presentation of some form of considered
'image' is unavoidable, indeed obligatory. My emphases
may not lie where some would wish to see them lie, nor
will my interpretations of Wagner's thought and music
satisfy everyone, but at no time have I sought to cross
swords with those who may believe otherwise. The reader
who wishes to see how varied the approaches to, and
judgements on, Wagner can be, has no shortage of
sources to turn to. The Bibliography at the end of the
book offers a selection of such works.

In the pages that follow, the life of Wagner the man, the
views of Wagner the thinker and the achievements of
Wagner the artist stand in the centre of the scene. I offer
no plot summaries, on the one hand, and no detailed
investigations into sources, no analyses, work by work, of
musical vocabulary and form, on the other. At the same
time the historical and cultural pressures of the age, the

day-to-day conditions in which, and against which, Wagner had to make his way, are inseparable from the biographical story and cannot but form part of any analytical narrative. Wagner was no remote, unworldly artist. He struck uncompromising attitudes towards the political and social events of his time, and without knowing something of the Revolution of 1848, of the developments that culminated in the political unification of Germany in 1871, of the problem of European Jewry and other issues that challenged the Germans in the nineteenth century, one would miss a complete dimension of his activity. Similarly, I have sought in my discussions of the individual operas, and especially of the intellectual impulses that inform their texts, to draw the underlying concepts into the broader context of nineteenth-century German art and thought.

The principal sources from which the story has been drawn are described in chapter-by-chapter bibliographical summaries at the end of the book. The emphasis lies on primary documents – Wagner's own autobiographical writings and letters, the testimony of friends and relatives such as his first wife Minna, Liszt, his second wife Cosima (Liszt's daughter), King Ludwig II of Bavaria and the philosopher Friedrich Nietzsche, together with contemporary accounts of the man and his music. The most recently published such source (1976-7) is the complete diary which Cosima Wagner kept from 1869 until her husband's death in 1883. If I can claim any advantage over earlier writers, apart from the privilege of being able to profit from their work, it is perhaps the availability of this remarkable material.

Contention surrounded Wagner's music at the time and still surrounds it today. But gladly as I would have given way to it, I have resisted the temptation to analyse at length the anatomy of this contentiousness. To do so would have meant writing another book, a very different one from this. However, for those who may be interested to look more closely into the nature of the argument, I have assembled in a Postscript a number of passages from the writings of prominent thinkers in order to show how the intellectual battle-lines are drawn.

I am greatly indebted to The British Academy for its support of my research. My thanks are due to Mrs Rosemarie Ash for her help with the typing of the book, while to my wife, who not only typed much of the manuscript but also made many salutary criticisms of it, I owe a special debt of gratitude. Among the many who generously made information and material available to me I should like to mention in particular my friend and former colleague Professor P. L. Jaeger of Cologne, and the late Mr Henry Reynold of Brighton, who was one of the most knowledgeable Wagnerians of my acquaintance. A warm thank-you also to Mr Antony Wood of Elek, who invited me to write the book and whose keen scrutiny of my successive drafts was of immense help to me.

My old friend Mr Kenneth Pearson, of the British Council, did me the great service of reading the proofs and making valuable comments on matters of presentation.

Learning that I was at work on this book, friends and colleagues too numerous to mention have at one time or another given me the benefit of their knowledge and opinions on Wagner the man and Wagner the artist. Perhaps they will recognize here and there their contributions to my argument. To all of them my sincerest thanks.

R. T.

CHAPTER ONE
Child, Schoolboy and Student

The lives of the world's great artists and thinkers are
sometimes fascinating, sometimes boring, sometimes vital
to their work, sometimes seemingly irrelevant to it. If, for
one reason or another, an artist's life seems outwardly
uneventful, and if his biography consists largely of a
domestic diary, a catalogue of his employers and patrons,
and a chronicle of his works, we accept the situation and
receive his art almost in a vacuum, as it were – something
self-sufficient and absolute. The music of Bach, for example. By the same token, when we see how inseparable
from personal vicissitudes, as from contemporary social,
intellectual and spiritual pressures, is the work of a
Wordsworth, a Victor Hugo, a Delacroix, a Liszt, we
know that an understanding of this work requires involvement on our part with the circumstances that attended its
birth. The more agitated the artist's personal and historical circumstances, the more deeply will they penetrate the
fabric of his art, and the greater the insight we, as
interpreters of that art, need to acquire into them.

Wagner forces us both to enter his personal world and
to follow his involvement in the historical and cultural
events of his age. He made these demands on his contemporaries. But the demands made by his art are even
greater – immeasurably greater than those of any earlier
composer, even Beethoven, and still far greater than
those of most composers since. What these demands are,
why he made them, why the musical world continues to
argue over their plausibility and their propriety: such are
the issues that directly confront us as we contemplate this
most controversial and disturbing of musical geniuses.

* * *

'My name is Wilhelm Richard Wagner, and I was born in Leipzig on 22 May, 1813. My father was a registrar in the police department; he died six months after I was born.' With these words Wagner introduced himself to the world in his *Autobiographical Sketch* of 1843.

Leipzig, second largest town in the Protestant Kingdom of Saxony, then had a population of 33,000. From the Middle Ages it had been an important trading centre. The markets at Easter and Michaelmas quickly grew into the large-scale trade fairs whose tradition has survived war and political upheaval right down to the present day, as have certain specialized industries such as the manufacture of railway locomotives, scientific and musical instruments (Blüthner pianos are still made there), and above all the trades of bookselling and publishing, including music (Breitkopf and Härtel, Peters, Eulenburg). Luther's famous disputation with Eck in 1519 over the supremacy of the Pope took place here. Johann Sebastian Bach was appointed Cantor at the Thomasschule in 1723 and spent the rest of his life in the town. And for the first half of the eighteenth century, largely through the prestige of its rich university, it could lay fair claim to being the intellectual capital of Germany. Goethe had grown up in a well-to-do family in Frankfurt, a larger and more prosperous town, but when he arrived in Leipzig in 1765 as a sixteen-year-old student, he found that his new clothes were out of fashion, that the traces of dialect in his speech attracted unwelcome attention, and that his social graces left a lot to be desired. Not for nothing had this Saxon metropolis acquired the name 'Little Paris'.

The Leipzig into which Wagner was born, however, was concerned with other matters than 'Little Parisian' culture and elegance. In the spring of that year, 1813, Napoleon, with fresh troops levied in France after the disaster of his Russian campaign the previous year, was again advancing towards the Elbe, planning to use Saxony as a base for the recapture of Berlin and the reconquest of Prussia. Soldiers were everywhere, baggage trains and artillery columns streamed along the main roads, while civilian life tried to salvage as much of its normal activities and values as it could.

E. T. A. Hoffmann, author of the famous Tales, was in Dresden, the Saxon capital, at this time:

On the 3rd of May enormous Russian baggage trains were crossing the Elbe bridge all day and all night. On the 7th the Chancellor and the Counsellors of State left the city. From three o'clock in the morning on the 8th the artillery began to rumble through; at ten the King of Prussia rode through the city; by eleven the wooden parts of the bridge over the river were ablaze, together with the jetties and the barges, which floated downstream as they burned. The roar of the cannons shattered the windows of the houses by the riverside. At a quarter past eleven a French bugler and a French lancer rode through the streets, followed by cavalry and infantry, and at five o'clock, as all the bells in the city pealed out, His Majesty the Emperor Napoleon arrived, attended by an immense retinue of guards, officials and servants, and was welcomed by numerous delegations.

By October the fighting was centred on Leipzig and its environs. Here, during the three-day 'Battle of the Nations', Napoleon's vassal, the King of Saxony, was taken prisoner, his troops deserted to the enemy, and the Emperor himself was forced to retreat westwards with the remnants of his army until he was across the Rhine. The German War of Liberation was over. Less than six months later the Allied forces marched into Paris; Napoleon abdicated and was deported to Elba, and the First Empire was at an end.

The siege of Leipzig had left a legacy of appalling misery, above all in the form of a typhoid epidemic carried by the polluted waters of the Elbe, into which the bodies of countless soldiers and horses had been thrown. The French historian Thiers painted a grim picture of the town: 'The lack of sanitation, the overcrowding, the exhaustion, the shortage of food, the almost continuous rain of the last two months – all this had made people profoundly depressed, affecting in particular the sick and the wounded.'

To bring up a large family in such difficult and dangerous conditions was the exhausting task that fell to Wagner's father and mother. Nine children were born to them during the fifteen years of their marriage. The second, a boy, had died eleven years earlier, little more than a year old, but the other seven – two boys and five girls, aged between two and fourteen – were there when their new brother was born, and looked with curiosity at the little creature who was to make the family name famous.

The *paterfamilias* was Carl Friedrich Wagner, forty-three years old when Richard was born. He came of a Protestant family of Leipzig schoolmasters but was already settled as registrar in the law courts when he married Johanne Rosine Pätz, daughter of a master baker from Weissenfels, a small town some twelve miles from Leipzig. He was twenty-eight, his bride twenty-four. At the time of Richard's birth the family lived on the second floor of a four-storey house on the street Am Brühl, then, as now, the centre of the fur trade in Leipzig (the original house was pulled down in 1886).

By all accounts Friedrich Wagner sounds to have been a lively and entertaining character, an educated man with an over-riding passion for the theatre. This passion showed itself in various extrovert ways. His four daughters, for example, he christened after heroines from Goethe and Schiller – Rosalie (from Goethe's *Wilhelm Meister*), Luise (from Schiller's *Kabale und Liebe*), Klara (from Goethe's *Egmont*) and Ottilie (from Goethe's *Die Wahlverwandtschaften*). He had a great gift for mimicking contemporary actors, as E. T. A. Hoffmann recorded in his diary: 'Evening in the "Grüne Linde". Registrar

Wagner, an exotic fellow, taking off Opitz, Iffland and others – very skilfully, too. He seems to belong to the better school; *un poco exaltato* after imbibing a good deal of rum.'

Nor, it seems, did Friedrich Wagner's interest in the theatre stop at the dramas themselves. In his autobiography *Mein Leben (My Life)*, Richard Wagner makes rather sniggering reference to his father's predilection for the company of local actresses. His visits to a particular lady made him repeatedly late for lunch, and when he finally did arrive, it was with the not unfamiliar excuse that he had been kept late at the office. To prove his point he would wave his ink-stained fingers at the assembled family. 'On closer examination, however', wrote his tactless son later, apparently on the basis of what his older sisters told him, 'his fingers were found to be perfectly clean.'

But young Richard was never to know his father. In the late summer of 1813, with the epidemic at its height, Friedrich Wagner fell a victim to the typhoid infection. In November he died. Richard was just six months old.

As *Polizeiaktuarius* in Leipzig, Friedrich Wagner had earned an annual salary of 1,045 thalers*, which seems to have allowed him and his family a comfortable life. But his death left the family totally unprotected. All that his widow and her children were entitled to, as his legal heirs, was a single payment of 260 thalers for the quarter in which he had died. Not even Albert, at fourteen the eldest

---

* It is impossible to convert this figure into a realistic modern equivalent. For purposes of comparison we may observe that 800 thalers was considered a good salary for a civil servant; a sizeable family apartment could be rented for 12 thalers per month, and two furnished rooms for 4 thalers per month. Schiller said that a single man of his class could live in Jena on 270 thalers a month, and in Dresden on 400 thalers a month. 1 thaler=3 marks; 1 guilder=2 marks. In the values of the 1930s, 1 Reichsmark=1 English shilling.

son, was of an age to contribute much to the family budget.

The woman whose lot it was to try and cope with the situation does not, fortunately, seem to have been the worrying kind. Johanne Wagner was now thirty-nine, 'an odd mixture' as her son Richard later wrote, 'of hardworking housewife and keen listener to new ideas, although the fundamentals of a respectable education were totally lacking'. She became strangely embarrassed, he recalls, when talking of her background, even going so far as to confuse the children over her maiden name. She had no intellectual or social pretensions, yet she had been sent to an exclusive private boarding-school in Leipzig at the expense of a nobleman from the court of Weimar, a man she demurely described to her apparently sceptical son as 'an aristocratic fatherly friend'. The nobleman in question was Prince Friedrich Ferdinand Konstantin, younger brother of Karl August of Weimar, who seduced Johanne while she was a young girl, then made the conscience-prompted gesture of paying for her to be educated in circumstances above her station. Prince Konstantin's death a few years later put a sudden end to this, which may explain the remarkably patchy school knowledge which she is said to have had.

Be this as it may, Wagner's childhood memories of his mother convey a picture, not so much of a close personal understanding and tenderness as of a harassed, not overly affectionate woman, doing her dutiful best to raise a large family under difficult circumstances. 'I can scarcely remember that she ever caressed me,' said Wagner; 'in fact, there were never any displays of tenderness and affection in our family.' Her saving grace was her good humour and her dry wit, and her strong religious nature helped to give the children's upbringing a sense of direction and moral purpose, though few of these or any other of her characteristics found their way to her youngest child. Mrs Mary

Burrell, that redoutable lady of leisure whose pioneering research into the details of Wagner's early life is an adventure story in its own right, concluded as early as 1898: 'Richard seems to have resembled his mother in nothing but her small size and electric disposition.'

Indeed, she appears to have been quite remarkably small – 'a tiny, eccentric woman so diminutive, an eyewitness has told me,' says Mrs Burrell, 'that when she visited her daughter-in-law [Minna, Wagner's first wife] in 1845 at Dresden, the maid took her on her arm like a baby and ran up the stairs with her.' A portrait painted in the year her husband died shows a plain, fresh-complexioned, buxom, rather sensual-looking woman – a portrait ungenerously described by Wagner as 'flattering'. The artist was one Ludwig Geyer.

This colourful character, half actor, half society painter, played an important role in the childhood of Richard Wagner. Eight years younger than Friedrich Wagner, Geyer had come to know the Wagner family while he was a student at the University of Leipzig. For some years he supported himself by painting portraits to commission, portraits praised for their remarkable fidelity to the subject, with a judicious trace of subtly applied idealism.

In the early 1800s he discovered a talent for acting and worked in a series of touring companies, returning eventually to Leipzig in 1809 and living as a lodger in the Wagner home whenever his troupe was in town. He had a vivacious and affectionate nature and was generous to a fault, but his constitution was not strong, and the life of an itinerant actor had taken its toll of his health. He was slight of stature and his voice had no heroic ring, but his culture and his intelligence made him an admirable player of character roles. When his fellow-actors were relaxing, he, more often than not, was busy at work on a portrait, and now the death of his friend Friedrich Wagner added to the burden on his mind.

Geyer had become very attached to the Wagner family, in particular to Johanne. A month after her husband's death he wrote from Dresden, where his troupe was playing, offering to help her in her unhappy financial situation. As time went on, the tone of his letters became more and more openly affectionate. Even while his father was still alive, Wagner tells us, Geyer would come to the house and 'take over the father's role', as he somewhat suggestively puts it, while the titular head of the family dallied with his actress friends after the evening performance.

So it surprised no one – though it displeased some of the Wagner relatives – when in August 1814, nine months after the death of her first husband, Johanne Wagner married Ludwig Geyer in the little village of Pötewitz, some twenty miles from her birthplace. Six months later, in February 1815, she bore him a daughter, Cäcilie. Geyer now had the responsibility of providing not only for the seven Wagner children (a daughter, Maria Theresa, had since died, at the age of four) but also for the new baby of his own.

In *Mein Leben* Wagner calls Geyer his stepfather, but an exchange of letters with his half-sister Cäcilie many years later shows him still not certain about the nature of the association between his mother and Geyer while Friedrich Wagner was still alive. In 1878 he remarked to his second wife, Cosima, on the resemblance between their son Siegfried and Geyer. 'Geyer must have been your father,' said Cosima. 'I don't think so,' replied Wagner. 'But what about the resemblance?' 'My mother loved him at that time,' Wagner answered, jocularly yet evasively: 'elective affinities.'

Friedrich Nietzsche, on the other hand, whose later love-hate relationship with Wagner gives his utterances an irresistible penetration but also, at times, a vicious perversity, pronounced bluntly: 'Wagner's father was an actor called Geyer.' Psychoanalytical interpreters of Wagner's operas have since joined the fray, armed with the discovery that throughout his operas there runs the problem of identity, the problem of knowing who one really is – as in the first scene of *Siegfried* where the increasingly impatient hero keeps demanding from Mime an answer to the question that plagues him: 'Who were my father and mother?'

Nor do the implications of the matter end here. The name Geyer means 'vulture' and has Jewish associations; the name Adler, which means 'eagle', is confined almost exclusively to families of German-Jewish origin. In the passage where he makes his deliberately offensive assertion of Wagner's illegitimacy, Nietzsche adds, in a particularly nasty tone, playing on the two bird-names: 'A "Geyer" is all but an "Adler"' – thus insinuating that Wagner, who later made no secret of his anti-Semitism, had himself been half-Jewish. The fact that a vulture forms part of the crest which dominated the title page of the original private edition of Wagner's *Mein Leben* – the edition prepared for publication by Nietzsche – also comes into the argument.

This farrago of innuendos and half-truths still holds the fascinated attention of many who have come to the opinion that Wagner was somehow not *simpatico*, not, in spite of his immense genius – or perhaps because of it – a very nice or very good man. For reasons that range from the personal to the philosophical, from the social to the aesthetic, he arouses, and always will arouse, suspicion, resentment, opposition, sometimes outright antagonism, so that there is a continual, often subconscious temptation to give credence to any report that casts a slur on his character or suggests something not quite proper about his ambience. This may make for interesting psychology, but it contributes nothing to the real historical picture of Wagner's origins and upbringing.

So for the record let us observe that there is not a single Jew to be found among Geyer's ancestors; that the surviving portraits, far from showing a resemblance to Geyer, place Richard firmly in the lineage of the Wagners and thus stultify the physiognomical pseudo-evidence that his nose, in particular, 'looks Jewish'; that, whatever her relationship to Geyer, Johanne Wagner lived with her husband right up to his death, so that Geyer is no more likely to have brought Richard into the world than his legal father; and that Nietzsche's attacks, on which many of the subsequent onslaughts against Wagner have been modelled, are often the hysterical outbursts of a mind seized by an uncontrollable hatred. That until the age of fourteen or so, both at school and among his friends, he was known as Richard Geyer, not Richard Wagner, only reflects a convention as familiar then as it is now. From 1814 on, after all, legal responsibility for the whole Wagner family, which moved to Dresden after Johanne's re-marriage, lay with the new stepfather, and only after their return to Leipzig many years after Geyer's death did Richard revert to his original family name.

If Ludwig Geyer cannot be proven to have been Richard Wagner's father, nor, with absolute certainty, can Friedrich Wagner. What seems like the evasiveness, or at least the uncertainty, on Wagner's own part when the subject was broached during his lifetime, has itself spawned enthusiastic genealogical, phrenological, graphological and other researches, and provoked equally enthusiastic dealings in assumption, speculation and hearsay by hucksters of various persuasions. Johanne survived her second husband by over twenty-five years, but nobody learned her secret – if, indeed, there was a secret to learn. Unpublished letters by the players in the piece are still coming to light, and the last word has certainly not yet been spoken.

After his wedding in August 1814 Geyer took his new

wife and five of her children to Dresden, where his theatrical troupe was now based. Spirits were at a low ebb in the Saxon capital, and public entertainers like actors and musicians felt especially keenly the general apathy and depression. Their activities carried no special privileges, and they shared the social status of valets, grooms, gardeners and other servants of the court. However, Geyer seems to have been able to provide adequately for his newly-acquired family, as well as for his own little daughter; his painting proved a valuable supplement to his actor's salary, and he was also gaining a reputation as a writer of comedies.

Wagner was very fond of his stepfather, as indeed, were all the Wagner children, and 'Uncle Ludwig' had been virtually a member of the family for as long as they could remember. But he seems to have been especially anxious that little Richard should make something of his life. At first he thought in terms of his own artistic skills – painting and acting. As far as the former went, Richard showed no talent – indeed, never in his life did he respond eagerly to the visual arts. Characteristically, seeing the large oil portraits, in various stages of completion, standing in Geyer's studio, the boy picked up the brush and began to make bold strokes on the same scale, quickly losing interest when he was told to stop playing about and turn his mind first to drawing details, like eyes. Wagner always learned in his own way and would never submit to the 'proper' way of doing things. Even the techniques of musical composition he acquired largely on his own, and only one man – Theodor Weinlig, cantor of the Thomasschule in Leipzig – ever succeeded in giving him any formal musical instruction.

As to acting, the same independence characterized his one recorded appearance on the stage in a speaking role. The play was Schiller's *Wilhelm Tell*, and the seven-year-old Richard had the part of Tell's younger son,

Wilhelm; the elder son, Walther, was played by Richard's sister Klara, with Geyer as Gessler, the villain of the piece.

At the end of the first scene of Act Three, Tell, setting out for Altdorf, says goodbye to his wife and takes Walther with him. But little Wilhelm runs to his mother and cries: 'I'll stay with you, mother!' This is his only line in the play and the Wagner family saw no reason why their Benjamin should not cope with it. But when this point was reached on the evening of the performance, and Klara, as Walther, began to leave the stage with Tell, Richard panicked. 'If you're going, Klara', he shouted, 'I'm coming too!' And off he ran behind her. 'At least,' commented Geyer, half-irritated, half-amused, 'he has a gift for improvization.'

Richard was a small child, excitable and highly-strung, with striking blue eyes which were to enchant many, especially women, in the course of his life, but with a disproportionately large head set awkwardly on his shoulders. The ailments that plagued him throughout his life, in particular erysipelas and various internal disorders, may well have their origin in his weak health in childhood. 'After one illness,' he later wrote, 'I was so feeble that it seemed unlikely I would recover, and my mother told me that she almost wished I would die.'

Nor did he betray any signs of exceptional intellectual or artistic talent. Of his earliest school years we have no record, but he showed no gift for drawing or painting, as we have seen, and all he could do on the piano at the age of eight was play nursery rhymes and folk-songs. Mozart had composed his first pieces at the age of five and was giving piano recitals at six; Mendelssohn started playing in public at nine and had written many works before he was thirteen; Beethoven published his first piece at the age of twelve and was a continuo player and court organist at fourteen; Liszt gave his first recital when he was nine and stunned Vienna and Paris as an infant prodigy. Wagner, by contrast, was the most unprodigious of children, a sensitive, unpredictable, self-willed, sometimes rebellious boy whose abilities one could not identify and in whose future one saw little ground for optimism. 'How little talent Wagner had!' exclaimed Nietzsche years later, with his eye on *Rienzi*. 'Was ever a musician still so deficient at twenty-eight?'

The family was dominated by the theatre, and this formed something of a bond between the children. The eldest boy, Albert, was to become an operatic tenor and later a theatrical director, while the two eldest girls, Rosalie and Luise, both became actresses; like Ottilie, the youngest girl, Luise later married into the Brockhaus family, the well-known Leipzig publishers. Klara, the next in line, also went into opera. They were a harmonious family, and Richard kept his affection for them right through his life, though in many ways he was even closer to his stepsister Cäcilie, his constant playmate in these childhood years.

The assurance and contentment which the devotion of Ludwig Geyer brought to Johanne Wagner and her family were short-lived. Geyer contracted tuberculosis. He became subject to fits of asthma and fell into moods of deep depression. The tensions of his dual career and the demands of a large family bore heavily on him, and in September 1821, having become progressively weaker over the last six months, he died.

As Geyer lay on his death-bed, the eight-year-old Richard was called to perform for him on the piano in the adjoining room. Listening to the little popular tune the boy played, Geyer said to Johanne in a weak voice: 'Perhaps he might have a gift for music.' It hardly amounted to a vote of confidence. Johanne, still only forty-seven, was a widow for the second time, and Richard was fatherless again.

Mrs Burrell summed up his life to this moment with characteristic bluntness: 'For the seven years that Ludwig Geyer was his stepfather, Richard was looked after. Now began the knocking about that lasted for the rest of his life.' Johanne Wagner had shown an increasing dislike of the stage as a career. It had brought her nothing but irritation and suffering, and she was determined that Richard should not fall victim to the same lures. 'Something should be made of him', Geyer had said. Which meant first giving him a decent education.

Four months after his stepfather died came the earliest of Wagner's lasting musical impressions – a performance in Dresden of Weber's opera *Der Freischütz*. Carl Maria von Weber had been appointed director of the Court Opera in Dresden in 1817, with the formidable task of breaking the monopoly of Italian taste and establishing a national German opera. Seven years later, only thirty-nine years old, he died, but *Der Freischütz, Euryanthe* and *Oberon* are landmarks in the German tradition that culminates in Wagner, and it was a happy gesture of providence which brought Wagner back to Dresden in 1843 to stand on Weber's rostrum as *Hofkapellmeister* to the King of Saxony.

Richard had in his room a marionette show which had belonged to his father. As soon as he got home from the performance of *Der Freischütz*, he set about reconstructing the famous Wolf's Glen scene, cutting the scenery out of cardboard, making models of the animals, including a particularly impressive wild boar, and allocating the vocal roles to members of the family. By all accounts the show seems to have collapsed in a mixture of anger, scorn and laughter, but the strength of Richard's intention emerges clearly enough from the story.

What gripped him was not the music of *Der Freischütz* but the mystery of the subject matter, the eerie, ghostly atmosphere that surrounds the legend on which the opera

is built. His lurid imagination subjected him to endless
nightmares and fits of screaming, which made his sisters
refuse to sleep anywhere near him, and the magic motifs
of *Der Freischütz* could only stimulate this hypersensitiv-
ity. From his earliest dramatic works, through *Der
fliegende Holländer* and on to *Der Ring des Nibelungen*,
his operas show how readily he responded to the dark,
sinister, destructive forces embedded in the legends and
myths from which he took so much of his subject-matter.

It was this same susceptibility that put him under the
spell of the stories of the Romantic writer E. T. A.
Hoffmann, which had been the subject of fascinated
admiration and agitated discussion over the whole of
Europe during the past ten or so years. Wagner was later
to take material from some of these stories for *Tannhäuser*
and *Die Meistersinger*. For the moment, however, it was
Hoffmann's supernatural world of phantasy and mystery,
his tales of psychologically unbalanced musicians and
painters, his exploration of hypnotism, telepathy and
other uncharted areas of the unconscious, that seized the
young Wagner's imagination.

His 'knocking about', as Mrs Burrell called it, started
with a stay at the house of Karl Geyer, his late stepfather's
younger brother, a goldsmith who lived in Eisleben,
birthplace of Martin Luther. Richard's elder brother
Julius – who played practically no part in his life – had
earlier been apprenticed to Karl Geyer. Here Richard
attended a private school for a few months. But when Karl
Geyer decided to marry, Richard was unwanted, and was
sent to his elderly bachelor uncle Adolf Wagner in Leipzig. 'Uncle Adolf' was a noted scholar and translator
whose private library greatly impressed the young boy,
and who told him of his encounters with many of the
leading intellectuals of the day, including Goethe, Schiller, Fichte and Tieck.

But this great barn of a house overlooking the market

square in Leipzig, inhabited only by the middle-aged Uncle Adolf and his unmarried sister, was no place for a high-spirited young boy, and at the end of 1822 Richard was able to rejoin his mother and the family back in the old Geyer apartment, Waisenhausgasse 12, in Dresden. Here he became a pupil at the famous old Kreuzschule, where he stayed until he was fourteen. 'I started as the lowest pupil in the lowest class,' he says in *Mein Leben*, 'embarking on my intellectual education from the humblest of beginnings.'

There was no thought of music in his mind. Two of his sisters were having piano lessons at home, and he would listen to what went on, but not until he was twelve did he have lessons himself. When he did, his fumbling efforts provoked the disconsolate teacher to pronounce that, with his terrible fingering, he would never get anywhere. 'He was right,' admitted Wagner in his *Autobiographical Sketch*: 'I have never in my life learned to play the piano properly.'

He showed no intellectual promise at school. Subjects that held no interest for him, like mathematics, he pushed aside. With those that did attract him, he would fix on what he found most fascinating and explore it in his own way, without reference to the structure of the subject as a whole or to the discipline involved in studying it. Thus Greek mythology, he says, filled him with enthusiasm, and in his imagination he pictured noble heroes like Agamemnon and Menelaus striding to and fro, talking to each other in their native tongue. But in order to realize his dream, he would have had to study the grammar of their language, 'and this,' he said, 'far from being a worthy branch of study in its own right, would simply be an annoying hindrance' – an obstruction to that ideal empathy which he saw as the only true knowledge. It is the same attitude that lay behind his refusal to acquire a proper keyboard technique.

Johanne had sold the paintings that her second husband had left, and family friends had made gestures of help, but since Geyer's death the only regular income in the Wagner family had been what the eldest daughter Rosalie earned as an actress. In 1826, when she was twenty-three, Rosalie, by far the most beautiful of the Wagner daughters and extremely talented, was offered a better-paid engagement in Prague, so Johanne and the family had little alternative but to go with her, leaving only the thirteen-year-old Richard behind to continue his education uninterrupted in Dresden until he went to university. He, after all, had been the one whom Geyer wanted 'to make something of'.

He was lodged with an unprepossessing family called Böhme, who also had sons at the Kreuzschule. The Böhmes' apartment was small and shabby, the family itself noisy and none too particular in its behaviour. Richard was drawn, not unwillingly, one imagines, into all manner of pranks and escapades with his new companions but he missed the sensitive company of his sisters. This feeling, offset – or rather, perhaps, intensified – by what he calls his 'earliest adolescent memories of falling in love', exposed for the first time that dependence on feminine sympathy which was to remain so characteristic of him.

In April 1827 he was confirmed in the Kreuzkirche in Dresden as Wilhelm Richard Geyer – the last time, apparently, that he used this name. Later that year Luise was offered a theatrical contract in Leipzig, and her mother hastened to return there from Prague with her three younger daughters, taking an apartment on the first floor of a house in the Pichhof, near the Hallesches Tor.

Dresden was a Rococco *Residenzstadt* of gracious living with much of the self-assured conventionality and complacency of a nineteenth-century provincial capital. Leipzig, on the other hand, was a busy commercial centre, a university town with the colourful originality and disrespect for traditional propriety that are part and parcel of student life. As a pupil at the Kreuzschule in Dresden, Wagner had gone through the motions of studying, but his mind had been on other things, the sort of things that Leipzig, or Prague, where he had visited his mother and his sisters, had to offer, rather than Dresden. He was at a critical age: a teenage schoolboy, volatile and impulsive, passionately attached to the theatre, abnormally sensitive to the mysterious and the supernatural, with no father to influence either his thoughts or his activities, and living apart from his mother and the rest of the family. It was an uneasy, even dangerous situation, both physically and psychologically, a situation which he had to resolve in his own way before his life could go forward with any sense of purpose.

So just before Christmas 1827 he produced a cock-and-bull story to his teachers that he had suddenly been called to rejoin his mother in Leipzig. The school had no alternative but to let him go. Of the once large family there were now only three children from Johanne Wagner's first marriage still living with their mother – Luise, now twenty, Ottilie, aged sixteen, and the fourteen year-old Richard – together with Cäcilie, Ludwig Geyer's daughter, who was twelve.

Most of Richard's intellectual stimulus in Leipzig at this time came from his Uncle Adolf, who was still living in the same bachelor apartment overlooking the market, surrounded by his books. But of his schooling, first at the Nicolai-Gymnasium, from which he was all but expelled, then, for six months or so, at the prestigious Thomasschule – which, like the Dresden Kreuzschule, still has its famous choir – the less said, the better. He had the worst marks in the class of thirty-one boys for Conduct, Diligence and Progress, and when it came to the examination at the end of the school year, he simply stayed away.

'Non scripsit absens', reads the blunt entry in the class register.

A large part of the blame for this lamentable behaviour lay with a secret project, conceived back in Dresden, which Richard now thrust before an unsuspecting world – a monstrous five-act tragedy called *Leubald und Adelaïde*. 'Since the rows I had had in school,' he wrote in *Mein Leben*, 'I had been lavishing on this drama all the efforts that I ought to have been spending on my school work.'

This gigantic piece of boyhood folly became a favourite butt of Wagner's own wit. The principal ingredients, he says, were *Hamlet*, *King Lear*, *Macbeth* and Goethe's *Götz von Berlichingen*; the hero, Leubald, was a Nordic mixture of Hamlet and Hotspur, while the only reason for giving the heroine such an un-German name was his affection for Beethoven's song 'Adelaïde'. No fewer than forty-two characters die in the course of the action, he solemnly tells us, most of whom were obliged to return as ghosts in the later acts, or he would have run out of actors. In fact the play has a modest twenty principal characters, and although the carnage is suitably impressive, not all of them perish. Someone, after all, has to be left to point the moral of the sad tale.

This was not all. 'No one else knew what I knew,' confided the author, 'namely, that the work could only be properly judged when provided with the music that I had decided to write for it.' The model for this music – not a note of which, unsurprisingly, was ever written – was to have been Beethoven's music to Goethe's *Egmont*, no less.

Uncle Adolf, who, the young dramatist-cum-composer hoped, would introduce this masterpiece to the world, was startled and shocked by its violent and sometimes crude language (one can guess which parts of Shakespeare and Goethe's *Götz* had particularly impressed him). Likewise his mother and his sisters were appalled at the thought that this was what he now offered as his justification for ignoring his school work. *Leubald und Adelaïde* hardly heralds *The Ring*, or even *Rienzi*, but the four principal characters – the lovers Leubald and Adelaïde. Adelaïde's attendant Gündelchen and Astolf the frustrated lover – stand in remarkable parallel to their counterparts – Tristan, Isolde, Brangäne and King Mark – in *Tristan und Isolde*, forty years later. The conjunction in Wagner's mind of Shakespeare and Beethoven, the greatest of dramatists and the greatest of composers, Promethean figures who made their own rules and forced new canons of judgment on art, also has its symbolic significance.

All thoughts of staying at school were now finally banished. Wagner was determined to become a student at the University of Leipzig – a student of music – and everything was to be sacrificed to this end.

Since his return to Leipzig a wave of overwhelming musical experiences had swept over him. First there were the concerts at the famous Gewandhaus, given by an orchestra whose reputation has survived to this day. In *Mein Leben* Wagner makes caustic comments on the ineptitude of the Gewandhaus players, particularly when confronted with new and difficult music, but at the time it was the excitement of discovery that filled his mind, above all the discovery of Beethoven. The overture to *Fidelio*, the late String Quartet in E flat major, the incidental music to *Egmont* and the Piano Sonatas were among these powerful early impressions. 'He went to bed with the sonatas and rose with the quartets,' wrote a friend: 'the songs he sang and the quartets he whistled.'

Most powerful of all, however, was the impact of the Seventh Symphony. 'Its effect on me,' he said, 'was beyond description. It was accentuated by the famous portraits of the composer that I had seen, by my knowledge of his deafness and of the lonely, withdrawn life that he led, and I was filled with a vision of his sublime originality, a mind of incomparable supernatural power.' This vision merged with his vision of Shakespeare, and he imagined himself standing in the presence of the two gods, engaged in rapt conversation with them. It would have been interesting to hear Shakespeare's German.

It was the new dimension given to Goethe's *Egmont* by Beethoven's music which had suddenly shown him, as if through a message from the two gods of his dream, that he too must have music to his drama. But while a literate schoolboy can write dramas, novels or any other works whose medium is words, he cannot, without knowledge of technique and conventions, write music. So, as surreptitiously as he had written his gory tragedy, Wagner borrowed a manual on composition from a lending library in the town – owned, incidentally, by the father of Clara Wieck, the future wife of Schumann – and set to work. He also took violin lessons from one Robert Sipp, a member of the Gewandhaus orchestra. Sixty years later the indefatigable Mrs Mary Burrell tracked Sipp down and asked him about his sixteen-year-old student. 'He picked things up quickly,' replied Sipp, 'but was lazy and never bothered to practise.' Adding, with a laugh: 'He was the worst pupil I ever had!'

The 'borrowed' textbook on composition stayed in Wagner's possession until the loan dues amounted almost to the cost of the book itself. When he was forced to get his mother to pay off the debt, the story came out, and with it a further proof of how he had spent the time when he should have been doing his school work. He copied out various Beethoven scores and began work on a piano transcription of the Ninth Symphony. A few weeks before his sixteenth birthday he heard the leading dramatic soprano of the day, the twenty-four-year-old Wilhelmine Schröder-Devrient, as Leonore in *Fidelio*. The die was now finally cast. 'I am dropping everything,' he wrote,

'and doing nothing but music, without any instruction.'
Shortly afterwards came his first compositions – a piano
sonata in D minor, a pastoral play with music, based on
Goethe's *Die Laune des Verliebten*, and a string quartet in
D major. The year was 1829 – the year of Mendelssohn's
famous revival of Bach's St Matthew Passion in Berlin,
and the year of Rossini's *William Tell*.

A paradoxical, characteristically Wagnerian conjunc-
ture. Here was a headstrong youth, totally unconcerned
for his formal education, who had taught himself to read
music, had managed to get some of his own compositions
on to paper, was able to transcribe one of the most
complex orchestral scores that the world had seen, yet
showed not the slightest aptitude for learning an instrument, or the least willingness to accept formal instruction
in the disciplines of his art.

Behind this unbridled independence, this resolute nonconformity, lie the answers to many questions, such as
how the texts of his own music dramas have their moments of power and vividness alongside stretches of
embarrassing tedium and mawkish bombast. Or why his
cultural and political essays, with their forceful insights
and challenges but also their eclectic and often grotesque
manipulation of history and their lack of an elegant
conviction of presentation, cannot join the company of
the Bacons, the Montaignes, the Schillers or the Ruskins.
Or why his odes to Ludwig II of Bavaria and other
occasional poems have fire and passion but neither discipline nor refinement of language. Or how his music can
move from the sublime to the excessive, even to the vulgar
– a music almost out of control, a music no longer just
music, as Bruno Walter once said.

In 1876, the year that Wagner's Festival Theatre in
Bayreuth opened its doors, Nietzsche wrote his last essay
in praise of the master before becoming his bitterest
opponent. In this, *Richard Wagner in Bayreuth*, he said:

'Wagner's youth was that of a versatile dilettante who never seemed likely to make anything of his life. There was no artistic tradition in the family; painting, literature, music – they were all like parts of his standard education and development, and anyone who cast even a superficial glance at the situation would conclude that he was a born dilettante.' Thomas Mann, who has few rivals as an interpreter of the significance of Wagner in the context of German and European culture, took the motif of dilettantism even further: 'With a sense of wonder and passionate commitment on our part, we might well say that Wagner's art, starting with his concept of the fusion of all the arts in the so-called *Gesamtkunstwerk*, is dilettantism to the n-th power, the product of an immense strength of mind and will, dilettantism raised to the status of genius.'

The scattered, undisciplined, yet uncannily deliberate and determined activities of Wagner's youth do indeed look like the preparation for a career in dilettantism, and give no hint of genius. He learned in his own way, not in the way his despairing teachers thought he needed.

The same is true of his older contemporary, a composer whose path he was to cross several times during his life – Hector Berlioz. But Berlioz, who was twenty years old before he became a music student, taught himself the theory of music largely from books, whereas Wagner taught himself composition from the music of others, above all Beethoven. Both men built on the unconventionality of their autodidacticism to become revolutionary figures in the history of music, with all the animosity that such figures provoke, and both retained throughout their lives a constantly evolving originality, a natural exploitation of the unexpected. All originality is ultimately indefinable, but the sense of novelty and inexplicability that attends the musical languages of Berlioz and Wagner has a special penetration about it. They are languages with strange new accents and intonations which can only have come from within. A similar case is that of Delius at the end of the century, who, also with no formal musical teaching until his twenties, emerged from a random succession of influences with one of the most individual dialects in the whole of music.

However helpful, or unhelpful, the term dilettante may be in characterising the genius of Wagner, one can hardly call a boy musically uneducated who produces a piano transcription of the whole of Beethoven's Ninth Symphony before he is eighteen. Wagner sent the first movement to the publishers Schott, in Mainz, in October 1831, hoping they would encourage him to send the other three movements as well (this is the earliest letter of Wagner's that has so far come to light). They did not. However, he went on with the work and gave the finished transcription to the same publishers the following year. 'They replied,' he says in *Mein Leben*, 'that they had not yet decided whether or not to issue a piano reduction of the Ninth Symphony, but that they would like to retain my careful transcription, offering me in return a score of the *Missa solemnis*, which I was overjoyed to receive.' Breitkopf and Härtel, in Leipzig, also turned down his transcription of Haydn's 'Drum Roll' Symphony.

In February 1831, the year when Heine went into exile in Paris, when Goethe was completing *Faust*, and when Hegel died in Berlin, Wagner enrolled at the University of Leipzig as a student of music. Strictly speaking, he did not qualify for full student status, because he had never worked his way through the secondary school curriculum and earned the certificate which, then as now, entitled him to matriculate. But he was able to get himself registered in a category that allowed him to attend classes without the right to sit official examinations – a proviso hardly calculated to worry him.

Two small things about the manner of his enrolment

give us a glimpse of the Wagner who never changed. One is the date – a week before the beginning of the Easter vacation, with lectures almost at an end and when thoughts were rather of going down than going up. His reason? In order to be able to join the 'Saxonia', the *Burschenschaft*, or corporation, of Saxon students and wear in public its crest and colours, thus proudly demonstrating the company with which he wanted people to associate him. The other is the way in which, instead of going through the formalities at the university registry, he went straight to the Rektor, and presented his credentials for admission. He was never one to dally in the foothills: his ambition drove him to make straight for the summit, the only level at which he felt at his ease and from which he was likely to have what he regarded as profitable dealings with his fellow-men.

A few weeks before he entered the university, Wagner experienced a great moment – the first public performance of one of his works. This was an overture in B flat major, one of a number of concert overtures furtively composed at the expense of his school studies. His intention had been to write out the score in three different inks – red for the strings, green for the woodwind and black for the brass – in order to make things easier for students of his masterpiece, but his pictorial intentions were frustrated, he sadly admits, because he could not find any green ink.

The performance itself, part of a pot-pourri of literary and musical numbers given in the Altes Theater in Leipzig, was hilarious. The main section of the work was an Allegro in common time; at the end of each four-bar phrase came an extra, unrelated fifth bar, the second beat of which carried a motif played *fortissimo* on the tympani. Once the regularity, not to say monotony, of this obtrusive device dawned on them, the audience had ears for nothing else, receiving each fresh *fortissimo* outburst with growing mirth and leaving the utterly demoralized young composer to creep out of the theatre at the end with his tail between his legs. 'This overture,' Wagner admitted later, with the affectionate self-mockery of a man who can afford the luxury of frivolous condescension towards the excesses of his youth, 'was pre-eminent among my follies.'

Many find the friends of a lifetime at university. Wagner found nobody, and much of the hectic, senseless mob activity into which he now plunged was a pseudo-compensation for what he missed. Looking back thirty years later, he remembered what it had been like:

I wanted to write a work that would have been worthy of the great Wilhelmine Schröder-Devrient, but as I knew this was totally out of the question, I gave up all my artistic aspirations in despair and abandoned myself to an aimless existence, indulging in all manner of youthful excesses in the company of the strangest associates. This marked the beginning of a dissolute student life so unattractive and empty that it still astonishes me. It was the purest, most casual chance what companions I found myself with and I cannot recall being led to choose my friends out of any particular affection or attraction. I can only explain this indifference through the fact that I had not as yet made the acquaintance of anyone who meant anything to me, and that all I therefore needed was somebody who would join in my activities, somebody to whom I could pour out my heart without heeding how much of it he actually took in.

The frankness of this self-characterization is equalled only by its accuracy. A friendship with Wagner required the total subordination of the friend, for Wagner could only conceive a relationship in terms of his own domination of that relationship. This, in its turn, is a manifestation of that total, naive self-centredness – the natural egocentricity of genius, one might call it – which constitutes the essence of his being. All those, men and women alike, who befriended him, helped him, loved him, came to experience the suffering that accompanied a relationship, any relationship, with him. His school friend

Theodor Apel, his later patron the faithful Frau Julie Ritter, Liszt, Hans von Bülow, Otto and Mathilde Wesendonk, even members of his own family – all passed out of his life the moment he had sucked from them, like a vampire, whatever intellectual, financial or emotional sustenance they had to offer him.

Finding no such person – victim might be a better word – at the moment, he took refuge, as he says, in the activities of the mob. The great source of excitement among European students at this time was the Paris revolution of July 1830. King Louis XVIII had returned to his throne in 1815 after the defeat of Napoleon, but during the final years of his reign, and even more so under his successor Charles X, the heavy hand of reactionary government had acted with increasing harshness to suppress the spread of liberal views. Matters came to a head at the end of July 1830. In three days the Bourbon regime was shattered, the sovereignty of the people reasserted, censorship abolished once and for all, and Louis Philippe, the 'Citizen King', established on the throne.

When the news of the revolution reached Leipzig, Wagner was still, on paper at least, a pupil at the Thomasschule, though in his mind he already reckoned himself among the politically conscious and potentially revolutionary students in *Burschenschaften* like the 'Saxonia'. The July Revolution marked for him the beginning of modern history, the history of the glorious struggle of the people towards freedom and self-expression, the destruction of outworn modes of thought and social patterns, and the defeat of the forces of reaction.

After Paris came the unhappy revolt of the Poles against their Russian masters, followed by uprisings of similar inspiration in Belgium, Spain and elsewhere. A group of Polish refugees found their way to Saxony, and their dramatic appearance in Leipzig aroused sympathy and indignation. There were even demonstrations against the police, and a number of students were arrested after skirmishes in the streets. When this news got round, the students, young Wagner in their midst, formed up in columns and marched from the market square to the university building, singing the student National Anthem, 'Gaudeamus igitur' and demanding the prisoners' release. Actually the Rektor had already decided on this, and the demonstrators had no other choice than to go home, but they quickly found something else against which to protest.

This time the object of communal anger was an official in the Leipzig city hall, who, as the rumour ran, had used his position to prevent any legal action being taken against a certain brothel, where he was evidently a regular client. The mob marched on this establishment, smashed the door and proceeded to break the place up, attacking indiscriminately everyone they found. Although he had not the slightest reason to get involved, Wagner felt himself being dragged into this orgy of senseless destruction, and 'like a madman', he recalled, he rushed around the house with the others, smashing everything in sight and tearing down a red curtain as a trophy to prove his participation in these 'heroic activities'.

His gambling and drinking with the students of the 'Saxonia' were a natural complement to such adventures. Never one to hold back with his opinions, he acquired an impressive list of enemies. 'When the grog, which was the staple drink of these rowdies, began to take effect', he said, 'they would cast mysterious glances in my direction, and I overheard suspicious conversations of whose real significance I remained blissfully ignorant for a time, the vicious brew having so befogged my mind.' He also found himself with a number of duels on his hands, most of them wilfully provoked by his own frivolity, but by a series of remarkable coincidences and accidents his opponents were prevented from appearing at the crucial moment.

Duels, often artificially provoked by gratuitous insults of an incredible triviality, were a stock feature of German student life, and remained so right down to the Second World War, but except in form and ritual they bore little resemblance to the classic duel *à outrance* fought with lethal weapons. One should see them rather as a sport based on a test of personal courage, albeit a sport which, like many others, could cause serious injury.

On one such improbable occasion, as related in *Mein Leben*, Wagner nonchalantly presented himself at the appointed hour of ten o'clock in the morning to face his rival, a certain Tischer. Tischer, however, had started a drunken brawl in a local brothel the night before and been so badly beaten up that the police had to take him to hospital. Naturally, said his shamefaced seconds, he would be expelled from the *Burschenschaft* and sent down from the University, but in his present state he could not possibly fight a duel. Since Tischer had the reputation of being a strong and skilled swordsman, while the young Wagner was a veritable tyro, European music may well have cause to be grateful for Tischer's anti-social tendencies.

Wagner clearly enjoyed recounting such inglorious episodes from his student days, and they will not have lost anything in the telling; but there is no reason to disbelieve them. So it is with his account of how a compulsive passion for gambling suddenly took hold of him, to the complete neglect of duelling, drinking and all other vices. Heedless of his mother's worries, he would stay out all night playing cards, frantically scraping together enough money to stay in the game. Trudging back home at dawn, he would climb over the front gate and creep up to his room to sleep off the effects of his exertions: 'I was utterly impervious to the scorn even of my mother and of my sister Rosalie, who hardly deigned to glance at the pale, worried, impossible young rake who so rarely showed himself in the house.'

Almost at the end of his tether, he even wagered his

mother's monthly pension, which he had just collected for her. He was down to his last thaler, when all at once his luck changed and he gradually won back all he had lost. Next morning he confessed everything to his mother: 'She folded her hands and thanked God for his mercy towards me, saying she was sure I was now saved and could not possibly fall victim to such iniquities again.' 'And indeed', he confirmed, 'from now on such temptations had lost all power over me.'

The *studium generale* of philosophy and aesthetics which was supposed to occupy part of his time at the university suffered the same fate as his school work. Nothing but composition interested him. For some six months he took lessons from Theodor Weinlig, Cantor of the Thomaskirche in Leipzig, who, after a few stormy opening weeks, succeeded in making him realize the need to master certain techniques if he were to bring order to his unruly imagination and produce literate scores from which musicians could perform. One cannot teach composition, in the sense that one can teach Latin, or mathematics, or cookery. But one can make a young composer aware of the world of musical realities, the product of history and evolution, which exists beyond the confines of his own mind, and with which, be he duffer or genius, he will have to come to terms. This the skilful Weinlig seems to have done, not by teaching rules and precepts as from a grammar book but by making his headstrong student aware of the musical practice of Palestrina, Bach, Mozart and the other masters of the classical tradition. It was education by example, the complement to what he had already taught himself by copying and transcribing the works of Beethoven. Wagner remembered Weinlig with gratitude – not a statement that can be made about many who tried to teach Wagner anything.

Undeterred by the catastrophe of his Overture in B flat, with its mirth-provoking drum roll, he went on cheerfully composing through 1831 and 1832 – overtures to Schiller's drama *Die Braut von Messina* and Raupach's *König Enzio*, seven pieces inspired by Goethe's *Faust*, two piano sonatas, a fantasia for piano in F sharp minor, a sonata for piano (four hands) and a concert overture in D minor. With this last piece, a work composed under the shadow of Beethoven's Coriolan Overture, the Leipzig theatre decided to risk giving the ambitious young student a second chance. It was given a respectful hearing and even repeated at a Gewandhaus concert a few months later; a similar success attended a further overture in C major, also inspired by Beethoven. To have a piece performed at the Gewandhaus meant a great deal to any young composer, and although he did not have the precocity of a Mozart, or a Mendelssohn, or a Bizet, Wagner was still a very young composer.

To the publicity of performance was now added that of publication, when early in 1832 Breitkopf und Härtel accepted a piano sonata in B flat major and paid him twenty thalers for it. This is Wagner's first published work – a competent enough exercise in conventional form, which could have been written by Weber, Hummel, E. T. A. Hoffmann or any of a score of minor composers of the early nineteenth century. A sonata in A major, written a few weeks later, is in the same manner and no less competent, but although the score had lain for decades in the Richard Wagner Archive in Bayreuth, it was not made public until 1960. Such are the vagaries of publishing.

The most substantial of these early works, and one that carried Wagner's reputation beyond the borders of Leipzig and Saxony, is a Symphony in C, spiritual progeny of the ever-dominant Beethoven and the Mozart of the Jupiter Symphony. Cast in the classical four-movement form, it is scored for the conventional orchestra of two flutes, two oboes, two clarinets, two bassoons, four horns, two trumpets, two timpani and strings. It was first played by students of the Conservatoire in Prague during Wagner's visit there in the autumn of 1832 and had two performances in Leipzig shortly afterwards, one of them at the Gewandhaus, where it was well received. The journalist and novelist Heinrich Laube, an influential figure in German letters in the mid-nineteenth century, praised the vitality and energy of the work in his review for the *Zeitung für die elegante Welt*: 'The composer storms from one end of the work to the other. At the same time his basic themes have an innocence and freshness that make me feel great confidence in his ability.'

A few years later Wagner sent the score of the symphony to Mendelssohn, who became conductor of the Gewandhaus orchestra in 1835, but Mendelssohn did not perform the work, and the score has never been found. The printed score published in 1911 was prepared from the orchestral parts used for the performance in Prague.

From the time in the late summer of 1831 when he started composition lessons with Weinlig, Wagner turned his back on the student life which he had once been so eager to share. Apart from realizing the moral and physical harm that the 'Saxonia' was doing to him, he was shocked by the students' indifference towards the Polish refugees who had fled from the Russians and sought refuge in Leipzig after the fall of Warsaw in September. The publisher Friedrich Brockhaus, who had married Wagner's sister Luise three years before, was chairman of a committee set up to help the Poles, and in his house Wagner met Count Vincent Tyzkiewicz, one of the most distinguished of them. He had for some while been anxious to leave Saxony and see something more of Europe, so when in the summer of the following year the Count returned to eastern Europe, he offered to take Wagner with him in his carriage as far as Brno. From here Wagner took the coach to Vienna, carrying with him the scores of the three overtures that had so far been perfor-

med, together with that of the as yet unheard Symphony
in C.

He did not think much of Vienna. He had expected
Beethoven but was offered Hérold's *Zampa* and the
waltzes of Johann Strauss *père* instead. Visiting the conservatoire, he tells us in *Mein Leben*, he made the
acquaintance of a teacher who tried to get the student
orchestra to play his Overture in D minor. For reasons he
could no longer remember, nothing came of the plan, and
since he found Viennese cultural life in general 'not
particularly uplifting' – Chopin, who had played in the city
the year before, passed a similar judgment – he stayed
only a few weeks. It was long enough, however, for him to
be forced to borrow money when the allowance his
mother had given him ran out. 'I was still paying off these
debts,' he recalled, 'when I was Kapellmeister in Dresden.' That was eleven years later, and in the meantime he
had collected further debts in Magdeburg, Königsberg,
Riga, Paris and elsewhere. Well as he knew his *Hamlet*,
Wagner never found reason to dally over Polonius's
advice to his son: 'Neither a borrower nor a lender be.'

From Vienna he took a cheap but correspondingly slow
coach to Bohemia, to visit Count Pachta and his family on
their estate outside Prague. Wagner's youngest sister
Ottilie had come to know the Count's two illegitimate
daughters Jenny and Auguste, at the time when the
Wagner family moved to Prague after Geyer's death. On a
visit there when he was thirteen, the young Richard had
been dazzled by the beauty of the two girls. Now, six years
later, he fell hopelessly under Jenny's spell. In *Mein
Leben* he made light of the whole affair, but letters written
at the time to his friend Theodor Apel give a different
picture. In flowery language, inspired – if that is the word
– by the Romantic fiction in which he had steeped himself
from his schooldays, he pours out a mixture of hopeless
passion, indulgent self-pity and almost savage resentment

that Jenny Pachta did not throw herself at his feet: 'At last I saw it all. You can imagine the wounds that such a passion can inflict, but more terrible than anything is the way it can kill! So bear with me when I tell you: She did not deserve my love!'

So often, when his most intense relationships revealed what seemed to him to be less than utter devotion and self-sacrifice on the other's part, Wagner would burst into a rage, accuse the world of using him merely for its own advantage and cry that nobody 'deserved his love'. He was a creature of extremes, living on a series of love-hate relationships with those who came within his orbit – and also with himself. Much of what is seen as his unreasonable, often impossible behaviour in areas of human contact where 'normal' values are expected to prevail, has its origin in the total egocentricity of this psychological complex.

Theodor Apel, to whom he confided the story of his passion for Jenny Pachta, was Wagner's first real friend. The two had been fellow students at the Nicolaischule, but whereas Wagner afterward stayed in Leipzig, Apel went to study at Heidelberg. He was two years younger than Wagner and looked to him for a lead in following the literary enthusiasms that united them. He had been left a considerable sum of money by his father, a well-to-do poet and scholar who had been a close friend of Wagner's Uncle Adolf, and many times in the coming years he was to rescue Wagner, who sometimes seems to have resented his friend's prosperity, from desperate financial plights. During his stay with the Pachtas Wagner set to music a poem by Apel called 'Abendglocken' ('Evening Bells') and in 1835 composed an overture for Apel's play *Columbus*. Apel was his closest confidant throughout these years, but in 1836, at the age of twenty-one, he lost his sight in an accident. The two drifted apart after this, and the last time Wagner mentions visiting his blind friend is in 1842.

It was during these five weeks with the Pachta family that

his Symphony in C was given its first performance at the Prague conservatoire. Also during these weeks he produced a sketch for his first opera, *Die Hochzeit (The Wedding)*, 'a sinister work of dark and ominous hue', as he described it.

But *Die Hochzeit* was abandoned almost as soon as it was started. Its melodramatic plot, medieval in inspiration, tells of two feuding families. To bring their enmity to an end, the head of one family invites the son of the other family to the wedding of his daughter; the son assaults the daughter, who pushes him over a balcony to his death, then, as divine judgment falls on her, renounces her bridegroom and sinks lifeless on the body of the man she has killed.

When he got back to Leipzig, Wagner eagerly showed his sketch of this macabre tale to his eldest sister Rosalie, now an experienced actress and a person in whose judgment he had always put great faith. He had even started to write the music. But Rosalie disapproved of almost everything about the story, and Wagner 'with complete nonchalance', he assures us, tore it up.

Until this point in his life Wagner had been totally dependent on his family. His mother had little enough for herself, and without the contribution from Rosalie, who was still unmarried and working at the theatre, the situation would have been hopeless. Rosalie, Richard, their stepsister Cäcilie and their mother were now the only ones left in the Pichhof apartment: Albert, Julius, Luise and Klara were all married, and Ottilie, who was still single, had gone to live with Luise and her husband. When, therefore, Albert, who was with the theatrical company in the Bavarian town of Würzburg, invited his brother there and arranged a temporary job for him as chorus master from the beginning of 1833, it was a relief to everybody. The university had nothing more to offer him, his apprenticeship with Weinlig, if it can be given so formal a title, had served its purpose, and although he had no idea what course his life would take, he had resolved that it would be a life devoted to music.

In January 1833 he took the stage coach from Leipzig to Bamberg, the beautiful little Franconian town in which his idol E. T. A. Hoffmann had lived as Kapellmeister, then on to Würzburg, a charming old university town which had for a long while been the Jesuit stronghold in Germany. The most important item in his luggage was the text of a new opera, to which Rosalie had this time given her blessing, called *Die Feen (The Fairies)*. Barely a year later he had finished the entire work – libretto and music. It was his first complete opera.

CHAPTER TWO
The Young Professional

Albert Wagner had worked himself into a position of some importance in Würzburg. His wife, described by Mrs Mary Burrell as 'a hideous woman with a sinister expression, very untruthful and a perfect fury', had also been an actress. Fourteen years older than Richard, Albert spent his entire life in the theatre, first as a tenor in light opera and as an actor, later as a producer, *inter alia* at the Hoftheater in Berlin. The difference in their ages meant that the two brothers had scarcely known each other: 'My brother now came into my life virtually for the first time,' wrote Wagner minor in *Mein Leben*.

The bond between them now unexpectedly grew closer through the person of Albert's daughter Johanna, who was to become an immensely popular operatic soprano in Dresden, rivalling the great Wilhelmine Schröder-Devrient. She sang the role of Elisabeth in the first performance of *Tannhäuser* twelve years later and was in the cast of the first Bayreuth *Ring* in 1876. For a few weeks Wagner stayed with his brother's family in what he rather disparagingly called their 'not exactly spacious domestic conditions' in the Untere Wöllergasse, then moved into a small room of his own opposite the Hofgarten.

What was expected of the young Wagner in his first professional position turned out to be a good deal less demanding than he had at first feared. The Würzburg Stadttheater catered for only a small public and had no great standing in the country, either for its drama or for its opera, but its repertoire was entertainingly varied and must have kept the inexperienced new chorus master on his toes. Weber's *Der Freischütz* and *Oberon*, Cherubini's *Les Deux Journées (The Water Carrier)*, Rossini's *Tancredi*, Beethoven's *Fidelio*, Auber's *Masaniello* and *Fra Diavolo* and Hérold's *Zampa* were among the operas produced during the season, together with Meyerbeer's *Robert le Diable*. This last had been a brilliant success in Paris only two years earlier, but Wagner, expecting to be dazzled by its daring novelty and originality, found it flat, affected and totally unmemorable.

To be surrounded by the life of the theatre, and to be made responsible for part of its activities, ought, one imagines, to have given him a sense both of pleasure and of achievement. He was not yet twenty, yet he held a post which today could hardly be occupied by one so young. But the few letters that have survived from this year, 1833, show little sense of enjoyment or satisfaction; rather, he is worried about the future, sees that life is becoming a serious business, and realizes that he cannot live for ever on what his mother and his sister Rosalie felt they could spare him.

There was also the matter of military service. In Saxony he would now be liable to serve his time with the army, but as long as he stayed in Bavaria, he could keep this unwelcome prospect at arm's length.

Had the terms of his contract with the theatre been applied to the letter, neither he nor his family would have been able to sleep peacefully in their beds. On the one hand it defines him as a kind of theatrical office-boy, engaged principally for one purpose but expected to put his hand to any odd job that might turn up; on the other hand it imposes rules of conduct on him and his family which makes his status sound more like that of a juvenile delinquent on parole than a professional musician in the service of a local authority. This quaint document deserves to be quoted in full:

Under the personal pledge of Frau Johanne Geyer, of Rosalie Wagner, actress, both resident in the Pichhof, Leipzig, and of Herr Albert Wagner, singer, actor and producer, resident in Würzburg, for the punctuality and obedience of Richard Wagner, being in the age of minority, formerly *studiosus musicae* in Leipzig, son of Johanne Geyer, widow of the actor Ludwig Geyer, said Richard Wagner is engaged as chorus master at the Stadttheater in Würzburg from the first day of his employment until Palm Sunday 1834. The principal duties of said Richard Wagner will be those of chorus master. If necessary, he is also to make himself available for roles, both silent and spoken, in plays of all kinds and in the mime sections of ballets, as required: to this both he and the guarantors of his assiduousness have given their approval and consent.

In the event of indiscipline or infringement of the rules, the management shall have the right to deal with Herr Richard Wagner accordingly. Should the said Richard Wagner's income be insufficient to meet any fine that may be imposed, the aforementioned guarantors undertake to pay it to the management on his behalf.

Richard Wagner will place his entire efforts and services at the disposal of the management of the Stadttheater at all times. In return for the prompt execution of his duties, the management will pay him the sum of ten guilders Rhenish per month.

Since over half this salary would have gone on rent each month, it is scarcely surprising that Wagner's letters from Würzburg are not brimful of enthusiasm.

Wagner's engagement with the Stadttheater was only brief, and after his last month's salary had been paid, he again had to look to the generosity of his sister Rosalie. But these few months gave both the young man and the young musician a new confidence and self-awareness. For one thing they brought his initiation into practical music making, forcing him to study and interpret a wide range of vocal scores and launching him on the conductor's career which was to absorb a great deal of his energy throughout his life. On the personal plane he was beginning to assert himself in his dealings with his elders, and also, 'without deluding myself that I was at all good-looking', as he conceded, to attract the attention of the ladies. The two short-lived, innocent love affairs in Würzburg of which he tells us in *Mein Leben* are of no great interest in themselves, but although, with his overly large head, his projecting chin and short stature, he hardly had a physical advantage over his rivals, he did hold a peculiar fascination for women. This he knew and exploited with the self-assertiveness that marked all his dealings with his fellow-creatures. When, at the age of fifty-two, he began to dictate *Mein Leben* to his wife Cosima, he remembered his months in Würzburg as a time of dawning self-discovery: 'My unusual vivacity and constant excitability now made me aware, in my dealings with all those I came across, of a feeling that I had the power to carry my listless companions away or to dumbfound them.' Once aware of this power, he was to become highly resentful of those who were not prepared to be either carried away or dumbfounded.

His predominant concern in Würzburg, however, was his new opera, *Die Feen*, based on *La donna serpente*, a dramatized fable by the eighteenth-century Italian writer Carlo Gozzi. He had come across the name of Gozzi while reading E. T. A. Hoffmann, whose world of supernatural phenomena and fantastic spirits had held his imagination in its grip since his schooldays. Gozzi's plays do not move outside the realm of allegorical fantasy, and their characters have no developed psychological depth. But precisely because of this, as Hoffmann posited in his dialogue called *Der Dichter und der Komponist (The Poet and the Composer)*, there was scope for the librettist to intensify and make explicit in modern terms the significance of what lay before him, and it was a psychological intensification in this spirit that Wagner sought to give his text.

Styled 'Romantic Opera in Three Acts', *Die Feen* is based on the familiar fairytale motif of the love between a mortal and a fairy, symbolizing the conflict between the finite world of man and the eternal world of the spirits, with the achievement of salvation through the power of love. These themes are dominant in Wagner's work, and they are all clearly stated in his first opera. It is as though *Der fliegende Holländer, Tannhäuser, Lohengrin* and *Tristan und Isolde* already lay in embryo in his mind, the mind of an unknown, part-time chorus master who was still not twenty-one, yet who could compose an entire three-act opera, words and music, fully orchestrated and ready for performance, in barely a year.

The music of *Die Feen* was written in about ten months. Parts of the work sound like Rossini, other parts like Mendelssohn, there are moments of Weber and the ultra-Romantic Marschner, and moments of Beethoven. There are also moments of Wagner – a tentative use of the leitmotif, harmonic prospects of *Die Meistersinger*, a flavour of the chromatic progressions of *Tristan* – with some robust dramatic writing that would be appreciated by many an amateur operatic society. Excerpts from the work were given at a concert in Würzburg towards the end of the year that Wagner was there, but the complete opera was never performed during his lifetime.

In May the theatrical season came to an end, and with it Wagner's engagement, but he stayed in Würzburg till the end of the year in order to work uninterruptedly on *Die Feen*, living on an allowance from Rosalie and with occasional help from Albert. Back in Leipzig at the beginning of 1834, he moved into the family apartment again and faced with a new sense of confidence the relatives who had had little hope that he would make a successful career in music. 'I had now become a real musician,' he proudly recalled in *Mein Leben*, 'and had written a full-scale opera, parts of which had been performed, not without success. This gave me a pleasant sensation, and was no less a source of pride to my worthy relatives, who now recognized that what they thought would turn out a disaster had in fact led to a positive result.'

However, a real 'positive result' had yet to show itself. In spite of Rosalie's intercession the Stadttheater decided not to mount *Die Feen*, partly because, they claimed, it did not meet public taste, but also, in fact, because both the producer and the conductor had so many objections to the score. For the moment this refusal caused Wagner deep disappointment, but his characteristic impressionability quickly brought him new stimuli to ensure his uninhibited development.

One such stimulus came with a performance of Bellini's Romeo and Juliet opera *I Capuletti ed i Montecchi* in the Leipzig Stadttheater soon after his return to the city, with Wilhelmine Schröder-Devrient as Romeo. Her performance as Leonore in Beethoven's *Fidelio* five years before had sealed Wagner's determination to make music his life. Now, in a work of a totally different kind, her singing brought him face to face with an aesthetic problem which he needed to think through before he could take his own creative activity further. The problem was how, as he put it, 'so remarkable an effect could be achieved with such utterly insignificant music.'

Every concertgoer knows it – the technical wizardry on the violin, the pyrotechnics on the piano, the breathtaking virtuosity lavished on a flimsy trifle, received with wild applause to which even the cynic feels obliged to contribute his mite. The performing musician, like the actor, is an intermediary: he can make a lot out of a little, turn something apparently mediocre into something moving.

Wagner was worried by this and, with the fate of *Die Feen* fresh in his mind, resentful of it. But as he pondered this 'utterly insignificant music' of Bellini's he found himself forced to concede that it had a freshness, a spontaneity, what he called 'the warm glow of life', which the German operatic music of the day – not excepting even Weber – fundamentally lacked. On the basis of this judgment he put together some forthright observations on the lifeless state of German opera and what was needed in order to give it vitality, and published them anonymously under the title *Die deutsche Oper* (*German Opera*) in Laube's journal *Zeitung für die elegante Welt* in June 1834.

Theory and practice run side by side throughout Wagner's creative life. Music did not just 'come to him' in the way that inspiration seemed to 'come', with little apparent effort, to, say, Mozart and Schubert. Like Dante, like Michelangelo, like Beethoven, Wagner wrestled with his inspiring angel, fought his way through with remorseless strength of will to a final expression of his vision in intense and total commitment, often at a cost that included the peace of mind and emotional stability of others. The composition of his operas is accompanied by a ceaseless explanation of his procedures, a criticism of the musical world whose horizons he felt called upon to extend, a commentary on aesthetics, on culture, on politics and society, on musical ends and means, and on a thousand other subjects which, he insisted, had to be understood if the meaning of his music were to be grasped. Of the fourteen volumes of his *Collected Works* edited by Julius Kapp (1914), only three, together with part of a fourth, are needed for the texts of his operas, dramatic fragments and occasional literary works; the remainder are filled with his autobiographical writings, critiques and expository essays.

So in *German Opera*, his first published declaration of intent, he sets out the thoughts that were in his mind at the time of writing *Die Feen* and, a little later, *Das Liebesverbot*. The besetting sin of modern German composers, he claimed, was their desire to appear learned and intellectual. The age of Bach had been one of genuine intellectuality, its intellectual modes of expression, such as the fugue, being the common currency that everyone recognized and used; but things had changed, and in trying to turn themselves into something they were not, German operatic composers had only succeeded in making their music pedantic, unnatural and, above all, undramatic. The human warmth of Mozart's characters came from the beauty of Italian song. French opera had received a sense of dramatic purpose from Gluck, but Weber (Wagner is no longer the uncritical worshipper of *Der Freischütz*), Spohr and their contemporaries, whatever their other virtues, lacked both feeling for true vocal writing and a sense of real drama. If we acknowledge this, if we get rid of the unnatural cult of affectation and intellectuality, if we seek to capture 'the voice of the people' and grasp 'life in all its truth and fervour' ('*das wahre warme Leben*'), then honesty and authenticity will return, and with them the basis of a true operatic art.

Two fundamental elements of Wagner's major theoretical works of the 1850s and onwards are already here. One is his concern with opera as a unified work of art under the dominant principle of drama, nourished through its roots in a shared social reality. The other is his appeal to the qualities of the German *Volk*, that mystical national entity in which so many of the splendours of nineteenth-century German culture, but also so many of the evils and calamities of nineteenth- and twentieth-century German history, have their roots.

In a further article, *Pasticcio*, published in November 1834 in Schumann's journal *Neue Zeitschrift für Musik*, he implicitly raises the genre of opera to a position of pre-eminence above all other forms of art. For since the essence of drama lies in the exposition of human motives, action. and conflicts, and since, he repeats, the challenge to the operatic composer is 'to grasp life in all its truth and fervour', so opera, i.e. drama plus music, infused with the expression of human emotions in passionate melody, must embody life at its truest and most fervent. How to achieve drama in such a work, says Wagner, can be seen in Gluck; how to create warm, full-blooded characters through the power of melody and musical form is exemplified in Mozart. It is not a long step from this to Wagner's concept of the *Gesamtkunstwerk*, the union of the arts in a single, all-embracing enterprise.

Wagner's specific concern with German opera is, in its way, a reflection of the mounting sense of national identity that manifests itself throughout the age of German Romanticism. Herder, in the 1770s, had called on the Germans to look to their own national folk-culture, not to foreign models, as the foundation for their literature, and had thereby urged them to look inwards, both in personal, spiritual terms, and as a nation. An awareness of history developed, the German Middle Ages were rediscovered, a sense of national community began to dawn, and with it a political consciousness that grew through the Napoleonic era and the Wars of Liberation, through the age of Metternich, the 1848 Revolution and its defeat, until it finally achieved its goal in 1871 after the Franco-Prussian War.

Wagner lived through this whole period and shares its underlying political dualism. It was a dualism composed, on the one hand, of rising liberal thought in the social and political sphere, highlighted by events like the Hambach Festival of 1832 – a huge, open-air political rally on a hill in the Rhine Palatinate, heralded as the first great revolutionary assembly of the German people – and by the Revolution of 1848; and on the other hand, of the aggressive nationalism that eventually swallowed up the forces of liberalism from which, paradoxically, it had received much of its early energy. Indeed, Wagner's life has almost a paradigmatic quality in its absorption of the conflicts between idealistic social reform and the personal search for success and economic security, between the cosmopolitan values of political freedom and uninhibited self-expression, and identification with the rise of a disciplined nationalism. There is no reconciliation, nor was there in Wagner, between such antitheses.

Through the 1830s and beyond, Wagner's outlook on life was dominated by the attitude of the so-called Young German movement, in particular those of the novelist, dramatist, producer and editor Heinrich Laube. A sensuous, exuberant, extrovert character, Laube was a fluent publicist, with the public relations man's ability to get on well with people of all kinds. His five-volume novel *Das junge Europa (Young Europe)*, which Wagner read with enthusiasm, preached the twin virtues of Love and Revolution, and as editor of the *Zeitung für die elegante Welt*, he called on the young generation in the name of what was 'natural' and therefore 'good', to fight political tyranny and the artificial restrictions on personal freedom imposed by a narrow-minded, convention-ridden society, and to seek 'natural' happiness in a wholehearted commitment to the here and now. Under the inspiration of Saint-Simonism, a man-centred, life-centred philosophy-cum-religion which attracted the poet Heinrich Heine, the journalist Ludwig Boerne and all those associated with the Young German movement, Laube used his journal to propagate a heady doctrine of universal brotherhood, of man's historical predisposition to happiness, of free love and the right to self-fulfilment, and other articles of a libertarian creed.

Wagner and Laube were introduced to each other by Rosalie, who hoped that the influential editor and critic would help her brother's career, especially after his encouraging notice on the Symphony in C. But Wagner only ever accepted help on his own terms. After the Leipzig performance of the symphony Laube had offered him an operatic libretto to set, but he already knew that he alone was able to write the sort of text that his music could interpret, and he declined the offer. The cordial relationship between the two men lasted over thirty years, and many were the occasions when Laube helped to rescue his struggling, debt-laden friend from financial disaster.

Rights such as those demanded by the *Zeitung für die elegante Welt* could have found no more eager champion than Wagner in his twenties, with his scorn of authority, his insistence on doing things his own way, and his pride in having demonstrated that he was prepared to take to the streets if that was what the assertion of liberty required. Life was to be lived to the full, 'life in all its truth and fervour', and a strain of hedonism, self-indulgence – it has been called many things – runs right through his life, unbroken even at the moments of his most desperate poverty and most humiliating failure. Nor, as the events of 1848 and 1849 were to show, did he flinch from the social and political implications of such a philosophy.

This world of sensuous pleasure, with the moral problems that attend it, provides the substance of the opera *Das Liebesverbot (The Ban on Love)*, begun in June 1834 and completed, text and music, eighteen months later. Based on Shakespeare's *Measure for Measure*, the libretto of this 'frivolous item of juvenilia', as he later called it, amounts to a hymn of praise in the name of natural, free love and a condemnation of the hypocritical puritanism of society. Indeed, his new title itself shows how different a direction he took from Shakespeare. 'Measure for Measure' has a connotation of justice, of equitable judgment on rival claims, and the action of Shakespeare's drama takes place under the guiding power of the Duke, whose resolution of the conflicts before him is that of a presiding judge. Wagner does away with the character of the Duke, thus dissipating at once the whole ambience of justice and moral verdict. What we are left with is a dramatized illustration of the demand for the 'emancipation of the flesh', each man being free – or rather, being bound by his obligation to the laws of nature – to pursue the sensuous pleasures of the moment without false embarrassment or impertinent interference. In Shakespeare the immorality and decadence of the Viennese are mercilessly exposed as a vile offence before God and man, but Wagner – who moves the scene from Central European Vienna to Mediterranean Palermo, where passionate Sicilian blood demands its due – lays no accusations and apportions no blame. The only thing he 'measures' is the individual's degree of allegiance to the natural drives of his sensual nature.

In the context of Wagner's development as a whole the interest of *Das Liebesverbot* lies rather in this field of ideas and intellectual enthusiasms than in its music. Its musical lineage is that of Franco-Italian 'Grand Opera', theatrical, melodramatic. It is more chromatic in harmonic idiom than anything he had composed so far, more thickly scored and bearing the marks – scars might be a more apt description – of prodigious intellectual concentration. *Die Feen* had been derivative in its own way but it was also fresh and direct; *Das Liebesverbot*, whose two acts take almost twice as long as the three acts of *Der fliegende Holländer*, is more pretentious without being more original and already betrays, especially in the ensembles, that proneness to monumentalism which pursued Wagner throughout his life and is the heritage of composers of the Wagnerian succession.

Wagner quickly lost interest in the work and later waxed highly scornful at its expense – 'terrible, nauseating', he called it. But it did receive one performance, a month or two after its completion, and the ensuing fiasco has a place of honour in the impressive annals of operatic catastrophes.

The date was 29 March 1836; the place, Magdeburg, a sleepy provincial town with a cultural life which provoked a man of the theatre to remark that he would 'rather be a cabhorse in Berlin than a theatrical director in Magdeburg'. Wagner persuaded the company to round off the season with a benefit performance – he himself was to be the beneficiary – of *Das Liebesverbot*. Apart from the publicity and professional satisfaction that he anticipated, the proceeds, so he calculated, would help to get him out of the financial difficulties that were a persistent and apparently ineradicable feature of his condition. He always believed in living well, and never asked whether he could 'afford' it. To want something was to need it, and thus to be entitled to it, because his nature, his psychological disposition, and hence his destiny, so ordained. If the world thought otherwise, so much the worse for the world.

The first problem over *Das Liebesverbot* was the title, which the police, who had to give their approval to any public performance, found suggestive and quite inappropriate to Holy Week, the time of year in question. Wagner got round this by calling it *The Novice of Palermo*, after the principal female character, Isabella, dissuading the authorities from looking too closely at the subject-matter by pointing out that his libretto was based on a very serious drama by the great Shakespeare. Having won this round, he turned to the preparation of the performance itself, for which he was granted a princely rehearsal time of ten days. The libretto had not been published in advance so the audience had no idea what the work was about, and so hard did the singers find it to learn their parts that they were for ever faltering and looking to the prompter to help them out. The most spectacular offender was the principal tenor, who tried to gloss over his lapses of memory by stalking around the stage and tossing his cockade in the air, and by filling in with snatches of Auber's *Fra Diavolo*, Hérold's *Zampa* and any other works that happened to come into his mind.

The effect of this lamentable première was predictable.

A quarter of an hour before the curtain was due to rise on the evening of the second performance, there were just three people sitting in the auditorium. Suddenly a riot broke out behind the curtain. The leading lady had been having an affair with the second tenor; her husband, whose fury had smouldered on throughout the season, now finally lost control of himself, rushed over to his wife's lover and punched him on the nose. The wounded lover retired ignominiously to his dressing-room to wipe the blood off his face, while the cuckolded husband rounded on his wayward spouse so savagely that she fell into hysterics. Soon the rest of the cast felt obliged to join in the fight, taking advantage of the occasion to work off all the private grudges and feuds they had been nursing during rehearsals.

With two of the principal singers thus *hors de combat* – 'victims of the offended husband's "ban on love", so to speak', as Wagner caustically observed – and the other members of the company engaged in a series of brawls behind the scenes five minutes before the curtain was due to go up, there was obviously going to be no second performance of *Das Liebesverbot*. The manager appeared in front of the curtain and informed the diminutive audience that 'unforeseen circumstances' had made it impossible for the performance to take place.

Wagner's connection with the Magdeburg theatre dates from the summer of 1834, when, returning from a trip to Bohemia with Theodor Apel, he found he had been invited to become music director for the company's summer season at the little spa of Bad Lauchstädt, near Halle. The Lauchstädt theatre, a charming little classicistic structure, still almost unchanged today, was built under Goethe's direction in 1802 and had been regularly used for visiting performances by the Weimar troupe in the early years of the century. Here Wagner conducted an opera in public for the first time: Mozart's *Don Giovanni*. Over the following five years he worked for a succession of small provincial theatres and lived a life which, from the professional point of view, was no different from that of numerous other young musicians struggling to make a living out of a cultural system which could hardly sustain them.

His first need in Lauchstädt was to find a room. 'A young actor whom I had happened to know in Würzburg,' he relates in *Mein Leben*, 'offered to help me, saying that in taking me to the best house he knew, he would be giving me the added pleasure of settling me under the same roof as the prettiest and most charming girl in the town. Indeed, the self-same young lady met us at the door of the house. Her appearance and manner were a striking contrast to the unpleasant impressions of the theatre which I had gained that morning. Fresh and very attractive in appearance, the young actress displayed great confidence and assurance which gave her friendly demeanour a particular dignity, and her quiet, scrupulously tidy dress only added to the remarkable impression that this unexpected meeting made upon me.' The young actress was Minna Planer, later to become Wagner's first wife.

In the stormy relationship between Wagner and Minna, which miraculously survived, on paper at least, until within a few years of Minna's death in 1869, are to be found all the psychological traits, all the intellectual and emotional poses, all the modes of behaviour that characterize Wagner's life as a whole. At one moment Minna plays hard to get, driving the impassioned Wagner to distraction; at the next he commands her utter adoration and pretends to treat her with disdain; he follows her like a faithful dog, subordinating his career to his desire to be with her, then finds her intolerable and a hindrance to his advancement and his freedom. For Wagner there was ever only one admissible standpoint in any situation – his own.

Disillusionment and anger were bound to pursue him, abuse and deceit could not but become second nature to him, yet for thirty years he strove to keep up appearances with Minna. Although he had no doubt that his suffering was far greater than hers – for did not such suffering threaten the expression of his genius? – and although he more than once saw the only solution in divorce, he knew what practical value she was to him. Even when he did not want her with him, he wanted to know that she was being looked after, in spite of what he saw as her ultimate unworthiness of him.

Born into a factory worker's family in a village near Chemnitz (now Karl-Marx-Stadt), in Saxony, Minna Planer, baptized Christine Wilhelmine, was almost four years older than Wagner and had been an actress since her late teens. She had a fresh, pert attractiveness about her, and although Wagner maintained that she had little artistic talent and even less culture, her charm seems to have brought her offers of engagements at theatres in many parts of Germany, from Bamberg to Bremen and from Leipzig to Königsberg. With her attractive physical qualities went a demure modesty of manner, and there had been no lack of young men to show how inviting they found her. She lived with an eight-year-old girl whom she described as her younger sister, Natalie. In fact Natalie was her illegitimate daughter, the fruit of a half-seduction, half-rape by a Saxon officer when she was fifteen. Natalie was thus Richard Wagner's stepdaughter, but without knowing it, for her mother never revealed her origin to her. In her will she left her property to 'my sister Natalie', and Wagner, who seems to have known the secret early on, kept it to himself.

After the three months summer season in Bad Lauchstädt Wagner and Minna returned with the company to its base in Magdeburg, and Wagner took up his new duties there as regular music director. Still only twenty-one, he was fully at home in the world of operatic and orchestral scores, brimful of zest for the task and bursting with confidence. 'I managed very quickly,' he writes in *Mein Leben*, 'to acquire complete assurance in controlling the orchestra. It was not long before I became very popular with the players, and their excellent playing in certain energetic overtures, the end of which I usually took at an incredibly fast tempo, often roused the audience to deafening applause.' Conducting remained a vital part of Wagner's musical activity to the end of his life, and reports of concerts he conducted in Paris, London and elsewhere later in his career show that he never lost his early panache and dynamism.

Minna not unnaturally enjoyed the attentions of a number of admirers in the town, and Wagner became intensely jealous, using, as he was to do so often in his relationships with women, all kinds of strategems to invoke her pity and concern. Her sympathy was also aroused by his distressing condition during an attack of erysipelas, and shortly after she had nursed him through this, he wrote in a letter to his brother Albert, in February 1835, that they had become engaged. Almost two years were to pass, however, before they married.

They were two restless, worrying years. The Magdeburg theatre went bankrupt six months after Wagner joined it – his appointment to any official position was almost to acquire the status of the kiss of death – and he moved desultorily from one town to another, ostensibly looking for singers who might eventually come to Magdeburg if, and when, the theatre re-opened. First he went to Leipzig, staying with his mother and Rosalie again, then to Dessau, to Dresden, where Minna was with her parents, to Prague and Karlsbad, to Frankfurt, and finally back to Magdeburg, where the company was reassembling under the management of a civic committee. He had started another symphony and completed an overture to a

play by Apel called *Columbus*, but the constant to-ing and
fro-ing, and his ever-increasing debts, were hardly condu-
cive to sustained work.

Above all his passion for Minna left him no peace. 'She
loves me,' he wrote to Apel, 'and her love means everything to me at this time. My life revolves round her. She
gives substance and warmth to my life, and I cannot do
without her.' While he was wandering around Europe,
Minna had returned to Magdeburg to join the re-formed
company. But scarcely was he himself back in the town
than Minna, whose position as leading lady was
threatened by a rival, accepted an engagement in Berlin
and left Magdeburg in a huff. A torrent of love-letters,
openly sexual in their intensity, brought her back, but it
was only a matter of months before the two were separated again, when the company, now municipal, went
bankrupt a second time, the *coup de grâce* being the
spectacular flop of *Das Liebesverbot*. Already in 1836
public ownership seems to have been no guarantee of
economic viability.

Wagner and Minna were married in the Tragheimer
Kirche in Königsberg on 24 November, 1836 – but only
just. They went to the church the day before to arrange
the time of the wedding. 'The pastor kept us waiting in the
hall for an unconscionable time,' said Wagner in *Mein
Leben*, 'and we got involved in an argument which rapidly
deteriorated into a slanging match.' The immediate cause
of Minna's anger was that Wagner had just spent a lot of
money on a new apartment for them to live in – borrowed
money, of course, advanced by unwary tradesmen and
acquaintances. 'We were just about to rush out and go our
separate ways,' Wagner goes on, 'when the pastor opened
the door of his study. Somewhat taken aback by our
quarrelling, he invited us with a certain embarrassment to
join him, which forced us to put on a pleasant expression
again; realizing the tragi-comedy of the situation, we set

the pastor's mind at rest and fixed the wedding for one o'clock the next day.' A happier note was brought into the day's proceedings by a benefit performance of Auber's *Masaniello* that evening, the welcome proceeds of which, in accordance with theatrical convention, went into the grateful Kapellmeister's pocket.

But even now the happy event was not assured of a trouble-free conclusion: 'So absent were my thoughts during what seemed to me a set of totally incomprehensible proceedings, that when the pastor held out the prayerbook on which we were supposed to lay our two wedding rings, Minna had to nudge me with her elbow to remind me what to do.' Then, more seriously: 'Suddenly I had a vision. I saw myself divided into two parts, one above the other, each pulling me in a different direction: the top part was dragging me upwards towards the sun like a man in a dream, while the bottom part held me in the inexorable grip of a mysterious deep-seated fear.'

Perhaps one should not over-dramatize this vision. Yet when one charts the stormy course of their marriage, and when one remembers that whereas the attractive Minna was much sought after by theatrical managers, the debt-laden Wagner had no permanent job and was still struggling to make a mark on the musical world, one can imagine the conflicts in his mind between the ideal and the real, between what he felt he would become and what might threaten to restrain him from achieving it. At all events, both bride and groom showed sufficient human frailty to want to give their union a touchingly conventional image for the eyes of society. In the records Wagner gives his age as twenty-four instead of twenty-three, while Minna coyly admits to only twenty-three of her twenty-seven years.

The climate in Königsberg was bleak, the theatre dreary, and Wagner's musical development sluggish. The only piece he completed was an Overture called *Rule Britannia*, composed in a political spirit akin to that of his *Polonia* Overture of the previous year. *Rule Britannia*, based on phrases from Arne's tune, is Wagner's musical tribute to the land of democracy; it is scored for a large orchestra, including four horns, four trumpets, three trombones, ophicleide and a battery of percussion instruments, which join forces to produce a joyful noise of the species most resonantly represented by Tchaikovsky's *1812*. Wagner's starting-point for both *Polonia* and *Rule Britannia* was Beethoven's overture to Goethe's *Egmont*, a drama likewise devoted to portraying the fight for political freedom. Wagner planned a similar overture on the figure of Napoleon but never started serious work on it.

A few weeks after Wagner's official appointment the management of the Königsberg theatre declared the enterprise bankrupt. He had been relying on a steady income to restore his financial equilibrium, but since the theatre could not pay its debts, including the salaries of its employees, nor could Wagner pay his. Keeping out of the way of his creditors was becoming part of his way of life, but worse than this, he found out that, in her quiet, unostentatious way, his bride of six months was having an affair with a Königsberg businessman, one of the patrons of the theatre. In the course of the mutual recriminations that followed, Wagner threatened divorce, Minna took refuge with her parents in Dresden, Wagner pursued her there, consoling himself in the company of his sister Ottilie and her husband, Minna slipped away again with her lover, Wagner accepted a post as music director in Riga – the comings and goings, the arguments, the protestations, the disillusionments, even the hopes, all crowded in upon them at once.

During the first months of this crisis Wagner oscillated between apologies for his jealousy of Minna's past lovers, violence at her present infidelity and forgiveness of her frailty. Whether she was in as desperate a state as her daughter Natalie made out to Mrs Mary Burrell fifty years later, may be open to question. Natalie had a deep hatred of Cosima von Bülow, Wagner's second wife, and was always anxious to present Minna, whom she saw as her sister, in a favourable light. But the situation was clearly intolerable for both Minna and Wagner, and in a letter written in June 1837, begging her to come back to him, yet also insisting that she realize her responsibilities as his wife, he is blunt and uncompromising: 'By going on in your old way, you make things impossible for me, and rather than have this, I would say: Let us separate for ever.' That moment did not come for many years.

If Königsberg, as Wagner had said, was a hundred miles from German civilization, Riga must have seemed like a thousand. He travelled from Königsberg to Dresden – almost 400 miles, an immense distance at that time – to try and persuade the half-sulking, half-defiant Minna, who had gone back to her mother, to come with him to Riga. She refused. So he left alone, travelled northwards by coach to Berlin, thence to Lübeck, on the Baltic Sea, then by boat – the first of his invariably miserable sea voyages – to Riga, where he arrived in August. Later joined by Minna, he stayed here for two years, making himself a subject of conversation to passers-by through appearing at his window in flamboyant dressing-gown and Turkish fez, but also acquiring the respect of the German community through his work at the theatre.

Since 1710 Riga had been Russian. From its foundation in the twelfth century, however, its history had been essentially German; it had belonged to the Order of Teutonic Knights and been a Hanseatic port, and it was still a predominantly German town in Wagner's day. He took humble lodgings in the Schneiderstrasse, close to the theatre, and plunged enthusiastically into his work of preparing operatic performances and rehearsing incidental music to the dramas in the repertory.

Conditions in the theatre gave him a pleasant surprise. 'After the depressing experience I had already had of small German theatres,' he says in his autobiography, 'the conditions in this newly-founded establishment made a favourable and reassuring impression. A group of rich businessmen and well-to-do friends of the theatre had created a consortium which through its own initiative had collected the necessary funds to provide a firm foundation for the high-class productions it wanted to see mounted.'

The director, a colourful personality from Berlin called Karl von Holtey, was identified by Wagner as belonging to the guild of 'likeable libertines'. He knew exactly what his public wanted, namely, light musical entertainment in the French and Italian style, like the operas of Adam, Auber, Hérold and Donizetti, together with substantial portions of emotional melodrama like Bellini's *Norma*. Although his one-time enthusiasm for such works had now waned, Wagner studied and prepared them without reservation and made the most of the modest but willing choral and orchestral forces under his command.

The first comprehensive biographer of Wagner, Carl Friedrich Glasenapp, has an interesting passage on the Riga theatre.

The auditorium of the old Riga Stadttheater in the Königstrasse was a pretty gloomy place by present-day standards. It had only one block of stalls, and immediately above it was the gallery, particularly popular with middle-class families. Young and old ladies alike, equipped with their knitting and with the necessary refreshments, could be seen arriving early – the seats were not numbered – to make sure of a comfortable place, preferably in the front row of the gallery, and would sit there until the programme began. As to the auditorium itself, a native of Riga, who happened to be in conversation with Wagner many years later, compared it to a barn, and asked him how on earth he had been able to conduct there. Wagner replied that three things about this 'barn' had stayed in his mind: the first was the steeply rising stalls, rather like an amphitheatre; the second was the darkness of the auditorium; and the third was the surprisingly deep orchestra pit. If he ever succeeded in building a theatre to his own designs, he added, he would keep these three features in mind.

He did. It is a remarkable vision, thirty years before the event, of the principles on which the Bayreuth Festival Theatre was built.

When Minna, having extracted a pledge of forgiveness from her husband, arrived in Riga towards the end of the year, she brought her sister Amalie, whom Holtey had engaged as a soprano. Since the flighty Minna had finally agreed to give up the stage for good, and with it the fringe benefit of extra-mural sexual excursions, Amalie's earnings were more than welcome in the communal household, and the three were able to leave the drab rooms in the Schneiderstrasse for more attractive quarters on the outskirts of the town. However, incessant bickering between the two sisters made the atmosphere in the *ménage* increasingly unpleasant. The news of the death in childbirth of Wagner's favourite sister Rosalie depressed him still further. Rosalie had been the one person in the family in whose artistic judgment he had trust, and she had helped to support him during his student days and long afterwards. At the same time a diverting consolation arrived in the form of a huge Newfoundland dog called Robber, who ran away from his original master and attached himself so impulsively to Wagner that from now on he became part of the household.

Of Wagner's industry in Riga there can be no doubt. Despite his growing dissatisfaction with most of Holtey's repertoire, he rehearsed and conducted fifteen operas during his first year and twenty-four during his second, with a thoroughness that caused some members of the company to complain to Holtey that they were being overworked. Not content with his operatic work alone, he announced a season of subscription concerts which, unlike opera, would bring him the undivided praise of the public and also give him a chance to perform some of his own pieces. The *Rule Britannia* Overture and the Overture to Apel's *Columbus* were slipped into the programme in this way. Heinrich Dorn, writing in the *Neue Zeitschrift für Musik*, called their conception 'Beethovenian' and their development 'broad', but their tempi 'ponderous' and their length 'almost tiring'. Inevitably, this enterprise on Wagner's part was seen by his enemies as pure self-advertisement, and it helped to bring about his subsequent dismissal, for which Holtey and his party were to be chiefly responsible.

Whether in spite of his busy life as a practical musician or because of it, work on compositions of his own was almost at a standstill, and practically all he managed to achieve during these two years in Riga was Act One and most of Act Two of the opera *Rienzi*.

In his earliest operas, including *Rienzi*, Wagner's basic procedure was first to prepare a composition sketch on three staves, the top one carrying the vocal parts, and the two lower ones the fundamentals of the accompaniment, then to make from this the full orchestral score. From *Der fliegende Holländer* right through to *Parsifal*, his last work, he proceeded in three stages: first came the composition sketch, for the most part on two staves, containing all the thematic material and the basic harmony – the vocal line and text on the upper stave and the bass, with an occasional chord to mark the harmony, on the lower; this was followed by an orchestral sketch on two, three or more staves, according to the vocal and orchestral forces involved, with stage directions and other instructions; finally came the full score.

That the later stages of the composition process absorb

their predecessors is obvious. Less obvious, but equally important to an understanding of Wagner's finished product, is that the text already carries in it the seeds of the music which is to grow out of it. Put another way: his texts are not dramas in their own right, self-sufficient poetic works to be read or acted as they stand, nor, at the other extreme, are they mere perfunctory vehicles for the music that is superimposed on them; they are a kind of precondition for the musical expression, the necessary basis of the final dramatic *Gesamtkunstwerk,* in which each art requires, and is inseparable from, the other. This is why Wagner had to be his own librettist, and why he was rarely successful in setting words written by others.

His occupation with *Rienzi* had started in Dresden in the summer of 1837 during one of his periods of despair over how he and Minna could possibly survive together. Among the new books he had seen in the private library of his brother-in-law Hermann Brockhaus was a German translation of Bulwer-Lytton's *Rienzi: The Last of the Tribunes*, a long-winded historical romance on the life of the fourteenth-century Roman demagogue who rose to become a great republican leader, the darling of the masses, only to fall victim to his own lust for power and be killed by those who had once idolized him. Reading this story in his mood of depression, Wagner could share with Rienzia a defiant conviction that the times were out of joint, that petty-mindedness and intrigue governed the affairs of men, and that a new idealism, source of noble thoughts and deeds, must arise to restore the freedom and natural goodness of man. His mind went back to the student demonstrations in Leipzig, to the July Revolution in Paris, to the Polish uprisings, to the liberal-patriotic emotions of the Hambach Festival – challenges to the present decadence and a call to moral and spiritual renewal. Rienzi's concept of the *buono stato*, the 'good state', became for Wagner the problem of individual liberty and the establishment of a popular democracy that would guarantee this liberty.

But by the time the anti-Wagner faction managed to have him removed from his post in Riga, little of the five-act 'Grand Tragic Opera' *Rienzi* had been written. Wagner's relations with Holtey had been slowly deteriorating, partly because Minna had refused an engagement that Holtey had offered her, and partly because he resented Wagner's intercalation of his own pieces into his orchestral programmes and his refusal to write incidental music for Holtey's plays. Above all Wagner's artistic standards were simply too high for either Holtey or the performers to tolerate for long. Holtey himself was becoming unpopular in the town and realized that he would soon have to leave, but first he arranged for Wagner to be replaced by Heinrich Dorn, civic director of music in Riga, without saying a word to Wagner himself. Wagner, though enraged at his dismissal, was powerless to prevent it. In so far as he could be happy anywhere, he must have been almost so in Riga, with a regular income and the chance to develop his gifts as a conductor. At the same time it was all too provincial for him; young as he still was, he had already outgrown what the cultural life of Riga or any German town, Berlin alone excepted, could offer him.

At the back of his mind was the thought that the triumphant production of *Rienzi* in one of the great cities of Europe, preferably Paris, would assure his fame and solve his financial problems at a stroke. But these problems could not wait that long. The situation was made worse by the fact that permission for a resident to leave Russia could be granted only after the intending traveller had publicly announced his intention three times in the press, so that those with financial claims to make would have time to present them. This was the last thing Wagner could afford. Once he had decided that he and Minna should go to Paris, and since legal exit from the country was impossible, the question became, how could they smuggle themselves out?

Two circumstances were to help them. One was the opera's forthcoming summer season in the small town of Mitau (now Jelgava), thirty miles south of Riga, where police control of people leaving the country was less strict than in Riga; Wagner had already received his notice of dismissal, but it did not take effect until after the tour to Mitau, so it was a matter of course that he should accompany the troupe there. The other was the providential reappearance of Abraham Möller, one of his staunch supporters in Königsberg, who now proceeded to lay an elaborate plan to get the couple across the border and back on to Prussian territory.

The episode, told in detail by Wagner in *Mein Leben* and also in Heinrich Dorn's memoirs, has an air of comic solemnity about it. The enterprising Möller travelled up to Mitau in his coach, collected the two Wagners and the giant Robber, with whatever bedding, linen and other household goods they could carry, and set off back with them to Königsberg on a burning hot day in July. The three passengers and their luggage took up practically all the room in the coach, and to start with Robber had to gallop along beside it. But as the miles went by, the heat told on the poor dog. Wagner, who was very sentimental about animals, and whose household was not complete without at least a dog, stopped the coach and insisted that they make room for the huge creature inside. This done, the four passengers continued their journey, with Wagner in a mood of jubilation at having escaped from Riga and at the prospect of success in Paris.

On the evening of the second day they reached the Prussian frontier, where they were met by a friend of

Möller's whose task was to get them across. There was a ditch running the length of the frontier; Möller's friend bribed some of the border guards to look the other way, and when he gave the word, Wagner and Minna, with the mercifully silent Robber trotting beside them, made a rush for the ditch and lay down in it. The friend had a coach waiting on the Prussian side, and with the guards' attention again distracted, they scrambled out of the ditch and into the coach, which drove off at full speed to an inn in a nearby village, where the anxious Möller received them with great relief.

The next day they set out with Möller in an open cart for the little port of Pillau, on the Gulf of Danzig, since in Königsberg, as in Riga, there were creditors waiting to spring into action at the mention of the name Wagner. Just before reaching Pillau, the cart overturned, and Minna received such a shock that they had to spend the night in a peasant's cottage while she recovered. Finally they got to the coast, only to find that the cargo boat *Thetis*, the little sailing vessel which was to take them to London on the first stage of the journey to Paris, would be several days late in leaving. When at last the day came, they were rowed out to the *Thetis* in a dinghy before dawn and clambered on board, while Robber was hauled up the side of the ship. So their voyage to freedom began – freedom to starve, freedom to fail, freedom to be ignored.

But first there was an ordeal by ship to be undergone. Eight days out, en route for Copenhagen, they struck a storm in the Skaggerak which forced the *Thetis* to seek shelter in a Norwegian fjord for three days. It was a striking moment, which Wagner had good cause to remember in his autobiography: 'The huge granite cliffs echoed to the shouts of the crew as they lowered the anchor and furled the sails. The rhythm of their cry was like an augury of comfort and quickly took the form in my mind of the theme of the Sailors' Chorus* in my *Fliegen-de Holländer*, a subject that had been in my thoughts for some time.'

Four days of fair weather were followed by a second, even worse storm, during which Wagner and Minna were convinced they would all drown. The couple had to share the ship's one cabin with the captain and were regarded with suspicion by the crew. Their unpopularity reached its climax when Robber, who will hardly have enjoyed the voyage any more than his owners, began to attack the most drunken of the ship's drunken sailors. A third storm struck them off the east coast of England. The *Thetis* finally sailed up the Thames in mid-August, 1839, three-and-a-half weeks after leaving Pillau, a voyage that would normally take eight days.

Wagner and Minna stayed in London for a week, taking a room in a boarding-house in Old Compton Street. The strain of the escape from Riga had left Minna in a pitiful state, and she spent much of the week recovering, while her energetic husband set out to visit Sir George Smart, conductor of the Philharmonic Society, to whom he had sent his *Rule Britannia* Overture, and Lord Lytton, with whom he wanted to discuss *Rienzi*. Neither of those gentlemen was in London at the time, but his enterprising attempt to find Lord Lytton at the House of Lords led him to spend the afternoon in the Strangers' Gallery of the Upper House, listening to, though hardly understanding, a debate on the slave trade. After experiencing 'all the horrors of an eerie English Sunday', as he put it, they crossed the Channel to Boulogne, where Wagner worked on the score of *Rienzi* for a few weeks and showed parts of the opera to Meyerbeer.

*

The forty-eight-year-old Giacomo Meyerbeer, born Jakob Liebmann Beer, the son of a Berlin banker, had been undisputed king of the Paris Opera since his *Robert le Diable* in 1831. He had a remarkable flair for fusing a variety of theatrical and musical traditions to produce works of spectacular pageantry and effectiveness, containing something for everybody to whom opera meant primarily entertainment and display. The success of *Robert le Diable* was followed by that of *Les Huguenots* in 1836 and of *Le Prophète* in 1849 – all three of them to libretti by Eugène Scribe, who also wrote the texts of famous operas by Auber, Verdi, Donizetti, Rossini and many others. Meyerbeer was appointed Music Director in Berlin in 1842 but still spent much of his time in Paris, where he died in 1864.

It was pure chance that Meyerbeer happened to be in Boulogne when Wagner landed there. On the boat Wagner had met a Jewish woman who knew the Meyerbeer family and gave him an introduction to the influential Giacomo. 'He confirmed the reports I had heard about his generosity and kindness,' Wagner wrote in *Mein Leben*, 'and made a highly favourable impression on me in every respect.' It was an impression that quickly changed.

Having read Meyerbeer a good part of the libretto of *Rienzi* and left him the first two acts of the score to study, Wagner travelled on by coach to Paris, centre of the operatic world and of his designs for artistic conquest. But the defences of Parisian musical life were not destined to fall before the attacks of the young Wagner, nor were men of influence prepared to see in him the prophet of the music of the future. Meyerbeer had murmured complimentary things about *Rienzi* but did not turn his words into deeds. Like every metropolis, political, economic or cultural, Paris was a jungle, with each man scrambling to grab what would ensure his survival. Wagner, however, with that naïve sense of predestined greatness that is one

of the dominant features of his personality, unques-
tioningly assumed that those in the cultural corridors of
power would immediately sense the presence of genius
and prepare a path for it. It was neither the first nor the
last time that he learned the hard way.

Wagner's step-sister Cäcilie had recently become engaged to an employee of the publishing firm of Brockhaus
called Eduard Avenarius, who had been put in charge of
the firm's affairs in Paris. Wagner wrote from Boulogne,
asking him to find a hotel for Minna and himself and
Robber, and they arrived in Paris to find themselves
accommodated in the Rue de la Tonnellerie, near Les
Halles (the street no longer exists).

Having worked himself into a state of high enthusiasm
at the prospect of working in the great city, Wagner found
the place dirty and depressing. Everything seemed cramped, narrow and noisy; the legendary boulevards were far
less impressive than he had expected, and the well-known
Rue de Richelieu, where Avenarius worked, struck him as
far less impressive than the streets of London's West End,
which were fresh in his mind. However, above the entrance to his hotel there was a plaque inscribed 'Molière was
born here', with a bust of the dramatist. 'This favourable
omen,' he drily observed, 'afforded a measure of consolation for the poor impression the city made on me.'
Fortunately he did not know that as so often in such cases,
the plaque was affixed to the wrong house.

Through Avenarius, who was soon to experience the
special obligations, especially financial, that went with
being a brother-in-law of Richard Wagner, he made the
acquaintance of a pathetic, once well-to-do German who
gave expression to his alienation from society by using the
assumed name of Gottfried Engelbert Anders (German
anders = different). Anders, who had a minor post in the
Bibliothèque Royale, shared lodgings with an im-
poverished Jewish scholar called Samuel Lehrs, with

whom Wagner formed a friendship described in *Mein Leben* as one of the most moving he ever experienced, a friendship cut short by Lehrs' death from consumption little over three years later.

In these early days the two men called on Wagner in his hotel almost every evening. The nervous Anders, a man of fifty or so, was very uncertain on his feet and would make his way through the streets with a cane in one hand and an umbrella in the other. He was also afraid of Robber, and when Wagner opened the door, Anders would push Lehrs in first to distract the dog's attention, then try to creep in unnoticed. As a result Robber became highly suspicious of him, and Wagner was afraid that one day there might be a repetition of the attack on the sailor on board the *Thetis*. But fortunately there was not.

Two more men, both painters, came into Wagner's life at this time. One was Ernst Benedikt Kietz, from Dresden, who was apprenticed to the studio of Delaroche and later set up in Paris as a portrait painter. To Kietz we owe the earliest known sketch of Wagner, made in the winter of 1839. He lived in Paris until 1870 and was a faithful friend to Wagner throughout these years, especially during Wagner's later attempts to impress his musical personality on the French capital.

The other was Friedrich Pecht, also a student in Delaroche's studio, a less gifted painter and a far less intimate friend than Kietz, but a man to whom we owe a fascinating eye-witness account of the Wagner he knew in Paris.

He was strikingly elegant [writes Pecht], indeed aristocratic in appearance, in spite of his rather short legs, and with such an attractive woman on his arm that she alone would have made the couple interesting if Wagner himself had not had such an impressive head that one's attention was involuntarily fixed on him . . . He showed great wit and vivacity, and we soon became friends, and as I had all kinds of interests in common with him, since we were both seeking our fortune in Paris, I often visited him in the little fourth-floor apartment he had rented in the Rue du Helder [Wagner and Minna moved here in April 1840] and immediately re-furnished – on credit, of course. He obviously had an innate gift for running up debts – perhaps because of the old actor's blood in him. Here I saw and heard the opera taking shape [i.e. *Rienzi*] through which we had come to know each other. Unfortunately he was far too bad a pianist, and I too poor a musician, for me to be able to judge whether he really had creative genius. But his magic power of attraction and his lively ability in other respects were beyond dispute, as was the fundamental nobility of his character, which ensured that in spite of his boisterous passion and sparkling wit he never appeared rough or common.

Charles Hallé, at this time a rising young pianist, also remembered Wagner as a somewhat larger-than-life character. 'He rarely spoke of his aspirations,' wrote Hallé in his autobiography, 'but when he did so, it was usually in a strain which made us wonder if, as the phrase goes, he was "all there". We liked him as a most frank, amiable and lively companion, modest and full of enthusiasm for all that is beautiful in art. And he evidently felt at home with us.' When the two men met again at the first Bayreuth Festival in 1876, by which time Wagner had become the most famous composer in Europe, his first words were of those enjoyable evenings that he had spent with Hallé in Paris.

The most significant and far-reaching encounter of Wagner's years in Paris, however, was with Franz Liszt, though at the time there could have been no inkling on either man's part of how closely intertwined their lives were to become. In April 1840 Wagner secured an introduction to him through the publisher Maurice Schlesinger, but the meeting made no mark on Liszt. A year later they met again, at a crowded reception in Liszt's hotel, with a result little better than the first. Liszt was the great virtuoso, lionized by elegant society, the darling of the ladies, the epitome of success and grace, and extremely wealthy. A bigger contrast with the unknown and near-destitute Wagner, resentful of the prosperity and success of others, keeping himself from starvation by making arrangements of other composers' music and similar hack work, could scarcely be imagined. Not only did Wagner covet Liszt's success, he also found, along with the wild brilliance of Liszt's playing, something meretricious about it, suspecting that the self-centred Liszt pandered to that popular taste which he, Wagner, had now pledged himself to transform and transcend. The two men had their first serious exchange of views in Berlin the following year, but a close relationship between them did not develop until later.

In anticipation of getting *Das Liebesverbot* performed at the Théâtre de la Renaissance, to whose director Meyerbeer had given him an introduction, Wagner borrowed 400 francs from Eduard Avenarius and smaller sums from other friends, and moved into the bigger apartment at 25 Rue du Helder, off the Boulevard des Italiens, that Pecht remembered. He also reckoned on royalties from a group of French songs he had just completed, including a setting of a translation of Heine's famous poem 'The Two Grenadiers'. But *Das Liebesverbot* was turned down, and the songs, which he had had printed on his own initiative, though without picking up the bill, brought in nothing. Nor did his *Faust Overture*, his tribute to Goethe, the first version of which was finished at the beginning of 1840. He did, however, earn a little through hack work such as reading proofs, preparing piano reductions of orchestral material and making various other musical arrangements, while his real musical goal remained the completion of *Rienzi*.

The two-and-a-half years Wagner spent in Paris were a source of profound misery and bitter disillusionment. *Rienzi* and *Der fliegende Holländer* were both eventually completed there but neither was performed. In fact, the only hearing his music received was one miserable performance of the *Columbus* Overture. During the first months work on the score of *Rienzi* went more and more slowly, his financial situation became worse and worse, and his spirits sank lower and lower. He begged and borrowed from whomever he could, pawned all his and Minna's valuables, including their wedding-rings, then, when this money had gone, sold the pawn tickets. More than once he narrowly missed being imprisoned for failing to pay his debts.

Even such a circumstance as this he was prepared to put to his advantage. In October 1840 he had Minna write a pitiful letter to his old friend Theodor Apel to say that he had just been taken to jail, and could Apel, as he had done before, possibly bail him out so that he could return to his dear wife, continue work on his great opera *Rienzi*, and so on. Apel, together with Laube, lent what he could. But the circumstantial evidence suggests that Wagner was not in prison at all, and had merely told Minna to write the begging letter in such alarming terms so as to be sure of achieving the desired result.

A particular indignity came one morning in the form of a parcel from London. It contained the score of his overture *Rule Britannia*, returned by the Philharmonic Society. But there was a shipping charge of seven francs to pay, which he could not afford, so the parcel went back to London. He never saw the score again.

On top of everything, Robber ran away. A year later Wagner caught sight of the unmistakable giant in a Paris street and gave chase, but the great dog loped off whenever he got too close. 'I pursued him through a maze of streets barely recognizable in the fog,' he said in *Mein Leben*, 'until, out of breath and dripping with perspiration, I finally lost sight of him for ever by the church of Saint-Roche.'

A moment of pleasure came when he saw Heinrich

Laube again. Laube's political views had since cost him a year in jail in Berlin, but he now appeared in Paris as the husband of a wealthy young widow who was prevailed upon to offer some modest help to the down-at-heel musician and his wife. Through Laube Wagner met Heinrich Heine, who had been in political exile in Paris since 1831 and was to spend the rest of his life there, but the two men did not come close to each other. Heine, who was as difficult and unscrupulous a person as Wagner, commented: 'Do you know what makes me suspicious of that talented man? The fact that he is recommended by Meyerbeer.' Meyerbeer, the Jew, recommending Wagner, who later became a violent anti-Semite, and being sneered at by Heine, a fellow-Jew, for doing so – the situation is rich in the often unpleasant irony that surrounds Heine's personality and work.

Wagner also came to know Berlioz at this time, though there was no question of an intimate friendship. He respected Berlioz, the disturbing, uncompromising innovator, above all for his integrity as an artist, seeing him as the only man in the corrupt and mercenary world of Parisian music who did not pander to popular taste and compose just for money. Yet although he was impressed by *Romeo and Juliet* and *Harold in Italy*, his verdict on Berlioz's music has an interesting ambivalence about it which many have since shared. 'For all the power and grandeur of this inimitable music,' he wrote, 'I could not overcome a certain sense of trepidation when facing it. I shrank from it as though in the presence of something strange, something I could never really come close to, with the result that Berlioz's major works not only gripped me and inspired me but sometimes also repelled me, even – dare I say – bored me.'

There is in Berlioz, as in numerous writers, painters and composers of the time, including Wagner, a strong infusion of that Romantic passion for the grandiose which is so marked a characteristic of life and art in the nineteenth century. The middle-class parvenu culture of the July monarchy and the Second Empire of 1848 had to look outside for the qualities of grandeur and monumentality that it lacked in itself. In the theatre spectacle triumphed over drama, while opera, which offered even greater opportunities for ostentation and effect, acquired a special status. This Parisian Grand Opera, opera-as-spectacle, reached its summit in Meyerbeer, who, following Spontini, Auber and Rossini, composed mammoth works like *Robert le Diable, Les Huguenots, Le Prophète*, and *L'Africaine*, which embodied in their own way the principle of the *Gesamtkunstwerk* long before Wagner, and without any programme or body of theoretical doctrine. The opera-going middle classes wanted to be impressed, swept off their feet, and the Paris opera triumphantly fulfilled their need, as it did again twenty years later in the elegant frivolity of the operettas of Offenbach.

Such a situation provoked Wagner to resentment and anger, and in his depressing, at times desperate, living conditions, and his failure to make any impression on the musical life of the city he had been so confident of 'conquering', these years in Paris brought about the first real crisis of his mature intellectual life. This in turn induced a decisive change in his attitudes both to art and to society. His view of his own situation at this time, and the exposition of these socio-artistic attitudes, find their most attractive and effective expression not in any letters or autobiographic sources but in the three linked short stories that make up his little trilogy *Ein deutscher Musiker in Paris (A German Musician in Paris)*.

These charming cameos, strongly reminiscent in motifs and in manner of the stories of E. T. A. Hoffmann, were first published in serial form, in French translation, in the Paris journal *Gazette musicale* between November 1840 and October 1841. All three of them are first-person narratives, permitting a blend of the autobiographical and the imaginary, as Wagner, the 'German musician in Paris', writes about what is and what might have been. The first story, *Eine Pilgerfahrt zu Beethoven (A Pilgrimage to Beethoven)*, is of the latter kind, a reverential yet gently humorous account of a journey that he might have made to Vienna to visit the composer he worshipped above all others. The other two, *Ein glücklicher Abend (A Happy Evening)* and *Ein Ende in Paris (An End in Paris)*, are cast as dialogues between the narrator and his self-projection as the 'German musician in Paris', in which the narrator prompts his *alter ego*, called Robert, to talk of Mozart and Beethoven, of the nature of musical perform-ance, and above all of the intolerable situation where a young composer finds himself at the whim and fancy of a philistine public and a set of commercially-minded impre-sarios. The attractive figure of the 'German scholar' in *Ein Ende in Paris* is Wagner's tribute to Samuel Lehrs. Robber, the renegade Newfoundland, also makes his appearance at the end of the story, as the dying Robert, spurned by society and left to starve, recalls the exper-iences – Wagner's experiences – of his last months. 'Here I lie,' he says, 'determined to pass away in thoughts of God and pure music . . . I believe in God, Mozart and Beethoven, in the Holy Spirit and in the truth of a single indivisible Art.' With this creed on his lips, he dies.

The conditions that Robert describes, his anger at a social system that produces these conditions, and the articles of the faith that he affirms on his death bed, are all Wagner's own. 'Every word,' he said later, 'is a cry of protest against modern artistic conditions, and from this moment on I trod a new path – the path of revolt against the artistic establishment, against the attitude of the public to art.' Thus from the very beginning his protest at the position of art in society was linked with a rebellion against society itself, for the pursuit of art, as a public activity, could not be divorced from the values of the community that sustained it, or failed to sustain it. In the years that followed these sobering experiences in Paris the spirit of Wagner's rebellion became more and more political, reaching its climax in the events that followed the revolution of 1848, but in its origins it was a rebellion based on art. Equally important, his rebellion was the product, not of social theories or book knowledge – though these played their part in consolidating his views as the years went by – but of personal experience, the experience of his self-confident genius in conflict with the values, tastes and expectations of the decadent society that was his paymaster. He was a have-not, full of the have-not's envy and hatred of the haves who surrounded him.

As well as his three short stories the Paris *Gazette musicale* published a number of his essays, on a wide range of subjects, between 1840 and 1842 – *Über deutsche Musik (On German Music), Der Virtuos und der Künstler (The Virtuoso and the Artist), Über die Ouvertüre (On the Overture), Der Künstler und die Öffentlichkeit (The Artist and the Public)* and an essay on Weber's *Der Freischütz*, intended as an introduction to the first performance of the work in Paris in 1841 – all, of course, in French translation. Those that deal with aesthetic topics, and with the relationship of the artist to his public, show the influence of E. T. A. Hoffmann; in the more directly critical pieces his style is particularly indebted to Heine. Common to all of them, whether in an attempt to characterize the spirit of German music for the benefit of the French (*On German Music*) or in a sketch of the development of the overture from Handel to Beethoven (*On the Overture*) is a markedly subjective, almost autobiographical manner and an aggressive tone. As man, as critic, as composer, Wagner was always the centre of his own world.

These essays, like the stories of *A German Musician in*

Paris, brought in some money to add to the fees he received from copying and other musical chores, to the loans and gifts he extracted from Avenarius, Apel and Laube, and to the dwindling proceeds of visits to the pawnbroker. But ends would still not meet, especially as the apartment in the Rue du Helder was far too expensive. Minna took in two elderly ladies as lodgers, while Wagner made an unsuccessful attempt to get help from Abraham Möller in Königsberg and dropped equally unproductive hints, as he resentfully tells in *Mein Leben*, when his sister Luise and her rich husband Friedrich Brockhaus came to Paris on a quick visit.

Paris may have symbolized for Wagner the contemporary music industry at its most corrupt and despicable, yet the performances he saw at the Opéra, or Académie Royale de Musique, as it was officially called, taught him the value of painstaking rehearsal and attention to detail. The standards of singing, playing and production were far higher than anything he had known in Leipzig or anywhere else in Germany. At the same time these years mark his turn from *Die Feen*, based on Gozzi, *Das Liebesverbot*, after Shakespeare, and the Italian hero Rienzi to the Germanic world of *Der fliegende Holländer, Tannhäuser* and *Lohengrin*. It is here that he lays the foundations of that cultivation of Germanic myth and legend which issues in *The Ring*, here, scorned in the foreign world of Romance civilization, that he begins to feel his German-ness, a national pride in the 'holy German Art' of which the chorus sings at the end of *Die Meistersinger*.

But the earliest of his operas that people now remember is very different. *Rienzi* was completed in November 1840. In a fawning letter which contains the avowal – quite false – that he had always wanted the work to have its first performance in Dresden, Wagner besought King Friedrich August II of Saxony to issue a royal decree that this be arranged and asked the King's permission to dedicate the opera to him. He had to wait over six months for an answer – but it was the answer he had asked for. Meyerbeer too wrote a letter of recommendation to Baron August von Lüttichau, director of the Royal Saxon Opera, though the work did not have its première there until 1842.

Rienzi is a piece of pure grand opera à la Meyerbeer – 'Meyerbeer's best opera', Bülow called it. Flamboyance, theatrical display, bravura arias for vocal exhibitionists from coloratura soprano to basso profundo, great marches and processions for the serried ranks of the chorus, the obligatory Parisian ballet in the second act, violence, love, noble principles, baseness, arson, destruction – Wagner satisfied all the expectations and conventions of the day, partly because his desire for success made him fight grand opera with its own weapons, partly also because he wanted to link his work to a living art form, a living tradition. The general unmemorability of *Rienzi*, its paucity of thrilling moments, stem from the shortcomings of Wagner's musical imagination at this moment, but many of the commonplaces of the work – the use of diminished seventh chords and arpeggios to convey horror, syncopated rhythms to convey excitement – derive from the world of Parisian opera that is its spiritual home.

Yet Wagner's years in Paris mark his revulsion from the society that sustained this kind of art and found in it an expression of its values. His detestation, based on envy, of the aristocracy expresses itself in *Rienzi* through the antagonism of the Roman people to the nobility and through the attempted abduction, in the very first scene, of the pure Irene, Rienzi's daughter, by the nobleman Orsini – a theme which has behind it Lessing's *Emilia Galotti*, Schiller's *Fiesko* and the whole tradition of the so-called 'bourgeois tragedy'. His anti-establishment emotions also emerge in his presentation of the power of Papal

Rome as a force for backwardness and intolerance, 'feudal' in the worst sense, and allied with the political powers that be in the defence of reaction and obscurantism. So while the external form and the superficial means of presentation, including the musical style, reflect a short-lived ideal of convenience, the political commitment that dominates the last two acts represents a new Wagner, the Wagner of the revolutionary ideas on art and society expounded in the essays of 1848 and the succeeding years.

Not surprisingly, therefore, Wagner was later at pains to draw a line between *Rienzi* and everything that followed. And since the first work that did follow, *Der fliegende Holländer*, was complete almost a year before the first performance of *Rienzi*, one can see how rapidly the change took place. Indeed, 'change' is too mild a word to describe the violent spiritual process through which he went, a process equally compounded, as he said, of longing – the desire for renewal, constructive, idealistic – and repugnance – a revulsion from what was now behind him but in which his *Rienzi* had had its part. *Rienzi* is drama-with-music – cynics might say, pseudo-drama-with-music; the ideal which Wagner now began to see was music-drama. Though not to be put in the same basket as *Die Feen* and *Das Liebesverbot*, it has never been accepted into the true Wagnerian canon, and has never been performed at Bayreuth. Indeed, Wagner himself later excluded it, naming *Der fliegende Holländer* as the earliest of the works he wished to see brought into the Festival repertoire.

Many years later, when at work on the *Die Meistersinger*, Wagner remarked that *Rienzi* was so remote from him that it almost seemed to have been written by someone else – a comment all the more trenchant in that one of the psychological corollaries to his self-centredness was an inability to do justice to the music of others. Yet when someone was overheard to say something uncomplimentary about *Rienzi*, Wagner snapped: 'All right, you try and write one!'

In the spring of 1841, finally forced to admit that they could not possibly afford to go on living in the Rue du Helder, the Wagners moved away from the city and rented a small summer apartment in Meudon, a village some twelve miles out. At the time this must have seemed like yet one more inexorable proof of failure, especially as at one moment, having missed the official date for cancelling the rent agreement on the Rue du Helder, Wagner found himself threatened with having to pay for two apartments at the same time. A further galling irony lay in the fact that Cäcilie and Eduard Avenarius, who had recently married, also took a summer apartment in Meudon, where they enjoyed all the domestic security and settled comfort which the Wagners lacked but, proud in spite of their poverty, affected to share. In fact, the months at Meudon were to signal a gradual rise in Wagner's fortunes, his emergence from the misery and apparent hopelessness into which his personal and artistic career had slumped.

First came the acceptance of *Rienzi* for Dresden. Then came a financial windfall from *Der fliegende Holländer*. The idea for a work on this subject had, we know, been in his mind for some while, and already in the summer of 1840 he had prepared a scenario for a one-act opera and left it with the director of the Paris Opera, Léon Pillet. Now, a year later, Pillet declared his interest in the sketch but suggested that Wagner should sell it to him for use, in translation, by a French composer. At first Wagner indignantly refused. However, when he learned that others were also at work on what was, after all, a well-known story, and that the deal would leave him free to set his own German libretto at any time, he decided to accept the 500 francs that Pillet offered.

The French text was given to one Pierre Dietsch, whose opera *Le vaisseau fantôme*, produced in Paris in 1842, was poorly received. Dietsch later rose to the eminence of conductor at the Opéra, and it was he who conducted the famous riot-torn performances of *Tannhäuser* in 1861. Wagner, in the meantime, exhilarated at the freedom that Pillet's 500 francs had bought him, immediately rented a piano – a luxury he had to do without for months – and plunged into the composition of his own opera. He was a totally different person. 'Everything suddenly came to life again,' he exclaimed. 'People were amazed at my high spirits, and the Avenarius family in particular were convinced that I was now very well off, since they found me such jovial company.'

The music of *Rienzi* had taken over two years to write. That of *Der fliegende Holländer*, begun at the moment of elation when he heard that *Rienzi* had been accepted for Dresden, was finished in short score, apart from the overture, in a miraculous seven weeks, and fully scored only two months later, by the middle of October 1841. The overture, a perfect statement in miniature of the dramatic passion that surges through the entire work, was written the following month. On the title page he wrote: 'In darkness and misery. *Per aspera ad astra*. May God bless it.'

The legend of the sailor condemned by the Devil to a life of endless voyaging until released from the curse by a woman's love was so familiar that Wagner must have known it since his schooldays, but it was through reading in Riga the interpretation of it by Heine in his *Memoiren des Herrn Schnabelewopski* that he first felt gripped by its dramatic qualities. The terrible voyage from Pillau to London then exposed him to the fury of the sea and to the dangers that were part of all sailors' daily lives, and the dramatic power of the legend took an even tighter hold on his mind.

Wagner sees the Dutchman as a kind of 'Wandering Jew of the ocean', in Heine's phrase, a figure from the world of spirits who has been turned by his curse into an outsider, and in whom despair of human kind and human society has generated a death-wish. Yet Senta's pure, redeeming love too is doomed, in the tragic tradition of such Romantic tales, through its implication in the mysterious world of the spirits, the underworld. No human love can survive this experience. It is a love that can find no other fulfilment than in death – the theme of the *Liebestod*, the love-death, which haunted Wagner throughout his life and returns again and again in his operas, but which was already a motif in the stories of German Romantic writers earlier in the century.

The irreducible tragic conflict can also be presented in other ways. Senta sees the fulfilment of her love in earthly terms, in marriage, the natural culmination of the pledge of eternal fidelity that binds her to the Dutchman. But for the Dutchman her love means death, which in turn means the release he seeks from the curse that the Devil has laid upon him, his ultimate salvation. Senta throws herself into the raging sea to prove her love; the Dutchman, in his despair, seeks to save her from her sacrifice by rejecting her love and accepting the perpetuation of his curse. Or in other terms: the Dutchman belongs to a non-mortal world whose claims are absolute, the world of spirit, irreconcilable with the relativities of earthly existence, demanding everything and offering nothing in return. Senta – how can she do otherwise? – offers the most that a mortal can offer, but it is not in her power to penetrate the world of unyielding absolutes to which the Dutchman is subject.

Wagner related this world of the Dutchman to the world of his own life and art, and thus to the uncompromising claims which he himself made on those who were drawn into his orbit. In an extraordinary letter to Liszt in 1853 he even identifies himself with his 'sorrowful hero',

as he called him, seeing no salvation but in death, 'death
in the raging sea, not on a sick bed', and quoting the
passionate cry from Senta's ballad which he could not get
out of his mind: 'Would that thou couldst find her, ghost-
like sailor!'

Ach, möch-test Du, blei-cher See - mann, sie fin - den!

Yet the moment at the very end of the opera, as Senta
jumps to her death, and the Dutchman's ship, with all its
crew, is swallowed up and crushed by the waves, is a
moment of victory, of the transfigured union of the
Dutchman and his redeemer. Clasped in each other's arms
they rise in a vision above the wild sea that has brought
death to one but deliverance to the other, and the music
gently subsides as the woodwind, *piano*, play for the last
time the languorous redemption motif.

This, the first time that we have had cause to talk of the
Leitmotif, a term so intimately associated with the compositional technique of Wagner's operas, is perhaps an
appropriate moment to give a first glance at what the
technique involves. Neither the term *Leitmotif* nor, as a
principle, the practice it defines was invented by Wagner.
Wagner's own word for a musical theme that becomes
associated with a specific object, personality, situation or
idea was *Grundthema*, basic theme. As for the principle in
practice, it is present, for example, in *Don Giovanni*
(1787), where the same motif accompanies the two appearances of the murdered Commendatore; in Grétry's
Richard Coeur de Lion (1785), in which a theme described
as *'une fièvre brûlante'* is used nine times in the opera at
moments of particular intensity; and, outside opera, in the
idée fixe of Berlioz's *Symphonie Fantastique*. Closer to,
but still earlier than, Wagner, Glinka uses the device in *A*

Life for the Czar (1836), while among Wagner's contemporaries Verdi does so in *Ernani* (1844), and Schumann in *Genoveva* (1850).

Its fully developed form in later works, together with Wagner's own theory of its exploitation, will concern us when the time comes. But the basic quality of a leitmotif as a device of association, whether as a motif of reminiscence or of presentiment, and with the many possible derivatives and combinations of the two, does not change, and is as unmistakable in *Der fliegende Holländer* as in *Götterdämmerung*. Association with a person or an object is, of course, the simplest and most direct form that a leitmotif can take, but it is the association with ideas and with developing states of mind which brings that psychological intensification of the meaning of the action from which Wagner's mature works derive their musical depth and power.

In *Der fliegende Holländer* there are the familiar motifs associated with the Dutchman's endless wandering, with the concept of redemption, with Senta's eternal love and so on. But the retention of the formal eighteenth-century pattern of separate musical numbers in each of the three acts – Act One, for instance, is divided into introduction, Helmsman's Song, the Dutchman's recitative and aria, scene and duet (Daland and Dutchman) and Sailors' Chorus – inevitably works against the uninhibited employment of leitmotifs. Only when this conventionalism is abandoned and the integrated music drama achieved, with the psychological motivation generated from within and accompanied by the free-ranging 'endless melody' of Wagner's fully developed style, does the leitmotif technique come into its own.

Der fliegende Holländer, as its title says, is a 'romantic opera', in the tradition of Weber's *Der Freischütz*, with touches of Mendelssohn and even of Meyerbeer, but above all with a rich harmonic vocabulary whose chromaticism goes far beyond Weber (the duet between Senta and Erik in Act Two is a beautiful example) and already carries in it the seeds of *Tristan und Isolde* and *Parsifal*. So much else in *Der fliegende Holländer* besides the music also points to the future – the text, for example, which Wagner now saw as a poem, not as a libretto: 'This was the moment when my career as a poet began and when I ceased being a producer of libretti.' And Senta, the character from whom the drama really springs, is described by Wagner as 'woman *per se*, woman in all her infinite femininity, woman as yet unknown but intuited, longed for – in short, the woman of the future.'

Wagner's original scenario for *Der fliegende Holländer* had been in one act, and he always viewed the work as an indivisible whole; the three-act form in which it was first given, and is usually given today (except at Bayreuth), he saw as merely an irritating concession to the conventions of the theatre. *The Dutchman* is the earliest of Wagner's works admitted into the Bayreuth canon, but it was the last work to be so admitted: Cosima Wagner introduced it into the Bayreuth Festival of 1901, for the first time in the single-act form in which her husband had conceived it.

Like *Rienzi*, *Der fliegende Holländer* was to have its first performance in Dresden, where Berlioz saw both operas. 'Whatever opinions one may have of the merits of these works,' he wrote in his *Premier Voyage en Allemagne*,

it must be admitted that men capable of twice performing this dual literary and musical feat successfully are not common, and that Herr Wagner has demonstrated a talent more than adequate to command both attention and interest . . . The score of the '*Dutchman*' I thought remarkable for its dark coloration and certain storm-effects motivated by the story, but I could not help also noticing an excessive use of *tremolo*, which had already disturbed me in *Rienzi* and which implies a kind of intellectual laziness. Of all orchestral effects sustained *tremolo* is that which one tires of most quickly; what is more, it requires no imagination on the composer's part if there is no outstanding musical idea either above or below it. Be this as it may, we must, I repeat, give all credit to the King of Saxony for his patronage, which has saved a young and highly gifted artist for posterity.

By talking of *Rienzi* and *Der fliegende Holländer* in the same breath, Berlioz draws attention to a striking fact about the operas of the first half of Wagner's creative life, down to 1849, namely that they come in pairs. *Die Feen* and *Das Liebesverbot* were written in quick succession; a few years later came *Rienzi* and *Der fliegende Holländer*, which, despite the great intellectual and artistic divide between them, lived side by side in Wagner's mind for so long that it was only external circumstances that caused the one to be finished before the other. Likewise *Tannhäuser* and *Lohengrin* belong together, both chronologically and in terms of Wagner's aesthetic and spiritual development.

What lies behind this phenomenon, which is not yet part of the world of Wagner at his maturest and greatest, is a set of complex, fluctuating values not yet fully resolved, values which derive on the one hand from the demands of the dramatic material – that is, from the judgments of Wagner the poet-dramatist – and on the other hand from the realization of the content of the drama in musical terms, the search for the all-encompassing musical correlative, so to speak. One needs to proceed with delicacy, even diffidence, in these matters, for it is all too easy to be tempted along the path of facile distinction-making and false classification. In much the same way the chase for leitmotifs in Wagner's works has unleashed innumerable huntsmen whose zeal and industry have not always been matched by the subtlety of their discrimination or the accuracy of their aim. But it may be plausible to claim that in *Die Feen* and *Lohengrin* the scope given to *musical* expressiveness is greater than in their chronological partners *Das Liebesverbot* and *Tannhäuser* or in *Der fliegende Holländer*; these latter bear in their turn, perhaps, a heavier accent on the presentation of human drama, philosophical conflict and the other problems with which Wagner was wrestling *qua* dramatist and poet. His goal, intuited rather than perceived at this moment, was a new form of art, the *Wort-Ton-Drama –* *word-note-drama*, the fusion of poetic drama and music. It would not be surprising if in his advance towards this goal it should at times be the *Wort* that predominates, at times the *Ton*.

While the atmosphere in the great metropolis of Paris grew colder and colder around me, the acceptance of *Rienzi* in Dresden was like an unexpected gesture of affection from Germany. A profound patriotic yearning came over me which I had no idea I could feel, a yearning brought about by feeling so forlorn and homeless in Paris. Yet it was not a yearning for old things that I wanted to regain but rather an inkling of something new, something I desired, albeit as yet unknown and still to be acquired, but which at least I knew I would never find in Paris.

This is how Wagner described his mood in the last months of the nightmare year of 1841 in *Eine Mitteilung an meine Freunde (A Communication to my Friends)*, the further fragment of private autobiography written ten years later. Once again he is on the point of giving himself over to presentiments, to fate, following his instincts with no clear idea of where they would lead him, but with no hesitation, no thought that it might be more prudent to do something else.

During the early months of 1842 the outlines of *Tannhäuser* began to form in his mind. Linked with his growing unhappiness in Paris, and feeding his nostalgia for Germany, had been the vision of the German Middle Ages which reading the history and the legends of those times had evoked – history and legend being inseparable, each contributing its own form of 'truth' to the total picture. One of the historical works that Lehrs had given him to read had stimulated him to write at the beginning of 1842 the prose draft of a five-act opera on Manfred, son of Emperor Friedrich II, called *Die Sarazenin (The Saracen Woman)*, but he carried the idea no further. His final contribution to the *Gazette musicale* was an essay on the Franco-Jewish composer Jacques Halévy, with whom he had struck up a cordial relationship.

The long-delayed but long-predicted decision to leave Paris was finally made. On 7 April 1842 Wagner and the submissive, though not entirely unresentful Minna said goodbye to the consumptive Lehrs and the equally pitiable Anders, and, seen off by the faithful Kietz, left in the coach on the first stage of the 400 miles to Dresden.

The journey, for which Friedrich Brockhaus had provided the money, took five days and brought Wagner two great experiences. One was his first sight of the Rhine, traditional frontier between France and Germany. 'As I saw the river for the first time,' he wrote, 'tears came to my eyes and I made a vow, poor artist that I was, to be eternally faithful to my native German land.' The other was a view of the famous turretted fortress of the Wartburg, near Eisenach, which sent a flood of memories of the Minnesinger, of Hoffmann's story of the Song Contest, of Heine's poem on the medieval minstrel called Tannhäuser, of the legend of the alluring Queen Venus and the Venusberg, pulsing through his mind. One particular aspect of the castle was still in his mind's eye when he set the scene of Act III of *Tannhäuser* in 'A valley beneath the Wartburg'; a forest ridge of the nearby Hörselberg he made into the Venusberg of the opera.

Otherwise it was an unpleasant journey. Wagner described it as a similar experience to that nightmare voyage in the *Thetis* from Russia to London. And to start with he found Dresden far from congenial. Even the Saxons –

after all, he was one himself – struck him as crude and offensive: '*schmierig, plump, dehnig, faul und grob*' ('greasy, crude, boring, lazy and coarse') is his list of choice epithets. Moreover he still had no professional position and no regular income, though the forthcoming performance of *Rienzi* was at least some testimony to his ability, and the members of the family were beginning to realize that their youngest member had something to give to the world.

Since Minna's parents, who still lived in the town, were too poor to put them up, Wagner took a couple of rooms at Töpfergasse 7 for seven thalers a month, installed Minna there with the household chattels they had brought from Paris, then set off to see his family in Leipzig. Since Rosalie's death in childbirth seven years earlier, Johanne Wagner had been provided for by the Brockhaus family. She was now living in a spacious apartment with her second son Julius, enjoying at the age of sixty-eight a quiet, comfortable life which she could hardly have dreamt of in the years when she struggled to raise her ten children. It was six years since Wagner had seen her. 'When I unexpectedly entered the room,' he said, 'she looked first startled, then highly delighted. Any bitterness between us had completely vanished; her only regret was that she could not have me stay with her instead of my brother Julius, who had failed in his intended career as a goldsmith and did not offer her any real company.'

But it was the future of *Rienzi* and *Der fliegende Holländer* that really occupied his thoughts. The première of the former was scheduled for the coming October and he involved himself enthusiastically in the preparations. A journey to Berlin to try to get the *Dutchman* performed there proved fruitless, and a call at the same time on Mendelssohn, whom he had first met long ago in Leipzig, also seems to have been a somewhat frigid occasion. In contrast, his various brothers-in-law, no doubt in response to the pleadings of their wives, showed an increasing cordiality towards him. At the instance of Hermann Brockhaus, Ottilie's husband, who was now Professor of Oriental Languages at the University of Leipzig, they joined forces to give him 200 thalers to tide him over until the royalties from *Rienzi* materialized. 'Tiding over' was the way Wagner too saw his repeated borrowings; the difficulty, especially for his creditors, lay with the infinite elasticity of the concept.

The enthusiasm that greeted the first performance of *Rienzi* seemed to all who had shown confidence in him, from the King of Saxony and his artistic advisors to Minna, the Wagner-Geyer family and a handful of friends, to demonstrate how right they had been. His friend Ferdinand Heine, a stage designer at the Dresden Court Theatre, told a charming story of how, to pay her own symbolic tribute to her husband's success, Minna put laurel leaves in his bed, so that when he got home after his triumph, he might literally 'rest on his laurels'.

Wilhelmine Schröder-Devrient, operatic idol of Wagner's young days, sang the dramatic contralto part of Adriano and the tenor Josef Tichatschek – the first to sing the role of Tannhäuser, and a lifelong friend of Wagner's – that of Rienzi. The performance started at six and finished at midnight, and Wagner, worried how the audience would react to this prodigious length, anxiously watched it from a box in the company of Minna, his sister Klara and the Heine family. Its reception left him in a daze: 'I did not notice the applause, and when, at the end of each act, the audience cheered and shouted for me to take a bow, my friend Heine had to shake me to my senses and push me up to the stage.' Not until the première of the *Die Meistersinger* twenty-five years later did he experience such a success again. Small wonder that Minna, who for six unhappy years had been following her impetuous, near-destitute husband across Europe with little hope of domestic security, continually urged him to 'write another *Rienzi*'.

Naturally enough the success made the Dresden authorities eager to stage the first performance of *Der fliegende Holländer* also, which they did a mere ten weeks later. Ironically, it did not make the same impact as *Rienzi* and was given only four performances, whereas *Rienzi* had found a permanent place in the repertoire. The presence of Wilhelmine Schröder-Devrient could not of itself guarantee success; the preparation seems to have been inadequate, and the performance of Michael Wächter as the Dutchman had not the brooding intensity that the role requires. In particular, Wagner had difficulty in getting both principals to bring to their singing that declamatory power which he demanded. Well-established singers that they were, they felt little inclination to change their style when audiences liked them very well as they were.

Above all, the public appeared less drawn to this gloomy, disturbing, psychologically problematical story than to the flamboyantly open tragedy of the Last of the Tribunes, which conformed more closely to what audiences expected of an opera. After the fourth performance of the *Dutchman* Schröder-Devrient left the Dresden company for a year, and the work was not performed there again until 1865.

Within three weeks of the première of *Rienzi* two of the leading musicians at the Dresden Court Theatre, both Italians, suddenly died, leaving the opera without a director or a senior conductor (*Kapellmeister*). The incumbent second *Kapellmeister*, Karl Gottlieb Reissiger, who had rehearsed and conducted *Rienzi*, took the senior post, leaving his own position vacant. It was now offered to Wagner.

He hesitated, and it is important to understand why. On the one hand it meant a permanent salaried job, the first in his life, and the first opportunity to break with the eternal borrowing, the hack work and the distasteful features of his hand-to-mouth existence. Minna, not surprisingly, implored him to accept; so also did Carl Maria von Weber's widow, who went so far as to maintain that, if Wagner really respected her husband's memory, it was virtually his duty to take the post that Weber had once held.

Yet at the same time he had a nagging feeling that the routine of being a public servant, the pressures to conform, the ordered life he would be expected to lead, would cramp his spirit and make inroads into the time and energy he needed for realizing his creative plans. He felt, as he put it, 'the temptation to be unfaithful to my inner voice', the voice which said that Dresden would soon cramp his genius.

In the end, under pressure from all sides, he accepted, consoling himself with the thought that he could at least make something worthwhile out of the players and singers he would have, and being assured that he would have time to work on his own operas. On 2 February 1843 he was appointed *Königlich Sächsischer Hofkapellmeister* for life with an annual salary of 1,500 thalers, 'to start with – I shall need more soon,' he said, 'I am still paying off debts, debts and more debts.' It did not help him to know that Mendelssohn received an annual 3,000 thalers jointly from Dresden and Leipzig, the Dresden producer Eduard Devrient also 3,000, and Wilhelmine Schröder-Devrient 4,000 thalers, excluding guest fees.

Fitting public acknowledgement that Wagner had finally 'arrived' came in the form of an invitation from Laube to write an account of his career for the *Zeitung für die elegante Welt*. The two parts of this *Autobiographical Sketch*, a sober, factual chronicle of names and events from the first thirty years of his life, with 'I', 'me' and 'my' in almost every sentence, were published at the very moment of his appointment in Dresden, accompanied by a reproduction of Kietz's portrait sketch. Laube introduced the *Autobiographical Sketch* with so telling and entertaining a description that it has its own place in the story of Wagner's life:

I have known this young musician, who has become famous in the last two months through the Dresden theatre, for ten years. His boundless energy, the product of a determined and ceaselessly active mind, always fascinated me, and it was my constant hope that a man so imbued with the culture of the age would eventually compose fine contemporary music. For a while he disappeared from my view, strange adventures taking him as far afield as Russia, when suddenly, to my considerable surprise, he appeared in my room in Paris one winter's day in 1839. With his wife, an opera-and-a-half, a handful of small change and a huge, ravenous Newfoundland dog, he had voyaged through storm and tempest from the Dvina to the Seine in order to seek fame and fortune in Paris. But in Paris, where half Europe is clamouring for success, everything, however excellent it may be, has first to be paid for before it can be put on the market and make any impression. Heinrich Heine, not a man usually given to worry, put his hands together and offered up a silent prayer at the sight of so much self-confidence in a German. Trust an artist to behave like that!

Well, he did not succeed, but he did not fail either, and two years later, poorer in body but richer in spirit, our wandering musician was back in Saxony, where he was welcomed as he deserved.

Tannhäuser and *Lohengrin* were to be written in Dresden, and the foundations laid for much else.

CHAPTER THREE
Art and Revolution

Whenever Wagner decided to do something, he did it with total commitment and with all the energy at his command – which was immense. Profitable or disastrous, far-reaching or of only short-lived effect, a decision, once taken, was like a dazzling light from which he could not turn his eyes, both the end that he sought and the means by which to reach that end.

So having overcome his hesitation and accepted the post of second Kapellmeister at the Royal Saxon Opera in Dresden, he immediately set to work to build up again what Weber had started twenty years earlier but had been allowed to slump back into the bad old ways since Weber's death in 1826. Even during Weber's time the musical forces available in Dresden were conservative in outlook and mediocre in quality, and in his own interest he had the premières of his three great operas given elsewhere – *Der Freischütz* in Berlin, *Euryanthe* in Vienna and *Oberon* in London. But with soloists like Wilhelmine Schröder-Devrient and Joseph Tichatschek at his disposal, an orchestra of seventy players and a chorus of forty-four, Wagner enthusiastically set about raising the reputation of Dresden in the musical world – 'putting one over on the Philistines and educating popular taste to appreciate the noble things in art', as he wrote to the Berlin music critic Karl Gaillard. Dresden had a population of some 70,000 at this time, with the reputation of being a more genteel and highly-cultured community than most German cities.

The 'Philistines', of course, i.e. the bourgeois theatre-goers for whom opera was a social occasion seasoned with a little light musical entertainment, had no desire to be educated in this way, by Wagner or anybody else, nor had the personnel in the theatre, including the singers and players, any wish to find their cosy mediocrity disturbed by a fiery, brilliant intruder with very different notions of what opera was about. 'So what was the first thing I encountered?' he went on in the same letter: 'Envy! As long as I was a poor, unknown musician who had suddenly had great success with an opera, everything went perfectly. But when this success led to my receiving a lifetime appointment with a salary of 1,500 thalers a year, the milk of human kindness turned sour!' As always, however, his scorn of all opposition enabled him to shrug off this resentment and criticism, and he set about preparing an adventurous repertoire that was to include Beethoven's *Fidelio*, Marschner's *Hans Heiling* and *Adolf von Nassau*, Cherubini's *Les Deux Journées*. Spohr's *Jessonda*, Rossini's *William Tell*, Halévy's *La Juive*, Gluck's *Armide* and *Iphigénie en Aulide*, and Verdi's *Ernani*.

An interesting picture of a provincial orchestra like that in Dresden emerges from a report, *Die Königliche Kapelle betreffend (Concerning the Royal Orchestra)*, which Wagner submitted to his employers some three years after his appointment. A different play, opera, ballet, concert or vaudeville entertainment was put on each night, which meant that the musicians were confronted with a bewildering variety of pieces, ranging from tragic opera to light music, not only in the performances themselves but also in the round of intervening rehearsals. Moreover different works required different orchestral forces. Wagner proposes in his report a total string band of forty-four (twelve first violins, twelve second violins, eight violas, seven cellos and five double-basses), all of whom would only be needed for large operas, while light comic operas could be performed with twenty-eight (8, 8, 5, 4, 3) and incidental music for plays with fourteen (4, 4, 2, 2, 2). Being concerned to recruit players of high quality, he suggests salaries graduated from 600 thalers for the front desk to 300 thalers for the less experienced players at the back. A similar range of salaries should apply to woodwind and brass players; quadruple woodwind, four trumpets, three trombones and two tympanists make up the rest of Wagner's standard orchestra. He also recommends that a further tenor trombone and a new set of tympani be bought, and that a second tympanist and a full-time harpist be added to the complement.

Finally, he insists, musicians, like anyone else, must be paid their due: 'It has been repeatedly shown that at the time when the orchestra's salaries were fixed at their present levels, the cost of living in Dresden was considerably lower than it is now . . . On this point the orchestra can only console itself by considering all the other court employees who are equally affected by the rise in the cost of living.' *Plus ça change* . . .

Wagner's return to Dresden stood in the divided shadow of his experiences in Paris. He had gone there as a would-be conqueror, had suffered there both physically and psychologically, and had left the foreign field, defeated, to rejoin his native German tradition. But Paris had been metropolitan; Dresden was provincial, and Wagner was not interested in provincial successes. After the triumph of *Rienzi* he had tried all possible ways of getting *Der fliegende Holländer* accepted in Berlin, and it was only because his efforts failed that it had its première in Dresden. Grandeur – of achievement, of life-style, of success – was part of his nature, a nature which, in this as in other things, both reflects and helps to constitute the cultural image of the mid-nineteenth century. Dresden, he knew, would quickly become too small for him; indeed, it was too small from the beginning. Wagner as Kapellmeister – the very phrase shows in its improbability how provisional, transitional this period in his life would be.

Memories of Paris returned when Berlioz came to

Dresden in February 1843 to conduct two concerts of his own music. The two men were utterly different in character and temperamentally ill-equipped to understand each other's music; Berlioz spoke no German, and Wagner, in spite of his three years in Paris, had learned very little French. With the suspicion that often accompanies ambitious plans and grand visions, Wagner believed, as he wrote to Lehrs in Paris, that Berlioz was envious of the success of *Rienzi* and *Der fliegende Holländer*. In the same letter he claims that Mendelssohn too is 'more than jealous' of him – though after the first Berlin performance of *Holländer* in the following year Mendelssohn was one of the first to congratulate him. Wagner for his part probably envied Berlioz's superior skill in orchestration, and was perhaps rather put out that the independence of action he demanded in his dealings with the musical world had already been claimed by the non-conformist Frenchman in his equally bitter fights with the musical establishment.

In fact, the historical vantage-point reveals quite a few parallels between the two men: both were iconoclasts, *enfants terribles* to their contemporaries; both were drawn to Goethe and wrote works on his *Faust*, and both shared an enthusiasm for Shakespeare; and although they were both active as conductors of their own and other composers' work, neither of them was an instrumentalist. Above all, both, in a way easier to sense than to define, have something of the uncut diamond about them, the autodidactic genius, a powerful rebelliousness reminiscent of the amateur who is impatient with the smoothness of professionalism and intolerant of the 'proper' way to do things.

In their domestic life these early years in Dresden marked a contentment and serenity that the Wagners, especially Minna, had not known before and would not know again. After a modest start elsewhere they acquired a spacious apartment at Ostra-Allee 6, with a view of the famous Zwinger, where Minna could enjoy a new sense of security and play to the full the role of the wife of the Royal Court Kapellmeister. Wagner bought a grand piano – partly, inevitably, on credit – and began to build up a library, collecting in particular works dealing with the culture of the German Middle Ages. In succession to Robber they added to the household a spaniel called Peps and a parrot called Papo. 'Since there is still no prospect of human progeny, we continue to make do with dogs,' Wagner wrote, half in sadness, half in bitterness, to Cäcilie.

That Minna never bore him a child was a source of deep sorrow to him, and may well have been one of the factors that forced them even further apart in the years to come. For all his professional ambition, his egoism, his often thoughtless treatment of those near to him, his many incidental love-affairs, Wagner was a family man, and when, during the liaison that preceded his second marriage to Cosima von Bülow, he did become a father, he showed the love and concern that he would always have shown.

Wagner's insatiable if eclectic reading and his proneness to be overwhelmed by enthusiasms of the moment are recorded by his Paris friend, the painter Friedrich Pecht, who recalls in his memoirs an amusing visit to the Wagner apartment in Dresden at this time:

One day when I called on him, I found him passionately absorbed in Hegel's *Phenomenology*, which, he assured me with characteristic extravagance, was the best book ever published. To prove it, he read me a passage that had particularly impressed him. I did not completely follow it, so I asked him to read it again. This time neither of us could understand it. He read it a third time, then a fourth, until in the end we looked at one another and burst out laughing. That was the end of phenomenology.

His appearance during those Dresden years is described by Eliza Wille, a rich Hamburg lady who, with her husband

François, was to see a good deal of him later in Zurich and elsewhere. He was distinguished, she wrote, by 'his lithe, elegant figure, his very high forehead, his sharp eye and the vigorous lines round his small, firmly-closed mouth. A painter sitting next to me also drew my attention to his jutting chin, which seemed to be carved out of stone . . . He had an extremely lively manner, full of self-confidence yet also charming and natural.' But his health was not good. The strain of the Paris years had produced certain internal disorders: he was suffering from haemorrhoids and was often struck with sudden pains. Apart from his work in Dresden itself there were now performances of *Der fliegende Holländer* to conduct in Berlin and a long journey to Hamburg for a production of *Rienzi*.

On top of these physical troubles came psychological worries, caused once more by his ever-looming debts. The success of *Rienzi* and his appointment to the Dresden court had had the ironical result of disclosing, not only to his recent Paris creditors, but also to long-suffering lenders in Magdeburg, Königsberg and Riga, where their quarry could be found. His comfortably-established sisters Luise and Ottilie made regular monthly contributions to the Wagner family budget for a while, and the singer Wilhelmine Schröder-Devrient lent him 1000 thalers with which to buy himself out of the most threatening of his obligations. When three years later she sued him for the return of the money, plus the accumulated interest, he paid her by taking out a further loan from the theatre pension fund.

His professional career too had a somewhat chequered appearance. *Rienzi* in Hamburg had been a depressing occasion, the principal culprit, according to Wagner, being the 'voiceless, bloated old tenor' in the title role, 'who was so intolerable that I thought of letting the Capitol crash to the ground as early as Act Two, so that he would be buried in the ruins.' As to the performances of

Der fliegende Holländer in the Schauspielhaus in Berlin, the public received the work warmly, and Mendelssohn, who attended the first evening, came up to him afterwards and said: 'You have good reason to be pleased!' The critics, on the other hand, judged it harshly, and after four performances it was taken off. It was not produced again in the Prussian capital for twenty-five years.

In Dresden Wagner's work with the orchestra and chorus met with general satisfaction, and the future seemed assured. At the end of February 1844 Liszt visited the city, and at his request a special performance of *Rienzi* was put on. This was the time of his affair with the notorious 'Lola Montez', the Irish courtesan 'whose reputation automatically made you think of bedrooms', as Aldous Huxley put it. In Paris Wagner had been spellbound by Liszt's virtuosity and suspicious of the use to which it was being put, but Liszt was now spending less and less time on his concert career. The two men had not yet made real intellectual contact with each other, but after he became Kapellmeister at Weimar in 1848, Liszt persistently used his influence to get Wagner's works performed, both in Weimar and elsewhere.

Shortly after Liszt's visit Wagner began to plan in earnest a project that he and others had cherished for some while – to bring the body of Weber back from London to Dresden and re-bury it there. Weber had been Hofkapellmeister in Dresden for the last ten years of his life. He was North German by birth, however, and since he had moved from one place to another in the course of his restless career, there was no overriding reason why Saxony should claim him as her own. Wagner's own motives were personal: on the one hand his special admiration for a pioneer in the field of German opera, on the other his sense of satisfaction at standing in the line of Weber's successors.

Against a certain amount of opposition, he and his

supporters finally got their way. Weber's son Max, at that time a student in London, arranged for his father's remains to be exhumed from Moorfields Chapel, and on a dreary December day the party arrived in Dresden to be greeted by a torchlight procession and the sounds of a piece by Wagner for eighty wind instruments and twenty muffled drums, based on motifs from *Euryanthe*. The next day Weber's body was buried in the Friedrichstadt cemetery Wagner delivered a passionate funeral oration, and a male voice choir sang a dirge which he had composed for the occasion.

At the end of this same year, 1844, Robert Schumann and his wife moved from Leipzig to Dresden, and the two men met from time to time. But though more cordial than that with Mendelssohn, Wagner's relationship with Schumann did not rise to the level of intimacy. Wagner was irrepressibly loquacious, Schumann was taciturn. As in his dealings with Mendelssohn, indeed with almost everybody, Wagner set the pace, a breakneck pace, which most could not, and many would not, follow.

Schumann had published a number of articles by Wagner in his *Neue Zeitschrift für Musik* in the 1830s, but in Wagner's eyes his music was unfairly ignored by that journal. When he sent Schumann a copy of the full score of *Der fliegende Holländer*, Schumann characterized the music as 'gloomy' and saw echoes of Meyerbeer in it. Presented with a copy of *Tannhäuser* two years later, he conceded that Wagner was 'certainly a clever fellow and adventurous to a degree' but, like so many young composers, was 'weak in harmony and the art of four-part writing'. In 1853, five years after *Lohengrin* – which he knew from the score but never saw performed – Schumann still claimed that Wagner was 'not a good musician' and that his music was 'often quite amateurish'. In sum: 'It is an unfortunate sign of perverted judgment if such works are extolled at the expense of the masterpieces of German drama.' Wagner the amateur, the dilettante, the apostle of perversity and decadence: such hostile epithets, picked up by Nietzsche and later developed and analyzed by Thomas Mann, had been thrown into the arena long before.

A far closer relationship that began in these Dresden years was that between Wagner and Dr Anton Pusinelli, his and Minna's physician and one of his many creditors – 'a life appointment in each case', Ernest Newman caustically observed in his biography. Pusinelli was among the many who sacrificed themselves so utterly to Wagner in the name of his art that they were prepared to accept almost any exploitation, any humiliation and cruelty if it were needed for the Master's self-fulfilment – or self-indulgence, as it must sometimes have seemed. As Wagner's correspondence with Liszt, with Bülow and with the publishing houses of Breitkopf and Härtel and Schott provide a commentary on his professional career, the fate of his music and his dealings with society, so his letters to Pusinelli give insights into his private fears and anxieties over a period of more than thirty years.

Two other intimate friends from these years, of a very different kind, were August Röckel, musical assistant at the theatre and later a leader of the Dresden revolution into which Wagner was also drawn, and Theodor Uhlig, a violinist in the Dresden orchestra, with whom Wagner discussed his theories of opera and his ideas for the reform of the theatre, and who was to be entrusted with preparing the piano reduction of *Lohengrin*. We shall meet both these men again shortly.

In any serial account of a man's life and works the impression will involuntarily arise from time to time that one work follows another in simple linear succession, each exercise only being embarked upon when the preceding task has been completed and the finished product laid aside. Some artists do work in this manner, totally absorbed in the demands of the moment, heedless of where the impulse for the next work will come from. But Wagner was not like this. We have already seen how, as he concentrated on one opera, plans for others were already crystallizing in his mind. In the middle of composing the music of *Rienzi* he sketched and finished the libretto of *Der fliegende Holländer*, as well as writing the Faust Overture, various other compositions, the short story *A Pilgrimage to Beethoven* and sundry essays; before finishing *Holländer*, he was planning *Die Sarazenin*; the subjects of *Tannhäuser*, *Lohengrin* and *Die Meistersinger* all overlapped in his mind, while both conception and composition of *The Ring, Tristan und Isolde* and *Parsifal* are inextricably linked.

The reason behind this interlocking of works is thematic. Certain ideas, concepts and problems pursued Wagner throughout his life. From the time of his very first opera, he planned the entire work himself and wrote his own text, presenting these ideas and problems in a series of different yet related historical or mythological settings, and ultimately conveying through the music the deepest meaning of the passions and conflicts in the work. *Tannhäuser* is present in *Tristan und Isolde* and *Parsifal*, so is *Der fliegende Holländer*, and Wagner himself was shattered to realize that the Amfortas of *Parsifal* was his Tristan of Act Three raised to a higher power. 'In my end is my beginning' says T. S. Eliot in *East Coker*. The world of Wagner's later works is prefigured, pre-existent in the works that come before.

Already in *Die Feen*, for example, then in *Der fliegende Holländer*, and in its fullest glory in *Tristan und Isolde*, the theme of redemption through the love of a woman runs right through his work. The man's love too has as its goal, not the beloved who stands before him but the salvation that lies beyond. As the Dutchman sings to Senta: 'This smouldering pain I feel – shall I call it Love? But no, it is a longing for Salvation. Would that it could be granted to me through the presence of such an angel!' From this springs the inexorable association of redemption with death, the love-death, and with it the motif of liberation from a curse – the curse that Arindal lays on Ada in *Die Feen*, the curse on the Dutchman, on Tannhäuser, on the Nibelung's ring, on Kundry in *Parsifal*. Like Schopenhauer, who was later to make such a great impact on his mind, Wagner was a man whose patterns of thought were already formed in essence in the early years of his intellectual development, and as one follows this development, one witnesses, not a series of reactions, experiments or changes but the refinement and intensification of values conceived as early as the moment when he finished the score of *Der fliegende Holländer* in November 1841.

Thus although he might appear to be preoccupied with the problems of one particular work, he was at the same time solving in a mysterious way problems in works which had not yet been written yet which already lay in embryo in his mind. *Tristan und Isolde* interrupted the completion of *Siegfried*, which was not completed until four years after *Die Meistersinger*, the first prose sketch of which had been made before even *Tannhäuser* was performed; *The Ring* was there while he was working his way through *Tristan*, over which, as already over *Lohengrin, Parsifal*, his last drama, cast its shadow. In some uncanny way everything had its place in his order of things, be that order conscious or subconscious. In a letter to Hans von Bülow in 1862, at the time he was working on the music of *Die Meistersinger*, he wrote that *Parsifal* would be his last work. Twenty years later it became just that.

So while he was still scoring *Der fliegende Holländer* in Paris and toying with plans for *Die Sarazenin*, chance gave into his hands the medieval legend of Tannhäuser and Venus, the story of the Knight who is torn between the pleasures of the flesh and repentence for his sins, who is finally pardoned but has already gone back to the Venus-berg in despair and never learns of his forgiveness. Wagner's Paris friend Samuel Lehrs also brought him, in this moment when his thoughts were turning wistfully to the homeland in which alone his gifts could flourish, the stories of Lohengrin and of the medieval Song Contest on the Wartburg. This latter he already knew through the tale by his beloved Hoffmann, while the Tannhäuser legend had reached him through Tieck's story *Der getreue Eckart und der Tannhäuser* as well as through the Tannhä-user poem by Heine.

The two German legends of Tannhäuser and of the Minstrels' Song Contest have nothing at all to do with each other historically, and it had not occurred to anybody before Wagner to link them. The catalyst was the sight of the romantic castle of the Wartburg, which he and Minna had passed on their journey from Paris to Dresden. The world of the Minnesinger who used to gather here at the court of Hermann von Thüringen; the historical Tannhä-user, knight and poet, whose restless wanderings had made him the archetype of the hero caught up in the dichotomy of spirit and flesh, goodness and sin; Hoff-mann's story *Der Kampf der Sänger*, in which a similar conflict is played out between the forces of light and darkness, openness and mystery – these motifs suddenly found themselves arrayed in a single constellation in Wagner's mind, a world of German realities, German symbols, German values.

Two months after arriving in Dresden he had finished the first draft of the text, and a second draft was ready two weeks later. In the forefront of his mind from the begin-ning was the Tannhäuser theme itself, the lure of sensual-ity, the agony and ultimate redemption, through the love and death of a woman, of the penitent sinner. He thus intended to call the work *Der Venusberg*.

It still bore this title when he took the score to the music dealer C. F. Meser in Dresden, with whom he had made an agreement for the publication of his operas at his own expense – or, more accurately, at his creditors' expense. Meser, however, objected to the title, saying that it would give rise to obscene jokes, especially in medical circles. To call an opera *Mons Veneris*, as a present-day Meser might point out, would provoke associations of *Oh, Calcutta!* rather than of Tannhäuser. So Wagner hastily removed the offending word and gave his work the composite title that it now bears: *Tannhäuser und der Sängerkrieg auf der Wartburg (Tannhäuser and the Song Contest on the Wartburg)*.

In the Tannhäuser story physical love is embodied in the figure of Frau Venus, who holds court in her sinister mountain fastness and lures the erring knight to a life of erotic pleasure. In order to personify the conflict in Tannhäuser between the spirit and the flesh, Wagner created a character of pure, ideal love to set against the sensual enticements of Venus – the figure of Elisabeth of Hungary, later canonized as Saint Elisabeth. Thus a further antithesis, that between Christian asceticism and pagan hedonism, is brought into the motivation, an antithesis characteristic of Heine, Laube, Gutzkow and the other writers of the Young German movement whose modes of thought still had their hold on Wagner's mind. Tannhäuser's divided consciousness has sometimes been made explicit in performance by having the same singer take the roles of both Venus and Elisabeth.

Out of these transmuted elements Wagner built the drama of sin and repentence, of human love and divine intercession, that is the life of his hero. Tannhäuser's submission to Frau Venus may motivate the Pope's refusal to pardon him, but Wagner was hardly the man to regard surrender to the pleasure of the senses as the ultimate offence. It is as unthinkable that he should have had Tannhäuser damned for giving way to his animal instincts as that Goethe could have allowed Faust to perish through his insatiable questing after experience and knowledge. At the same time Tannhäuser is guilty of the grievous offence of casting as the object of his carnal love a woman who is not just Elisabeth, niece of the Landgrave, but Saint Elisabeth, divine mediator, the angel who intercedes for the penitent sinner's deliverance from perdition. The 'objective' situation of the second act of the opera, with the promise of Elisabeth's hand to the winner of the song contest and the declaration of the love between her and Tannhäuser, is left far behind. As her dead body is carried from the Wartburg, he falls lifeless beside her with the words 'Saint Elisabeth, pray for me' on his lips. At this very moment the band of young pilgrims arrives from Rome bearing the Pope's staff, which has miraculously put forth green leaves as a symbol of his redemption. Through this fusion of elements Wagner has created a drama which is imprinted with his own intense preoccupations yet also presents an objective conflict between sacred and profane love, between sacrilegious rebellion and final repentance, between expected damnation and the miracle of salvation.

According to *Mein Leben* Wagner finished the text of *Tannhäuser* on his thirtieth birthday, 22 May 1843. The short score of Act One took him from November to the following January, Act Two a mere six weeks in September and October 1844, and Act Three was finished by the end of the year. The fully orchestrated work was ready by April 1845, and Wagner had a hundred copies printed at his own expense, counting on using the proceeds from the sale to offset his losses on *Rienzi* and *Der fliegende Holländer*. Three months later he had already written the prose sketch of all three acts of the *Die Meistersinger*, and a bare two weeks after that the prose sketch of *Lohengrin* lay finished on his desk.

At the first performance of *Tannhäuser* on 19 October

1845 Tichatschek, who had created the part of Rienzi, sang the title role, and Wilhelmine Schröder-Devrient the role of Venus. The part of Elisabeth was sung by the nineteen-year-old Johanna Wagner, daughter of Richard's brother Albert, whose musical talent Wagner had discovered on a visit to his brother in Halle four years earlier.

The work left the audience baffled and dissatisfied. Technically the first performance seems to have had many shortcomings. The portly Schröder-Devrient hardly embodied the voluptuous charms of Venus, and Tichatschek sang, or shouted, himself hoarse while trying unsuccessfully to convey the tragic psychology on which the meaning of the part rests. The other soloists, schooled in the operatic convention of recitative and aria, could not come to terms with the Wagnerian arioso style, the incipient 'endless melody' that lay midway between the two; and the décor created the wrong atmosphere. The second performance a week later, however, proved more convincing, and from the third onwards its place in the Dresden repertoire was secure. Wagner subsequently made the meaning of the final scene more explicit by having the body of the dead Elisabeth actually carried into view, and by bringing Venus on to the stage in person to try to tempt Tannhäuser back into the Venusberg, instead of leaving us to imagine the struggle going on in his mind. These modifications smoothed the path towards the full acceptance of the work by a public whose attitudes Wagner was persistently seeking to change.

The measure of Wagner's success in weaning the public from the operatic pabulum to which it had grown accustomed can be judged from a notice in the Leipzig journal *Signale für die musikalische Welt* in February 1847: 'It is a noteworthy phenomenon,' says the anonymous writer, 'that the cool and unexcitable Dresden theatre public has been transformed by Wagner's operas into a fiery and enthusiastic body such as can be found nowhere else in Germany. When has it ever been known for the composer of an opera that has been in the repertoire for over a year to be called on to the stage three times, as happened after the recent performance of *Tannhäuser*?' Within ten years *Tannhäuser* had been given in most opera houses throughout Germany.

Schumann's reaction to the work illustrates what has since become a characteristic phenomenon. After studying the score, a copy of which Wagner had sent him in the summer of 1845, he wrote to Mendelssohn: 'Wagner is certainly a lively fellow, full of extraordinary ideas and as bold as brass, but for the life of him he cannot write four consecutive bars of music that are decently thought out, let alone beautiful. It is scarcely better than *Rienzi* – duller and more affected, if anything.' Yet three weeks later, after seeing an actual performance, he wrote again to Mendelssohn: 'I must take back much of what I said when I read the score. On the stage everything is totally different. It greatly moved me.' Criticism, suspicion, even antagonism towards the music, and the man, in the cold solitude of intellectual analysis, then the experience of the living work in performance, the emotional impact, the confrontation with an unyielding spiritual reality – it is a familiar dichotomy in the history of the reception of Wagner's works. Schumann is only one of the countless musicians whose vaunted critical faculties have crumbled under the pressure of the aesthetic and spiritual experience itself.

Compared with *Der fliegende Holländer*, the music of *Tannhäuser* is more 'of a piece', more like the seamless garment of vocal and orchestral sound that envelops the works of his supreme maturity. There is a breadth of phraseology, an air of expansiveness, to which in particular the sonorous choral writing, a denser, fuller harmonic structure and the development of far larger orchestral forces contribute, which is not to be found in any of his earlier operas. Striking signs of the chromaticism which he later so ruthlessly exploited in the psychological delineation of his characters are also to be found, as in the wonderful modulations in the middle section of the Pilgrims' Chorus:

Durch Sühn' und Buss' hab' ich ver - söhnt den

Her — ren, dem mein Her - ze fröhnt.

Yet there is still a great deal in *Tannhäuser* that shows its line of descent from *Holländer*, and makes us 'feel' it, together with *Lohengrin*, as a superb refinement of an earlier tradition rather than the beginning of something new. Beneath the mesh of the musical web the conventional shapes of recitative, aria and ensemble are still visible, and in the harmonic realm the chord of the diminished seventh is still the basic vehicle for conveying fear, anxiety and other forms of emotional agitation. Much of the melodic idiom also still belongs to the tradition of Italian *bel canto* opera, and much else to what Italian and French nineteenth-century opera have in common. At the same time there is a broad strand of unmistakably German music running through the work, beginning and ending with the Pilgrims' Chorus – the opening bars of the overture and the final ensemble of the whole opera.

Set against the solid grandeur of this 'German' music of Wolfram von Eschenbach and the pilgrims, in deliberate, symbolic counterpoint, is the original, rhythmically varied, almost abandoned music of the Venusberg, a music of sudden darts and thrusts, which, as in the juxtapositions in the overture, can as readily merge back into the world of the Pilgrims' Chorus as break away from it into the seductive realms of excitement and sensual delight. Small wonder that men like Schumann and Mendelssohn were unsettled by this music.

A few weeks after the first performance of *Tannhäuser* Wagner finished the text of *Lohengrin* and read the whole work to a literary and philosophical circle in Dresden – the young composer Ferdinand Hiller, the architect Gottfried Semper, designer of the splendid new Dresden theatre, Schumann, the writer Hermann Franck, the sculptors Ernst Julius Hänel and Ernst Rietschel, and painters such as Julius Schnorr von Carolsfeld and Friedrich Pecht. 'It was adjudged striking and worthy of high praise,' said Wagner. It even won the approval of Schumann, who however, although he knew *Tannhäuser*, was still looking in opera for a sequence of set numbers and therefore could not grasp the underlying musical form that Wagner had in mind. The basic musical sketch was made during a three-month vacation which he and Minna spent in the summer of 1846 in a village near Pillnitz, some three hours ride from Dresden. The short score of the three acts of the work was written at intervals over a period of a year, but the full score was not complete until April 1848.

One reason for the erratic progress of his work on *Lohengrin* was the amount of time taken up by the concerts and operas that he rehearsed and conducted in Dresden. Two occasions stand out. One was his performance of Beethoven's Ninth Symphony on Palm Sunday 1846 and his establishment of a tradition, against considerable opposition from both the court and the town, that this symphony be regularly performed at the annual Palm Sunday concert in future. It was a work hardly known at that time in Dresden, or, for that matter, anywhere else in Germany; its idiom, like that of the late quartets, was still largely incomprehensible, and its performance posed difficulties which hardly any instrumentalists or singers of the day could cope with. Such performances as had been given earlier, like the two in Dresden under Reissiger in 1838, only succeeded in conveying to the audience the sense of bafflement and confusion that the players themselves felt.

Wagner was determined to put matters right. For weeks he subjected orchestra, soloists and choir to a barrage of the most strenuous rehearsals. He had the platform in the hall rebuilt so that the audience would be exposed to the full power of orchestra and chorus, and prepared the way for the actual performance with a series of notices in the *Dresdner Anzeiger*, the local paper. The occasion was a huge success. The hall was packed. Among the audience were Hans von Bülow, then a boy of sixteen, and Ludwig Schnorr von Carolsfeld, later to become a famous Wagnerian tenor, and the applause went beyond anything the authorities – but not Wagner – had expected.

How much the occasion meant to him, both at the time and later, is vividly conveyed in his enthusiastic description in *Mein Leben* of the triumphant performance and the preparation that had gone into it. It is not difficult to understand his aggressive self-confidence: 'The event served to strengthen the pleasant sensation that I had both the ability and the power to achieve with irresistible success whatever I seriously wanted.' To nobody's surprise, the opposition to seeing the Ninth Symphony as a regular feature of Palm Sunday concerts quietly disappeared.

The other outstanding moment was his revival of Gluck's *Iphigénie en Aulide*. German by birth and education, Gluck wrote all his operas to French or Italian texts, and the cadences of a Romance language became superimposed on a basically German musical vocabulary. His operas for Paris had to comply in their formal arrangement with what the French eighteenth-century public expected and since its first performance there in 1774, *Iphigénie en Aulide*, a work full of the rough, unpolished dramatic power which sustains Gluck's best operas, had become steadily more encrusted with these fossilized conventions, even in performances in Berlin and other German cities. Wagner went back to Gluck's original score, read Euripides' *Iphigenia* tragedies and conducted his re-dramatized arrangement of the work before an admiring Dresden audience in February 1847. His niece Johanna sang the title role, Wilhelmine Schröder-Devrient that of Clytemnestra. A further month's work on the music of *Lohengrin* followed, then came the second annual Palm Sunday performance of Beethoven's Ninth Symphony, and after that three more months on *Lohengrin*.

Between these two works, Beethoven's Ninth Symphony and *Lohengrin*, there is a special affinity which Wagner makes explicit in one of his introductory notices in the *Dresdner Anzeiger*. In this he speaks of Beethoven's world of spiritual loneliness, a loneliness which he desperately sought to overcome, reaching out to his fellow-men and to nature through the sublime message of hope, joy and universal brotherhood proclaimed by his last symphony. This loneliness also besets Lohengrin, the Knight of the Swan, who seeks release from the isolation of his divine perfection through the love of a pure woman. But he cannot betray his origin, and his tragic fate is pre-ordained. Similarly Wagner, the artist, knew the loneliness to which every artist is committed, and the impossibility of escaping from this loneliness without betraying his art, his gift from God. Moreover Wagner was becoming increasingly alienated from his fellow-musicians at Dresden, at times taking refuge in the past, in literature, in myth and symbolic legend, at other times feeling himself drawn to politics and the problems of society.

The social conditions under which he found himself forced to work were also becoming irksome. His report *Concerning the Royal Orchestra*, proposing reforms in the status and constitution of the orchestra, was ignored, as were other practical suggestions he made for the administration of the theatre and its orchestra, and he became more and more frustrated. Particularly galling was the appointment of the novelist and journalist Karl Gutzkow to a position as dramaturge in Dresden, which resulted in what Wagner witheringly called 'the brutal despotism of total incomprehension'. Gutzkow, who had an insatiable desire for power, disliked both Wagner and his niece Johanna, and repeatedly tried to curb the influence of the former and the theatrical career of the latter.

The annual rent of 220 thalers for the rooms in the Ostra-Allee proving too much to pay, Wagner and Minna moved in April 1847 into a converted apartment in the old Marcolini Palace in the suburb of Friedrichstadt, which cost only 100 thalers but left Wagner with a long walk to the theatre each day. Some of his debts in Paris, such as to his friend Ernst Benedikt Kietz, to his tailor and to his shoemaker, had been paid, and 300 thalers for the performing rights in Dresden of *Rienzi*, together with a presumably similar sum (the exact figure is not known) for *Der fliegende Holländer*, had supplemented his Kapellmeister's salary. Such amounts, however, made little impression on his overall indebtedness to creditors in Magdeburg, Riga and elsewhere, not to mention friends like Theodor Apel and relatives like Eduard Avenarius and Friedrich Brockhaus. There was also the matter of the furniture for the apartment in the Ostra-Allee, including the grand piano and the ever-growing library, while the generous life-style he permitted himself made its own deep and regular inroads into his salary. We are not surprised that Wagner was perpetually in debt, and nor was he, so he never drew a veil of shame or uneasiness over his beggings and borrowings. After all, he would say, one cannot take a moral stance over a law of nature.

In September and October 1847 Wagner was in Berlin, accompanied by Minna, to rehearse and conduct *Rienzi*. First impressions suggested that conditions for a musician in the Prussian capital might now be more congenial than in Dresden; he had a cordial meeting with Meyerbeer and also visited the venerable poet and storyteller Ludwig Tieck, now seventy-four, with whom he discussed problems concerning *Lohengrin*. But the intrigues in the theatrical world and the unsavoury compromises he found himself forced to make if he was to get anywhere with his preparations for *Rienzi*, quickly showed him that Berlin was no different from Dresden in its attitude towards art and artists. The King of Prussia, Friedrich Wilhelm IV, did not, as Wagner had hoped, come to hear the opera, nor was he granted an audience in order to read the libretto of *Lohengrin* to His Majesty. The final irony of the Berlin *Rienzi*, tolerably well received by the public though disparaged by the critics, was that he received no fee for rehearsing and conducting the three performances that were given, because he had come at his own request and not been formally invited.

Gutzkow's behaviour showed little sign of becoming more amicable, and twice Wagner wrote resentful letters of Lüttichau, director of the theatre, threatening to resign to Gutzkow were not put in his place. Towards the end of the year he demanded a rise in salary from 1500 thalers to 2000 thalers, which was not granted as such, although he did receive an *ex gratia* sum of 300 thalers specifically to help redeem his known outstanding debts, and a further once-for-all payment of 200 thalers out of the subscription concert fund. With this apparently generous gesture went a stinging criticism of his 'frivolous mode of life' in Paris, which had landed him in this sorry financial state, 'of which he can probably only be cured by such hardships as he is at present being forced to undergo'. Furthermore 'he has not appreciated his good fortune in being appointed Kapellmeister in Dresden' and has been encouraged by the sometimes exaggerated praise lavished on his works to develop too exalted an opinion of himself, expecting the sort of rewards that fall only to a Meyerbeer, and then only in places like Paris, or Berlin or London.

Such severity both astonished and offended him. To belittle his Dresden successes in this way, his *Rienzi*, his *Holländer*, his *Tannhäuser*, was an intolerable humiliation. And like a master's report on a naughty schoolboy, the document concludes with a recommendation that Wagner 'be threatened with instant dismissal should he get into further financial difficulties or be unable to meet his present commitments.'

Part of the opposition to Wagner, both as man and musician, must have been led, or at least encouraged, by Gutzkow. For one thing he rejected any idea of a union of the arts: drama must remain drama, he said, and opera must remain opera – by which he meant French and Italian opera. The uncritical adulation that Wagner's works attracted in some quarters also riled him. 'At every performance of a Wagner opera that I saw', he later wrote in his autobiography, 'there was indiscriminate and exaggerated applause from an organized claque which is active all over Germany and for which Wagner, Liszt and others will one day have to answer. Behind me in the audience a fanatical German-Russian family literally went mad with enthusiasm in their pursuit of this Wagner cult. The worship of Wagner's music is then carried from Dresden to other places by society ladies, loose-living characters and men of effeminate character.'

The vulgar imputation of licentiousness and homosexuality to one's opponents is familiar enough. More to the point is Gutzkow's confirmation that already in the mid-nineteenth century there flourished that violent enmity between pro-Wagner and anti-Wagner factions which has become so familiar a feature of the modern musical landscape. Innovation and novelty will always tend to polarize opinion, with the silent majority shrugging its shoulders in the middle. And in the past, as often today, conflict could be artificially generated, as it was in the famous literary 'Querelle des Anciens et des Modernes' in seventeeth-century France, and in the operatic 'war' between the rival supporters of Gluck and Piccinni in Paris in the 1770s. But the division forced by Wagner is real and deep, and will remain. It has nothing to do with fashion, and the challenge it lays down cannot be ignored or shrugged off. There cannot be Bachians and anti-Bachians, or Mozartians and anti-Mozartians, or Beethovenians and anti-Beethovenians, but there can be, and are, Wagnerians and anti-Wagnerians. To understand why is to penetrate to the very heart of his music and its meaning.

For the moment the mutual threats of resignation and dismissal were laid aside, and as the fateful year 1848 arrived, Wagner was working on the score of *Lohengrin* and rehearsing a series of three orchestral concerts. The first consisted of a Symphony in D by Mozart (possibly the Prague or the Haffner, but we do not have the details), Bach's motet *Singet dem Herrn ein neues Lied*, a scene from Cherubini's opera *Medea*, and Beethoven's Eroica Symphony; the second included Haydn's Symphony No. 104 in D, Gluck's *De profundis* for chorus and orchestra, Mendelssohn's setting of the 42nd Psalm, and Beethoven's Seventh Symphony; and the third consisted of Mendelssohn's Symphony No. 3 in A minor (The Scottish), Palestrina's *Stabat Mater* and Beethoven's Fifth Symphony. At the Palm Sunday concert that year Wagner conducted Beethoven's Eighth Symphony, and Reissiger conducted a performance of Mendelssohn's *Elijah*.

The emphasis on Beethoven in these concerts needs no explanation. That Mendelssohn should figure so prominently – a composer Wagner greatly admired, though Mendelssohn did not return the admiration – was in the nature of a memorial tribute. The previous November, only thirty-eight years old, Mendelssohn had died in Leipzig, where he had founded the Conservatoire and been conductor of the Gewandhaus concerts for twelve years. Though polite and proper in his dealings with Wagner – who describes him in *Mein Leben* as 'cold' – Mendelssohn had never given much thought to either Wagner the man or Wagner the composer. He did not begrudge Wagner the success of *Rienzi* and *Der fliegende Holländer*, but the classical refinement and delicacy of his own musical world was a far cry from what he felt as Wagner's thrustful, unsubtle, overpowering musical manner.

While busy preparing for these Dresden concerts, Wagner received the news of his mother's sudden death. 'I hurried to Leipzig at once for the funeral,' he wrote, 'and was deeply moved by the soft, wonderfully serene expression on her face. Whereas her earlier life had been a busy and restless one, she had spent her latter years in peace and contentment, indeed, in a state of quiet, almost childlike other-worldliness. Her last words, spoken in a tone of demure humility and with a blissful radiant smile on her face, had been: "How beautiful, how lovely, how divine! How have I deserved such mercy?"' Wagner does not linger over the occasion in *Mein Leben*. Johanne Wagner had virtually passed out of her son's life many years before, and it was now only a formal link that was being severed. Her children had long since made their own lives, leaving her to pass her final years in an untroubled serenity which, as she looked back on her struggles to raise her ten children, must have seemed like paradise. Wagner's own links with his brothers and sisters also became weaker with the years; even his favourite sister Cäcilie he did not see for over twenty years, until she visited him at Tribschen in 1869.

The score of *Lohengrin* was finally completed at the end of April 1848, though the work was not performed for another two years. It was given as the main item in the annual celebration of Goethe's birthday on 28 August 1850, in the Court Theatre at Weimar. The conductor was the Weimar Hofkapellmeister, Franz Liszt. But Wagner was by then a political exile in Switzerland.

In German literature the story of Lohengrin, Knight of the Swan, first appears at the end of Wolfram von Eschenbach's epic *Parzival*, written in about the year 1210. A young princess of Brabant refuses all offers of marriage, saying that she will only give herself to a man sent by God. From the temple of the Holy Grail a knight arrives in a boat drawn by a swan and is hailed by the princess as her God-sent husband. He marries her but makes her promise that she will not ask his name or origin. Some years later, unable to restrain her curiosity any longer, she asks the forbidden questions, whereupon the swan returns and carries the knight back to the Grail castle. His name was Lohengrin (i.e. Garin le Loherain, Garin of Lorraine), and he was the son of Parzival, King of the Grail.

The events of this story are expanded in an anonymous strophic epic, composed between 1275 and 1290, which, in a modern German version, was Wagner's principal source. This Middle High German epic is closely related to the contemporary poem of the Song Contest on the Wartburg, the so-called *Wartburgkrieg*, in which the Lohengrin story is related by Wolfram von Eschenbach.

Wagner had already drawn on the *Wartburgkrieg* for *Tannhäuser*, and would do so again in the *Die Meistersinger*.

The story rests on two legendary motifs – the metamorphosis of human beings into swans (in Classical mythology the swan was the bird of Apollo) and the curious wife whose question brings disaster (Cupid and Psyche). But the medieval Christian background of the story as he found it was too restrictive for the interpretations Wagner wanted to give the story. For Wagner the tragedy of Lohengrin's situation lay in his loneliness. As a divine creature among men, he can never become part of human life, never be drawn into a human relationship, and Elsa's love for him is as doomed as Senta's for the Dutchman. Indeed, by daring to love Lohengrin and subject the supernatural to human terms of reference, Elsa herself incurs a tragic guilt, as Tannhäuser had done by longing for Elisabeth as though she were a mortal. Lohengrin, too, was aware from the beginning of the incompatibility of his mission with a pledge to a human institution such as marriage, and sows the seeds of his own suffering as the swan returns to bear him back to the castle of the Grail. Like Anselmus, the young hero of Hoffmann's tale *Der goldene Topf*, who has to sacrifice the security of domestic happiness to the higher call of his utopia on the island of Atlantis, so Lohengrin, envoy of the utopia that is the kingdom of the Grail, can never commit himself to the values of earth, even to the highest of those values, human love.

In this complex of irresistible demands and forced sacrifices, of guilt for situations inaccessible to influence, and of desires that clamour for fulfilment, Wagner saw the embodiment of his own fate – his bourgeois existence as a husband and as a paid servant of society, the incompatibility between the creative force within him and the circumstances within which it was confined, the conflict between the finite, relative realities of life and the absolute, unconditional, because divine, reality of art. Then, arguing back to the work from its egocentred significance, he sees Lohengrin as a paradigm of the tragic predicament of the modern artist, who desperately needs, but can never find, true understanding and sympathy from the world, as Lohengrin longs to be received into the community of mortals to which he does not belong. Added to this is a political dimension, borne in the opera on the one hand by Ortrud, a demonic, 'reactionary' woman, as Wagner calls her, fearful in her lovelessness and her political emancipation, and on the other hand by King Henry the Fowler, with his patriotic pride and his determined defence of his German realm. For Wagner this became part of the revolutionary situation which came to a head in 1848 and which was soon to absorb his entire energy and commitment.

Unusual about the musical composition of *Lohengrin* is the fact that the last act was written first. Only when this third act was complete did Wagner turn to the first, then to the second, and finally to the Prelude, which is not a full-scale, articulate 'Overture', like that to *Der fliegende Holländer* or *Tannhäuser*, which presents the motifs that accompany the dramatic action to follow, but an adagio, mood-setting evocation of a world of perfect love, the world of the Grail, home of the Knight of the Swan. This is indeed Grail music, the static music of a world that is, not of a world that is becoming, an ethereal music of serenity and bliss, the spiritual forebear of the prelude to *Parsifal* – not a Christian music, any more than the meaning of the text can be circumscribed in terms of Christian versus pagan, but assuredly a religious music, again like that of *Parsifal*.

Schumann had been disconcerted at not being able to detect in the libretto of *Lohengrin* any implied division into arias, ensembles and other set numbers. The music is as much of a piece as the text. 'It has such a unity of conception and style,' said Liszt, 'that there is not a melodic phrase, still less an ensemble, in fact not a single passage that can be properly understood apart from the work as a whole.' It is above all this one-ness, the flowing unity of each 'through-composed' scene, that marks the advance of *Lohengrin* over *Holländer* and *Tannhäuser* and shows us the Wagner that is to come.

Whereas from *Das Rheingold* onwards the orchestra dominates more and more, in *Lohengrin* the voice still reigns. The full-bloodedness of the work, the declamatory passion of its ariosos, its rich orchestral sonorities, its juxtaposition of high drama and appealing lyricism – this is what makes it the most frequently performed of all Wagner's operas. Yet *Lohengrin* is still grand opera rather than music drama, the end of one phase in Wagner's life rather than the beginning of another. And after finishing the score in April 1848, he composed hardly a note of music for five years.

There had never been such a silence in his musical life before, nor was there ever again. Other things drove music from his mind during these years. But his musical development had itself reached a turning point, and what was driven out could never return. It was a very different Wagner who in September 1853 suddenly heard in his mind the opening bars of *Das Rheingold*, the E flat major chord out of which *Der Ring des Nibelungen* was to grow.

The Germany into which Richard Wagner was born was a Germany of political confusion – or, more accurately, non-political confusion, for not even in the most advanced of the thirty-five states and four free cities that constituted the German Confederation after 1815 was there what we would call a popular political awareness. The absence of a national civic consciousness left a political vacuum. This vacuum came to be filled in the course of the nineteenth century by the rising self-confidence of the German people, that is, the rise of nationalism, and public expression of this national sentiment reached its apogee with the proclamation of the Second Reich under Bismarck in 1871. Prussia dominated the development towards unification from the year 1810 when the philosopher Fichte, one of the most important figures at the newly-founded University of Berlin, preached the liberation of the German people through the embrace of the Prussian military ideals of duty, service and honour, down to the moment when the German victory over France in the war of 1870 made Germany the strongest power in Europe.

Yet it was a national strength based, not on firm inner social and political virtues, civic institutions evolved to give expression to the liberal ideas which fed the early rise of national feeling, but on a sense of military achievement and a shared suspicion of the outside world, the product of an uneasy inkling of inferiority. Prussia, the home of the *Aufklärung*, domain of the most enlightened of 'enlightened despots', Frederick the Great, had a history of liberal and progressive thought which none of the other states could match, and from the middle of the eighteenth century Berlin had drawn intellectuals, scientists and artists towards itself like a magnet. The University, first named after the then King Friedrich Wilhelm III, and now called after its founder, Wilhelm von Humboldt, attracted famous names from the beginning – philosophers like Fichte and Hegel, jurists like Savigny and Eichhorn, classical philologists like Bekker and Böckh. As the century progresses, the list becomes endless – the brothers Grimm, Schelling, the physicist Helmholtz, the historians Mommsen and Treitschke, Robert Koch the bacteriologist, Rudolf Virchow the pathologist and many others.

But Prussia was not Germany. Many of the smaller principalities were still virtually feudal in their administration. Austria, the only power of real European status among the German states apart from Prussia, was a conservative monarchy with as little sense of corporate constitutional life as any other German state. Metternich, the Austrian chancellor, emerged as the strong man of the Confederation after the Congress of Vienna in 1815, but his almost pathological fear of any movement that might remotely be called liberal turned him into a repressive reactionary, concerned with the application of political censorship to all published matter and the stifling of the incipient liberal movement in the universities. This authoritarianism was embodied in the Karlsbad Decrees of 1819, a reassertion of the holy alliance of 'throne and altar' formulated by Metternich and imposed on all the other German states. It was these decrees that led to the ban on the writers of the Young German movement and sent Heine, Boerne and others into exile.

Nor must one forget that Germany in the first half of the nineteenth century was still predominantly an agricultural country – indeed, it remained so well beyond the middle of the century. There were no great industries and no independent class of prosperous manufacturers or merchants; only a quarter of the entire population lived in towns. According to the historian Golo Mann, there were barely a million factory workers in Germany in 1848, far more craftsmen than factory workers, and more peasants than craftsmen and factory workers put together. The tenor of life was set, particularly in the smaller states, by the ruler and his court. Intellectuals wrote their books for their court and for their fellow-intellectuals; there was no 'public', no open body of consumers, either of ideas or of works of art, in the modern sense. This hollow core, this emptiness of the middle ground, was to prove one of the most depressing realities that the makers of the revolution of 1848 were compelled to accept.

In this confusion of conservative and radical pressures, of particularist loyalties and incipient nationalism, of individual brilliance and corporate backwardness, of a society in which aristocratic sources of power were weakening but no clearly defined forces were there to take their place, a man of Wagner's generation could not but be thrown to and fro between conflicting attractions. It was a potentially explosive situation which, nationally, did not explode, but which forced open many individual minds. The old conditions appeared intolerable, reforms long overdue, but the misty idealistic visions of the reformers were utterly unrealizable. The answer to an impossible present was an equally impossible future, and whereas a sensitive young mind might support a movement for change, such a man also wished to retain what he valued in the status quo.

So we find Wagner behaving at one moment like a revolutionary, at the next like a prince. As a have-not, he developed the snarl of the underdog and made free with Proudhon's famous battle-cry 'Property is theft'; as a have, he was to claim the silks, the satins, all the luxuries and extravagances which he felt to be the legitimate accoutrements of his vocation. He was both an opponent of his age and a product of it. He reviled it, despised it, rejected it, yet needed it and eventually grew prosperous on it. And as his life, so his art. The revolutionary programmes, the imperious sweep of the arm to brush away the ostentatious, popular but, to him, frivolous and vain operatic successes of the day, and at the same time the Romantic luxuriance of his music, the self-indulgence in the glorious warmth of plush, velvet scoring. And dominating everything the cult of grandeur, the commanding gesture, the total commitment. Some call it megalomania; others, the all-embracing demand of genius.

Back in his student days in Leipzig, in the wake of the Paris Revolution of 1830, Wagner had already marched in the cause of political revolution, and he had since read authors who provided a framework of theory for such actions. From the time when Heinrich Laube came to Leipzig as editor of the *Zeitung für die elegante Welt* in 1833, that journal had been a mouthpiece for the progressive ideas of the so-called Young Germans, a loosely knit group of writers, anti-Romantic and anti-idealist in outlook, pledged to the overthrow of conservative politics and the rejection of conventional morality. It was this latter, with its hedonistic praise of sensual pleasure for its own sake, that first fired Wagner's enthusiasm for a libertarian ethic and a wholehearted acceptance of life as one finds it, life 'as it is'. Wagner always believed that art was part of life, not separate from it, let alone antagonistic to it, as a once fashionable Romantic doctrine had taught. It thus followed that only the uninhibited expression of life, the free movement of society, could create a world in which art could flourish and be what it was meant to be.

From his appointment to the Dresden court in 1843, at the age of twenty-nine, and through to his flight into exile in 1849, Wagner found the ethos of genteel bourgeois society and the role of art within that society increasingly intolerable. His report *Concerning the Royal Orchestra* had shown what he thought of the state of music in particular, and what he proposed should be done to improve the situation in a technical sense. But since the malaise of art reflected the malaise of society, reform had to be directed at the latter. And art itself had its part to play in this reform. Never would Wagner countenance 'writing down' to the level of an ignorant public: it was the task of true art to raise minds to its own level, to create its own new public through its purity and its refusal to compromise. He knew exactly what he was aiming at, and anyone who performed his works had to know too. As he wrote a few years later: 'I do not care in the slightest whether my works are performed. What I do care about is that they are performed as I intended them to be. Anyone who cannot, or will not, do so, had better leave them alone.'

A set of practical proposals establishing the theatre on a sound and reputable basis, and hence also raising the standard of public taste, is contained in his *Entwurf zur Organisation eines deutschen Nationaltheaters für das Königreich Sachsen (Draft of a Plan for a National German Theatre for the Kingdom of Saxony)*, which he submitted to the King in May 1848. A kind of companion piece to *Concerning the Royal Orchestra*, and similarly destined to collect dust on an administrator's shelves, it proposes the removal of the theatre from the control of the court, a democratic association of dramatists and composers which should elect the director and determine artistic policy, and the foundation of a theatre workshop to train young artists, producers and technicians. It sounds almost like a theatrical commune – a concept which would have been far from alien to the Wagner of 1848.

'As I reflected on the possibility of a fundamental change in the situation of our theatres,' he wrote three years later in *A Communication to my Friends*, 'the full awareness suddenly dawned on me of the barrenness of the contemporary political and social situation, which could not but lead to just those conditions in the world of art that I was attacking. The realization of this fact was decisive for the whole of my future development.' In *Mein Leben* he tried to make out that he had not really believed in the serious possibility of revolution in 1848, but the *Communication*, written with the excitement of the events still fresh in his mind, tells a different story.

So too does a characteristic letter of November 1847 to the Berlin music critic Ernst Kossak. After telling Kossak how pleased he was with the performance of *Tannhäuser* in Dresden the previous evening, at which King Friedrich Wilhelm IV of Prussia had been present, Wagner bursts out: 'My dear friend, what is the use of all our preaching at the public? There is a wall to be broken down, and the way to do it is by revolution. We must first achieve a solid foundation. What we consider right and good must become our starting-point, our firm, unshakable base, then all the bad features of the contemporary situation will easily be overcome.'

The idea of revolution dominates Wagner's mind in these years, though in reality he was not so much a revolutionary as a rebel. Passionately committed to reform, yes, but quite unsystematic in his notions of how to achieve it and quite unwilling to throw in his lot with any organized movement, group or party. Like Heine, he feared that his individual genius would be swamped by the mediocrity that rules any mass movement, and his impulsive involvement for a few days in the street fighting in Dresden during the popular uprising of May 1849 quickly gave way to a dissociation from the activities of the revolutionaries and to a personal stance of 'reform from a distance'. In the essay *Über Staat und Religion (On State and Religion)* written in 1864, he gives his final verdict on the matter: 'Those who invested me with the mantle of a political revolutionary and included my name in the lists of such revolutionaries, obviously knew nothing at all about me and based their judgment on what the circumstances *appeared* to be. This might well mislead a police official, but hardly a statesman.'

Yet the works he read during these last years in Dresden, the friends he made and the views he expressed, as in the letter to Kossak, all point to the conclusion that, though not a professional revolutionary or agitator, he had adopted a philosophy of radical and more-or-less violent social change. The laissez-faire morality that had attracted him to the Young German movement now found a political counterpart in the inflammatory ideas of early socialists and anarchists such as Proudhon and Bakunin, with support from the man-centred, atheist philosophy of Ludwig Feuerbach.

Of these three influential thinkers the only one Wagner

met personally was the Russian anarchist Mikhail Bakunin, but it was an encounter that left a deep mark on him.

Bakunin was a strange mixture of a man, 'a really kind and sensitive person', Wagner called him, who preached the political gospel of violence for its own sake and laid down a strategy of terrorism for forcing the collapse of bourgeois regimes. Born of an aristocratic family, he left Russia after a period in the Imperial Guard, went to Germany, where he studied Hegel in Berlin and met the members of the Young German movement, then joined the radical intellectuals assembled in Paris, among them Proudhon and Karl Marx.

Bakunin followed Proudhon in his insistence on individual freedom, in his anti-dogmatism and his opposition to authority and state, and this inevitably put him in opposition to Marx. The early history of communism and anarchism shares common ground and the terms often seem interchangeable, but after the founding of the First International in 1864 the incompatibility of Bakunin and Marx over the issue of dogma and individual freedom became absolute. 'Marx called me a sentimental idealist,' said Bakunin, 'and he was right. I called him morose, vain and treacherous, and I was right too.'

Bakunin's fellow anarchist Pierre Joseph Proudhon, a less violent yet no less radical opponent of privilege, authority and dogmatism, did not have so direct an influence on Wagner, but like all aspiring young reformers of his day, Wagner knew Proudhon's revolutionary tract *De la propriété*, published in 1840. The slogan 'Property is theft' was calculated to evoke the full-throated approval of all those, like Wagner, who had no property. By 'property' Proudhon meant, in fact, not personal possessions, which are every man's right, but land, capital, with the associated structures of credit and finance, like banks, which are the agents of exploitation by an immoral capitalist system. At the very end of his life, economically assured and the most talked-of composer in Europe, Wagner could still exhibit a combination of envy, sentimentality and the urge to destruction. 'All that is property,' came his surly voice, as he surveyed the villas of Venice (he was living in one himself), 'the source of all ruin!' Then, bringing some of his other basic prejudices into the context, he added: 'Proudhon tackled the matter far too materialistically, far too superficially. Concern for property is what determines most marriages, and consequently what causes the degeneration of racial types.'

The attraction of all this to Wagner, as he looked for ways of reforming art in society, needs no labouring. And when Bakunin arrived in Dresden at this time, fleeing from the Austrian police for his part in the Slav demonstrations in Prague, Wagner felt himself in the presence of an immensely powerful man. Bakunin found refuge in the house of Wagner's friend, the violinist August Röckel, who committed himself wholly to the revolutionary cause in 1848 and 1849 and had a good deal to do with the ways Wagner thought and acted during these agitated years.

Röckel, son of an opera singer and brother-in-law of the composer Lortzing, was the same age as Bakunin, that is, one year younger than Wagner. He had been in Paris at the time of the 1830 Revolution and was as outspoken as Wagner in his scorn of an effete nobility and his demands for the radical reform of society and the artistic conditions governed by it. But he carried his political convictions further than Wagner. In 1848 he launched a political journal called *Volksblätter*, in which, building on the doctrines of Proudhon, he urged the overthrow of bourgeois capitalism and its replacement by 'a new moral world order', a slogan characteristic of woolly-minded and sometimes dangerous utopians. Wagner contributed a number of anonymous articles to the *Volksblätter* and even took over responsibility for publishing the final issue in April 1849, while Röckel was trying to co-ordinate plans for revolutionary action in Prague. When the fighting broke out in Dresden on May 3, Röckel returned, was arrested four days later and, together with Bakunin, sentenced to death for plotting a *coup d'état*; his sentence was commuted to one of life imprisonment, and he was released in 1862. Wagner continued to write to him in jail, and he was one of those to whom Wagner sent a privately-printed copy of the complete libretto of *Der Ring des Nibelungen* in 1853. The friendship was brought to an unhappy end when, a few years after his release, Röckel saw fit to add his voice to the gossip over Wagner's affair with Cosima von Bülow. He died in 1876, two months before the opening of the first Bayreuth Festival.

The revolutionary movement that swept through Europe in 1848 started in France, but that it travelled so fast and so far, and that leaders like Louis-Philippe, his prime minister Guizot and the Austrian chancellor Metternich should have given up so quickly, shows how universal was the expectation of, and preparedness for, revolt. It also shows how resigned to it were those who sensed that their power would soon be no more. In the same month, February 1848, as France took to herself the constitutional principle of the sovereignty of the people, there appeared a pamphlet that was to change the face of the world. Its authors were two German exiles called Karl Marx and Friedrich Engels; its title: *Manifesto of the Communist Party*.

This particular revolution was not for the bourgeois Germany of 1848. What was now primarily at issue in each of the thirty-nine self-governing units of the Confederation was, as in France, the establishment of a constitution and an elected assembly. This actually brought little real change, since in each state the dynastic principle, the basis of particularism, still prevailed, and consequently the sources of effective power, like the army and the police, remained in the same hands as before. But on 18 May

1848 elected representatives of the individual German states, among them some of the noblest and most distinguished intellectuals of the day, gathered in Frankfurt to work out a constitution for a state that did not yet exist: a new, unified Germany. Because they had no power, except the power to talk, they failed, and by the summer of 1849 the last radical remains of the Frankfurt Assembly, brave monument to the idealistic futility of intellectual revolution, revolution in the mind, had been swept away. The romantic liberal path to one Germany became a dead-end, and soon the Germans found themselves marching down a hard, authoritarian road towards the national unity that fate had so long denied them.

The day before the National Assembly met in the Paulskirche in Frankfurt, Wagner sent a letter to Dr Franz Wigard, one of the Saxon delegates, threatening that there would be trouble if the Assembly did not assert its supremacy over the separate states, immediately establish a 'citizens' army', and form an alliance with France. The following month he delivered a speech on 'Republican Tendencies and the Monarchy' to the Vaterlandsverein, a left-wing political association.

It is a speech that epitomizes Wagner the revolutionary. In the style of the true demagogue he demands one-man-one-vote and the abolition of inherited wealth and power, then calls on the aristocracy to surrender its position of privilege and share the life of the common people in a spirit of mutual respect. The crux of his argument – we can hear the shrill voice of Proudhon in the background – is the passionate claim that the source of all human misery, all degradation and moral depravity, is money. Take away the power of money, and our sickness will be cured. Society rests on people, not on money: this is the meaning of the emancipation of the individual and of society. It is a vision, like Proudhon's, that rests on a utopian faith in human nature; no compulsion was needed, no class warfare, simply the removal of the conditions and pressures that prevented man from being what he was created to be. 'God,' said Wagner, 'will light our way towards the true law . . . the true emancipation of mankind, the fulfilment of the teaching of Christ in all its purity.' Three years later he wrote in *Communication to my Friends*: 'In all this I took it for granted that there would be a peaceful solution to the problems, which called for reform rather than revolution.'

Here, as elsewhere, Wagner oscillates between gradualism and upheaval, between persuasion and force. In moods of rage, often produced by the frustrations of his own life, he would shout revolution and destruction; at other times, as before the Vaterlandsverein, he would temper his anger with appeals to man's better nature and turn away from the clamour for violent change. Likewise the language of Christianity keeps company with the materialism of Feuerbach. Consistency was never one of Wagner's characteristics.

At no time did Wagner's political ideas coalesce into a system. Indeed, his whole approach to politics was basically unpolitical. Thoughts jostled each other in his mind, and it was often the circumstances of the moment that dictated which of them should be uttered. Furthermore his first instinct was to refer external events to himself, to their implication for his own immediate purposes. Even the revolution, committed and active as he was in its cause, he seems at times to regard less as an end in itself than as a concomitant of his own projects for the reform of art and of the social context of art.

The address to the Vaterlandsverein caused considerable irritation to the King and the court, but he had no intention of turning back. Of Wagner's visit to Vienna in July 1848 to discuss matters of theatre reform, the critic Eduard Hanslick noted: 'Wagner was all politics.' This was no doubt why Franz Grillparzer, Austria's greatest classical dramatist, whom Wagner tried to impress with his ideas on society and the theatre, reacted with barely-disguised disapproval and indignation.

Wagner's revolutionary journalism reached its climax in an unsigned article for Röckel's *Volksblätter* called *Die Revolution*, published in April 1849. Here, in high-flown, rhapsodical style, barely pausing for breath from beginning to end, revelling in a purple-patch phraseology that moves between the embarrassing and the risible, he pours out his enthusiasm for the socialist utopia of his dreams:

I seek to destroy root and branch the order in which we live, for it is the product of sin. Its flowering is misery and its fruit is crime; but the seed has ripened, and I am the reaper. I will root out all the false thoughts in men's minds and destroy the domination of one man by another, of the living by the dead, of the spiritual by the material. I will shatter the power of the mighty, of the law and property. Man's sole master shall be his own will, his own desires shall be his only law, and his own strength his sole possession. For the only divine power is a free man. There is nothing higher than he.

Small wonder that Bakunin, interrogated after his arrest about his relationship with the other Dresden revolutionaries, said: 'I immediately recognized Wagner as an impractical dreamer, and although I talked with him about politics, among other things, I never committed myself to any joint action with him.'

There was no music in his mind at this time but there were plans for dramatic works in which his political preoccupations were bound to show themselves. One of these works was to deal with the Emperor Friedrich Barbarossa, the great medieval leader, who, as the legend has it, will rise from his grave in the hour of Germany's need and save his people. But this plan was soon absorbed and transfigured by the legend of Siegfried and the Nibelungs, the subject that left him no peace until, over twenty-five years later, he wrote the final bars of *Götter-dämmerung*, the last of the four parts of *Der Ring des Nibelungen*.

Exactly when Wagner decided, or even half-decided, to write a drama on the Nordic saga of the Nibelungs, we do not know. The subject had been common currency since the time when the Romantics, as part of their cult of the Middle Ages, stimulated interest in medieval epic and lyric poetry, and Wagner tells us in *Mein Leben* that in 1843, while he was working on *Tannhäuser*, he carried Jakob Grimm's *German Mythology* with him wherever he went. This collection of German myths and legends was at his elbow as he worked on the idea of *Der Ring des Nibelungen*, and in the summer of 1848 he produced an essay called *Die Wibelungen*, in which he sought to link the Wibelungs (Ghibellines) of history with the Nibelungs of legend.

But the first written proof of his intentions is a detailed prose sketch, *Der Nibelungen-Mythus (The Nibelung Myth)*, written in October 1848, which contains in essence, albeit with a few vital differences, the entire action of *The Ring* as we know it. A few weeks later he drafted a prose version of *Siegfrieds Tod (The Death of Siegfried)*, then turned this into a poetic libretto, a mixture of free verse and the alliterative principle found in pagan Germanic poetry. At the end of the year he read this text to a group of friends in Dresden, among them the architect Gottfried Semper, also a worker for the revolution, Wilhelm Fischer, conductor of the opera chorus, the producer and stage designer Ferdinand Heine, and the eighteen-year-old Hans von Bülow, a sickly, nervous boy who had already alienated his family by his passion for Wagner's music and whose sad life was to become tragically linked with Wagner's own.

Siegfrieds Tod, later called *Götterdämmerung (Twilight of the Gods)*, now stands as the last of the four dramas that make up *The Ring* for in order to make its meaning clear, Wagner was to find that he had to work his way back through the story and explicitly reveal, rather than just allude to, the events which issued in this climax. The death of Siegfried he subsequently motivated in *Der junge Siegfried (Young Siegfried,* now just *Siegfried,* the third part of the tetralogy), then moved further back still with *Die Walküre (The Valkyrie)* and finally added, as a prelude to the action as a whole, *Das Rheingold (The Rhinegold).* The text of *The Ring* as a whole, finally completed in 1852, was thus written from end to beginning.

As Wagner originally conceived it, his drama was to present through the events of the epic myth the establishment by the gods of a utopian society through the agency of man – specifically, through the two figures of Siegmund and his son Siegfried, the latter portrayed as a shining hero inspired by the ideals of the revolution of 1848. The race of the toiling Nibelungs represents the proletariat, the giants the propertied exploiting class. Siegfried is a *Sturm und Drang* character, prototype of the new, natural man who has shaken off the dross of false convention but, like all heroes too big and too good for this world, is fated to be murdered by the forces of evil that cannot tolerate such grandeur and goodness. Brünnhilde is made to see, through her love for Siegfried, the nature of these forces, and at the end the two transfigured lovers rise triumphant in a vision above the funeral pyre. The ring itself, forged by the Nibelung Alberich, father of Siegfried's murderer, Hagen, symbolizes the rule of money, the subjection of human life to the false philosophy of getting and spending, and the ultimate destruction of that life. Unlike the end of *Götterdämmerung* as Wagner finally made it, not only are the Nibelungs released from their bondage but the gods, purged of their guilt by Brünnhilde's self-immolation, still live on, their rule now established on a true and noble basis.

At this time, his eyes set on the revolutionary message of

Siegfrieds Tod, Wagner could not see how to make his meaning clear, above all because of the dichotomy between the myth of the gods from which he had started out and the essentially human tragedy of the New Man, Siegfried. He therefore put the whole project on one side. When he returned to it three years later, his perspective had completely changed. But the anti-capitalist spirit of 1848 is embedded in the work, and its social revolutionary meaning could never be lost.

Another significant product of the revolutionary spirit, and directly stimulated by his reading of the Gospels, was Wagner's plan for a five-act drama to be called *Jesus von Nazareth*. Although the project did not get beyond the stage of a lengthy prose draft, it is as fascinating an example of his infusion of artistic plans with political content as is the Nibelungen material. Like David Friedrich Strauss's shattering and shocking *Critical Study of the Life of Jesus*, published in 1835, Wagner's text sees Jesus as man, not as God. Barabbas is plotting a revolt of the Jews against their Roman overlords, but before Jesus enters Jerusalem, the plot is discovered and Barabbas arrested; the people look to Jesus to become their revolutionary leader, but the Pharisees set them against him, and in the end he acquiesces in his own murder, while the people, manipulated, like all mobs, by the Pharisees and their political cunning, clamour for the release of Barabbas. In Wagner's words: 'Jesus's self-sacrifice is an imperfect expression of the human urge to rebel against a callous society. This the lone individual can accomplish only by self-destruction, which, however, amounts only to a rejection of such a society.' On the one hand Jesus seeks to lead men to a community based on an ethic of love, not on the cold rule of law; on the other hand he is driven by the death-wish which, as a motif, held an almost obsessive attraction for Wagner at this time. Behind this human Jesus, the social reformer, lurk the figures not only of the humanist theologian David Friedrich Strauss but also of the materialist Feuerbach – both of them directly descended from Hegel, whose work Wagner was reading at this time – and of Proudhon.

Bakunin, who took no interest in Wagner's artistic enterprises, merely advised him to make Jesus a weak character. His musical advice was simplicity itself: 'Let the tenor sing "Behead him!" and the soprano "Hang him!", with the bass singing "Fire! Fire!"'. A philosophy of violence has rarely stimulated the creation of an artistic masterpiece.

Wagner's relations with the Dresden theatre had by now become cool, almost perfunctory. In the early months of 1848 he had diverted his thoughts from the subject by immersing himself in *Lohengrin*; since then he had lived for politics, keeping the company only of Semper, Ferdinand Heine and a few other close friends. In August, however, he made an excursion to Weimar to see Liszt. Liszt did not yet have the influence he was to acquire in the 1850s, when he did for Wagner's music what no one else had ever done, but the roots of the personal and professional understanding between the two men were laid in this year of 1848. Their friendship was sealed the following February, when, after conducting the first performance of *Tannhäuser* to be given outside Dresden, Liszt wrote: 'From now on count me among your most enthusiastic and devoted admirers. Whether you are close at hand or far away, depend on me and use my services as you will.'

The one remaining moment of achievement for Wagner in Dresden was the performance of Beethoven's Ninth Symphony on Palm Sunday 1849. The final rehearsal was listened to by Bakunin. At the end of the work he strode through the auditorium towards the stage and shouted, as Wagner joyfully recalled, 'that even though all our music might be lost in the impending holocaust, we should join forces to ensure, at the risk of our lives, that this sym-phony survived.'

In April 1849 King Friedrich Wilhelm IV of Prussia was offered the Emperor's crown by the Frankfurt Assembly in a final effort to achieve a united Germany, excluding Austria. He refused. He would not, he said, 'pick up a crown from the gutter' at the request of a body of butchers and bakers who were offering him something that did not belong to them: only crowned heads could offer crowns. This was the end of the liberal revolution towards national unity. By rejecting the imperial crown, the King of Prussia rejected the proposed new constitution, and although the assemblies of twenty-nine states, including Saxony, had individually already agreed to this constitution, the King of Saxony now destroyed it by dissolving the state assem-bly and calling on the help of Prussian troops to deal with any popular revolt that might break out.

And it did. On 3 May the citizens of Dresden poured on to the streets, to be confronted by the Saxon infantry. Barricades were put up and attempts made to distribute weapons among the population. 'But what stayed in my mind,' said Wagner, who gives a long and graphic account of these events in *Mein Leben*, 'was the impression of utter confusion . . .

Suddenly the alarm bell in the tower of the Annenkirche nearby began to toll, the signal for the revolt to start. This sound went right through me. It was a bright, sunny afternoon, but suddenly I had the same sort of experience as Goethe describes when he heard the cannons going off at the Battle of Valmy. The whole of the Postplatz in front of me seemed to be bathed in a dark yellow light, almost brown, like an eclipse of the sun that I once experienced in Magdeburg . . . Making my way to another part of the city, I came across a detachment of the people's militia which had been attacked with grapeshot by the soldiers. I saw a militiaman, supported by one of his comrades, trying to march briskly along, although his right leg dragged along lifelessly behind him. Seeing patches of blood on the cobblestones, people in the crowd shouted: 'He's bleeding!' The sight of this man made me extremely agitated. All of a sudden the cry went up: 'To the barricades! To the barricades!' And, as in a daze, I was dragged along by the crowd as it surged back to the town hall.

In the small hours of the following morning the King and his ministers slipped out of the city, and later that day, to the ringing of bells and the cheering of the crowds, the rebels proclaimed from the town hall balcony the establishment of a Provisional Government led by Samuel Tzschirner, a lawyer, Karl Gotthelf Todt, mayor of Dresden, and Otto Leonhard Heubner, a state official who was also a member of the Frankfurt National Assembly. The next day, 5 May, after further skirmishes with the police, the rebellion broke out in full force. That night Wagner was detailed to keep a look-out from the tower of the Kreuzkirche for troop movements. On 6 May the Prussian soldiers joined the Saxon army in the suppression of the revolt. Clara Schumann, who recorded the events day by day, wrote in her diary:

We heard of the terrible atrocities committed by the troops. They shot every insurgent they could find, and our landlady told us later that her brother, who owned the 'Goldner Hirsch' inn on the Scheffelgasse, watched helplessly while the soldiers shot twenty-six students, one after the other, that they found in a room there. Then we heard they had thrown dozens of men out of third- and fourth-floor windows on to the street below. It is horrible to have to live through such things. This is the way men have to fight for their little patch of freedom. When will the time come when all men have the same rights?

On 7 May the opera house was ablaze, while more insurgents marched in from the surrounding countryside to reinforce the barricades. The lives of women and children were now also at risk, and that morning Wagner took Minna, together with dog and parrot, to the safety of his sister Klara's house in Chemnitz, some fifty miles away. When he returned alone to Dresden on the 8th, he found that Röckel had been arrested and the 'nervous Todt' and 'cowardly Tzschirner', as he called them, had fled. That evening the rebels gave in and the fighting stopped. The uprising had lasted a mere five days.

As a known friend of Röckel's and an undisguised supporter of the revolt, Wagner, like Bakunin, Semper and others, now had to get out of Dresden as quickly as possible. The morning after the fighting was over, he made his way to Chemnitz, where Klara's husband, a businessman called Heinrich Wolfram, helped him to get the post-chaise to Weimar, to the security and help that he knew Liszt would offer. On 16 May, three days after he arrived in Weimar, the police searched his rooms in the Marcolini Palace in Dresden and a warrant was issued for his arrest. He was described as 37-38 years old, of medium build, with brown hair and spectacles. The news of the police search and the warrant came in a letter which Minna, who had since returned to Dresden from Chemnitz, sent to Liszt, since she did not dare address it to her husband and thus betray his whereabouts.

Indeed, it was a miracle that he had not been caught already in Chemnitz. Bakunin and Heubner arrived independently in Chemnitz from Dresden that same night; a local inhabitant informed on them, and they were arrested in their beds in the inn where they were staying. Had Wagner been with them, he would have met the same fate. As it was, thinking it too dangerous to go straight to Minna at the Wolframs' house, he spent the night in a different inn. By the time he rejoined Minna the next day – she had no understanding of political events and deeply resented the way Wagner had sacrificed his secure, respectable job in order to play at being a revolutionary – Bakunin and his comrades were on their way back to Dresden to stand trial.

Weimar was the seat of the Grand-Duke of Sachsen-

Weimar-Eisenach, and thus outside the immediate juris-
diction of Saxony. But as soon as the warrant for Wagner's arrest became public knowledge, treaty obligations
would compel other states to look out for him and hand
him back to the Saxon authorities. After a few days in the
Erbprinz hotel in Weimar, where Liszt was also living,
and without having dared to show himself at the performance of *Tannhäuser* that Liszt had just conducted, Wagner
left for a country estate at Magdala, a village some ten
miles away, where he called himself 'Professor Werder
from Berlin'. In Magdala, with the help of sixty thalers
that Liszt had persuaded his mistress, Princess Caroline
von Sayn-Wittgenstein, to make available, Wagner celebrated his thirty-sixth birthday.

Liszt had come to Weimar as Kapellmeister at the
beginning of 1848, when he was thirty-six. From 1833 to
1844, the years of his international fame as a virtuoso
pianist, he had lived with the Comtesse Marie d'Agoult,
wife of an aristocrat in the French Army; the second of
their three daughters, Cosima, became Wagner's second
wife. Three years after his break with the Countess Liszt
met the Russian Princess Carolyne von Sayn-Wittgenstein, who left her husband and went to live with Liszt in
Weimar. She never succeeded in getting her husband to
divorce her, but she stayed with Liszt throughout his
twelve years in Weimar and afterwards went with him to
Rome. They never married, nor did they have any children. Throughout his life the need of the wayward, self-
centred, emotionally and spiritually insecure Liszt was for
a woman of a character stronger than his own, a woman –
preferably aristocratic: rank mattered to him as much as
beauty – who would provide a framework for his life and
work. He had already earned enough money from his
concert tours to live comfortably for the rest of his days,
and Wagner always envied him this security. What he
lacked, and found only in fleeting moments, sometimes in

personal relationships, sometimes in music, sometimes in religion, was peace of mind and spirit.

The value to Liszt of his position as Kapellmeister in Weimar lay above all in the stability it gave him to devote himself to composition, and it was during the Weimar years that he composed some of his most familiar works – symphonic poems such as *Ce qu'on entend sur la montagne, Tasso* and *Les Préludes*, the Piano Sonata, the *Faust* and *Dante* Symphonies, and some of the great organ pieces. At the same time it was through the music of Wagner that he found his true powers as a conductor, firstly with *Tannhäuser* in 1849, then with the première of *Lohengrin* in 1850. This latter, in particular, led him to look for new and unfamiliar works to include in the concert and operatic repertoire, works like Berlioz's *Romeo and Juliet* and *Symphonie fantastique*, Schumann's *Genoveva*, Weber's *Euryanthe* and Cornelius's *Barber of Baghdad*. Compositions such as these made great demands on the modest forces at his disposal – an orchestra of thirty-five, a chorus of twenty-three and a group of soloists of only local reputation. The names of the giants of Weimar Classicism – Goethe, Schiller, Herder – together with the appellation Weimar Republic to describe the period of German history between 1919 and 1933, may give the impression that Weimar had been a large, influential city since the end of the eighteenth century, whereas it has never been more than a small town. Its economic importance was, and still is, modest, and it has never had a university. In the mid-nineteenth century its population was a mere 12,000, less than quarter the size of Dresden and only one-twelfth that of Berlin. Thus Liszt by no means found himself in the musical capital of Germany, nor did he make Weimar so during his reign there. Successful and rich, he stood at a turning-point in his musical life, looking for new fields of expression.

What a contrast to the political fugitive who had suddenly arrived from Dresden! Wagner, poor and dependent, confident architect of his own artistic fortunes but now threatened with arrest and imprisonment as a rebel against society, had put composition on one side and left the power of music for the power of the word. Already in summer of 1848 he had written a begging letter to Liszt in the bluntest terms: 'I need 5,000 thalers. Have you got it? Can you find it, or is there someone who could produce it as a favour to you?' Now again, in the few days before his escape from Germany, he needed Liszt's help.

Liszt suggested that Wagner should go to Paris – not the direct route via Hessen and Baden, where the revolution was still flickering and the police were particularly vigilant, but through Bavaria and Switzerland. Magdala could only offer a temporary hideout, so on 24 May he took his leave of Minna and set out for Rudolstadt on the first stage of the long journey, for which Liszt, mortgaging the expected royalties from future performances of *Lohengrin*, had provided the money. As a further service a Swabian friend of Liszt's called Widmann, a professor at the University of Jena, gave him an old, expired passport of his own which might get him out of the country incognito.

From Rudolstadt he took the post-chaise to Saalfeld, thence via Coburg, Lichtenfels and Nuremberg to Lindau, on the shore of Lake Constance, where he arrived on 27 May. At the gate to the town, together with the other two travellers in the coach, he had to hand in Professor Widmann's passport for inspection. 'I vividly recalled Widmann's Swabian dialect,' he wrote in *Mein Leben*, 'and I began to imagine what it would be like if I had to explain to the Bavarian police why the passport was out-of-date. I spent a feverish night practising a Swabian accent, but I simply could not manage it, and I waited anxiously for the dawn.'

When morning came, the policeman returned the passports of the three travellers without a word. Wagner made his way cheerfully to the harbour and went on board the ferryboat. An hour later he landed at Rorschach, on the Swiss side of the lake, beyond the reach of his pursuers.

Hardly had he set foot on land than he sent the joyful news to Minna:

My own, true wife,

I have arrived safely on Swiss soil. I had hoped to be able to write a day sooner, but the journey took a very long time, with many stops and so on. In Lindau they only asked for my passport and gave me a visa for Switzerland without any trouble.

This morning I came across the lake from Lindau, and in half-an-hour I shall travel on to St Gallen and Zurich. I intend to rest awhile in Zurich and write to you more fully. I must close now.

I am safe. May God keep you in good spirits. I have worried a great deal about you, but I have now regained much of my *joie de vivre*. Farewell, my dearest wife, I shall write again tomorrow from Zurich.

Your
R. W.

He kept his word. He may by now have been able to live quite well without Minna, but he was still concerned for her well-being and he wrote her three long letters during the first ten days of his exile. It was to be six months before he saw her again.

So ended the drama of Wagner and the revolution. Even if one felt tempted to discount some of the more colourful autobiographical episodes he relates in *Mein Leben* and in his letters – it is a temptation one has every right to resist – there is enough evidence from other sources to show that he was thoroughly committed to revolutionary action, that he was constantly to be found in the company of the leading insurgents, and that his own life was more than once in danger. The charges, depositions, statements and other legal items produced at the trial of the revolutionaries who were caught, make frequent reference to Wagner and give ample proof, as do Röckel's *Revolt of Saxony* and other first-hand accounts, that he was as fully implicated in the events of May 1849 as they were. All this testimony was produced again in 1856 when he sent his first appeal to the King for an amnesty.

As for the other rebels, Röckel and Bakunin were in jail, together with Heubner, one of the leaders of the Provisional Revolutionary Government in Dresden; the other two leaders of the Government, Tzschirner and Todt, had been captured but managed to escape; Semper had avoided arrest and was on his way to Paris. Wagner, too, was now an exile, again on the run, again with no job, still living mainly on borrowed money.

His salary as Kapellmeister had been 1,500 thalers per year. At the time he fled from Dresden, according to his friend Friedrich Pecht, he owed an incredible total of 20,000 thalers. When debt reaches proportions like these, it seems to lose the earnest reality of what is credible in financial terms and recognizable as a moral issue. For Wagner there was financially nothing that could be done, and morally nothing that need be felt. Facing an apparently directionless future, he was determined, whatever his situation, never again to become an employee of the degenerate and Philistine society which he had tried, and failed, to destroy.

It was to be eleven years and three-and-a-half operas before he saw Germany again.

CHAPTER FOUR

Exile

Wagner's is a life of extraordinary contrasts. At one moment he is musical director of a nondescript little German provincial theatre, at the next he finds himself in Paris, languishing in the cultural bastion he had counted on taking by storm; at one moment he is a court Kapellmeister, at the next, a political refugee; in his forties a man close to despair, in his fifties suddenly the excited protégé of a Royal patron; now the composer in solitude, living for his art alone, now the creator of his own festival theatre, playing host to kings and princes and making himself the most talked-about composer of his age.

Yet, remarkably, this succession of oscillations lies within a symmetry of equal halves divided by the year 1849, the year of the Dresden rebellion. Wagner was thirty-six. Up to this time he had been in and of the society that surrounded him. To be sure, he had long been aggressively critical of that society and had radical ideas for changing it, but he had always worked within its framework, and in one way or another it had always been his employer. From this moment on, however, as a fugitive from his own country, scornful and bitter, he never worked for that society again, never again held an official position as a public servant. 'I had no alternative,' he declared in his *Communication to my Friends*, 'but to resolutely turn my back on a world to which in essence I had long ceased to belong.' Henceforth, and in full knowledge of what he was doing, he set a distance between his artistic world, the pursuit of his own musical and dramatic aims, and the outer world of professional music-making, with its stultifying restrictions and its demoralizing commercialism. Others might allow their souls to be destroyed. Wagner would not.

The full score of *Lohengrin* had been finished on 28 April 1848. Since then he had not written a note of music, yet plans for dramas and operas from the Germanic, the Biblical and the Greek worlds crowded his thoughts. Some of these came to nought, as one suspects he knew they would – *Friedrich der Rotbart* (on the subject of the Emperor Barbarossa), *Jesus von Nazareth, Achilleus, Wieland der Schmied* (*Wieland the Smith* – taken from the Scandinavian Thidrek saga). Others, above all the innumerable strands of the Nibelung complex, had yet to be drawn together in final form. But it remained for the moment a world of words, not of music, and there were controversial, challenging, even offensive opinions and theories in his mind that still had to fight their way out before the dominance of music could return.

As he stood on the free soil of Switzerland this May morning in 1849, Wagner felt a glow of liberation – not just in the obvious physical sense of having put himself beyond the reach of the Saxon police but as an experience that penetrated every part of his being. Goethe's '*Stirb und werde!*' is the command to which he now joyously responds – 'Die and be born again', the call to regeneration, to cast off the old Adam and learn the new truth by which man, both as individual soul and social animal, shall now live. He wrote in his *Communication*:

Nothing can be compared with that feeling of well-being which ran through me as I realized that I was free, free from the torment of desires destined to remain for ever unfulfilled, from the condition in which these consuming ideas had been my only sustenance. An exile and a refugee, once I was no longer forced to live a lie, once I could turn round on this hypocritical world and shout in its face how utterly I despised it, this world without a single drop of true artistic blood in its veins, powerless to utter a breath of true culture or beauty – then, for the first time in my life, I felt fully and completely free, restored in strength, happy, with no thought for where I would spend the next day, as I breathed the air of heaven around me.

The first 'air of heaven' he breathed was that of Zurich, which he reached by post-chaise from Rorschach on the evening of his first day of freedom. 'The moment I set eyes on the mountains surrounding the lake, bathed in the warmth of the sun's glow, I resolved, almost without knowing it, to avoid anything that could prevent me from making my abode here.' And indeed, Zurich, which, compared with Dresden, was little more than a cultural backwater, became the centre of his life for the next nine years.

'We are all of us men,' wrote Wagner in *Der Mensch und die bestehende Gesellschaft (Man and Contemporary Society)*, one of his essays for Röckel's *Volksblätter*, 'and all subject to the commands of the age.' For Wagner the age seemed to issue special commands, above all that destiny, fate – call it what we will – should create a set of circumstances which would ensure the protection of himself and his art. Relatives, friends, colleagues, patrons – someone was always on hand to see him through the financial crisis of the moment so that he could go where he wished to go, or do what he wished to do, where less favoured mortals would have been forced to capitulate before a stubborn and unsympathetic reality. In Chemnitz he had escaped capture through a coincidence that the best-laid plot could hardly have contrived, and the same benevolent hand had seen to it that, by a far from predictable turn of events, Liszt should take up residence in the little town of Weimar in the revolutionary year of 1848.

Now, in Zurich, he found an old friend from his Würzburg days called Alexander Müller, who was to do for him what he could not do for himself. Müller was a piano teacher and the conductor of a local choral society. Together with one of his pupils, Wilhelm Baumgartner, who had visited Wagner in Dresden some years earlier, he took Wagner to see two government officials, Jakob Sulzer and Franz Hagenbuch. The next day these officials handed him a Swiss passport, and with it his freedom of movement once more. Müller and Baumgartner were to be found in Wagner's company on a number of occasions during his years in Switzerland, but this was their great moment of service to the master. Sulzer was to remain equally loyal to him.

From this passport we have a closer description of Wagner's appearance than the police warrant gives. He was 5 ft 5½ ins tall, with blue eyes, brown hair and brown eyebrows, round chin and medium-sized mouth, while his nose, which, together with his high forehead, was always the most prominent of his features, is tactfully called 'medium'. His profession is given as 'compositeur de musique' and his destination as Paris. The same day as he received the passport he set out on his second campaign to conquer the musical capital of Europe.

It was a disaster. Little over a month later he was back in Zurich, Liszt having had to send him 300 francs for the return journey. As far as the world of art was concerned, hardly anything had changed in Paris since his first protracted failure there seven years earlier: the revolution was over, the power of bankers and industrialists was as firm as ever, and the ostentations of Grand Opera dominated musical taste as they had done in the days of the 'Citizen King', Louis Philippe. Wagner felt as though he had never left the place. 'A week was enough,' he said, 'to make me realize what a tremendous mistake I had made. During the last few decades operatic conditions, under the financial influence of Meyerbeer, have become absolutely execrable [*stinkend scheusslich*], and no self-respecting man can have anything to do with them.' His only pleasure – there was a cholera epidemic in Paris at the time, to add to the strain – was to see his fellow-exiles Gottfried Semper and Wilhelm Heine (son of his former colleague Ferdinand Heine), who had also escaped from Dresden with a price on their heads. His reading, he recalls, consisted of Proudhon's *De la propriété* and Lamartine's *Histoire des Girondins*.

Back in Zurich, living for the time being with Alexander Müller, Wagner set about persuading Minna to join him from Dresden. She needed a great deal of persuading. She had neither understood nor forgiven what she saw as his wilful sacrifice of a reliable position and domestic security to the self-indulgent pursuit of so-called revolutionary ideals. Wagner's letters from this time express an affection for her which cannot be gainsaid, but Minna was in no hurry to fall yet again into the snare of blind dependence and uncertainty. 'I hope you realize, my dear Richard,' she wrote in response to his entreaties, 'that it would be no small sacrifice for me to come and join you. What does the future hold in store? What can you offer me? It could well be two years at the very least before you have a proper income, and to have to rely on the generosity of one's friends is a miserable existence for a woman.' Wagner at his highest was, for her, Wagner the Kapellmeister, Wagner the triumphant conductor of *Don Giovanni* and Beethoven's Ninth Symphony, the respected, salaried servant of society. This is the sad measure of her spiritual limitation, the limitation later to be so cruelly exposed first by Mathilde Wesendonk, then by Cosima von Bülow.

But that autumn she did join him, accompanied by her ever-present daughter Natalie, the spaniel Peps and the parrot Papo. Liszt, at Wagner's request, had sent her money for the journey, and Wagner met them at Rorschach, where he himself had landed earlier in the year. Looking back on this moment in *Mein Leben*, he wrote:

I was quite moved as I watched them come ashore, this strange family of which half consisted of domestic pets. It was the dog and the parrot, I must admit, that gave me the happiest feeling. My wife at once introduced a chilly note into our reunion by threatening that, should I behave in an unseemly manner, she would immediately return to Dresden, where a great number of friends had offered her help and protection. Yet I only needed to look at her for a moment – she had aged considerably in a very short time – for my sympathy to be aroused and drive away my bitterness.

The Wagners moved into a small apartment at the back of a big house on the Zeltweg, in the fashionable Hottingen quarter of Zurich. Minna had been forced to sell most of their furniture in Dresden but managed to rescue some of Wagner's personal effects, including his grand piano and some pictures, among them portraits of his friends Wilhelm Fischer, the Dresden chorus master, and Ferdinand Heine, which he at once hung on the wall of his new quarters. Minna had sent his scores to Liszt some time earlier, and these too arrived soon afterwards. His small but precious library, however, Minna had entrusted to the Brockhaus family; when she later asked Heinrich Brockhaus to send the books, he refused, saying he would keep them until her husband repaid the 500 thalers he owed him. The debt was never paid, and Wagner did not see his books again.

The mixed tone of sympathy and amused detachment in which Wagner describes Minna's arrival in Switzerland shows how far they had grown apart. His letters to her are more affectionate than hers to him, and he continually seeks to reassure her. She, for her part, was suspicious, unsure both of him and of herself, while her grasp of his genius and of the demands it made remained as primitive as it had always been.

Outsiders too were aware of the disharmony. Carl Schurz, for example, the German revolutionary who later went to the United States and became Republican Senator for Missouri, was also a young political refugee in Zurich at this time. 'The most remarkable man I met during this period,' he wrote, 'was Richard Wagner. He had already composed some of his most important works, but his greatness was recognized only by a small circle. He was by no means popular with his fellow-exiles, being regarded as an extremely arrogant and domineering fellow of whom nobody could make a friend, and who treated his wife, a quite attractive, good-natured woman, though not particularly intelligent, in a very unkind manner. If anyone had predicted at that time how remarkable his career would be, nobody would have believed it.'

In Minna's eyes the blame for her growing estrangement from her husband lay with his involvement in the revolution. Liszt too saw Wagner's commitment to politics and ideological adventures as detrimental to his proper development and irrelevant to the pursuit of art. 'Away with this political claptrap!' he wrote impatiently to him. 'Stop this socialist cackle and these personal bickerings!' But although the time of Wagner's direct political action was past, the mood of social and aesthetic revolution persists unabated in two essays that he wrote in the latter half of 1849 – *Die Kunst und die Revolution (Art and Revolution)* and *Das Kunstwerk der Zukunft (The Work of Art of the Future)*, both published, like many of his essays, as separate brochures. 'My task,' he wrote defiantly to Theodor Uhlig, a violinist in the Dresden orchestra who became a close friend and admirer, 'is to make revolution wherever I go.' And as to why he chose to write about 'the work of art of the future' rather than compose it himself: 'This new art cannot at the present be created, it can only be prepared for – by provoking revolution, by smashing and destroying everything that deserves to be smashed and destroyed.'

These works show once more the persistent influence of

Bakunin and Feuerbach. Art, says Wagner, is a product of society: the rejection of the one entails the rejection of the other, and the 'work of art of the future' presupposes the 'society of the future'. 'Society', moreover, means the whole of society, not merely that privileged élite which has hitherto made up the consumer public of the art-industry, and the ideal of art in the service of the community demands the creative involvement of the entire spiritual energy of that community. The values of an industrialized society, a machine geared to soulless criteria such as 'productivity' and 'efficiency', must be overthrown, and utilitarianism discarded in favour of an aesthetico-spiritual idealism. Wagner's ultimate expectation, therefore, is of nothing less than the emergence of a new 'man of the future', in whom the old utilitarian, pragmatic motives will have been transmuted into new, spiritual 'values of the future'.

Here occurs for the first time in Wagner's writings the – for Wagner – technical term 'total work of art of the future' (*Gesamtkunstwerk der Zukunft*), which embraces both the union of the individual arts, a total aesthetic experience, and the communality of the participating artists, a collective creative enterprise. The bizarre utopianism of Wagner's concept – as many saw it – provoked a critic to coin the mocking counter-slogan *Zukunftsmusik*, literally 'music of the future', but with the ironical incredulity of something like 'never-never music'.

Feuerbach, to whom *The Work of Art of the Future* is dedicated, makes his presence felt in particular in the anti-Christian bias of *Art and Revolution*. Here, in a Romantic treatment of history which is selective to the point of falsification, Wagner professes to find in Greek antiquity the social conditions within which his ideal of art as the expression of a free and natural community was once realized. This predisposition to revitalize the artistic life of the nation through graftings of Classical stock is a recurrent feature in German thought, and sets Wagner in a tradition which can be traced back through Hölderlin, Schiller, Goethe and Lessing to Winckelmann. Forwards the line leads to Nietzsche, whose Hellenism, like Wagner's at this moment, was also violently anti-Christian. By the time of his essay *Heldentum und Christentum (Heroism and Christianity)* 1881, with its reference to 'the sublime simplicity of the pure Christian religion', and as his last, most sublime work, *Parsifal*, conveys, Wagner's attitude has become very different.

One concept that does remain firm in Wagner's mind, however, is that of the *Volk*. *Volk* means 'people', but the German word has an emotive, almost mystical overtone of national identity, a quality far more evocative than anything that the passionless word 'people' can command, and more self-consciously nationalistic than the slightly precious notion of the 'folk' from whom folk-tale and folk-song spring. Herder coined the word *Volkslied* in 1771, and the concept of *Volk* quickly became invested, above all through the activities of the Romantics, with a mystical aura of nostalgia for a pristine national unity that was now lost. This is the spirit in which Wagner, in *Art and Revolution*, rhapsodizes over 'the Greek *Volk* in its supreme beauty and truth' as he puts it. It is the same spirit that inspires in him the nationalistic pride which makes him so thoroughly German a composer. 'My ideal of art stands or falls with the rebirth of Germany and her rise to strength. Only in such conditions can it flourish,' he later declared. Small wonder that Wagnerian music-drama should come to be seen as the cultural counterpart to the establishment of German political unity under Bismarck in 1871. Small wonder also – in a different key but with the same, albeit often distorted themes – that Wagner and Bayreuth could be made to play a symbolical role in the National Socialist 'culture' of the 1930s.

Wagner received five Louis d'or for *Art and Revolution*

from the progressive Leipzig publisher Wigand, and another five for his earlier essay *Die Wibelungen (The Ghibellines)*, one of the preliminary studies for *The Ring*; the latter sold well enough to warrant a second impression. But sums like these, with the occasional help of Liszt and other well-wishers, could hardly keep the Wagner household going. This time the rescue operation was in the hands of two rich ladies. One was Frau Julie Ritter, a rich widow, mother of Karl Ritter, and a young friend and admirer of Wagner's from Dresden. Karl had been a member of the group – Semper, Bülow and Ferdinand Heine were others – to whom Wagner read the complete first draft of *Siegfrieds Tod* at the end of 1848. The other was Jessie Laussot.

Wagner's love affair with the rich Anglo-Scots girl Jessie Taylor, wife of the Bordeaux wine-merchant Eugène Laussot, was a hectic and melodramatic episode. Jessie had lived for a time with Frau Ritter in Dresden, had been at the first performance there of *Tannhäuser* in 1845 and had met Wagner in 1848, when she was nineteen. The following year she made an unhappy marriage with Laussot and settled in Bordeaux, together with her widowed mother, whose English husband, a lawyer, had left her very well-off. Here she heard of Wagner's plight and conceived the idea of joining Frau Ritter, with whom Uhlig and Ferdinand Heine had interceded, in making him an annual allowance – 500 thalers from Frau Ritter and 2,500 francs from the Taylor-Laussot family. 'These were the first signs of a new phase in my life,' Wagner later wrote, 'in which I grew to accept the fact that my outward fate was governed by inner laws which were to relieve me of the restrictions of domestic life.' Wagner responded warmly to sympathy; he responded even more warmly to sympathy accompanied by financial aid.

The largesse of Jessie Laussot and Julie Ritter came, ironically, at the moment when 'the restrictions of domestic life' were stronger than the 'inner laws'. For Minna, with her vision of Wagner as the operatic master of Europe, had almost made it a condition of joining him in Zurich that he should try yet again to make his mark in Paris. Liszt, whose tastes and attitudes were dominated by things French, was of the same mind and gave him 500 francs for the journey. So, putting what confidence he could in the still unfinished libretto of *Wieland der Schmied* – a Germanic subject totally unsuited to a Parisian milieu – he set out by train yet again for the French capital at the beginning of February 1850.

His old disgust immediately returned, this time under the particular stimulus of Meyerbeer's *Le Prophète*, which, he said, made him feel physically sick. The city he found intolerably noisy, and he had to drive around for a long time before he found a room in a quiet area. The cabbie found this search for quietness incomprehensible, muttering that if people wanted to live in a monastery, they did not come to Paris. Of his old friends, Semper and Kietz were still here, so was the pathetic figure of Gottfried Anders, the librarian. He worked on the prose draft of *Wieland der Schmied* and wrote an essay *Kunst und Klima (Art and Climate)* – but he need not have come to Paris to do this.

Then, in March, an unexpected letter came from the Laussots, inviting him to Bordeaux. Jessie, young, cultured, musical, seems to have thrown herself at him; finding in her the selfless commitment and total confidence in his art that Minna lacked, his professional future unsettled and his emotions under strain, and as always susceptible to the flatteries of female admirers, he responded with an instinctive romantic eagerness. They made plans to elope to Greece or Turkey, and he wrote to Minna that he intended to leave her; Jessie, meanwhile, confided to her mother that she had decided to desert her husband and go away with Wagner.

Nothing of the kind happened. In fact, the bizarre

three-month episode, which can be followed blow by blow, as it were, in the letters from Wagner to Minna, Minna to Wagner, Wagner to Kietz in Paris and Uhlig in Dresden, even between Minna, Jessie and Mrs Ann Taylor, has the character of a charade (no letters from Wagner to Jessie, or from her to him, have ever been found). First Minna hurried to Paris to have things out with her husband, but he managed to avoid her. Then Jessie's mother told Eugéne Laussot of his wife's infidelity, whereupon Laussot threatened to shoot Wagner. Finally, through the agency of Karl Ritter, Jessie wrote in June that she could no longer go through with the plan: the circumstantial evidence suggests that Minna and Jessie's mother had conspired to make Wagner look something of an ogre, and had made it clear to the infatuated young woman that she had better have nothing to do with him for at least a year. In a long letter to Minna at the end of June, which he saw as generous and genuinely affectionate, but which to her was full of reproaches and false accusations, Wagner ostentatiously put the whole affair behind him, and in July he returned to Zurich. Jessie later became the wife of the historian Karl Hillebrand and settled in Florence, where she played a prominent part in the musical life of the town. By a strange coincidence she and Hans von Bülow had both been pupils of the same piano teacher in Dresden, and in 1869-70, when the affair between his wife Cosima and Wagner reached its climax, Bülow often sought consolation in her company as a fellow-victim of the Master. She was at the première of *Die Meistersinger* in 1868 and met Wagner again in Florence in 1876, a few months after the first Bayreuth Festival.

It is easy to smile indulgently at this short-lived passion, and many have. It is equally easy to strike a tone of moral indignation over Wagner's attempted enticement of another man's wife and his shabby treatment of his own;

many have done this too. But Wagner and Jessie, for one brief moment, made common cause – in their love of music and in their disintegrating marriages, their bond being sealed by the hero-worship that turned to mutual passion. For a few short weeks Jessie understood Wagner, the man and the artist, in a way that Minna never could. By his lights, he could not have behaved otherwise, and certainly not better. The bitterness of seeing both financial help and passionate understanding being lavished on her husband by a younger, more attractive, more intelligent woman than herself was an experience that poor Minna was to suffer again a few years later when Mathilde Wesendonk appeared on the scene. Like his great friend and future father-in-law, Franz Liszt, Wagner needed, as man and artist, the constant presence of a woman.

All Wagner's personal dealings rested on an unquestioned inner conviction that it was *his* needs that were paramount, to the promotion of *his* art that the world should devote itself. Hence the harsh, pedantic tone of his writings on the reform of art and society, the intolerance of the intellectual who knows best, and knows that he knows best, and who regards the masses as an ignorant body it is his task to educate. Hence also the almost breath-taking equanimity with which he begged and borrowed from relatives, friends and acquaintances. For in his eyes the world did owe him a living. Moreover, subsidization of Richard Wagner, he insisted, was an investment, an excellent investment, since the royalties that eventually accrued from world-wide performances of his works would dwarf these gifts and loans into insignificance. Not many of his creditors took so rosy a view of the situation in 1850.

In Zurich Wagner conducted a number of concerts, and the occasional musical motif flickered through his mind, but he was still the writer, the man of ideas, the pamphleteer, not yet the composer again. The dramatic text of

The Ring, surrounded by unfulfilled projects like *Wieland der Schmied* and other themes from the world of Germanic mythology, was only laboriously taking shape in his mind, as he struggled to motivate the actions of the characters in his dramatic world myth. By contrast, his theories of art and society, his views on politics and the state of the world, still clamoured for expression, and two further essays from the years 1850 and 1851 stand out. One is *Oper und Drama (Opera and Drama)*, his most extensive and important statement of theoretical principle on the subject of opera. The other is one of the most controversial and in some ways most unpleasant of all his writings, an utterance as disturbing as it is psychologically revealing – the article *Das Judentum in der Musik (Music and the Jews)*.

Wagner and anti-Semitism, Wagner and Nazism, Wagner and Hitler – the slogans have a depressingly familiar ring, and much passionate ink has been spilt on such subjects by writers determined to press Wagner into service as some kind of forerunner of National Socialism. The extent to which a man may be held responsible for the subsequent perversion and distortion of his work is a subtle issue which needs to be approached with delicacy and open-mindedness. That it *is* a real issue with Wagner – and we need take it no further at this juncture – shows itself in the sober realization that, however vicious the means, Wagner's art could be, and was, perverted to an evil end, whereas Bach's, Mozart's or Beethoven's could not.

But what does Wagner actually maintain in this much vilified piece – as distinct from what many without reading his argument assume he maintains? For of many a critic of the work it may be said, as was said of Robert Owen, that he never thought differently of a book for having read it.

He claims, in a tone that is sneering and gratuitously offensive, that the great and true artist is one who, in expressing his own aspirations and conflicts, expresses those of his whole society, because he embodies at their most powerful the cultural values of a common heritage. He had argued the same case, the argument of the *Volk*, in *Art and Revolution*, and he returns to it in *Opera and Drama*. No Jew, he says, could enjoy such a position. The Jews of Europe had only recently been freed from their ghettoes and had no roots in the Gentile societies in which they now found themselves. There was intellect, culture and ability in plenty but no instinctual basis of creation, because no common basis of cultural or spiritual experience. Jewish composers like Meyerbeer and Halévy represented for Wagner Jewish self-assertiveness at its most meretricious, but even Mendelssohn, whose talent and taste he acknowledged, and whose artistic integrity he did not dispute, was denied, by his cultural rootlessness, the power to penetrate the heart of Western man's spiritual experience. A Jew living in the European tradition cannot be a true artist, let alone a great one – unless he ceases to be a Jew. Only by total assimilation, i.e. by renunciation and destruction of his Jewishness, can he be saved. 'There is only one thing – the same thing which redeemed Ahasverus – that can redeem the Jews from the curse that lies upon them, and that is their downfall.'

Discussion of anti-Semitism, or of any racial issue, tends to be conducted at white heat, and personal resentments and animosities smouldered in Wagner's mind as he wrote. Since he had only once had a secure and regular income, had even been close to starvation, he resented the prosperity of industrialists and financiers – many of whom were Jews. Since he had failed to impress the Parisian operatic world with his greatness, he resented the success of those who dominated this world, above all Meyerbeer and Halévy – both of them Jews. Meyerbeer, indeed, was doubly cursed, in that his father was a banker. It is at this level of personal frustration and envy that one must first understand Wagner's anti-Semitism, not in the realm of pondered theory, right or wrong. Its immediate context is thus very different from that of a classic racialist statement like Gobineau's *Essai sur l'inégalité des races humaines* (1853-5). Samuel Lehrs, one of his closest friends from the dark days in Paris, was Jewish, so was the pianist Karl Tausig, a pioneer of Bayreuth and the man entrusted by Wagner with making the piano reduction of *Tristan*. Angelo Neumann, the first to produce the complete *Ring* outside Bayreuth and the only producer in whom Wagner had any real confidence, was Jewish, so were Hermann Levi, conductor of the première of *Parsifal* at the Bayreuth Festival of 1882, and the later Bayreuth conductor Felix Mottl. Neumann, Levi and Heinrich Porges, a Jewish musician and critic, were among the twelve pall bearers at Wagner's funeral.

Wagner went on saying spiteful things about the Jews to the end of his life, even in their presence, but the prime irritant was his memory of Paris, 'Grand Opera', Meyerbeer and that whole complex of frustrations. Because he despised Parisian Grand Opera, and because its leading practitioners were Jewish, he ascribed all its abhorrent features to Jewry. He refused to forget the personal harm he was convinced the Jews had done him; at the same time undisguised self-interest and practical reality asserted themselves when circumstances changed. The two Nibelungs Mime and Alberich, like Beckmesser in *Die Meistersinger*, are Jewish caricatures.

But beyond the patent prejudices and the egregious offensiveness which have prevented many people from seeing the wood for the trees, *Music and the Jews* presents an historical argument. The Jewish composers of Wagner's day, of whom Mendelssohn was the greatest, belonged to the early generations of emancipated Jews, and as artists – the distinction between artists and intellectuals is important in the argument – they could not feel truly part of the tradition in which they now found themselves. In time, of course, they assimilate, and become part of, their new tradition, and the two greatest Jewish composers of modern times, Mahler and Schoenberg, belong as completely to the world of Western European music as any of their Gentile contemporaries.

In other words, what Wagner was looking at, with hate-filled eyes, was a period of transition, though he could not see it as such. As orthodox Jewry declines, so does the obtrusiveness which Wagner goes out of his way to identify and mock. *Mutatis mutandis* the contribution of the Jews to the culture of the society into which they are being assimilated becomes greater, generation by generation. What this has come to mean to the arts in Germany by the twentieth century finds its tragic expression in the flight of numerous writers, painters, musicians, actors and other creative artists from the country of National Socialism in the 1930s.

The origins of Wagner's anti-Semitism, as of practically all his public stances, were personal. But that there *was* a Jewish problem in the mid-nineteenth century is clear enough from the writings both of racialists and radicals – and of Jews. And because of their particular involvement in the business and financial world, the Jews had acquired a special status in, a virtual identification with, the structures of capitalist society, which meant in its turn that no discussion of economic matters could leave the Jews untouched. Karl Marx, son of a Jewish lawyer, regarded usury and self-interest as the driving forces in Jewish life, and the Jew's real God, not as Jehovah but as Mammon. In a society in which private usury had been abolished, the Jews could not have acquired the influence they did, and with the destruction of the capitalist system, as Marx saw it, the Jews would experience their true emancipation, an emancipation not cultural in nature but economic and social. In terms of hostility towards the Jews and what they represent there is often little to choose between Wagner and Marx.

The other substantial essay, *Opera and Drama*, completed in January 1851, is a social document to the extent that, as always in Wagner, art cannot be separated from social life, and 'the music of the future' must rest on 'the society of the future'. Its essence lies, however, in its detailed programme for the restoration to opera of the true quality of drama, a theoretical framework, set around with historical arguments of varying degrees of credibility, for 'the art of the future'. And since this framework amounts to a statement, not just of an ideal vision but of the intentions that he himself was about to pursue, it constitutes a *credo* of 'the artist of the future', of Wagner himself.

'Here is my last will and testament. Now I can lie down and die.' With these half-serious, half-jesting words Wagner sent a copy of *Opera and Drama* to Uhlig. Scarcely a single letter written in the weeks leading up to its completion and in the months that followed fails to make reference to it in one way or another, so preoccupied was he with its message. This message can be stated with embarrassing simplicity, almost triteness, yet it will always remain a challenge. Opera, says Wagner, is properly a musical form of drama – no more, no less. Its recent history has been perverted, in that what should be a means of expression, namely the music, has become an end in itself, while the proper end, namely the drama, has been made into a means. Gluck stood for modern opera as it should be, opera as drama; Rossini and Meyerbeer represented undramatic opera, opera as empty spectacle and ostentatious vocal display. Wagner would have accepted the formulation of Walter Felsenstein, the great postwar producer at the Komische Oper in Berlin; 'Music that does not grow organically out of the events being portrayed on the stage has nothing to do with drama.'

Wagner always accepted the postulate – a postulate purely psychological in origin, like the pessimism of Schopenhauer, which was soon to exert a powerful influence over him – that drama is supreme among the arts. With that strange confusion of inspired insights, semi-truths and shameless eclecticism which distinguishes most of his excursions into historical analysis, he selects Greek tragedy as the summit of human artistic creativity. His reasons, or pseudo-reasons: it was an art form that involved the whole community – his familiar argument from *Art and Revolution, The Work of Art of the Future* and other essays; its subject matter was drawn from the myths, religious in significance but human in application, that formed the spiritual fabric of that community; and it represented a fusion of the arts – poetry, music, dance – in a single dramatic purpose.

Time, argued Wagner, has seen the progressive disintegration of this Greek unity, and the individual arts have gone their own ways, becoming more and more remote from the community and contributing to the breakdown of a common consciousness. The need is for a return to the real values of the past through the creation of a new musico-poetic art form that shall assimilate and re-express the great moments of European art since Antiquity – Shakespeare, Beethoven, Goethe, Schiller and the Greeks, all in one. In characteristic erotic imagery he describes his vision of the union of poetry and music in a letter to Liszt: 'If one is to ensure that music, being female, duly conceives through her union with the poet, the male, one must take care not to deliver this noble creature into the hands of the first libertine who comes along. She must only become pregnant by the man who really loves her and yearns for her with an uncontrollable passion.'

As a challenge to the operatic composer to 'think dramatically', and as a compendious exposition of how dramatic words can be expressed in dramatic music, how a dramatic libretto should be constituted, how the psychology of the action and the inner drama in the characters' minds can be expressed through the use of recurrent leitmotifs, how the orchestra should be employed for dramatic effect, and other technical matters, *Opera and Drama* still has its fascination today. And as a statement of intent, it has to be set alongside Wagner's music dramas themselves. But the notion that an agglomerate of poetry, music, visual spectacle and acted stage-drama embodies the highest aspirations of artistic creativity and is the art of the future, has something bizarre about it. Would *Hamlet* be greater if it had music, or Beethoven's Eroica Symphony be greater if it were accompanied by a stage drama? Is there not an autonomous set of values within each art, the product of the autonomous development of that art? Is Goethe's poem 'Erlkönig' somehow incomplete without Schubert's music, or Büchner's drama *Woyzeck* inferior to Alban Berg's opera?

In its own way Wagner's concept of the *Gesamtkunstwerk*, the union of the arts, is as much an expression of the nineteenth-century cult of grandeur, of size for size's sake, as the 'Grand Opera' of Meyerbeer about which Wagner waxed so scornful. So too, again in their own way, are Wagner's works themselves, with their inordinate length and their extraordinary demands on performers and spectators alike. The idea that bigger means better is what Thomas Mann called 'the bad, mechanistic side' of the nineteenth century. But the greatness of Wagner's operas does not prove the greatness of his theory – it simply proves the greatness of his operas. That this greatness is a greatness in music, not a greatness in some composite dramatic 'art of the future', is a reality experienced by anyone who has surrendered to Wagner. Indeed, *The Ring* is epic rather than drama. Moreover, to return to the historical terms of Wagner's own argument, anything more different from Greek tragedy than Wagnerian opera would be difficult to imagine.

Wagner lived in perpetual fear of being misunderstood, both as man and artist, and felt bound to issue commentaries and instructions from time to time in order to set the record straight. Some of these pieces convey his thoughts on the interpretation of other composers – his various essays on Weber, on Gluck, Spontini, Liszt's symphonic poems, and above all on Beethoven. Others deal with the explicit ways in which he wished his own operas to be understood and interpreted. An extended personal and artistic apologia from these years in Zurich is *Eine Mitteilung an meine Freunde (A Communication to my Friends)*, written and published in 1851, the second of the autobiographical essays that precede *Mein Leben*. As 'friends' – in this he never changed – he defines all those prepared to devote their lives to promoting his music.

Claiming that the man and the artist cannot be separated in him, and that only those who love him as a man can understand him as an artist, Wagner surveys his career up to the turning-point in his life when the vision of a new art of drama in a new society began to take firm shape in his mind. Of particular significance are the final paragraphs of the *Communication*, in which he tells of his work on the Nibelung saga and makes explicit his plans for the entire *Ring*, both in conception and in performance:

I intend to present the myth of the Nibelungen in three complete dramas (I have given up writing 'operas') with an extensive prelude. But although each of these dramas is a self-contained unit, they are not intended as individual 'repertory pieces' in the modern sense. Instead I envisages a festival, specially arranged, at which each of the three dramas will be performed on a separate day, with the prelude on the first evening.

This is 1851, twenty-five years before the vision became reality.

* * *

Apart from excursions to various other parts of Switzerland, to Northern Italy, to Paris and, in 1855, to London, Wagner stayed in Zurich until 1858. In 1853 he and Minna moved from Zeltweg 11 to a larger apartment on the second floor of Zeltweg 13, which he furnished lavishly in anticipation of royalties from performances of his works and fees for conducting. The following year he told Jakob Sulzer, one of the officials who had procured him his Swiss passport, that he owed a total of 10,000 francs but reckoned on receiving 21,000 francs from performances of *Tannhäuser* and *Lohengrin* in various German opera houses.

Various physical complaints and maladies continued to plague his day-to-day existence, in particular his recurrent erysipelas and acute constipation. He spent two months at a hydropathic clinic near Zurich, living on a strict diet, 'without wine, tea or coffee, surrounded by a terrible collection of incurables, with depressing evenings relieved only by games of whist, all intellectual activity banned, and my nerves increasingly under strain'. The treatment had little effect beyond causing him to lose weight, and when he describes in *Mein Leben* his return to Minna and their little apartment in Zurich, the sense of relief is unmistakable.

But his depression persisted. 'My life is decaying day by day,' he wrote to Liszt in November 1852. 'I am living an indescribably useless existence, totally bereft of pleasure. It will not be long before I am in a state of utter ruin.' 'I wept bitter tears over your wounds and torments,' replied Liszt from Weimar, 'but I fear your only remedy is to suffer and be patient. How sad that a friend can say no more than this!' Liszt then quickly turned to his own worries and his own plans, offering Wagner a few crumbs of comfort with the prospect of performances of some of his works. He ends his letter, not with words but with notes, 'for one single chord brings us closer together than all the verbal expressions in the world' – a melancholy, pining chromatic sequence that does indeed say all:

The civic Music Society in Zurich had a small orchestra of professionals and amateurs, and there was a privately-run theatre – the theatre, strangely enough, where Wagner had been offered the post of Kapellmeister when he was in Würzburg twenty years earlier. Though reluctant to accept a permanent commitment, he conducted many concerts and operas here over the years – operas by Mozart, Weber, Bellini, as well as *Der fliegende Holländer* and *Tannhäuser*. Of the four performances of *Holländer* that he conducted in 1853, he wrote to Liszt: '*The Flying Dutchman* has left an indescribable impression here. Philistines who could never be induced to go to a theatre or a concert went to every one of the four performances and are now regarded as having gone mad. Piano scores sell by the half-dozen. With the women too I am making a great hit. At the moment I am staying in the country [he and Minna were spending a few weeks in a pension on the Zürichberg] and feel in good form.'

Three special concerts of excerpts from *Rienzi, Holländer, Tannhäuser* and *Lohengrin*, given in 1853 as a kind of miniature Wagner festival, were received with equal enthusiasm, though the box-office takings did not equal the expenses. He also used his position to launch the careers, as conductors, of the twenty-one-year-old Hans von Bülow and of his young Dresden friend Karl Ritter, whose mother, unmoved by the rumpus of the Jessie

Laussot affair, still paid Wagner an annual allowance, and continued to do so until he left Zurich.

Meanwhile news of his works was spreading across Germany, and theatres in Berlin, Prague, Breslau, and elsewhere announced their wish to stage *Tannhäuser*. Since he dared not set foot on German soil, he could not have directly involved himself in these productions. But with his almost pathological anxiety lest his work should be mangled to the point of unrecognizability by producers incapable of grasping a new operatic idiom, he wrote in 1852 a long tract *Über die Aufführung des Tannhäuser (On Performing Tannhäuser)*, giving detailed instructions to producer, stage manager, conductor and performers about how they should carry out their task. Ironically, those who read this handbook of instructions – and many, if not most, ignored it – were put off rather than stimulated, so categorical and disturbingly new were its demands. Wagner insisted that his singers must first absorb the text, and with it the spirit and meaning of the drama; the actual singing of the parts would then present no problems, and the music would become what it should be – the vehicle for conveying dramatic meaning, not a display of empty virtuosity. Neither managements nor performers were pleased to be shaken out of the ways in which both they and their audiences regarded the art form of opera, and the Leipzig theatre, for one, took fright at the prospect of attempting what Wagner demanded, and decided not to produce the work for the present.

The beauties of the surrounding countryside led Wagner, since his youth a tireless walker, to explore the Swiss mountains, sometimes in the company of friends, sometimes alone. With Uhlig, who had arrived from Dresden to spend a holiday in Switzerland, he visited the famous spots around the Lake of Lucerne associated with the story of William Tell, and later, by himself, tramped southwards to Interlaken and the Bernese Oberland, arriving eventually at Lugano. Another frequent companion was the one-time revolutionary poet Georg Herwegh, whose involvement in literature and politics in the wake of the July Revolution of 1830 made him a perfect foil for the Wagner in whom the ferment of 1848 had far from died down. Through Herwegh Wagner was introduced to the circle of intellectuals that had gathered round the former Hamburg newspaper editor François Wille and his rich wife Eliza, a circle that included his old friend Semper, the Dresden architect, the historian Theodor Mommsen, with Gottfried Keller and Conrad Ferdinand Meyer, the two greatest Swiss writers of the nineteenth century. It was Herwegh too who initiated a few years later the most profound intellectual experience of Wagner's whole life – his encounter with the philosophy of Schopenhauer.

A few weeks after the three successful concerts of his music, in May 1853, Wagner completed his first musical compositions since 1848 – a polka and a sonata, both for piano. In July his spirits rose further when Liszt arrived for a week's stay. 'Since my financial situation had unexpectedly improved as a result of the steadily increasing number of performances of my operas, I abandoned myself more and more to my predilection for attractive and comfortable furnishings, making my apartment so fine with new carpets and items of furniture that even Liszt, on entering the room, was struck with surprise and admiration, calling it my *"petite élégance"*.' The two men, accompanied by Herwegh, made excursions into the nearby mountains and sealed their friendship by toasting each other as *Du* on the Rütli, the mountain where, in the story of William Tell, the Swiss freedom fighters swore their oath of brotherhood and freedom. Later, after Liszt had returned to Weimar, Wagner and Herwegh made their way to Chur and St Moritz, Wagner hoping that the spa waters and the mountain air would benefit his uncertain constitution, but they had little effect. Nor did a trip that autumn to Genoa and La Spezia, paid for by the wealthy merchant Otto Wesendonk, an admirer of his work, whom we shall meet again shortly.

Wagner's exhilaration at Liszt's visit was to be repeated in the autumn of 1856, when Liszt, in the company of his Princess, came to Zurich again and celebrated his fifty-third birthday in the famous Baur au Lac hotel. Before a large gathering in the hotel they improvised a perform-ance of Act One of *Die Walküre*, with Wagner singing the parts of Siegmund (heroic tenor) and Hunding (bass), and Liszt playing the orchestral score on the piano.

The text of *Götterdämmerung* (still called *Siegfrieds Tod*) had lain complete since 1848. More than once since then Wagner had written to Liszt and others that he was poised to start work on the music; in 1850 he had started a composition sketch for two scenes, and the following year he jotted down the theme of the Ride of the Valkyries. The Weimar court even made him an offer of 500 thalers for the completed work, to be paid in four instalments. But it was the intellectual meaning, the myth, the concep-tual allegory that still filled his mind and had first to be made explicit. 'Once the poem is finished,' he wrote to Uhlig in 1852, 'I shall become entirely a musician again, and then remain solely a performer.' The prose sketch of *Siegfried* (still called *Der junge Siegfried*) was written in a bare week, and the complete text over the following three weeks in May and June 1851; the texts of the first two parts of the tetralogy, *Das Rheingold* and *Die Walküre*, were not finished, however, until November of the follow-ing year. In February 1853, at considerable personal expense, which he airily dismissed, he had fifty copies of the complete *Ring* poem printed on fine paper for presen-tation to his friends, including Liszt, Bülow and Röckel, and to influential figures whose interest he hoped to arouse.

This gesture met with scarcely any response beyond that

of polite acknowledgement. Even Liszt, to whose sympathetic understanding Wagner attached so much importance, seemed uncertain what to say, and for a long while, to Wagner's chagrin, he said hardly anything. Yet it could scarcely be otherwise. The text of *The Ring* is so far removed from what the nineteenth century expected of an operatic libretto that readers could not see how the music could possibly grow out of it – or, as they would have said, was to be superimposed on it. For although these texts are inconceivable as stage plays in their own right (a few misguided attempts have in fact been made to mount them as such), they also clearly stand as creations utterly different, in conception and in form, from the libretto of a Scribe or a Boito, waiting to be set to music by a Meyerbeer or a Verdi. Gone are the regular flowing lines of *Tannhäuser* and *Lohengrin*, with the dependence on symmetry and rhyme. In their place come short, jerky lines, uneven in length, and rich, not in the poetic device of rhyme, Christian in origin, but in assonance and alliteration, formal features of pagan Germanic poetry, the poetry of the world of Siegfried, Brünnhilde and Wotan.

Different as they are, however, from the conventional operatic libretto, intrinsically more dramatic, more self-consciously 'literary', Wagner's texts have no more claim to an independent existence apart from their music than others. Indeed, since in some miraculous way that defies description, the music is nascent in the poem, already dwells in the words, the indivisibility of the operatic 'total work of art' is even more absolute than when, as has been the rule throughout the history of opera, the libretto is written by one man and the music by another. As Wagner worked at the composition of *The Ring*, the orchestra became more and more dominant, absorbing the vocal parts, arrogating to itself the deepest meaning of the work, and thus undermining the autonomous validity of the words still further. It is this totality of conception that made it impossible – his handful of attempts shows how impossible – for him to compose music to words written by other poets. (That the Wesendonk Songs come closest to being an exception tells its own story.) Even less thinkable, for the same reason – though the annals of opera know of many cases of multiple setting – in that his texts could be set to music by another composer.

The writing of the poem of *The Ring* spanned a period of over five years of extreme agitation in Wagner's mind, and that the last of the four parts, *Götterdämmerung*, was the first to be written is only the most obvious of the reasons why, in its final form, the work should have taken new courses and acquired new meanings. Wagner had read the principal German and Scandinavian sources of the Nibelung saga while working on the score of *Lohengrin*, and the heroic figure of Siegfried, with all the mythological significance that his actions and his fate could be made to bear, became a dominant image. Wagner expressed the philosophy of his task thus: 'I had always been attracted by the glorious figure of Siegfried but only now did I realize how he could be made the hero of a drama. The poet-composer has to express human values in their purest form, free of all convention.'

This 'purest form, free of all convention' is myth. The power of mythology resides in its presentation of characters and situations in which successive generations recognize their own condition. The characters and situations themselves, while having an identifiable historical or legendary origin in a given set of circumstances, possess a relevance beyond these circumstances and convey a symbolic meaning that transcends time and place, a meaning that rests on changing yet ever-valid psychological motivations. The contingencies and relativities of history give way to the absolutes of symbolic truth. Myth leads into the world of ideas, of objective and universal truths. It stands for more than it is, and means more than it says. It is at once the creature of human minds and, once created, an influence upon those minds, an influence that persists from generation to generation.

So from the Nibelung myth of giants and men, of dragons and dwarfs, of love and hate, murder and vengeance, Wagner took first the figure of Siegfried, portraying him as the revolutionary hero, the fighter for the new social order that shall arise above the ruins of capitalist slavery. 'Through the revelation of the initial evil, which gave birth to a whole universe of evil,' as he put it, 'we are to learn how to recognize evil, how to extirpate it and how to build a just world in its place.' The evils of greed, theft and treachery set the scene in *Das Rheingold*, where not only the perverted, power-hungry dwarf Alberich but even Wotan, greatest of the gods, pursues his ends by foul means as readily as by fair. The gods are supreme, but their supremacy rests on a history of ruthlessness and cunning. They themselves are party to the evil and the injustice that they seek to eradicate, and the curse that rests on the Nibelung's ring, symbol of wealth, power and exploitation, exacts its price from them as from the others who possess it.

'This treasure of the Nibelungs,' wrote Wagner to August Röckel in jail, 'is a symbol of extraordinary significance. It becomes the focal point of all manner of crimes.' In the 1930s a German lawyer called Ernst von Pidde wrote a book called *Richard Wagner's 'Ring des Nibelungen' and the German Criminal Code*, in which he demonstrated that the total punishment for the crimes committed in the course of the action – murder, kidnap, incest, arson, robbery with violence and the rest – would amount to five sentences of penal servitude for life (Alberich, Fafner, Fricka, Hagen, Brünnhilde) and up to ninety years imprisonment or penal servitude for the other criminals. Even Wotan cannot right an old wrong without committing a new one. The need is thus for a New Man, a child of the gods, invested with their divine power but bending this power to his own free will, and through this transcendent free will redeeming them from the guilt which they themselves can never purge.

Siegfried, while bearing the original sin of his incestuous provenance, is this New Man, an amalgam of trust in instinct and man's natural sensual being (Feuerbach), of the will to destroy a sick and diseased society (Bakunin), and of an utopian faith in the emergence of a new world order based on a new morality (Proudhon). He shares the national reformatory zeal of the Young German movement and breathes the social-revolutionary air of Wagner's *Jesus von Nazareth*. He knows no fear, and now uses the power he has received from the gods to assert his authority over them, splintering Wotan's spear with his sword. Love becomes omnipotent, the love that demands sacrifice in life but is victorious in death, *Liebestod*, love as redemption, as fulfilment, as transcendence. Here it is the love of Siegfried and Brünnhilde, as it had earlier been the love of Lohengrin and Elsa, and was to be the love of Tristan and Isolde. (A further recurring Wagnerian pattern may be seen in the Siegmund-Sieglinde-Hunding triangle in *Die Walküre*, the Dutchman-Senta-Erik triangle in *Der fliegende Holländer*, the Tristan-Isolde-Mark relationship in *Tristan und Isolde*. In each case the romantic outsider invades rule and convention to claim the love of a woman by the force of his passion, as Wagner was to claim Mathilde Wesendonk and Cosima von Bülow.)

'In Siegfried,' wrote Wagner to Röckel, 'I have sought to portray my ideal of the perfect human being, whose highest consciousness manifests itself in the fact that all consciousness can find expression only in living and acting in the present.' But this optimism, this *Sturm-und-Drang* confidence did not last. Wagner was highly impressionable, given to sudden enthusiasms but equally sudden depressions, and a ready prey to discontent and disillusion. His life is littered with dashed hopes, from the frustrations of his career in Dresden, through the collapse of the national reform movement of 1848 and 1849 to the fluctuations of his relationship with Ludwig II and his disenchantment with Bismarck's Empire of 1871. Disillusionment is, after all, the ever-present obverse of utopianism – the despairing admission of frustrated hopes. And Siegfried himself is guilty of criminal acts.

The longer Wagner pondered the events of the Nibelung myth, the larger loomed the character of Wotan. Siegfried signalled the advent of the new age, but the weight of the drama was shifting towards the passing of the old age, towards the tragedy of Wotan the Wanderer, as he becomes in *Siegfried*. The power of the gods, far from being restored, is now broken for ever, and Walhalla goes up in flames. On the one side the inevitable destruction of the old world, the corollary to Wotan's tragic renunciation; on the other the redemption of the world by love, the annunciation of a positive future. How to absorb the drama of Siegfried into the tragedy of Wotan now becomes Wagner's problem. 'My poem encompasses the beginning of the world and its destruction,' he wrote to Liszt. 'Pay good heed to it!'

The key to Wagner's answer lies in the figure of Brünnhilde. By defying Wotan and defending Siegmund in his fight with Hunding, she achieves her individuality at Wotan's expense and reduces him to impotence; but at the same time, as his daughter, she is part of him, and he looks to her for the act that will lift the curse and bring the peace for which he and the world yearn. For Siegfried himself, made unfaithful to Brünnhilde through the philtre, symbol of the wiles of the world, becomes a victim of the hubris that is the occupational hazard of all heroes, and Wotan sees his hopes destroyed again by the power of the curse. Brünnhilde, made strong by her suffering, brings about the final catharsis by the pure, selfless love that leads her to join Siegfried in death, by the will to renounce, the will to die and thus transcend the values of earth. By her death she achieves redemption for Siegfried, for herself and for the gods. Peace is denial of the world, forgetfulness of self, nirvana. A current of pessimism always ran close to the surface of Wagner's spiritual life; here art and life flow in a single stream.

A year after the private printing of the poem of *The Ring* Wagner read Schopenhauer's *Die Welt als Wille und Vorstellung (The World as Will and Idea)*. He was overwhelmed. 'I recognized to my amazement,' he said, 'that what had gripped me about Schopenhauer's theory had long been familiar to me in my own poetic text. Only now did I understand my Wotan.' As so often, the insights of the artist and the constructs of the philosopher share a common world of experience.

So *The Ring*, among the other meanings that the myth, as Wagner uses it, can legitimately bear – the evil of man's domination of man, whether by capitalist exploitation or any other exercise of force, even in the name of benign altruism; man's conquest of nature for his own purposes; sin and the inevitability of retribution; the nemesis of power – becomes an allegory of self-discovery and self-understanding, which is to say, the discovery and understanding of life itself, the life of the collective unconscious. 'What we must learn from the history of man,' wrote Wagner to Röckel, 'is to will what is necessary and to bring it to pass.' At the end of *Götterdämmerung* pure, ageless Nature is restored, and the Rhine Maidens frolic around their gold as they had done at the beginning of *Das Rheingold*. Between this beginning and this end the whole drama of the world is played out through the conflict between power and love, and in the final bars of *Götterdämmerung* the violins soar above the Walhalla-motif and the song of the Rhine Maidens with the leitmotif of Redemption, bringing peace and serenity back to the world.

Like all great works, *The Ring* lives on a hierarchy of levels. The order of precedence within the hierarchy may be disputed, and the sparks that fly as zealous young producers grimly grind their axes in Bayreuth, Berlin or London, ensure that there is a good fire to go with the smoke. But – assuming their percipience and integrity – such interpreters have only ignited something that was meant to burn.

'Once again,' wrote Wagner towards the end of his *Communication to my Friends*, 'in an irritable frame of mind, utterly dejected over my inability to carry through any artistic project, I felt compelled to confess that my creative life was at an end. But then a friend came to lift me out of my depression, assuring me with all the earnestness and enthusiasm at his command that I was not alone but was truly and profoundly understood, even by those who seemed most remote from me. He it was who made me an artist again – a new and complete artist. This wonderful friend was Franz Liszt.' The reference is to the year 1849. In February of that year Liszt gave the first performance of *Tannhäuser* outside Dresden, following it with a long and enthusiastic article on the work in the *Journal des débats* in Paris (French was Liszt's chosen language, both for intellectual discourse and in day-to-day life). In 1850 he conducted the première of *Lohengrin*. With these performances, and with planned productions of *Tannhäuser* in Berlin, Breslau, Prague and elsewhere, Wagner's fame, and with it his contentiousness, steadily grew.

Perhaps there has been a tendency to present Liszt as a man of immense influence on German musical life at this time, a man who, by giving his accolade to *Tannhäuser* and *Lohengrin*, had at a stroke guaranteed recognition of Wagner's greatness once and for all. In fact, what happened in the musical life of Weimar caused scarcely a ripple on the surface of German music as a whole. Had Weimar been Berlin, it would have been a different story. As Liszt wrote: 'The performances of *Tannhäuser* in Frankfurt, Breslau, Schwerin and so on are very welcome, but the most important place for you is Berlin. The impression your works make there will be the decisive influence on your whole reputation at this stage.'

But Wagner desperately needed some outside gesture of support at this moment, a moment, he wrote, 'when it seemed abundantly clear to me that none of my dramatic works would enjoy any public success'. By breaking a lance for these two operas, Liszt, more than anybody or anything else, restored to Wagner the confidence to face the challenge of his vision. And when, at the height of his powers, he suffered fits of black despair over the course of his life and the value of the works he was producing, it was still to Liszt that he confessed his anxieties.

Liszt had been with Wagner in Zurich in July 1853, and his presence hovers over that moment of radiance when, during a trip to Italy in September, Wagner suddenly felt the power of music surge through him again – the long E-flat-major chord that opens the Prelude to *Das Rheingold*. In October they met again in Basle, when Bülow and the violinist Joachim were also present; from there, accompanied by Princess Carolyne von Sayn-Wittgenstein, they went together to Paris. The evening after their arrival Wagner dined with Liszt, the Princess and Liszt's three children by his first mistress, the Countess d'Agoult. This was his first sight of the fifteen-year-old Cosima, but although he describes the occasion in *Mein Leben*, he does not mention her name. During his stay he saw the old faithfuls, Kietz and Anders, again, and Minna joined him for the last eight days.

Back in Zurich, he set to work on *Das Rheingold* in earnest, completing the musical sketch, which contained all the basic thematic material, in nine weeks. The final score was ready in September 1854, and by then the composition sketch for the first two acts of *Die Walküre* had also been made.

Symbolic of the emergence of the new music drama, of the Wagner whose five years of musical silence since *Lohengrin* were now finally and triumphantly broken, is the different technique of composition that he now began to develop. Broad as the sweep of his earlier operas had been, he could not have started writing the music of *Das Rheingold* as though it were the natural successor to *Lohengrin*. Already in 1848, with the text of *Siegfrieds Tod* complete, he must have known intuitively that the huge task on which he had just embarked was one for which he did not have, as yet, commensurate musical powers. And even without the political preoccupations of the past five years, there would surely have had to be an interregnum in which he forged new musical techniques which would lead him beyond the lyricism of *Lohengrin* into the epic and dramatic world of *The Ring*.

First and foremost it was a matter of sheer size, of the immensity of his total vision. This compelled him, as he described in *Mein Leben*, to change his whole method of composition:

I saw how awkward it would be to sketch the orchestral prelude to *The Rhinegold* on two staves, as was my usual practice, and I had to use full-score paper from the outset. This led me to make my musical sketches in a new way, *viz.* by hastily jotting down the rough outlines in pencil to work out in the complete score immediately afterwards. This brought considerable difficulties in its train, since the slightest interruption in my work often caused me to forget the meaning of these rough sketches and made me struggle desperately to bring it back to mind. By 14 January 1854 I had sketched the music of the whole work; this meant that, in its essential thematic relationships, the plan of the entire musical structure of the tetralogy was now laid down.

The thematic material of *Das Rheingold* has a tautness and conciseness which, explored and exploited in the symphonic fabric of the work, symbolizes how far Wagner has come since *Tannhäuser* and *Lohengrin*. Nowhere is this more striking than in the leitmotifs, now the informing principle of a huge musical argument.

From *Der fliegende Holländer* to *Lohengrin* the leitmotifs are essentially vocal in origin, self-sufficient musical phrases linked to specific characters and ideas, not evolving as the character or the significance of the idea evolves but recurring throughout the work in their original form and thus evoking each time their original associations. Such are the Redemption motif from Senta's ballad and the related motif of Faithfulness in *Der fliegende Holländer*, the Repentence, Love's Magic and Love's Renunciation motifs in *Tannhäuser*, Elsa's Prayer and the Grail motif in *Lohengrin*, and a host of others. It was the obtrusion of such motifs throughout Wagner's *oeuvre* that provoked Debussy to call them 'visiting cards', and led the violinist Joachim, we are told, to rise from his seat at the recurrence of each leitmotif, make a slight bow and murmur 'Pleased to meet you'.

These earlier leitmotifs are usually extended melodic phrases wedded to a text of comparatively long, rhyming poetic lines. A glance of comparison at the short, ejaculatory, alliterative lines of *The Ring* is sufficient to show how different the melodic idiom is now bound to be. The motifs become shorter, more concentrated, rarely more than two bars in length and often only one. Nor are they by any means essentially vocal themes; and even where they are vocal in origin, they are often not lyrical or vocal in nature but part of a broad musical canvas dominated by the orchestra. If we except *Die Meistersinger*, as we so often must, from such generalizations, there is more than a grain of truth in Cecil Gray's deliberately disparaging characterization of Wagner's operas as 'works which are to all intents and purposes symphonic poems to which voice parts have been not always too skilfully added'.

The orchestral forces also become correspondingly lavish. For Bayreuth Wagner posited one hundred and six players – fifteen woodwind, four horns, five tubas (including the so-called Wagner tubas, tenor and bass), four trumpets, four trombones, four percussionists, six harps and sixty-four string players.

In *The Ring* the leitmotifs guide the listener through the action, interpreting, anticipating, accompanying the psychological development of the characters and the ebb and flow of the drama, subtly changing in melodic or rhythmic outline, in harmony, in dynamics, in orchestration, to convey the emotional and situational changes in the work. The formal variations in the individual motifs present a depth psychology in music, a pattern of forms released by the physical and psychological action but at the same time expressive of inner musical values and obedient to – better, perhaps, creative of – the laws of an inner musical logic. This music does not illustrate: it *is*. The text, by itself a half-creature, finds its full meaning and function through the music that absorbs and expounds it, and the spiritual experience that Wagner's work brings us issues not from an experience in drama, or in *Gesamtkunstwerk*, or in the significance of myth, but from an experience in music.

Strictly speaking, *Das Rheingold*, which has more physical action than any of the other parts of *The Ring*, is not the full first movement of the symphonic programme but the 'Vorabend', as Wagner called it, the introduction to the in-depth psychological drama that opens in its full intensity with *Die Walküre*. Here the breadth of vision, the richness, the audacity, the demands on performer and listener alike become even greater, reaching their wonderful climax as Wotan kisses his daughter Brünnhilde and sends her into the sleep from which she will be awakened by Siegfried.

Die Walküre, full of character study and passionate relationships – the story of Siegmund and his twin sister Sieglinde (the incest motif that also occurs in *Rienzi*, *Die Sarazenin* and *Die hohe Braut*), the fate of Brünnhilde, above all the tragedy of Wotan, compelled to kill his Siegmund and banish his Brünnhilde – is the most frequently performed of the parts of *The Ring*. Apart from its sheer musical and dramatic quality, it is the most tautly constructed of the four dramas, and its stage demands have not the frightening excessiveness of the other three. Much of this tautness of construction derives from Wagner's concentration of the dramatic action into extended duets within each of the three acts – the confrontation and psychological development of Siegmund and Sieglinde, Siegmund and Brünnhilde, Brünnhilde and Wotan, duologues linked by the theme of woman's love and informed by the passion which, for a brief moment, had linked the fates of Wagner and Jessie Laussot, and was about to unite Wagner and Mathilde Wesendonk.

As the orchestra becomes more dominant – this is one of the most vital changes that take place between *Lohengrin* and *Das Rheingold* – so not only do the leitmotifs lose their basically vocal origins and associations but the weight of the musical argument shifts from the realm of melody to the realm of harmony. This in turn brings a greater depth and intensity to the emotional experience, a depth and intensity embedded in the increasingly chromatic vocabulary and the growing opulence of the orchestration. Chromaticism undermines key relationships: familiar and often predictable associations disappear, and feelings of uncertainty and uneasiness insinuate themselves, finding peace only when diatonicism is restored and dissonance resolves into consonance.

Wagner had been made aware of new areas of harmonic experience through Liszt, in particular through the Faust Symphony and the Dante Symphony, parts of which Liszt played to him on his visit to Zurich in the autumn of 1856. But Wagner was to penetrate into these areas more deeply than Liszt or any other composer of the nineteenth century. It is at moments such as that when, at the end of *Die Walküre*, Wotan sends Brünnhilde to sleep and kisses her eyelids with the beautiful words:

Denn so kehrt der Gott sich dir ab,
         (So the God turns from thee
So küsst er die Gottheit von dir!
       and kisses thy godhead away.)

that Wagner's chromaticism breaks into its full glory:

When *Das Rheingold* and *Die Walküre* were both complete, he approached the Leipzig publishers Breitkopf and Härtel. With characteristic self-confidence he suggested that they buy the entire *Ring* for 10,000 thalers, 5,000 to be paid on the spot for the two finished parts, and 2,500

for each of the other two parts, which at that time he thought he could deliver in another two years. Breitkopf and Härtel knew that Wagner's reputation was growing, but they shrank from so substantial an outlay for a work which might never be finished. Even receiving a copy of the complete poem of *The Ring* could not persuade them to take the risk. There, after an ill-tempered exchange of letters between composer and publisher, the matter ended, and *The Ring* was eventually published, not by Breitkopf but by Schott of Mainz. It is not something that Leipzig cares to be reminded of.

Homesickness for Germany, as he had felt it in Paris, now came over Wagner again in his Swiss exile, above all because he was cut off from personal contact with German opera houses, and thus from potential performances of his operas. With the presentation copy of the complete poem of the *Der Ring des Nibelungen* that he sent to Liszt, he enclosed a letter begging his friend to arrange for an invitation to Weimar, from where he naïvely thought he could return to Dresden. A few weeks later he urged Liszt again – there are often two or three letters of Wagner's to one of Liszt's, now as at all times – to secure Karl Alexander's intervention with the Saxon authorities to have him granted a pardon. 'Your letters are sad – your life still more so,' wrote Liszt in reply. 'It is your greatness that causes your misery – the two are inseparable and cannot but torture and torment you until you absorb them in a new faith, a faith in happiness. I cannot expound this to you or preach you a sermon, but I will pray to God that His radiance may shine into your heart and that he may give you faith and love.'

The Saxon government responded to the Duke's pressure by reissuing Wagner's description and the warrant for his arrest. He was even prepared, he told Liszt, to admit that his involvement in the Dresden uprising had been a youthful indiscretion – 'provided they do not subject me to the shame of being forced to sign some declaration of repentance'. The authorities remained unmoved. During a two-month visit to friends and relatives in Germany in the autumn of 1854 Minna made her own appeal to the new King Johann of Saxony, who had recently succeeded his brother Friedrich August, for proceedings against her husband to be dropped. Again the plea fell on deaf ears, and not until 1862 was he finally granted permission to return.

To take Wagner's testimony of his years in Zurich at its face value would leave a picture as of almost unrelieved misery and frustration. Yet to others he looked far from the unhappy professional exile. Eliza Wille, who, with her husband, François, saw a great deal of him and constantly sought to help and encourage him, wrote in her memoirs: 'I have never been able to agree with statements I have heard and seen from time to time that Wagner experienced all the miseries of banishment in Zurich. He was held in high regard by all, had a settled home of his own and friends to intercede on his behalf. He knew nothing of the sad lot of the political exile, looking hopelessly for sympathy and knocking at doors that were often barred to him.' Gottfried Keller, who saw a good deal of him in Zurich, also found him lively and entertaining company (Wagner did not return the cordiality). But to the man who was forced to live it, it was inwardly a life of worry and frustration which he sought to express, and thus to sublimate and to transcend, in the writings and musical works in which his genius found its liberation.

The composition of *Das Rheingold* and *Die Walküre*, neither of which was performed for another fifteen years, was the great achievement of Wagner's years in Zurich. Only rarely, at any time from *Rienzi* and *Der fliegende Holländer* onwards, did he turn from work on his large-scale operas to compose smaller occasional pieces. One such, however, an interesting link with the past, is the

Faust Overture, originally written in Paris in 1840. Liszt conducted this first version (which has since been lost) at Weimar in 1852, and it was 'a sensational success', as he wrote to Wagner. Stimulated partly by Liszt's Faust Symphony, partly by the hope of selling the *Faust Overture* to Breitkopf and Härtel, Wagner set about rescoring it and turning it into a more substantial work, an orchestral tone-poem – he describes it thus himself – of the genre inaugurated by Liszt. He finished it, in its definitive form, in January 1855 but always saw in it an expression of that special enthusiasm for the titanic dynamism of men like Goethe, Shakespeare, Beethoven – and Faust – which he had felt when he first conceived the work. Whatever revisions he made, he never wanted the sight of these origins to be lost.

At the same time his growing reputation as a conductor was bringing him invitations to give concerts in Zurich and other towns in Switzerland, and in February 1855, at the invitation of the Philharmonic Society, he went to England to conduct a series of eight concerts at the Hanover Square Rooms in London. Each concert contained a major work by Beethoven; there were also pieces by Mozart, Mendelssohn, Weber, Cherubini, Spohr and contemporary English composers (Cipriano Potter, MacFarren, Charles Lucas), together with the overture to *Tannhäuser* and excerpts from *Lohengrin*.

London music critics unburdened themselves of their suspicion of this colourful composer-conductor by giving him a generally hostile press, taking exception in particular to his unconventional tempi. The Allegros, they said, are too quick, and the Adagios too slow: a symphony is torn apart by such exaggerated contrasts. They also found his use of rubato excessive and his dynamics too extreme.

Without a recording, we cannot know what Wagner's performance of say, the Eroica Symphony sounded like. (Edison demonstrated his phonograph in December 1877, so there could, theoretically, have been cylinder recordings of music he conducted at Wahnfried – and also of Liszt's playing.) But the critics' remarks point in an unmistakable direction, a direction that leads where we would expect it to lead, namely, to a conception of the Eroica Symphony as drama, as the conflict of themes, whose individuality has to be made explicit. The expressive meaning of the music has thus to be drawn out in all its intensity if the nature of the drama is to be demonstrated.

The tendency of the time was to 'unify' a symphony by minimizing the differences between the movements. The range of tempi and dynamics was narrowed, and most conductors – Mendelssohn lent his considerable authority to this practice – took the whole at a brisk moderato-cum-allegro and more-or-less uniform mezzo forte. This had the further advantage of not revealing the limitations of the players more than could be helped. By contrast, Wagner's treatise *Über das Dirigieren (On Conducting)*, written in 1869, shows his concern to penetrate the in-dwelling *melos*, the melodic soul, of what he was performing, which involves surrendering to the ethos of the movement, the section, the phrase, even the individual bar, laying bare its innermost nature. This means that a particular group of notes, or a particular tempo, or a particular dynamic acquires its character in the first place from its context, and in the second place from its composer; Allegro in Mozart has a different meaning from Allegro in Beethoven. Even a given metronome mark in two different pieces, says Wagner, cannot be slavishly followed and expected to demonstrate the one and only 'correct' tempo in both cases. Whatever the form his interpretations took, Wagner's demands on the conservative and slightly aggrieved members of the Philharmonic Society orchestra, as well as on the London music critics, make it clear that, as conductor no less than as man and composer, he forced the world to accept *his* terms and do things *his* way.

Years later, in Munich, conducting a rehearsal in the energetic manner captured in contemporary drawings and cartoons, Wagner once alarmed his players by almost falling off the edge of the rostrum. Checking himself just in time, he called out to them: 'Gentlemen, I am accustomed to standing on the edge of a precipice.' One wonders whether the orchestra, enjoying the joke, knew how earnestly he meant it.

Wagner had come to London as a conductor, but the press took care that the public should also be informed of some of their visitor's less admirable qualities. *Punch* of 31 March 1855 carried the following none-too-kindly item:

We do not know what Herr Wagner's new musical theory may consist of, but we think that the notes of 'The Music of the Future' must be mainly promissory notes, payable at two, three or six months after date.

However carpingly the critics received Wagner's concerts, public enthusiasm grew from one to the next. The seventh was attended by Queen Victoria and Prince Albert, who summoned the conductor to the royal box during the interval. 'The Queen has a highly-developed taste for the most trivial things,' he recalled. She also suggested, undoubtedly in all seriousness, that it would be nice if his operas could be translated into Italian and performed in London. What makes the Queen's remark memorable is not its mildly comical inappropriateness – La Scala, Milan has resounded many times to *Tristano e Isotta*, *L'Olandese volante* and *Il Crepuscolo degli Dei* – but the assumption that opera, by natural law, was in Italian. It was an assumption that rested on over a century of operatic history leading back to the days of Handel.

At his final London concert, which ended with Beethoven's Fourth Symphony and Weber's overture to *Oberon*, Wagner received a great ovation. The series as a whole also brought him a welcome fee, and he was 1,000 francs* the richer when he returned to Zurich. Among the guests at his farewell banquet were Berlioz – who had also been invited to London to conduct a number of concerts which included excerpts from his own works – and a young pianist, a pupil of Liszt's, called Karl Klindworth, 'in appearance the very image of my Siegfried', said Wagner. Klindworth moved in and out of Wagner's life over the next twenty years or so; he prepared the piano score of *Siegfried* in 1871, and became after Wagner's death the foster-father of Winifred Williams, the British girl who married Wagner's son Siegfried in 1915 and controlled the Bayreuth Festival from 1930 until 1944. A highly controversial figure, tainted by her relationship to Hitler from the 1920s onward, the eighty-one-year-old Winifred Wagner still lives in the grounds of Wahnfried, the family villa in Bayreuth.

English life and the English temperament had nothing to offer Wagner. He found the English totally impervious to culture, a people interested only in balance sheets and profit-and-loss accounts. 'I cannot imagine anything more repellent than the true, authentic Englishman,' he wrote to Otto Wesendonk from his flat in Portland Terrace. 'He is like a sheep, with the sheep's practical instinct for sniffing out its food in the field – except that the beautiful field itself and the blue sky above are beyond his perception.' He might have stopped to wonder why the 'sheep' applauded his concerts so enthusiastically. Apart from the necessary official engagements connected with his concerts, his personal dealings were almost entirely with old German friends, like Semper, who were in England at the time, and with French and German émigrés. Among these latter was the remarkable Malwida von Meysenbug, an aristocratic Communist sympathizer who had left

---

*About £60 in the values of the 1930s. 1 Swiss franc = approx. 1½ French francs in the mid-nineteenth century.

Germany in 1848 and was now living in London as a teacher and as governess to the children of the Russian writer Alexander Herzen, himself also a political refugee. Malwida von Meysenbug, who admired Wagner's revolutionary writings and was overwhelmed by his music, remained part of his life until the end, leaving in two volumes of memoirs fascinating sketches of Napoleon III, Mazzini, Wagner, Liszt and others.

But neither his public success in London, nor its financial rewards, nor any personal experience could lift the weight off Wagner's general depression and disillusionment. Every day he read a canto of Dante's *Divine Comedy*, identifying his own situation with the world of the *Inferno* and becoming more and more convinced of the emptiness of worldly values. His chronic attacks of erysipelas caused him considerable pain and made work almost impossible. Various nervous disorders and allergies also appeared, which were, however, alleviated to some extent the following year when he spent two months at another hydropathic clinic, this time at Mornex, near Mont Blanc. For his forty-second birthday, which fell during his London visit, he sent himself a cynical little rhyme, starting with the first line of a well-known poem by Heine:

> Im wunderschönen Monat Mai
> Kroch Richard Wagner aus dem Ei:
> Ihm wünschen, die zumeist ihn lieben,
> Er wäre besser drin geblieben.

> One beautiful May morning
> Wagner broke out of his shell.
> 'He should have stayed inside the egg!'
> Said those who loved him well.

This black mood was compounded of two inseparable elements, the one personal, the other philosophical, each nurturing the other but at the same time feeding on it, and both nourishing the roots of his art. The personal element was his love for Mathilde Wesendonk; the philosophy was that of Schopenhauer.

'I was totally absorbed in my work. On 26 September I completed the fair copy of the score of *Das Rheingold*. Then, in the peace and serenity of my home I became acquainted with a book which was to acquire a profound significance for me. The book was Schopenhauer's *The World as Will and Idea*,' so wrote Wagner in *Mein Leben*. The year was 1854. Schopenhauer's *magnum opus* had first appeared in 1818 but at the time it created scarcely a ripple on the surface of philosophical thought. The aftermath of the Congress of Vienna and of the Wars of Liberation, the Hegelian consolidation of the line of philosophical idealism, the accelerating pace of scientific advance and industrialization – this was no moment to preach a message of pessimism and self-denial.

But thirty years later the Germans, particularly young Germans whose ideals had disintegrated in the disillusionment of 1848, suddenly found relevance in a doctrine which, identifying Will with the ultimate Kantian *Ding an sich*, the primary world-purpose, made this Will both metaphysically irrational and senseless, and ethically wicked. The individual's pursuit of 'the right to live', together with the cultivation of his powers and abilities, is thus not only meaningless but offensive, destructive. We must seek to transcend the senseless suffering that is life, must destroy the individual will, reject the quest for happiness and nobility, renounce love; in place of these false values now come self-abnegation, resignation, asceticism – an ideal virtually identical with that of the Buddhist *nirvana*, the state in which all desires and passions are extinguished and the perfect bliss of oblivion attained. In Schopenhauer's pattern there is an intermediate stage in the attainment of this perfect condition, a point of refuge from which we can sense the complete *nirvana* beyond, namely art and aesthetic contemplation. In his supreme moments the artist achieves a state of self-absorption in his art which comes near to self-destruction; the realm of art, above all of music, is the infinite, and to create art is to be granted a glimpse of the absolute.

'For years,' wrote Wagner in *Mein Leben*, 'Schopenhauer's book was never completely out of my mind, and by the following summer I had studied it from cover to cover four times. It had a radical influence on my whole life.' No intellectual experience, before or after, made a comparable impact on Wagner's mind. But it would hardly have been so if his condition, material and spiritual, had not been such as to render him susceptible at that moment to the pessimism that Schopenhauer preached. Schopenhauer's effect on him, as Wagner saw it, was not to change completely the direction of his life but to express and justify in philosophical terms a change of direction that he had subconsciously already made. It was as though he had been a Schopenhauerian without knowing it. As Theodor Weinlig, his old teacher of composition in Leipzig, had set him to study the principles behind the music that he had absorbed through his feelings, so now Schopenhauer gave him the intellectual key to an understanding of his emotional and spiritual situation.

The spiritual kinship between Schopenhauer and certain Eastern philosophies, in particular the concepts of *nirvana* and metempsychosis, is mirrored by Wagner's attraction to Buddhism at this time. While recovering from one of the attacks of erysipelas that plagued him during the winter of 1855-6, he read Burnouf's *Introduction à l'histoire du Bouddhisme*. Shortly afterwards, between finishing the full score of *Die Walküre* and starting work on *Siegfried*, he planned a Buddhist drama, sustained by the themes of sensual renunciation and self-denial, called *Die Sieger (The Victors)*. It never got beyond the stage of a prose sketch, evidently because Wagner could not envisage how it could be given operatic form, but the thought of it stayed with him to the end of his life, and elements of it, notably its mystical aura and the theme of self-realization through renunciation and the attainment of purity, are central to *Parsifal*, his final work. Indeed, the plan of *Parsifal* itself, the story of which he had last read in Marienbad at the time when the *Die Meistersinger* and *Lohengrin* were first conceived, sprang fully-formed from his mind barely one year later, though the poem was not to be written for another twenty years and the opera not finished till a year before his death.

Out of the understanding that Schopenhauer had given him, and as he continued to work at the music of *Die Walküre*, which was finished in March 1856, there grew on the one hand the background to Wagner's involvement with the young Mathilde Wesendonk, wife of his most generous benefactor in Zurich, and on the other hand his conception of a drama on the subject of Tristan and Isolde. 'Since I have never enjoyed in life the real happiness of love,' he wrote to Liszt, 'I will erect to this fairest of all dreams a memorial in which that love shall drink its fill.' It was a love which, from the beginning of its life in Wagner's mind, as in the Tristan legend itself and its treatment in medieval epic, could find fulfilment only in death, *Liebestod*.

Wagner's earliest sketches for *Tristan und Isolde* date from the summer of 1857, while he was in the middle of the musical draft of *Siegfried*. But *Tristan* now thrust the whole *Ring* conception out of his mind. Act One of *Siegfried* was already finished in full score; the orchestral sketch of Act Two was also complete. Not for seven years did he go back to it, and not until another five years after that, in March 1869, did he start work on Act Three. By that time he had written both *Tristan und Isolde* and *Die Meistersinger*.

Indeed, at this moment, in the summer of 1857, Wagner seems to have resigned himself to seeing *The Ring* remain a massive torso. 'I have finally decided,' he wrote in a long letter to Liszt in June, 'to abandon the idea of finishing my unmanageable *Nibelungen*. I have brought Siegfried to the wonderful solitude of the forest [at the end of Act Two], left him there beneath the linden tree, and taken my sorrowful farewell of him. He is happier there than anywhere else.' Proud bearer of the new-forged sword Nothung, Siegfried, the man who has never learned the meaning of fear, has now killed the dragon Fafner and the dwarf Mime; in possession of the Tarnhelm and the ring, heir to Alberich's curse yet himself guiltless, he follows the forest bird – one of the most attractive pieces of tone-painting in all Wagner's operas – as he sets out on his quest for Brünnhilde. The final stage direction of Act Two, the point at which Wagner broke off, reads: 'He runs after the bird, which teases him for a while by flying in different directions, then finally takes a definite course towards the back of the stage. Siegfried follows. The curtain falls.'

One force behind Wagner's decision to abandon *The Ring* was as real as it was mundane – the realization of the virtual impossibility of ever getting such a gigantic work as the complete *Ring* actually performed, a realization confirmed by the refusal of Breitkopf and Härtel to advance him any money against the completion of the first three parts. Beyond this Wagner seems to have felt, after the four intensive years that had produced the complete *Rheingold*, the complete *Walküre* and now the orchestral draft of the first two acts of *Siegfried*, that he had 'written himself out' as far as the realm of the Nibelungs was concerned, and needed the stimulation of a different world – the world, first of *Tristan*, then of *Die Meistersinger*. The music of Acts One and Two of *Siegfried* belongs to the intense, passionate dramatic context of *Das Rheing-*

old and *Die Walküre*, that of Act Three – which will concern us in due course – has a markedly more 'operatic' quality, like *Götterdämmerung*, which was to follow.

When Wagner returned to *Siegfried* in 1869, the inroad made into his consciousness by his encounter with Schopenhauer showed itself in a dichotomy of optimism and pessimism, of confident hope of change and resignation to the will of fate. *Siegfried*, like its never-written fellow *Jesus von Nazareth*, stands for positive, progressive values, for the man who says 'Yea' to life and puts his confidence in the human will. But as *The Ring* progresses, Siegfried, like Wotan and Brünnhilde, lives only for his end; he no longer qualifies for the status of tragic hero, because, never having learned to fear, he yet knows that better than a life in fear is death, and this is what he now wills. In a passage that Wagner added to the text of the final scene of *Götterdämmerung* but did not set to music when the time came, Brünnhilde proclaims the highest meaning of the myth in terms which show how far Wagner was later to retreat from the all-conquering world of Siegfried as the liberated and liberating New Man, in whose certain victory lay the future of mankind:

> Alles Ew'gen
> Sel'ges Ende,
> Wisst ihr, wie ich's gewann?
> Trauernder Liebe
> Tiefstes Leiden
> Schloss die Augen mir auf:
> Enden sah ich die Welt.

> (The blissful end of all eternity –
> know ye how I attained it?
> The deep suffering of a grieving love
> opened my eyes, and I saw the world
> come to an end.)

It is pure Schopenhauer.

At Christmas 1845 Wagner sent Schopenhauer one of the fifty luxuriously-printed copies of the poem of *Der Ring des Nibelungen*, inscribed 'With reverence and gratitude'. To judge from his comments in the margin, the old philosopher was not too impressed – indeed, one would hardly expect him to be. 'Apparently the "work of art of the future",' he noted, 'is quite extraordinary.' Four years later Wagner also sent him one of the first printed copies of the text of *Tristan*, but we do not know how he responded. It seems unlikely that he ever heard any of Wagner's operas – which, since his own musical idols were Mozart and Rossini, is probably just as well.

'So often do I cast my yearning gaze towards the land of Nirvana. But Nirvana quickly turns into Tristan again.' Wagner's philosophical quest for *nirvana* had been in the company of Schopenhauer. His immediate, most intense artistic expression of the ideal was *Tristan und Isolde*. The emotional experience which brought him the personal knowledge of love and its renunciation centred on the woman to whom these words were written – the rich and attractive young Mathilde Wesendonk.

The Wesendonks – Otto, two years younger than Wagner, German partner in a New York firm of silk merchants, and his second wife Mathilde, twenty-three at the time Wagner first met her – belonged to upper-middle-class Zurich society. They first met Wagner in 1852, two years after arriving in Zurich, and quickly became ardent champions of his music. Otto financed both personal and professional activities of Wagner's with remarkable generosity, ultimately providing him and Minna, at a nominal rent, with a little house on a hill in the fashionable Enge district, where he was building himself a new villa. Wagner always called the Wesendonk estate the *Grüner Hügel*, 'Green Hill', and his own house the *Asyl*, 'Refuge'. (The Wesendonk villa is now an historical museum belonging to the city of Zurich, but the Asyl, alas, is no more.) Wagner took such generosity as his due, and Otto Wesendonk was only one of a number of Zurich patricians who were called upon at one time or another to supplement his regular allowance from the faithful Frau Julie Ritter. 'I cannot sleep on straw and drink bad whisky,' he said; 'I must be coaxed in one way or another if my mind is to perform the forbiddingly difficult task of creating an as yet non-existent world. Above all I must have money – but what is the good of hundreds, when thousands are needed?'

Another of the Wesendonks' gestures was to present the Wagners with a spaniel, called Fips, to fill the gap left in their life by the death of old Peps in the summer of 1855. Papo, the parrot, had died four years earlier and been succeeded by Jacquot. For Wagner and Minna, who had no children, these pets fulfilled a vital emotional need.

From the very beginning the 'Wesendonk affair' involved all four members of the Wagner and Wesendonk families. Mathilde Wesendonk was overwhelmed by Wagner's genius; he, for his part, found in her the attentive female sympathizer he always needed, a woman to whom, unlike Minna, he could read his works, teach the symphonies of Beethoven and explain the philosophy of Schopenhauer. On the manuscript of the Prelude to *Die Walküre* he wrote the motto 'Blessed be Mathilde', and under a revised version of his *Faust Overture*, made in 1855, he added 'To the memory of my beloved Friend'. Otto was devoted both to his young wife and to Wagner's music, a man whose selflessness and understanding, even at the moments of greatest strain, were almost beyond belief. For poor Minna, the last of the quartet, the experience was a nightmare which left her humiliated, enraged and exhausted. In breadth of personality and in culture she was far inferior to the other three; she was also a sick woman, suffering from heart disease and chronic insomnia, and incapable of coming to terms with what she saw as the insults to which her husband and above all Mathilde subjected her.

In *Mein Leben* – it is far from being the only time he behaves in this way – Wagner professes the innocence of his 'friendly relationship' with Mathilde Wesendonk. But his letters, the testimony of Mathilde herself, the letters of Minna, together with the reminiscences of third parties and a mass of circumstantial evidence, all show how deep their passion ran, a passion exposed to the world in all its glory in *Tristan*. The forbidden love of Tristan and Isolde, with their betrayal of King Mark, is a situation already foreshadowed in the triangle of Siegmund, Sieglinde and Hunding in *Die Walküre*. Behind it, linked in a relationship of creative suffering, stand the figures of Richard Wagner, Mathilde Wesendonk and her husband Otto.

The mutual attraction that developed between Wagner and Mathilde Wesendonk was no secret to the world around them. Minna was forced to watch it grow, a spectacle made all the more bitter by the friendliness that had linked her and Mathilde at the beginning, as well as by the indebtedness of her husband and herself to their benefactors. Visitors to the Wesendonk villa realized what was going on, while Mathilde, a gentle woman of complete honesty and sincerity, made no secret to her husband of her feelings for Wagner.

The Master, as always, saw the whole pattern of events as a constellation revolving round himself, and was convinced that, although the affair could not but cause worry and unhappiness – and were not his own worry and unhappiness the greatest of all? – he had acted quite blamelessly at all times. Overwhelming as was his need for Mathilde, he had assured Minna that he would not abandon her, and had even been willing, at one stage, to leave Zurich for a few weeks so that, as he put it, 'the suffering of the good-natured Otto could be relieved to some degree'. Haunted, as he was, by the tragic story of

Tristan and Isolde, the love that could only find fulfilment in death, he talked a great deal about renunciation and self-abnegation, but his instinct was that others should renounce, not he himself. Indeed, how can an artist renounce his 'Muse', as he called Mathilde, and still remain true to his art?

In the autumn of 1857 the love between Wagner and Mathilde Wesendonk reached its climax. 'A year ago today,' he reminisced in his diary on 18 September 1858, as though talking to her,

I finished the poem of *Tristan* and brought you the last act. You led me to the chair by the sofa, threw your arms round my neck and cried: 'Now I wish for nothing more!' This day, this hour marked my rebirth. A sweet creature, demure and coy, plunged into a whirlpool of pain and suffering to make this wonderful moment possible and to say to me: 'I love you.' Since that time there has been no more conflict in me. Perplexity and torment might be our lot, but never, not for a single, terrible moment, could my love for you lose its fragrance, even the smallest particle of that fragrance. I always knew with absolute clarity that your love was the supreme thing in my life, and that without it my existence was a contradiction in terms. Take my thanks, O sweet, loving angel.

A week or two before this incident of the *Tristan* poem there had been in the Wesendonks' villa a social encounter, natural in the circumstances but almost bizarre in retrospect, between three women who are linked in history by their individual attachments to Wagner. The first was the twenty-eight-year-old hostess, Mathilde Wesendonk, without whom we might have had no *Tristan und Isolde*. The second was the ailing, suspicion-laden Minna, now forty-eight, the life companion who never understood what her husband's genius was about. The third was Cosima, nineteen-year-old daughter of Liszt, who was on her honeymoon with Wagner's disciple Hans von Bülow, who, after studying with Liszt in Weimar, was now a piano teacher at the Stern Conservatory in Berlin. Cosima's thoughts were of her new husband, Minna's were of herself and her wounded feelings, Mathilde's were of the composer of *Tristan*, who, making himself the centre of attention as always, dazzled the company by playing from his manuscript some of the recently completed parts of *Siegfried*. When Hans and Cosima von Bülow returned to Berlin, they took with them a complete copy of the text of *Tristan*. (When Wagner read the poem aloud to a group of friends shortly afterwards, Gottfried Keller was one of those who warmly applauded; Semper, on the other hand, found the whole thing 'far too serious'.) Less than ten years later Minna was dead and Cosima was living with Wagner. Mathilde, like her husband, remained a faithful supporter of the cause of Wagner's music until her death in 1902.

In January 1858 Wagner wrote a desperate letter to Liszt, asking for a loan of 1000 francs and begging him to meet him in Paris: 'It is with you that I want to talk over my whole position, so that whatever I decide to do has the complete agreement of the only friend I have.' Liszt had the money sent to Paris but did not go there himself. Wagner had to borrow the cost of the journey from Semper, for as usual he had made his plans without considering what they would cost to carry out. He took a room in the Grand Hôtel du Louvre, enjoying the frequent company of Blandine Ollivier, Liszt's eldest daughter, and her husband Emile, a lawyer, and spent a good deal of time reading the plays of Calderón, which helped to calm his agitated mind.

In the company of Madame Hérold, widow of the composer of *Zampa*, he heard Haydn's *Creation* for the first time and later, at a soirée in the house of the Erards, the famous manufacturers of musical instruments, he met again the widow of Spontini, a composer for whose work he always had a special affection. When Madame Erard made him a present of one of the firm's fine grand pianos, worth 5,000 francs, he could hardly believe his good fortune. 'This gesture seemed to illuminate the obscure purpose of my whole visit to Paris,' he wrote in *Mein Leben,* 'constituting its real success and making everything else look illusory.' The piano was delivered to him in Zurich a few months later.

He also called on Berlioz, who was at work on *The Trojans* and whom he had last seen in London three years before. We know now that Liszt's mistress, Princess Carolyne von Sayn-Wittgenstein, who never liked Wagner or his music, supported Berlioz in the hope of checking Wagner's rapidly growing popularity, and had cast *The Trojans* in the role of rival to *Der Ring des Nibelungen*. Whether Wagner knew this or not – it would have depended on Liszt and his divided loyalty to his friend on the one side and his mistress on the other – he was totally unimpressed by Berlioz's libretto of the work, which the author read aloud to him with poetic pride.

Wagner's dependence on the friendship of Liszt during these years in Zurich speaks out of almost every letter he wrote to the man who, though only two years his senior, personified the success, the security, the popularity for which he himself yearned. Often, inevitably, it was material assistance he asked for – and received, but at its deepest it was a relationship based on a spiritual need, a need, one might almost say, for a father-figure such as neither his real father nor his stepfather had been allowed to become, and which no personality from his formative years had been able to represent. His self-surrender to Liszt at this time was almost complete. 'If,' he wrote on New Year's Day, 1858, 'I so thoroughly resent your innumerable commitments and engagements, then, as you must have noticed, it is for one very special reason – that it takes you away from *me*. Our contact with each other means everything to me – it is like a spring from which all else flows.'

He returned to Zurich in February. Later that month

there was a performance of *Lohengrin* in Munich, attended by the Baroness Meilhaus, governess of the young Crown Prince Ludwig of Bavaria. The Baroness's excited account of the performance to her impressionable young charge now linked the name of Wagner with Ludwig's favourite legend, a conjunction whose profound consequences were to emerge eight years later. But Zurich was not Munich. Wagner could not break with Mathilde Wesendonk, yet they could have no future together. He worked intensively at the score of the first act of *Tristan* and finished setting to music the five poems by Mathilde, the so-called 'Wesendonk Lieder', which he had started before going to Paris and which both biographically and musically belong to the world of *Tristan*.

Mathilde's poems, inspired by her love for Wagner and by the text of *Tristan*, have a wan charm, with their naïve melancholy and their sensitive, if conventional imagery and manner. Wagner's music, on the other hand – and this was one of the very few occasions when he set words other than his own – has all the chromatic sophistication and emotional intensity of *Tristan und Isolde*, the voice weaving its arabesque of 'endless melody' above the rich harmonic texture. Indeed, the Wesendonk Lieder are a classic example of a familiar phenomenon – that a beautiful song may as well be written to a mediocre poem as to a great one. All the songs contain moments of the *Tristan* music, but two of them are directly linked to the opera. 'Im Treibhaus' ('In the Hothouse') is a complete sketch of the orchestral prelude to Act Three, and 'Träume' ('Dreams') contains the germ of the love-duet in Act Two – 'O sink' hernieder, Nacht der Liebe' ('O descend upon us, night of love'). 'Träume' was already in fair copy by December 1857, and two days before Christmas a group of players performed an orchestral version of it beneath Mathilde's window in the Wesendonk villa as Wagner's present for her twenty-ninth birthday.

R.W.–H

The first performance of the whole cycle was given in July 1862 by Emilie Genast, sister-in-law of the Swiss composer Joachim Raff, at a country house belonging to Franz Schott, the publisher. The young pianist Wendelin Weissheimer, who was among the guests, recalled in his memoirs the difference between an emotional and a commercial response: 'Tears poured down Cosima von Bülow's face. Herr Franz Schott rubbed his hands in glee and immediately locked the manuscript away in a drawer.'

Suddenly the 'Wesendonk affair' exploded and Wagner's choice was made for him. For months Minna had watched jealously as Mathilde çame across from the villa to visit him in his room on the first floor of the Asyl – Minna herself lived on the ground floor. She would also watch Wagner hurry across to the villa to see Mathilde, 'particularly,' she noted, 'when the good Otto was not at home.' Minna discovered from the servant at the Asyl that when he opened the door to Mathilde, she used to forbid him to divulge that she was upstairs with Wagner. One morning in April 1858 Minna intercepted a messenger in the garden on his way to the Wesendonk villa with.a roll of music paper. It contained the original pencil draft of the Prelude to *Tristan*, and concealed inside it was a long letter to 'Madame Mathilde Wesendonk'.

The letter never reached her. Minna opened it, found that parts of it implied a passionate relationship between her husband and Mathilde of the kind she had always suspected, and rushed up to his room to confront him with it. Wagner tried to calm her. He knew that she was unwell, and he showed a genuine fear about her condition. He arranged for her to take an extended rest cure at Brestenberg, on the Hallwyler See, and a few days later she left Zurich, but not before she had stormed into the Wesendonk villa, flourished the letter at Mathilde, then at Otto, not knowing that Mathilde had never concealed the affair from him.

During the weeks that Minna was away, Wagner worked on the music of the second act of *Tristan* and received a number of welcome visitors – the tenor Josef Tichatschek, who had been the first Rienzi and the first Tannhäuser; Albert Niemann, a tenor from Hanover, who was to become famous in the roles of Tannhäuser and Siegmund; and above all the flamboyant young Polish-Jewish pianist Karl Tausig, who became as close a personal friend of Wagner's as the short-lived Samuel Lehrs, also a Jew, had been in Paris during the miserable years from 1840 to 1842.

Far from restoring her health and her composure, Minna's stay in Brestenberg only made her the more bitter towards both her husband and Mathilde Wesendonk. 'It is really terrible,' she wrote in June to the wife of Wagner's friend and fellow-exile Georg Herwegh, 'how shabbily Richard treats me, after making me so ill. A week last Sunday I went home, barely for one day. I wish I had never gone: Richard vented his anger on me till two in the morning.' So when she got back to Zurich in July, the situation was as intolerable as ever, and the final dissolution of the Wagner household in the Asyl only a matter of time. To the end Minna saw her husband as a weak, spiritless creature and Mathilde as a spiteful, predatory serpent. 'Richard has two natures,' she said in another letter: 'he has been caught in someone else's snare and only clings to me out of habit. I am now resolved, since this woman cannot bear my living with my husband, and he is weak enough to give way to her, that I shall live by turns in Dresden, Berlin and Weimar until either Richard or God calls me away.' Wagner did not see why he should not have Mathilde as his 'Muse' and Minna as his house-keeper, while Minna, on her side, could not bear the thought of divorce.

By August he could endure the situation no longer. After the last of his various house-guests had left – Hans and

Cosima von Bülow, on another visit from Berlin, Cosima's mother, the Countess d'Agoult, and the pianist Karl Klindworth, who accompanied Wagner as he sang through the principal roles of *Das Rheingold* and *Die Walküre* from his manuscript – he put the unfinished score of *Tristan* in his travelling trunk and took the train to Geneva; from there in the company of Karl Ritter, who joined him from Lausanne, he travelled to Venice. Here he was to spend the next six months, living on his memory of Mathilde Wesendonk and wrestling with the music of *Tristan*. 'This is where I shall finish my *Tristan*,' he wrote in his private diary of passionate conversations with Mathilde, 'in spite of the raging world outside. And when I have, I shall come back to you with it, to comfort you, to make you happy.'

It was not to be. He did not finish *Tristan* in Venice. And when, 'not in the slightest degree embarrassed', as he put it, he did go back to see the Wesendonks the following year, the fever had gone out of the affair and the unpleasantness left by Minna's behaviour was forgotten. What now mattered in Italy was the freedom he had gained, freedom from Minna and the impossible circumstances of the Asyl. 'As I took my leave of Minna,' he said, 'I was deadly serious, bitter, sad – yet I could not weep. In this frame of mind I set off on my journey, and I cannot deny that a feeling of well-being came over me and that I now breathed freely. I was travelling into solitude: that is my true home.' Solitude meant renunciation – not a negative surrender but a positive commitment, a Schopenhauerian renunciation of the physical presence of the beloved in the name of a higher spiritual reality, a union in grief and suffering which, like that of Tristan and Isolde, carried in itself the promise of eternity.

Although her personality cannot but gain from a comparison with the uncultured and sometimes vulgar Minna, time may have cast a soft, slightly unreal glow of idealized perfection on the figure of Mathilde Wesendonk. Yet what she meant to Wagner, and thus to *Tristan und Isolde*, perhaps also to parts of *Die Meistersinger* and of *Parsifal*, is beyond dispute. Genius is not always solicitous of the well-being of others, and art often rides rough-shod over human susceptibilities. It was Wagner's personal tragedy that this love, so necessary to him as an artist, should have brought so much bitterness into his life and been the catalyst to destroy finally any hope that a community of interest between himself and Minna might survive.

Minna herself, having attended with a somewhat ostentatious air of grief and injury to the practical aspects of vacating the house, left the Asyl for Dresden two weeks after Wagner. Before she did, determined to fire the parting shot in the war with her hated rival, she wrote a savage letter to Mathilde. It began:

Dear Madam,

Before I leave, I must tell you, with bleeding heart, that you have succeeded in estranging my husband from me after a marriage of almost twenty-two years. I trust that this noble act will help to bring you happiness and peace of mind.

'She is past saving,' Wagner said, 'but I cannot take revenge on the unhappy woman – she must pass her own judgment on herself.' Years later, when, long after the passion had gone out of the 'affair', Minna's suspicions still persisted, Wagner's tones sharpened as he made the results of her actions clear to her:

Your blindness and false suspicions will never force me to give up my sincere and intimate relationship with that family which, husband and wife, has shown such unwavering devotion towards me. So I command you to hold your peace and never to mention the matter again – not because there is anything dubious or suspicious about it but because you cannot and will not recognize the true situation.

The Asyl had become anything but a refuge.

CHAPTER FIVE

Career Without a Centre

Until the providential moment in 1864 when King Ludwig II of Bavaria entered his life, the movements of Wagner's public career had been governed by the exigencies of withdrawal and flight. First in Magdeburg, then in Königsberg his theatre went bankrupt; he was dismissed from Riga and smuggled out of Russia like a criminal; Paris starved him into defeat, and revolution drove him out of Dresden. Now the impossibility of ever claiming Mathilde Wesendonk as his own, with the equal impossibility of ever rescuing his relationship with Minna, had turned him out of his Asyl, where he had completed the poem of *The Ring*, composed the music of *Das Rheingold*, *Die Walküre* and the first two acts of *Siegfried*, and finished the composition sketch of *Tristan und Isolde*.

Yet his decision to leave was as inevitable as it was a relief. He recalled in *Mein Leben*: 'I cannot remember that I shed a tear or even looked back at Minna as the train drew away, which almost alarmed me. But I could not repress a growing satisfaction; it was obvious that all the suffering of recent years had been to no avail and become unbearable. Only by tearing myself away from such conditions could I pursue the purpose of my life.'

The immediate 'purpose of his life' was dominated by Mathilde and by the urge to complete *Tristan*. For some eight months after leaving Zurich he chronicled his emotional life in the form of unsent letters to Mathilde; she too kept a private diary, but for the first months of their separation she agreed, at Otto's behest, to have no direct communication with him. When she agreed to receive his letters again, his tone became less and less passionate, more and more intellectual; after January 1859 he even renounced the intimate *Du* form of address for the formal *Sie*. And in March of that year, when he visited the Grüner Hügel for a day, he described his meeting with her and her husband as 'sorrowful but in no way embarrassing'. The Wesendonks continued to befriend and support him till the end of his life.

From the beginning – Germany still being barred to him – Italy had been for Wagner the obvious place to which to escape from Zurich, and when Karl Ritter, who had joined him at Lausanne, urged that they should make for Venice together, he willingly agreed. Here he took two large rooms in the secluded but dilapidated Palazzo Giustiniani, on the Canal Grande, at the end of August 1858 and settled into a daily routine. Each morning he worked at the score of *Tristan*; his own Erard grand piano was brought from Zurich in October. At two o'clock he would take a gondola to the Piazzetta San Marco and walk across to the Albergo San Marco, on St Mark's Square, to have lunch with Ritter; then a stroll to the Giardino Publico, sometimes with Ritter, sometimes alone, and at dusk back by gondola to his rooms. In the evening he would do a little more work, then Ritter would come regularly at eight o'clock, and the two friends would finish the day talking together and drinking tea. Occasionally he would vary the pattern by going to the theatre or listening to the excellent Austrian military bands that played in St Mark's Square. He met only very few other people, chiefly through Ritter, who led the life of a gentleman of leisure.

Apart from the endemic money troubles, including that of providing for Minna back in Dresden, Wagner was afflicted in Venice by gastritis and by a painful carbuncle on his leg, which took four weeks to heal. There was also another cause for worry. Venice belonged to Austria, and Austria was the second largest state in the German

Confederation, whose members were supposed, in theory, to unify their foreign policies and cooperate with each other in domestic matters. This cooperation included the extradition to a member state of anyone required to answer a criminal charge in that state, and Wagner knew that the Venetian police were watching him. For the moment, however, the Venetian Chief of Police, one Angelo Crespi, clearly impressed by the genius of the 'criminal' who was temporarily living in his city, and assured that Wagner had no intention of involving himself in political activity, resisted pressure from Vienna to move against him. Similarly, the Saxon government, nine years after the event, saw little point in making an issue of the matter, and no one interfered with him. But only for the moment.

His anxiety over whether he would be allowed to stay in 'the quietest, most tranquil city in the world', as he called it, fills his letters to Liszt at this time. But Liszt had troubles of his own. As Dresden had been too small for Wagner, so Weimar was becoming too small for Liszt. Personal rivalries in the theatre, resentment of his autocratic manner and personal dislike, both at court and in the town, of the man and his mistress grew to the point where, at the end of 1858, he handed the Grand Duke his resignation. He and his Princess stayed on in Weimar for a time, then went together to Rome. Wagner, like most people close to Liszt, regarded the Princess as the real cause of his troubles and of his sometimes unpredictable, even unsympathetic attitude towards his friends. She was jealous that Wagner's reputation as a composer was growing, while Liszt's was not; she was also jealous of the Comtesse d'Agoult, mother of his three children, and forced him against his nature to treat them with a harshness provoked by her jealousy, where Liszt himself wished to be affectionate and understanding. Indeed, she bent his will entirely to her own in his dealings with others.

Liszt stayed in Wagner's life till the end. He came to Bayreuth to see the Master's triumphs and was with him in Venice to within four weeks of Wagner's death there. But the presence of the Princess, which Wagner had found it easier to accept in the years when his spiritual dependence on Liszt had been at its height, became more oppressive as time went on. An instinct now made him hold back, stop short of absolute candour in his dealings with the man to whom, at one stage, he had owed his artistic survival.

At the moment he left Dresden, ten years earlier, Wagner had sworn that he would never again take a salaried position, and now, little nearer to an adequate income than he had been then, his determination was as firm as ever. 'You must take me at my word,' he wrote to Liszt in January 1859, 'when I tell you that the only thing which really gives my life purpose is my irresistible urge to complete the series of works I have conceived. I have come to recognize with absolute clarity that to occupy myself with and finish these works is the only thing that satisfies me and makes me want, in some inexplicable way, to go on living. The prospect of actually seeing these works performed, on the other hand, is something I can quite do without.' The possibility of an amnesty did not interest him if it were linked to any form of contractual engagement: 'Never can I accept, or shall I accept, a regular position or anything approaching it. What I require is the guarantee of a respectable allowance for the one and only purpose of enabling me to create my works of art without disturbance and entirely independent of external circumstances.' It is the cry of the creative artist from time immemorial.

As to his work on *Tristan*, he wrote in his Wesendonk diary: 'What music this is going to be! I could spend my entire life just working on this music, so profound, so beautiful will it be! Never before have I done anything like this; I am totally immersed in this music, and I do not want to hear anyone else ask me when it will be finished. I shall live in this music eternally.' He had started the orchestral sketch of the second act of *Tristan* in July 1858; it was not until March of the following year, sending the full score to Breitkopf and Härtel almost folio by folio, that he finally solved the musical problems that it set him. But once finished, it made him aware of what he had achieved: 'It is the highest point I have yet reached in my art,' he wrote to Mathilde Wesendonk.

By now political events had left him little chance of staying in Venice much longer. Sardinia, with Cavour at its head, allied itself with Napoleon III to liberate Italy 'from the Alps to the Adriatic', an aim which amounted to a declaration of war on Austria. When, after the defeat of the Austrians, peace was made in the spring of 1859, Lombardy, including Milan, passed to Sardinia, but Venice was retained by Austria. The instability of this situation, particularly in view of his own dubious political status, made Wagner decide to leave the city.

In March, having sent off his grand piano in advance, he set off for Lucerne. Here he spent a lonely six months as a resident of the Schweizerhof Hotel. But it was a fertile loneliness, for out of it the last act of *Tristan* was finally born. 'The gentler mood of that part of the work which now occupied my mind sent me, despite its atmosphere of melancholy, into a state of almost ecstatic peace and serenity, in which I completed the music at the beginning of August,' he wrote in *Mein Leben*. At half-past four on the afternoon of 6 August 1859 he finished the full orchestral score.

Of all Wagner's works, *Tristan und Isolde* is the closest to the experienced reality of his life, the most directly expressive of the emotional strains and spiritual pressures that gripped him during the years of its gestation. His passion for Mathilde Wesendonk, which could culminate only in renunciation and self-denial, is poured into the tragic love-story which embodies the archetypal myth of adultery, of forbidden love. The myth itself, in the form given to it by the early thirteenth-century poet Gottfried von Strassburg in his epic poem, was one of those that Wagner had come across during his study of European mythology in Dresden. But we are not facing some kind of modern version of the Tristan legend, as *Tannhäuser* and *Lohengrin*, in their way, are re-presentations of the events of original stories. *Tristan* is a spiritual drama, a statement of a human situation in its stark spiritual reality, of a passion which must die in earthly form but which finds its transcendent fulfilment in death. 'With utter confidence,' recalled Wagner, 'I immersed myself in this spiritual world and proceeded to boldly create its outward form from a position at its very heart. Life and death, together with the meaning and existence of the external world, are utterly dependent on inner spiritual development.'

Thus the magic potion given to Tristan and Isolde by Brangäne, which in the classical story is the agent that causes them to fall in love, becomes in Wagner the mere external symbol of the passion that they themselves have kindled. The drama rests on knowledge, therefore on responsibility and choice. The lovers know what binds them, know that they are betraying King Mark, know that there can be no happy resolution; they are human beings in a human context, gripped by passion and an awareness of guilt, by the consummation of their bliss and their agony of conscience, with no gods or supernatural spirits either to appeal to or to be judged by. The loneliness of the heroic individual, of the heroes identified in the titles of so many of Wagner's works – *Rienzi, Der fliegende Holländer, Lohengrin, Siegfried, Parsifal* – becomes here the loneliness, the isolation of the pair, for Tristan and Isolde do not, like the characters in *The Ring*, embody different forces but are incarnations of a single, passionate love. 'Love in its fullest reality,' wrote Wagner, 'is only possible in the framework of sex. The most vital human love is possible only between man and woman: all other love is merely a result, a derivate or an imitation of sexual love.'

As the writing of *Tristan* cannot be divorced from the personal drama of the relationship between Wagner and Mathilde Wesendonk or from the sombre mood of uncertainty and frustration that accompanied the condition of exile, so the intellectual sub-structure of the work is dependent on the philosophy of Schopenhauer. The meaninglessness of external events and the emptiness of a faith in progress and achievement; the conquest of the individual will and the joyful acceptance of self-abnegation; suffering as a positive force, and music as the symbolic reflection of world-purpose, the 'objectification of the Will', as Schopenhauer put it: this laid out in systematic terms a world-picture of whose truth Wagner's reading of his own experience had already convinced him. Thomas Mann, looking back over half a century of German history after Wagner's death, gave his development paradigmatic status: 'He went the way of the German middle-classes – from revolution to disillusionment, to pessimism and to a resigned, impregnable inwardness.'

Wagner described the process of writing *Tristan* as an urge 'to pour myself out in music, as though I were writing a symphony.' And inasmuch as the opera is a triumphant achievement, a completed and living masterpiece, whereas the love between Wagner and Mathilde Wesendonk was doomed from the beginning, art is the victor over life. More exactly, the victory is that of music. For *Tristan*, to a greater extent than any other of Wagner's operas except, perhaps, *Parsifal*, is totally in the grip of music, subject to musical modes of experience and expression. 'Malwida von Meysenbug once told me,' said the French novelist and critic Romain Rolland, 'that at the

Bayreuth Festival of 1876, while she was following one of the scenes in *The Ring* very attentively through her opera glasses, two hands were suddenly laid over her eyes, and she heard Wagner say impatiently: "Don't look so much at what is going on. Listen!"' It would be even truer counsel for *Tristan* – and, later, for *Parsifal*.

The libretto which Wagner gave to Mathilde in September 1857 shows this – shows how different is the conception of the lyrical, elegiac *Tristan* from the epic dramas of *The Ring* into which it intrudes. Gone are the hard, jagged, totally rhymeless lines of *Die Walküre* and *Siegfried*, and although alliteration still plays its part, rhyme, which Wagner had last used in *Lohengrin*, now reappears, bringing softer, more gentle contours to the prosody at high moments such as the love-duet in Act Two and Isolde's *Liebestod*.

But the heart of the action and the meaning lies in the music, music of a kind the world had never heard, a profoundly disturbing music which carries the psychological movement of the work and the pessimistic fatalism of its immoral passion. And the core of this music is its harmony, its development of a chromatic vocabulary utterly new in European music.

It is not difficult to point to antecedents of this chromaticism – Berlioz, Chopin, Liszt, moments in J. S. Bach and even in the sixteenth-century madrigalist Gesualdo di Venosa have all been adduced by musicologists anxious to demonstrate the continuity of musical history and the dependence of Wagner, like any other composer, on the past. What matters, however, is the fact, felt by any open-minded music lover capable of distinguishing between Bach and Irving Berlin, that the idiom of *Tristan und Isolde* is totally new, and with it – which is the heart of the matter – the psychological and spiritual realities that it expresses. What happens in the score of *Tristan* is something that had never happened in music before. The action and meaning of the drama are enmeshed in the web of the orchestral score. And as the lovers' passion is immoral, their self-absorption so complete, their anguish so intense – does *passio* not mean suffering? – and their tragic fate so inescapable, so the music rests on ambiguous harmonies, half-resolved dissonances, interrupted cadences, long, soaring melodic arcs, dense orchestral textures, a ceaselessly flowing, inward-looking music that expresses the ebb and flow of desire and its consummation in death. 'What Fate rent asunder on earth,' wrote Wagner later in a programme note, 'receives new life, transfigured, in death: the gateway to union has been opened. As she lies on Tristan's dead body, the dying Isolde feels the blissful fulfilment of her burning desire, eternal union in infinite space, free and unrestrained, conjoined for ever.'

As the drama presented on the stage is the externaliza-tion of the drama embodied in the music, so, reciprocally, the music becomes its own stage and imposes its own laws on the enacted drama. The economy of the dramatic construction – one single scene for each of the three acts, the almost exclusive domination of the stage by the two main characters, and the peripheral musical role of the few other *dramatis personae* – intensifies the assertion of musical values.

The seamless web of the musical fabric, 'endless melody' at its most perfect, is the 'art of transition' which Wagner identified as the most vital feature of the work. 'I now recognize,' he wrote to Mathilde Wesendonk, 'that that particular quality in my music which my friends regard as so new and so significant derives from the utmost refinement of emotion which shows me how to link together the most extreme and divergent elements. My art at its most subtle and most profound is what I would call "the art of transition": the entire fabric of my art consists of such transitions. I have come to dislike abruptness and suddenness, and although violent changes are often inevitable and necessary, they should only occur when the atmosphere has been so well prepared for them that it actually calls for them.' This art carries every inflection of emotional experience, making the musical expression the complete correlative of the spiritual meaning, the total union of acted drama and musical drama. Here Wagner achieves his complete, integrated music-drama, the antithesis of traditional opera with its separate numbers and its pursuit of self-contained, self-justifying musical values.

Hence the remarkable oneness of *Tristan*, based on the embracing chromaticism which induces that sense of unease and helplessness which is the psychological foundation of the work, 'shrouded, as it is,' said Wagner later, 'in violet, a hue of deep lilac'. Chromatic melody and harmony destroy the familiar landmarks of the diatonic world and provoke a subconscious yearning to see these landmarks restored. Discovery can only start from a known point, and the new can only be understood in terms of the old. Every listener experiences the contrast when he moves from the oppressive chromatic realm of *Tristan* to the open diatonic world of *Die Meistersinger*, from the sinuous, inward-looking, agonized Yearning-motif in the first bars of the *Tristan* prelude

– to the fresh, buoyant, relaxed opening of *Die Meistersinger*:

Sehr mässig bewegt, durchweg breit und gewichtig

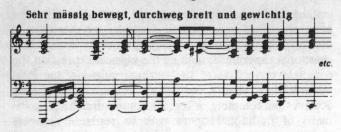

etc.

The tempo markings tell the same story – *Tristan*, 'Slow and languishing', *Die Meistersinger*, 'Molto moderato, with breadth and gravity throughout'. Not only the musical markings but also the stage directions, here as in all Wagner's works, contain a wealth of insights into his detailed intentions and conceptions, theoretical, even philosophical, as well as practical.

Yet whatever these intentions and conceptions may be, the experience that the listener receives from a performance of *Tristan* is an experience in *music*. The theory of *Opera and Drama* may require music to serve, like the other arts involved in the composite work of art, an alleged central dramatic purpose, and the presence of the theory in Wagner's mind can hardly have been without influence on the course of his musical composition. But at the end, whatever the theory says, the music dominates, as it must do. That a union of poetry and music will always result in the subordination of the former to the latter – a fact that his earlier theories could not admit – is a principle which Wagner subsequently concedes in his Beethoven essay of 1870.

At the same time the effects of *Tristan* go far beyond the musical, in that mysterious, sinister way which led Thomas Mann – he was thinking of Wagner – to call music 'daemonic territory'. It was the penetration of our consciousness by the unsettling, insidious power of chromaticism that led a famous conductor to murmur, as he walked home one night through the quiet streets of Munich with Mann, after conducting a performance of *Tristan*: 'That is just not music any more.' It is a remark that strikes to the heart of the Wagnerian experience.

Wagner had wanted peace and solitude to complete *Tristan*, and the months in Lucerne, the quiet little town by the lake, had served their purpose. He had no hope of seeing the work performed, but his need now was for the challenge of practical music-making again, the preparing and conducting of his own and others' works. This meant living and working in a large town. With Germany barred to him, and with Liszt continuing to urge what he had always urged, it was almost inevitable that the name which had repeatedly spelt disaster should again stare him in the face – Paris.

To pay for his fare this time he sold to Otto Wesendonk the publishing rights of *The Ring* for some 6,000 francs per score, which, since *Das Rheingold* and *Die Walküre* were both finished – the latter copied out with a superb gold pen which Wesendonk had given Wagner in Zurich – brought him in an immediate 12,000 francs. He spent three days with the Wesendonks on the Grüner Hügel – 'well looked after', he remarked, and clearly in a relaxed atmosphere free of animosity or dissimulation – where he saw his friends Semper, Herwegh and Gottfried Keller again, then set out in September for Paris. First he took rooms in the Avenue de Matignon, off the Champs-Elysées, then found a house for Minna and himself at 16 Rue Newton, near the Etoile. This cost him 4,000 francs a year; he had it redecorated at considerable expense and engaged the domestic servants to whom he considered himself entitled, including a personal valet.

Minna, accompanied by the family dog and parrot, arrived from Dresden in November and moved into the rooms on the top floor of the house; Wagner occupied the first floor, and the ground floor was taken up by two reception rooms. He was happy to have the practical side of his life attended to, but he was also genuinely worried, with good cause, about Minna's state of health, and knew that alone in Dresden, a prey to fantasies and jealousies, she could only sink deeper into physical and psychological ruin. Minna, for her part, played on her husband's inability to abandon her: 'Her arrival,' he wrote in *Mein Leben*, 'involuntarily put me in mind of the time she landed at the harbour in Rorschach ten years earlier. Just as she had done then, she now made it immediately clear to me that she had not come out of necessity, adding that if I did not treat her properly, she knew very well where she would be made welcome.' Indignant at the unnecessary lavishness with which he had equipped the house, she sacked the valet and the chambermaid – whose real function she suspected of being something different – and launched into the familiar tantrums which quickly disabused him of any hope that the outside world might believe that the marriage was a true one.

Those who saw a lot of the Wagners were not deceived. Malwida von Meysenbug, who recognized the absolute claims of Wagner's greatness while yet sympathizing with Minna's inadequacies, wrote in her memoirs: 'I did what I could to make her understand her role in life better, but of course it was no use. She had not understood it after twenty-five years of marriage, and it was just not in her to do so.'

Wagner took his mind off these domestic irritations by occupying himself with various musical projects and getting himself introduced into influential Parisian society. He wrote a new ending for the overture to *Der fliegende Holländer*, and an ending for concert performances of the prelude to *Tristan* (in the opera the prelude leads straight into the first act). He visited Berlioz and tried to interest Léon Carvalho, director of the Théâtre-Lyrique, in *Tan-*

nhäuser; he also sold to Schott in Mainz the score of *Das Rheingold* for 10,000 francs – with the permission of Otto Wesendonk, to whom he had already sold both this and *Die Walküre* (selling the same product more than once was a skill at which he excelled). Most important of all, he prepared with the help of Bülow a set of three orchestral concerts of his own music to be given in the Théâtre Italien – the former Théâtre de la Renaissance, which, ironically, had accepted *Das Liebesverbot* for performance in 1840 and then gone bankrupt.

Every Wednesday he held soirées in the Rue Newton which were attended by those, important and unimportant alike, who had heard his music, or at least heard of his reputation. Among the visitors to the Wagnerian *salon* after the concerts of January and February 1860 were Gounod and Saint-Saëns, Gustave Doré, the novelist Jules Champfleury and the poet and editor Catulle Mendès, together with many other writers, musicians, artists and intellectuals, including Liszt's eldest daughter Blandine Ollivier and her husband. 'Wagner dominated the company so completely,' recalled Malwida von Meysenbug,

that one had eyes and ears only for him. On one occasion, I remember, he talked of how rare was the state of what people call happiness, quoting the words of Eleonora d'Este in Goethe's *Tasso*: 'Who can say he is happy?' I knew what he meant, but I found it strange that he said so many wonderful things in the presence of so many people who I could see from their faces did not understand him, and I thought to myself: Why does he cast his pearls before swine? But then perhaps it is in the nature of genius to create without heed to who is watching or listening, just as the sun shines on good and bad alike.

Malwida von Meysenbug, friend of Michelet, Alexander Herzen, Mazzini, Nietzsche and many other European intellectuals, is only one of the multitude who, then as now, saw Wagner's creative genius as a self-justifying force, beside which any defects of character or disagreeability of behaviour, even if one were to concede such phrases, appear totally irrelevant.

The alarming intensity of Wagner's commitment to his own music was witnessed by one Agéner de Gasperini, a young French doctor and friend of Bülow's, who arranged introductions for him to the artistic *haute volée* and tried to interest them in his operas. At a meeting with Carvalho at the Rue Newton, writes Gasperini, Wagner plunged into a performance of the finale of the second act of *Tannhäuser*: 'He sang, he shouted, he threw himself about, he played the piano with his hands, his wrists and his elbows, he smashed the pedals and ground the keys. In the midst of this chaos M. Carvalho showed no emotion, waiting with the patience of a Greek hero for the orgy to end. When the last page was reached, he stammered a few polite words, turned on his heel and disappeared.'

For the first part of this extraordinary performance, Carvalho himself remembered, Wagner wore a blue jacket with red braid and a yellow Greek cap with a green fringe. 'Then, dripping with perspiration, he went out, returning this time in a red cap with yellow braid and wearing a yellow coat with blue braid. In this costume he sang for me the second part of his opera. He roared, he flung himself about, he hit all manner of wrong notes and on top of everything he sang in German! And his eyes! The eyes of a man possessed! I dared not interrupt. He frightened me.' Fortunately Carvalho's fright was not so great as to scare him from promoting the cause of *Tannhäuser* in Paris.

Wagner's three concerts, which he conducted without a score, each consisted of more or less the same programme – the Overture to *Der fliegende Holländer*, the Prelude to *Tristan und Isolde*, and excerpts from *Tannhäuser* and *Lohengrin*. 'At the first concert,' he wrote in *Mein Leben*,

'I had the remarkable experience that one of the pieces, the march from *Tannhäuser*, was interrupted in the middle by a burst of wild applause.' Among those in the well-filled hall who shared in this excitement were Berlioz, Auber, Gounod and Meyerbeer, the last-named still king of the Parisian operatic world and manipulator of the press, and suspicious of Wagner's exercises in self-advertisement.

So a similar situation arose to that of Wagner's London concerts in 1855. The audiences were enthusiastic – except about the *Tristan* Prelude, which left them bewildered (Berlioz said he did not understand a note of it) – while the critics, whom Wagner had again deliberately offended by not sending them complimentary tickets, could find scarcely a good word to say. Hostility from intellectuals, enthusiasm from the theatre-going public; resentment of an art that undermines the authority of the critical faculty, self-abandonment to the sensuous appeal of spectacle and sound: the antitheses are familiar. But nowhere in the realm of great art do they have the starkness, the intolerant intensity generated by the music of Richard Wagner.

A week after the last of his Paris concerts Wagner received a letter.

I am not of an age at which one still amuses oneself by writing to eminent men, and I should have hesitated a long time to express my admiration if I did not come across, day after day, absurd and disgraceful articles which seek in every possible way to cast a slur on your genius . . . It seemed to me that this was my music, and I recognized it the way everyone recognizes what he is destined to love . . . What struck me above all was its grandeur. It represents what is great, and its aims are great . . . There is everywhere something elevated and elevating, something reaching out to infinity, something superhuman, something superlative.

Without doubt there are others like me. At all events you must have been content to observe that the instinct of the public was superior to the false so-called learning of the critics.

The letter was signed: Charles Baudelaire.

Baudelaire was thirty-nine, certainly no longer 'of an age to amuse himself by writing to eminent men.' The revolution of 1848 had spurred him, as it had spurred Wagner, to fight against monarchist establishmentarianism in the search for a new and better life, and his spirit of nonconformity had already expressed itself in *Les fleurs du mal*. Baudelaire 'discovered' Wagner for France as he 'discovered' Edgar Allan Poe, and as he introduced E. T. A. Hoffmann and other German Romantic writers to the French public. He soon joined Wagner's weekly *soirées*, and the following year he sprang to Wagner's defence in a pamphlet called *Richard Wagner et le Tannhäuser à Paris*.

The concerts may have added to Wagner's artistic following but they did nothing to repair his battered finances. After the box-office takings were set against the cost of hiring the hall, the fees of the orchestra and the singers and the other expenses, there remained an uncomfortable deficit of 10,000 francs.

Once again a rich benefactor, an admirer of his genius, suddenly appeared to relieve him of his burden. This time salvation came in the person of Madame Marie Kalergis, niece of Graf Karl Robert von Nesselrode, the Russian chancellor, who had eagerly followed Wagner's career since his Dresden days. The moment she learned of this latest debt, Madame Kalergis presented Wagner with the 10,000 francs from her private purse. He eagerly accepted the gift, yet somehow without surprise that providence had rescued him yet again. 'I felt,' he said in *Mein Leben*, 'as though it were merely the fulfilment of what I had considered myself entitled to expect all along.' Nevertheless he showed his gratitude to Madame Kalergis in a striking way, with an improvised performance of Act Two of *Tristan und Isolde* in the house of the famous soprano Pauline Viardot-Garcia. Mme Viardot – somewhat half-heartedly, it seems – sang the female roles, Wagner the others, while Karl Klindworth, who had come especially from London at Wagner's expense, accompanied at the piano. Apart from Marie Kalergis the only member of the audience was Berlioz, who at the end merely vouchsafed a sour comment on the 'passionate intensity' of Wagner's performance.

More generous was the reception given to Wagner by the great Rossini, now close on seventy and long retired from active musical life. The two men met for the first and only time in Rossini's house in March 1860. Their artistic worlds were poles apart, and Wagner, in his article on Halévy in 1842, had been none too complimentary about the limitations of Rossini's talent. But Rossini, who, as he put it, respected any man, like Wagner, 'concerned to extend the scope of his art', allowed none of this to cloud their meeting, and received his ebullient, controversial guest with warmth and sagacity. Wagner recalled this kindness in a memoir for the *Augsburger Allgemeine Zeitung* after Rossini's death eight years later.

One of Wagner's ways of attempting to meet a debt, other than by begging a gift or a loan from a friend, was to mortgage the expected proceeds of his next activity – expected but not often forthcoming. Before Madame Kalergis came to his rescue over the Paris concerts, he had eagerly risen to the suggestion that he should repeat the programmes in Brussels: the profit, he reckoned, would cover the expenses still unpaid in Paris. He had also expected these concerts to pay the 6,000 francs he owed Otto Wesendonk for *Das Rheingold*. He now proceeded to mortgage to Wesendonk the publishing rights of *Götterdämmerung*, not a note of which had yet been written.

His Brussels contract made him responsible for the costs of the musical side of the concerts – the performers' fees, provision of orchestral parts and the like – so that in spite of a full house and a suspended subscription list at the first concert, his profit was practically nil. Since the subscription list was restored for the second concert, he again received hardly anything. He therefore cancelled the third concert and returned to Paris thoroughly disgruntled. 'Take my word for it,' he wrote some years later to Hans Richter, first conductor of *Der Ring des Nibelungen* and later conductor of the Hallé orchestra: 'You can't rely on any country where French is spoken.'

Yet despite such familiar discouragements there were also influential people, chiefly in republican circles where progressive ideas in politics and art were discussed, who took up Wagner's cause. One was Princess Pauline Metternich, wife of the Austrian ambassador in Paris and daughter-in-law of the once mighty Chancellor whose power had been broken by the revolution of 1848. The Princess made herself Wagner's special protector and succeeded, with the help of the Prussian ambassador Count Pourtalès and others, in winning the support of Louis-Napoleon and the Empress Eugénie for his work. In March 1860 the Emperor announced that he wished *Tannhäuser* to be performed at the Opéra. Even more important for Wagner, in July the Saxon ambassador brought him the news that his exile had been lifted for all the German states except Saxony, where his involvement in the uprising of 1849 still rankled. Shortly before he learned of this, Minna, whose heart condition was slowly getting worse, had left Paris for a stay at the spa of Bad Soden in Hessen. His first visit to Germany for eleven years took him first there, then, together with Minna, to Frankfurt, to visit his brother Albert. From here he went to Baden-Baden to pay his personal respects to another of his supporters, Auguste von Sachsen-Weimar, Princess Regent of Prussia, who had been a prime mover in securing his amnesty and had obtained a Prussian passport for him.

Returning to Paris by way of Mannheim and Cologne, after a journey by steamer down the Rhine, he at once began rehearsals for the command performance of *Tan-*

Wagner in his twenties. Drawing by Behr

Minna Wagner (*née* Planer), Wagner's first wife. Oil portrait by Alexander von Otterstedt, 1835

Franz Liszt in middle life. Drawing by George T Tobin from a photograph of uncertain date

Friedrich Nietzsche as a young man. Photograph from the 1860s, when he first came to know Wagner

Stage set of Act Two (The Hall of the Wartburg) of *Tannhäuser,* as produced in Paris in 1861. Photograph of a diorama

Cosima, daughter of Liszt, married Wagner in 1870 after her divorce from Hans von Bülow. Oil portrait after Franz von Lenbach, 1870

Mathilde Wesendonk, whose relationship with Wagner coincides with the years (1857-59) when he was writing *Tristan und Isolde.* Portrait in oils by C Dorner

Wagner in 1865. Photograph by Franz Hanfstaengl, Munich

Caricature from the humorous magazine *Punsch*, Munich, 1867. Wagner knocks at the door of the Bavarian Treasury. The caption reads: 'Just a passing visit'

Ludwig II as King Lohengrin, watched by Wagner in the moon. Caricature from the magazine *Der Floh*, Vienna, 1885

Tribschen, the villa outside Lucerne where Wagner and Cosima lived from 1866 to 1872. Today it is a Wagner Museum and also houses a collection of old musical instruments

The Bayreuth Festspielhaus in 1881. The so-called 'Königsbau' had not yet been added to the bowed front of the building

Interior of the Bayreuth Festspielhaus before the seating had been installed. Drawing of 1875/76

The orchestra pit in the Bayreuth Festspielhaus during rehearsal, with Hermann Levi conducting and Wagner gesturing through the hatch in the canopy that conceals the orchestra from the auditorium. Pen-and-ink drawing (1882) by Josef Greif, a member of the orchestra

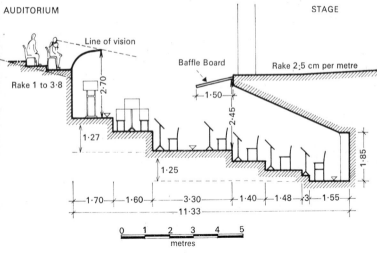

Cross-section of the orchestra pit in the Festspielhaus

Stage set by Josef Hoffmann for Act Two of *Götterdämmerung* at the première in Bayreuth, 1876

Wagner with friends at Wahnfried. Left to right: Franz von Lenbach, Emil Scaria, Cosima with Siegfried, Amalie Materna, Franz Fischer, Wagner, Fritz Brandt, Hermann Levi, Liszt, Hans Richter, Franz Betz, Countess Marie von Schleinitz, Albert Niemann, Countess Hildegard von Usedom, Paul von Joukovsky. On the wall is a portrait of King Ludwig. Engraving after a picture by G Papperitz

Facsimile of the last page of the autograph score of *Götterdämmerung*. The final inscription reads: 'Completed at Wahnfried on 21 November 1874. I shall say nothing more. RW'

nhäuser and worked at the same time on an extensive revision of the first scene, which he had long intended to expand. Fulminate as he might against the undramatic ostentations of grand opera and its mandatory ballet, his visits to the Paris Opéra had shown him for the first time the potentialities of ballet as a medium for making explicit, through graphic physical movement, the meaning of the musico-dramatic stage work of which it was part. No self-respecting Parisian would accept as true opera a work that did not have a full-scale ballet in the second act; many dandies even regarded it as a point of honour not to appear in the theatre before the second act, seeing the action of the opera before and after the ballet as a tiresome irrelevance.

Wagner had no intention of ruining the dramatic structure of *Tannhäuser* by inserting a ballet merely to satisfy an idiotic social convention. At the same time he realized that a choreographic representation could heighten the audience's experience of the struggle between the sensual and the spiritual in the soul of Tannhäuser. For the Paris production he therefore expanded the Venusberg scene, adding a Bacchanal full of creatures drawn from Classical, Nordic and other mythologies, and extending the long scene (Act One, Scene Two) between Tannhäuser and Venus. He also made changes in the Song Contest of Act Two.

'The scene at the court of Frau Venus,' he wrote to Mathilde Wesendonk,

Was the obvious weak point in my work. I had left the Venusberg nebulous and vague, with the result that the vital background to the ensuing tragedy was lacking . . . I now realize that at the time I wrote *Tannhäuser*, I was not yet able to provide what was necessary in this area. I needed a greater ability, an ability I have only now acquired; only since composing Isolde's transfiguration have I found the proper ending for *Der fliegende Holländer* Overture and portrayed the horrors of the Venusberg.

And it is, indeed, from the music of Venus, from the portrayal of the voluptuous and the erotic which make up the world of ballet – in short, from its commitment to what Goethe called 'das Ewig-Weibliche', the seductive principle of the 'eternal feminine' – that the new *Tannhäuser* draws its meaning, a meaning linked in the symbolism of the new text and the chromaticism of the new music to *Tristan und Isolde*. Now, even more than at the time of the original Dresden version, it deserved its first title, *Der Venusberg*.

In effect, the Paris Venusberg scene is almost an independent work-within-a-work which cannot but betray the sixteen years that separate it from the rest of the opera. Conceptually it can be read as an intensification of the spiritual conflict, a linear emotional extension of the original argument, but the music, fascinating in its novelty and technical subtlety, is the music of a new Wagner, a Wagner whose musical language now says very different things from those native to the idiom of the Dresden Kapellmeister. He himself declared the Paris *Tannhäuser* to be the sole authentic version, and when Cosima introduced the work into the Bayreuth Festival of 1891, it was the Paris version, naturally, that she adopted. Ironically, by the time Louis-Napoleon made known his imperial wish concerning *Tannhäuser*, it was rather *Lohengrin* – which he had still not heard – and even more *Tristan*, that Wagner was longing to see performed.

For the role of Tannhäuser himself Wagner engaged Albert Niemann, from Hanover, who some time ago, like Tichatschek, Anton Mitterwurzer (who had both been in the cast of the first *Tannhäuser* in Dresden in 1845) and a number of others, had declared their willingness to come and sing for him in Paris if his operas were accepted there. The parts of Venus and Wolfram were taken by Italians, Elisabeth by a Frenchwoman, Mme Fortunata Tedesco. Everything, of course, was sung in French. The musical direction – unhappiest of omens – was put in the hands of the official conductor of the Opéra, one Pierre Dietsch, who in 1842 had conducted, to a totally apathetic audience, his opera *La vaisseau fantôme*, composed to the French translation of Wagner's *Der fliegende Holländer*.

Rehearsals started in September 1860, Wagner himself dominating the proceedings from the stage. By the time of the première six months later there had been no fewer than one hundred and sixty-four rehearsals for various groups, interspersed with arguments over the conventional ballet, squabbles between composer, producer and conductor, complaints from the histrionic Niemann that parts of his role were unsingable, Wagner's growing impatience with Niemann's proneness to look for easy vocal effectiveness at the expense of inner dramatic meaning, and a host of other incidents, that threatened to bring the whole enterprise to a halt. Finally, on 13 March 1861, Paris saw *Tannhäuser* for the first time. It has become one of the most famous scandals in theatrical history.

Everyone was there – the Emperor with the Empress Eugénie, Princess Metternich, Wagner's champion, courtiers, aristocrats, ambassadors. Wagner's old friend Ernst Benedikt Kietz also came, so did Hans von Bülow and Malwida von Meysenbug, both of whom, like Minna, left eye-witness accounts of what happened. But also present was a detachment from the Jockey Club, an association of aristocratic young dandies and ballerina-fanciers, who, having learned that this monstrous German upstart had dared to dispense with the sacred ballet in the second act, intended to make their indignation as public and as vociferous as possible. Among the allies of these trouble-makers were, predictably, the press, whom Wagner had treated with his usual disdain, certain courtiers who resented Princess Metternich's sponsorship of an artist who was the epitome of everything non-French, and even some of the musicians, including the conductor himself, who had smarted for months under the lash of Wagner's intolerant tongue.

The overture and the Venusberg scene passed off without incident. But when the Bacchanal was over and the shepherd boy appeared at the beginning of the third scene, the trouble started. The young men of the Jockey Club had provided themselves with whistles, and the moment the notes of the shepherd boy's song were heard on the cor anglais, they set up a furious whistling and howling. The majority of the audience, who wanted to give the opera a fair trial, shouted them down, and the performance continued. But after a while the whistling broke out afresh, to be met again by cries of protest from the rest of the audience. So it went on throughout the evening. Somehow or other the singers managed to struggle through to the end, but so mangled was the performance that no one could have formed an opinion of the work. To the extent that the performers had carried on to the end, the pro-Wagner camp could claim to have won the battle; on the other hand, by reducing the evening to chaos and ridicule, the Jockey Club too had achieved its purpose. Even Berlioz, from whom one might have expected greater magnanimity, made no attempt to conceal from his friends his malicious satisfaction at Wagner's downfall, as his letters show.

'The following morning I went to Wagner's house', wrote Malwida von Meysenbug,

and found him calm and composed. Indeed, even the most hostile reports in the newspapers admitted that he had faced the storm that evening with the utmost dignity. He wanted to withdraw the score and prevent a second performance, for he saw clearly that he had no chance of success with the public of the Opéra. But those of us who were his close friends opposed this idea, cherishing the hope that success would ultimately come our way. So passionately involved were we that we did not pause to consider that in fact such a thing was totally out of the question.

Five days later, again in the presence of the Emperor, the second performance took place. If the first performance had been chaos, the second was a riot. The overture was applauded, so was the septet of Tannhäuser, the Landgraf and the Knights in Act One, Scene Four. But in the second act, their fury rising as they remembered that there was no ballet to come, the rowdies of the Jockey Club went into action again. Whistles and catcalls filled the auditorium, followed by the angry protests of the offended majority. 'The row was beyond belief,' wrote Albert Niemann to a friend, 'and even the presence of the Emperor could not restrain it. Princess Metternich, to whose patronage the production of the opera is largely due, was compelled to leave the theatre at the end of the second act because people kept turning round towards her box and jeering at her.' At one stage Niemann himself became so enraged that he hurled his pilgrim's hat into the audience. Yet again the singers and players miraculously survived to the end of the performance.

Wagner had no stomach for the third performance the following week, nor had Princess Metternich and her party, for whom two evenings of public insults from the Jockey Club had been more than they could stand. To judge from accounts by Malwida von Meysenbug and others, the entire evening was sheer pandemonium. The noise of whistles, catcalls, hissing and shouting drowned the music and forced the singers to break off sometimes for as long as a quarter of an hour before they could fight their way to the end of the scene. The next day Wagner wrote to Alphonse Rayer, director of the Opéra, withdrawing the work.

One hundred and sixty-four rehearsals – all but nine of which Wagner himself had attended – and three near-fiasco performances: such was the history of the Paris *Tannhäuser*. 'What will Europe think of us,' wrote Baudelaire in his essay *Richard Wagner et le Tannhäuser à Paris*, 'and what will people in Germany say about Paris? This handful of scoundrels has brought down infamy on the heads of all of us.'

The costs of the production were enormous, yet the takings from the three performances met almost a quarter of these costs, and had the run continued for the ten weeks of Niemann's engagement, the Opéra would certainly have made a handsome profit. As it was, the singers received their fees – Niemann's and Madame Tedesco's were 6,000 francs a month – while Wagner, after deducting his innumerable expenses, was left with a paltry 750 francs.

In April 1861, knowing, as he always had, that the future of his operas could only lie in Germany, and now having freedom of movement there, except in Saxony, he went to Karlsruhe, where the possibility of *Tristan* being staged had once before been raised. The influential names of French music, men like Meyerbeer, Berlioz and Auber, let alone the administrative establishment, would do nothing for him in Paris. He did, however, take with him a charming compliment from one great composer. 'I was told,' he wrote in *Mein Leben*, 'that Gounod had enthusiastically taken my part at all social gatherings, and that on one occasion he had cried: "If only God would grant *me* a disaster like *Tannhäuser*!" I valued his attitude all the more,' Wagner added, 'since no obligation of friendship had been able to persuade me to go and see his *Faust*.'

In Karlsruhe the young Grand Duke Friedrich von Baden showed himself interested in *Tristan*, and in May Wagner travelled to Vienna with the Grand Duke's support to try to recruit his singers. The Viennese opera was among the best in Europe. In Wagner's honour they mounted a performance of *Lohengrin* which was rapturously received – 'one of those continuous, warm-blooded ovations such as I have ever only experienced with Viennese audiences', he described it – and he acknowledged the applause from his box. It was the first time he had heard the work in its entirety. Its success led to talk of staging *Tristan* in Vienna as well, but the administrators of the Opera refused to allow Wagner to borrow their star singers for a première elsewhere. So, after a short visit to Zurich, where he celebrated his forty-eighth birthday in the company of old friends – Otto and Mathilde Wesendonk, Semper, Georg Herwegh and Gottfried Keller – he went back to Karlsruhe empty-handed.

Not, however, before renewing his acquaintanceship with a man who was something of a *bête noire* to him – the music critic Eduard Hanslick. Today Hanslick is remembered as the man largely responsible for instigating a ridiculous feud later in the century between so-called Brahmsians and Wagnerians. In 1846 the twenty-one-year-old Hanslick had been overwhelmed by *Tannhäuser* in Dresden and wrote a series of wildly enthusiastic articles on Wagner in the *Allgemeine Wiener Musikzeitung*. Since then, partly because of what he saw as the megalomania and intolerable self-righteousness of *Opera and Drama, The Work and Art of the Future* and other writings of Wagner's, and partly because of a sense that Wagner's appeal was unhealthy, dangerous, somehow 'extra-musical', he had turned against him. Wagner, of course, knew this and deliberately snubbed Hanslick when he came up and presented himself at a rehearsal of *Lohengrin*. Not for nothing, in the original text of *Die Meistersinger*, is the character who later became Beckmesser, archetype of the soulless, carping critic, called Hanslich; indeed, it was only on legal advice that Wagner changed the name.

The same day as he arrived back in Karlsruhe, Wagner travelled on to Paris. Minna was still living in the Rue Newton – but not for much longer. However cruel a blow the *Tannhäuser* débâcle had dealt to his pride, its impact on his purse was little short of catastrophic. He had scarcely any revenue from performing rights at German theatres; the publishing rights of *Das Rheingold, Die Walküre* and *Tristan* had been sold and the money spent, while *Götterdämmerung*, which he had not even begun, was already mortgaged. To stay in Paris was out of the question. But was there a town in Germany that offered him anything better?

There was not. And for the next three years Wagner wandered from one European city to another, as his Dutchman had roamed the ocean in search of deliverance. Yet although roaming may not merit the epithet dynamic, neither is it static, and Wagner's restless to-ing and fro-ing between Germany and Italy, Russia and Hungary, Austria and Switzerland at least enabled him to believe that his musical life was in motion, and to present to the world, with the confidence in his destiny that never deserted him, the irrepressibility and gaiety which fill his account of these directionless years in *Mein Leben*.

With the help of Liszt, the publisher Flaxland, to whom he sold the French and Belgian property rights in *Tannhäuser, Lohengrin* and *Der fliegende Holländer* in 1860, and a number of well-wishers from the Paris embassies of various German states, Wagner was able to meet some of his most urgent debts and pay for Minna to go back to Bad Soden for further treatment. He disposed of their apartment in the Rue Newton, lived for a few weeks as the guest of Graf Albert de Pourtalès, the Prussian ambassador, spending much of his time in the company of aristocratic supporters like the Metternichs and admirers like Champfleury, Saint-Saëns and Gustave Doré. Then, in August 1861, he travelled via Bad Soden to Weimar on the first of the innumerable journeys that were to fill the unsettled three years to come.

In Weimar Liszt gave Wagner a room in his house and

played host at a musical evening attended by Hans and Cosima von Bülow, Peter Cornelius, Tausig, Leopold Damrosch, Emile and Blandine Ollivier and other friends. Liszt himself, however, was on the point of leaving for Rome, where Princess Carolyne had taken up residence over a year ago.

During this year, away from the constricting influence of the Princess and her mystical religious obsessions, Liszt had returned to the free, hedonistic life with which the world associated him. His extravagant manner and irregular relationship with the Princess had always been something of an irritant to the inhabitants, although his contribution to the cultural life of the Grand Duchy could not be gainsaid. One side of his being craved for the peace of religious experience; the other sought the stimulus of social flattery and snobbery, of alcohol and of the company of women. What one saw when one looked at him depended on which side he presented, and even those well acquainted with his circumstances confessed their bewilderment. Peter Cornelius, who knew the Liszt *ménage* as intimately as that of the Wagners, said: 'The Altenburg [Liszt's house in Weimar] is an enigma to me.' And when, after this year of his old, pleasure-seeking ways alone in Weimar, Liszt left in August 1861 to join the Princess, he took his leave of Cornelius with the words: 'Now I am going to Rome for my wedding!' He may have meant it, or he may, as so often, have been posing. At all events, even after Prince Wittgenstein's death in 1864 removed the last of the hindrances, no marriage ever took place.

Wagner too, whose personal relationship with Liszt underwent many fluctuations, knew how hard it was to get to the 'real' Liszt. Shortly before coming to Weimar this time, he wrote to Hans von Bülow, with a touch of irony but no less sincerely for that: 'I wish I knew how to be something to Liszt. But he has other, profounder criteria for what he does than a poor plebeian like myself can fathom.' From Liszt's letter of July 1861, asking him to come to Weimar, until Wagner's invitation to Liszt in May 1872 to attend the foundation-stone ceremony at the Festspielhaus in Bayreuth, not a single letter passed between the two men. It is an eloquent silence.

After a few days Wagner moved on with the Olliviers to Nuremberg and to Munich, then to the spa of Bad Reichenhall, where Cosima was taking a milk cure. From there he went by pony and trap to Salzburg, and finally, in mid-August, arrived back in Vienna, still hoping to rouse interest there in *Tristan*.

Sitting in a café on the Stephansplatz the next afternoon, he suddenly saw a man enter whom he had met earlier in the year, when he had been in Vienna to look for singers for *Tristan*. The man was Dr Josef Standhartner, personal physician to the Empress Elisabeth and an enthusiastic follower of Wagner's music. He insisted that Wagner should come and stay with him while his family was away, and Wagner made Standhartner's house his own for over a month, visiting the aristocracy, making new acquaintances, like that of the dramatist Friedrich Hebbel, discussing the world with his old friend Heinrich Laube again, now director of the Vienna Burgtheater, and trying to get *Tristan* finally performed.

But nothing went right. Suitable singers, above all a tenor for the title role, were either unavailable, like Tichatschek and Schnorr von Carolsfeld, or diplomatically 'indisposed'; the music was again adjudged unplayable, and the whole opera unperformable. 'It became clear to me,' he said in *Mein Leben*, 'that my position was utterly desolate. The whole world seemed to have given up interest in me.' The same self-pitying tone fills a long letter to Minna at the time: 'My new works are far, far in advance of the time and far beyond the capabilities of our theatres . . . Nobody asks for me. I shall have to start again from the very beginning.'

When the Standhartner family returned from vacation, Wagner moved into the Kaiserin Elisabeth Hotel in the Weihburggasse, which quickly proved far too expensive. At the invitation of the Wesendonks he spent a week with them in Venice, then returned to Vienna. But this time with a new purpose in mind – to carry *Die Meistersinger* through to the end. In November he wrote a fresh scenario; in December, back in Paris at the invitation of the Metternichs, he started the poem, and the complete libretto was ready by the end of the following January. He kept Schott, the publishers, well informed of his progress, less from a desire to communicate his plans than with the intention – successful – of extracting some money from them. This time his particular ploy was to emphasize that, unlike the 'unperformable' *Tristan*, the new *Meistersinger* would be eminently accessible, presented no conceptual problems and, while being technically well within the reach of a humble provincial theatre, also left ample scope for the larger companies to lavish their skills on it. The complete work, text and music, he assured Schott, would be in their hands by the end of September.

As Wagner expounded his plans, so, true to character, his enthusiasm and confidence – or rather, self-deception – grew. For although the final poetic text of *Die Meistersinger* was complete in January 1862, only the Overture and fragments of the opera proper had been composed by the end of the year; it was to be 1866 before Acts One and Two were finished, and October 1867 before the last note of the full score was written. Franz Schott's financial patience, not unreasonably, gave out well before this. Indeed, in a letter of October 1862 he delivered a classic judgment on the image Wagner presented to the outside world. 'Let me assure you,' he said, 'that there is not a music publisher on earth who can satisfy your requirements. Only an immensely rich banker, or a prince with millions of marks at his disposal, can do so.'

Both the conception and the execution of *Die Meister-singer* are intimately linked with *Tannhäuser*. Both are set in the German Middle Ages, both have their action in fixed geographical localities, both present poets known from history, both draw on the same stories of E. T. A. Hoffmann, on the scholarship of Jakob Grimm and on direct medieval literary evidence. Wagner's first draft of *Die Meistersinger* had been made while he was on vacation in Marienbad in 1845, three months after the completion of *Tannhäuser*, and had already concluded with the famous lines (slightly modified in the final version):

> Zerging' das Heil'ge Römische Reich in Dunst,
> Uns bliebe doch die heil'ge deutsche Kunst.

> ('Let the Holy Roman Empire fall apart,
> We still have our Holy German Art.')

And it was among the ruins of the Paris *Tannhäuser* of 1861 that he finally forged the poem of the most direct and unproblematical of his mature works, with its solid, realistic characters, its concrete imagery and its symmetrical, rhymed diction.

In mood and design, conceptually and musically, emotionally and spiritually, *Die Meistersinger* is an open pageant, a comedy of frankly and fully expressed conflicts, a warm statement of a confident, yea-saying faith – everything, in short, that the tragic *Tristan, Der Ring des Nibelungen, Der fliegende Holländer* – and *Tannhäuser* – are not. And by a supreme paradox, this sureness, this optimism, this profound serenity is the creation of a man without security, without a true context for his music, a man sitting at his desk in a hotel room and looking out over the city that has just hissed his work off the stage.

Indeed, these experiences at the hands of a foreign public played their own constructive role in the creative process. *Die Meistersinger* is rugged, Northern European

art, the antithesis of Mediterraneity; it is bluntly Protestant, like its sixteenth-century hero Hans Sachs, champion of Luther and the Reformation, and breathes a
different air from French Catholicism. Above all it embodies the nineteenth-century German dream of nation-
hood, of political unity, here expressed in the terms of art,
'Holy German Art', which transcends petty political bar-
riers and makes every German aware of the spiritual
world to which he belongs. Wagner returns to his romantic concept of *Volk* from the revolutionary days of 1848, a
paternalistic ideal to be achieved not by movement from
below, from the roots of the *Volk* itself, but from above,
through the enlightened and imperious vision of leaders,
of men of genius, whose vocation was to inspire and to
command. Rienzi had been such a leader. And in his
address to the Dresden Vaterlandsverein on *Republican
Tendencies and the Monarchy* at the same period, Wagner
had similarly spoken of 'revolution from above'. When,
under Prussian leadership, German political unification
finally became a reality in 1871, it was also brought about
'from above'.

At the centre of the action of *Die Meistersinger* – the
only opera of Wagner's, incidentally, not based on epic
source material – stands the figure of Hans Sachs, cobbler,
dramatist and Mastersinger of Nuremberg. In his *Communication to my Friends* of 1851, Wagner wrote: 'I
conceived Hans Sachs as the supreme embodiment of the
artistic spirit of the people, setting him against the arid,
narrow-minded pedantry of the Meistersinger as personified by the figure of the *Merker* (adjudicator).' The
Merker, Sixtus Beckmesser, had in the meantime turned
into a caricature of the critic Hanslick and become the
spokesman for non-art, or anti-art – which, to be fair, is
not what the Meistersinger represented, or what Wagner
makes them out to represent. Beckmesser is thus caught
up in a double conflict: on the one hand he stands for a

technical, soulless, small-minded view of art against the magnanimity of Sachs and the Meistersinger tradition at its best; on the other he is the crabbed, resentful, pitiful would-be lover condemned to ridicule in the presence of his dashing young rival Walther von Stolzing with his Prize Song.

Sachs, wise, tolerant, firm, representative of all that is best in his productive environment and his people, is an idealized self-portrait of the mature Wagner, the master of his art, the benevolent overseer of the emotional, spiritual and artistic well-being of the community. His counterpart, the young Wagner, the passionate lover, the artist in the making, is the knight Walther von Stolzing, wooer of the goldsmith Pogner's daughter Eva, for whom Sachs, too, cherishes a secret love. But Sachs, experienced in life as in art, knows that Eva's love belongs, as it should, to Walther, not to him. So he renounces – not as one withdrawing into a fatalistic loneliness, like Lohengrin, or pursuing the nirvana of a *Liebestod*, or possessed by the demon of despair, like Kapellmeister Kreisler and other heroes of Wagner's beloved E. T. A. Hoffmann, but positively, a man in whom passion, a sense of the tragic and of other forces whose dominance means destruction, have been brought together in serene synthesis. As the fatalistic, Schopenhauerian *Tristan* had been an image of self-abandonment to passion, of negative renunciation, of Wagner's yearning for Mathilde Wesendonk, so *Die Meistersinger*, in its own way, mirrors his positive renunciation and self-conquest in his love for Mathilde, the almost enchanted spiritual contentment which, transcending his material disasters, suffuses so many of the letters that he wrote to her throughout 1860 and 1861.

'Watch your heart with Sachs,' he once said to her; 'you are bound to fall in love with him.' And many who find it difficult to stomach the march-like, four-square choruses of praise for German art and the German spirit in *Die*

Meistersinger, or who grow impatient at the romanticized tableaux of Meistersinger life – the musical cousins of the massive frescoes by Moritz von Schwind, painted in the Wartburg Castle only a few years earlier – can still find an affectionate smile for this most honestly attractive of Wagner's heroes.

'My furniture is all packed up and stored in the depository here. God knows where it will be unpacked again – probably I shall never see it any more. I want my wife to move to Dresden and have it with her there. For my own part I cannot see myself settling anywhere.'

Melancholy lines like these, from a letter written in Paris to Mathilde Wesendonk in July 1861, could have been written at almost any time during the three years following the *Tannhäuser* disaster of March 1861. In the past Wagner had been able to turn to Liszt in such moods, but Liszt was no longer there. Friends and patrons, when directly approached – and Wagner never suffered from false modesty – found one reason or another for not being able to offer him accommodation. Only his sister Cäcilie Avenarius and her husband, now in Berlin, showed any willingness to have him, albeit on condition that he did not bring Minna; when Minna learned of this, she wrote a furious letter to Wagner, who realized that to accept Cäcilie's offer would lead to endless nagging and bickering, and therefore declined it.

Since *Die Meistersinger* was to be published by Schott of Mainz, who, Wagner hoped, would make him further advances as the work progressed, he decided to rent rooms on the first floor of a villa in Biebrich, a little town on the Rhine near Wiesbaden. In February 1862 he had part of his furniture installed, including his Erard grand, sent the rest to Minna in Dresden and settled down to work.

But things did not turn out as he had planned. Hardly

had a week gone by when, without warning, Minna appeared. He had written to her in Dresden to say that he had established himself in Biebrich, but his tone made it clear that he did not welcome the prospect of her joining him. Instead of replying by letter, she came in person. There followed what he described as 'ten days of hell', with Minna continuing to rave about 'the Wesendonk woman', from whom, as fate would have it, two letters were delivered within a few days of her arrival. From *Mein Leben*, and from Wagner's account of the affair in a letter to Peter Cornelius, we get a picture of a distraught and neurotic woman, creating scenes at the slightest provocation, with the abused husband heroically trying to reassure her. A letter from Minna to her daughter Natalie, however, written the day after her return to Dresden, describes Wagner as angry and abusive, while she, the sad, maligned wife, maintained a stoical silence.

No doubt it is all true, in part. Separation was, and had been for a long while, the only tolerable relationship between them. At the time of their silver wedding the previous November Wagner had written to her from Vienna: 'My dear, I almost think it would be best for us to take no notice of our anniversary this year.' But Minna had never been able to face the prospect of formal divorce, and Wagner, who half started proceedings more than once, shrank from inflicting this final blow on the poor, sick woman whose only companion was her 'sister', Natalie. Shortly after the 'ten days of hell' in Biebrich he wrote to Dr Pusinelli, their family doctor of long standing, asking him to consult with his sister Luise Brockhaus over persuading Minna to accept a legal separation. A passing fancy for an actress called Friederike Meyer, whom he met in Frankfurt in March, may have stimulated this urge for freedom, but at Minna's indignant rejection of the idea, he let the matter drop.

Visitors to Biebrich included Hans and Cosima von

Bülow and the tenor Ludwig Schnorr von Carolsfeld and his wife Malwine. Wagner took the Schnorrs through the score of *Tristan und Isolde* in great detail; they were to sing the title roles at the first performance three years later, and Ludwig, now with the Dresden opera, became Wagner's ideal of the *Heldentenor* – Lohengrin and Tristan above all – that he needed for his operas. In Biebrich he also received the news that his request for an absolute pardon for his offences in the Dresden revolt of 1849 had finally been granted, leaving him free to return permanently to Saxony – a freedom, however, he had no intention of exercising. The memory of these days was vividly brought to his mind by a visit from his revolutionary comrade August Röckel, who had just been released from the penitentiary at Waldheim – a fate which, had he not managed to escape to Switzerland in time, Wagner would have shared. As it was, Wagner had just received his freedom by royal amnesty, while Röckel had earned his through thirteen years as a convict. The most suitable job for him now, Röckel commented sardonically, would be prison governor.

An interesting portrait of Wagner at work comes from one Wendelin Weissheimer, a rich young musician whom he had first met in Zurich, then again in Weimar the previous year. Weissheimer, who had a position with the opera at the nearby town of Mainz, now joined the impressive ranks of those who provided Wagner, or persuaded others (in this case Weissheimer *père*) to provide him, with funds for his day-to-day life. Weissheimer writes:

Sitting at the piano, Wagner worked at the Prelude to his *Mastersingers*, producing first a very precise sketch, which looked like a piano score but contained all the doublings and inner parts ready to be written out in full orchestral score. 'The more precise the sketch,' he said, 'the easier and more confident the instrumentation. Young people often make the mistake of working too hastily.' He always used the piano when preparing the sketch; it was the *actual* sound that counted, not the sound in his head, so he never wrote down any particular doubled chord or modulation before trying it out and being satisfied with the sound. To make things easier, he let the front lid of the piano project above the keys, so that it was more convenient to write on. He struck individual chords with his left hand, or tried things out with both hands until he had got the passage right, then wrote it down immediately without needing to get up and walk across to a desk. This very deliberate manner of working naturally meant that he did not make very quick progress. But once he had written something down, it was there once and for all, and only rarely did he need to alter anything. The scoring then followed comparatively rapidly: he told me he could do about six pages a day without exerting himself.

It was at this time that Wagner met another of the women who in their different ways – Minna, Jessie Laussot, Mathilde Wesendonk, later Cosima von Bülow and Judith Gautier – fulfilled his need for feminine company at crucial moments in his life. Her name was Mathilde Maier, and when Wagner met her, she was twenty-nine. Her father had died at an early age, and she lived in Mainz with her mother, a younger brother and sister, and two aunts. She had known Schopenhauer, and was anxious, as Weissheimer put it, to meet Schopenhauer's 'spiritual brother'; later she came to know Nietzsche, who also responded to her perceptive intelligence and her attractiveness.

A sense of sympathy and understanding grew out of their first meeting at a reception in Schott's house in Mainz, and for over a year, on and off, Wagner toyed with the idea of setting up house with her in Biebrich. Throughout this time, 1862-3, he still confided many of his deepest worries over his life and art to Mathilde Wesendonk, while Friederike Meyer brought him a moment of more light-hearted, theatrical pleasure. But where with Mathilde he had pledged himself to renunciation, like Hans Sachs in his love for Eva, and where Friederike offered little more than a brief adventure, Mathilde Maier, like Jessie Laussot, had both the nature and the will to meet him on more than one level. For one brief moment she responded in her heart to the cry that he uttered in a letter to her:

There is nowhere I belong – I do not mean in the geographical but in the personal sense. Next May I shall be fifty. I cannot marry again as long as my wife is still alive, and to divorce her in her present state of health (advanced dilation of the heart), when the slightest upset could cause her death, is something I cannot bring myself to do. At the same time she will accept any other solution, as long as legal appearances are maintained. It is a situation that is driving me to ruin. I need a feminine presence, a woman who in spite of all would resolve to be what a woman *can* be to me in these lamentable circumstances – indeed, *must* be, if I am to survive.

Towards the end of 1862 Wagner finally set foot in his native Saxony again. He first visited his sister Ottilie and her husband Hermann Brockhaus in Leipzig, then, at a Gewandhaus concert arranged and subsidized by Weissheimer, conducted to an almost empty hall the first performance of his newly-completed overture to *Die Meistersinger*. In Dresden he stayed with his sister Klara, where Minna was also living. It was the last time he saw her. After visits to friends like the Schnorrs, old Ferdinand Heine and Dr Pusinelli, he went back to Biebrich. Here his landlord claimed that he wanted Wagner's rooms for himself and refused to renew the lease. The attractions of a ménage with Mathilde Maier still tempted him, and Friederike Meyer continued to flit in and out of his life. Meanwhile Schott refused to subsidize him any further until he produced some more of *Die Meistersinger*. He offered them the five Wesendonk Lieder as a substitute, which they accepted as a partial discharge of unfulfilled obligations but not as a justification for a further advance.

Against this background of depression and confusion he decided, on the strength of an unexpected gift of 1,500 marks from the Grand Duke of Weimar, to make another assault on Vienna, and on Boxing Day 1862 he conducted the first of three concerts of excerpts from *Das Rheingold, Die Walküre* and *Die Meistersinger* in the Theater an der Wien. At his bidding these excerpts had been arranged for concert performance by Peter Cornelius, Tausig, Weissheimer and the twenty-nine-year-old Brahms, who had been recommended to him by Tausig as 'a very good lad'. Indefatigable commentator on his own work, he also produced extensive programme notes for the audience's benefit.

One might have guessed what would happen. Royalty and aristocracy in the boxes, ovation after ovation from the audience, almost unrelieved hostility from the critics, led by Hanslick, and financial disaster. The pattern was repeated at two further concerts. Of the 'Ride of the Valkyries', which brought the house down, the dramatist Friedrich Hebbel, who had little time for Wagner's theories and whose own trilogy *Die Nibelungen* had just been seen on the Viennese stage, wrote:

Wagner's followers, most of them his own pupils, claim that 'The Ride of the Valkyries' is a music of blood and iron that leaves Handel and Gluck, Mozart and Beethoven far behind. His opponents say he has rediscovered the trumpets of Jericho . . . At all events, 'The Ride of the Valkyries' forms a splendid overture to the Viennese Carnival. There is a whistling, a buzzing, a hissing, a ringing and a roaring as if the very stones are about to burst into song. The only surprise is that the final chord does not blow composer, theatre, audience and everything else sky-high . . . For my part I would not venture to decide whether the music grips the soul more than it strikes at the spine.

In February Wagner received 1,000 guilders from a concert in Prague arranged by Heinrich Porges, a musician who became a faithful friend of Wagner's and was one of the pall-bearers at his funeral. Among the viola players in the Prague orchestra was Antonin Dvořák.

It was now over five years since Wagner had written a note of *The Ring*. First there had been *Tristan*; now, in his thoughts but not yet on paper, there was *Die Meistersinger*. Yet at this moment, ten years after the first, private edition of the poem of the complete *Ring*, he sat down to write a lengthy preface to a new edition. The moment had not yet come when he could pick up the music of the interrupted *Siegfried* again, but there were so many facets to the huge *Ring* project besides the obvious ones of the words and the music that his thoughts were continually returning to one aspect or another of the realization of his great dream.

This new preface to the poem of *The Ring* contains his most explicit statement so far of how he envisaged the ideal conditions for producing his 'Stage Festival' (*Bühnenfestspiel*) called *Der Ring des Nibelungen*. The standard repertory theatre, he maintains, is tied to a routine which makes it totally unsuited for mounting such a work; what is needed is a specially-erected theatre, humble in size and basic in construction, in one of the smaller cities of Germany, where the best singers, players, producers and technicians can be brought together for the sole purpose of preparing *The Ring*. The design would be that of an amphitheatre, with a hidden orchestra, giving the audience a clear view of the stage without the distractions of orchestra pit and conductor. 'I have in mind perhaps three performances in all [i.e. of the complete cycle of four works] – *Das Rheingold* on one evening and the three main parts, *Die Walküre*, *Siegfried* and *Götterdämmerung*, on the three succeeding evenings . . . The invitations to attend would be offered to the German public as a whole.'

That so special and extravagant an enterprise could by its nature hardly be for the 'public as a whole' was an irony that probably never crossed Wagner's mind. Its appeal was, and only could be, to an élite – a different élite, to be sure, from the bourgeois opera-going public of the nineteenth century which Wagner so despised, but an élite none the less. It is in the nature of art that it should be so. But it is a long way from the utopia of 'art for the community' which had roused Wagner's passions in the 1840s.

The cost of the project, he considered, could be borne either by a consortium of wealthy patrons or by a German prince; whoever it turned out to be, he was convinced, could only gain in prestige by subsidizing such a high-class venture. A postscript, delivered in a doleful tone of voice quite unlike the characteristic optimism of the rest of the preface, confesses his disillusioned resignation to never actually seeing his 'Stage Festival' performed, not least because of doubts that he would ever be able to complete the music.

Meanwhile, through the influence of his tireless supporter Marie Kalergis, Wagner received an unexpected invitation to conduct two concerts in St Petersburg in February 1863. The long train journey took him through Königsberg, where he was forced to spend the night, but as the uneasy memory of his earlier escapades spread through his mind, he feared to show his face in the town and did not venture outside his hotel room. The next day, as the train approached the Russian border, he thought of his hair-raising escape from Riga with Minna and their great Newfoundland, Robber, and anxiously scanned the faces of his fellow-travellers for any sign of suspicion towards him as a foreigner. Nobody took any notice of him, however, and once in St Petersburg, he found himself in congenial aristocratic company. His concerts were warmly received and, for a change, financially successful, as were three further concerts, largely of his own music, that he conducted in Moscow, followed by two more in St Petersburg on the return journey. By the time he got back to Germany at the end of April, he was 4,000 thalers the richer.

But less than five months later this, together with the remains of sundry fees and loans, had disappeared, most of it swallowed up by the expenses of a large, handsome apartment in a villa at Penzing, some five minutes ride from the beautiful palace of Schönbrunn, just outside Vienna. Biebrich had become petty and provincial, no place from which to launch an offensive against the theatrical establishment of Europe. The choice of Vienna was motivated by two thoughts: one was the lingering hope of seeing *Tristan* performed there; the other, as he put it in *Mein Leben*, was because 'with no other German city had I developed so close an artistic relationship'. Here, in the company of Cornelius, Tausig, Standhartner and others, and waited upon by a servant couple who remained faithful to him for a number of years, he celebrated his fiftieth birthday in grand style. 'Wagner is just like a child when he has money in his pocket,' said the Viennese conductor Heinrich Esser, who was to have directed the first performance of *Tristan*, 'and it does not seem to enter his head that it will not last for ever. And then he claims that he cannot work at all unless his rooms are luxurious and unless he has exclusive use of a large garden – in a word, unless he can live like a lord.' Part of the life-style of a lord involved ordering, first for the apartment in Penzing, later for his house in Munich and for Tribschen, the hundreds upon hundreds of yards of satin, brocade and other fine materials which he bought – and often could not pay for – from the milliner Bertha Goldwag. His letters to Bertha, the *Putzmacherin*, between 1864 and 1868 have become a *locus classicus* of Wagner's breathtaking prodigality and irresponsibility in such matters. Concerts of his music in Budapest followed, then in Prague once more, in Karlsruhe – where he was again fêted by the nobility and where he met the Russian novelist Turgenev – and in Breslau.

This hectic round of concert-giving consumed Wagner's energies for the whole of 1863. He made hardly any progress with *Die Meistersinger* – though whether this was a cause or an effect, his ceaseless travels distracting him from composition or being a substitute for his inability to do so, may be debatable. His move to Vienna did, however, provoke him to write yet another essay, *Das Wiener Hofopern-theater (The Vienna Court Opera House)* on the nature and the problems of opera, since a new opera house was in process of being built in the city. But the minds of the Viennese establishment proved no more receptive than those of other official bodies to whom he had preached reform.

A friend who came more and more into Wagner's life at this time, and remained his faithful, though not uncritical, supporter – few had the devotion and energy to do so – until his premature death in 1874, was the composer Peter Cornelius. He was eleven years younger than Wagner and had studied *inter alios* with Liszt at Weimar; he first met Wagner in 1853 at a gathering in Basle attended by Liszt, Bülow, the violinist Joachim and other celebrities. As a composer – he also wrote poetry and music criticism – he is remembered today only for the carol 'Three Kings from Persian lands afar' and the comic opera *The Barber of Baghdad*. This was given a hostile reception at its first performance – the only one to be given in the composer's lifetime – in Weimar in 1858, though the hostility seems to have been a calculated demonstration against the art and life-style of Liszt rather than a genuine response to his pupil's opera. The particular value to Wagner of Cornelius's friendship, like the interest of his letters and diaries to the biographer, lay in his independence of mind. He knew that he was a musical dwarf in the presence of a giant but he never fawned, pretended not to hear what displeased him, or shrank from questioning the Master's work and character. And as one who followed from close quarters the drama of the Wagner-Cosima-Bülow triangle, he left a frank testimony of what he saw.

Many who had helped Wagner in the past with loans or outright gifts of money now refused to do so any more, some because they disapproved of his continual love affairs and his unstable, extravagant mode of life, subsidized too long by the misplaced generosity of third parties, others because of doubts, seeing the antagonisms that his works always incited, whether this really was the 'music of the future', since it had not even been the music of the present. Henriette von Bissing, for instance, the rich, widowed sister of his patron Eliza Wille, whom he seems to have conceived a fantastic idea of marrying for her money, explained her refusal to help by saying to her sister: 'Even if I do help Wagner, he will only go on loving the Wesendonk woman in the end.'

Of those whose attitude was commercial rather than philanthropic and who looked for actions rather than words, Schott, the publishers, were at this time among the most important. But tact and delicacy were not high on the list of Wagner's virtues. The conductor Heinrich Esser was only one of the many who saw, and found distasteful, the totally self-centred nature of Wagner's personal relationships: 'He has the objectionable habit,' wrote Esser to Franz Schott, 'of favouring people with his friendship for just as long as he considers they can be useful to him, and dropping them the moment the lemon has been squeezed dry.' And although Esser can hardly rank as a dispassionate observer, he was only representing a common view when he indignantly described Wagner's predisposition to 'embark on amorous escapades in every town where he happens to be staying'.

But as his numerous promissory notes became due, and creditors began, as creditors will, to tighten the screws of extortionate rates of interest, friends pressed him to leave

Vienna quickly while they tried to extricate him from the consequences of his folly. He made first for Mariafeld, on Lake Zurich, home of François and Eliza Wille, then for Stuttgart, to visit the local Kapellmeister, Karl Eckert, who had been at his Karlsruhe concerts the previous year. He took a room in the Hotel Marquardt and telegraphed to Wendelin Weissheimer in the hope that he would come and keep him company, planning to escape with Weissheimer to the loneliness of the Swabian hills, away from fear of pursuit. His savage self-pity found expression in a bitter little epitaph:

> Hier liegt Wagner, der nichts geworden,
> Nicht einmal Ritter vom lumpigsten Orden;
> Nicht einen Hund hinter'm Ofen entlockt'er,
> Universitäten nicht 'mal 'nen Doktor.

> (Here lies Wagner, a man of no fame,
> He made no impression, Herr What-was-his-name;
> Not even the dogs were curious to see
> This creature who failed to take his degree.)

'If a miracle does not happen this moment, everything will be finished,' he wrote to Cornelius.

On the evening of 2 May 1864 Wagner was sitting with the Eckerts when a man presented himself at the house and gave the servant a visiting card inscribed 'Franz von Pfistermeister, Secretary to the King of Bavaria' to be handed to Wagner. At once suspecting that this man represented some creditor or other, Wagner told the servant to say he was not there. When he got back to his hotel, he learned that a man from Munich had been enquiring for him. With some apprehension he made an appointment to see this man at ten o'clock the next morning.

When morning came, Pfistermeister was shown into his room: he had gone first to Vienna, he said, then to Mariafeld, and had now tracked Wagner down at last, to his great pleasure; he was there on the instructions of the young

King of Bavaria, Ludwig II, from whom he brought a ring, a portrait and a message expressing his admiration for Wagner's work, together with his desire to do everything in his power to help Wagner carry out his artistic plans; if Wagner were willing to accept this offer, said Pfistermeister, he would accompany him to the King the next day.

Eckert, Weissheimer and the other friends to whom he excitedly gave the news at lunch that day were, as he described it, 'delighted and astonished'. The next morning he and Pfistermeister took the train to Munich, and the following day he had his first audience of his new patron. Within a week he received 4,000 guilders from the King's privy purse to cover his outstanding debts, and a few days later was installed in a country villa near the King's residence by the Starnberger See.

At this moment of climax – could any be more appropriate? – *Mein Leben*, the frank, fascinating, often witty, always entertaining autobiography of this extraordinary man comes to an end. There could never be an 'easy' life for such a man: indeed, without obstacles and strains, not infrequently of his own wilful creation, his life would have lacked the goads of frustration and anger, the personal and artistic tensions, that it needed for its foundation. But it is not difficult to feel, and to share, the relief and the satisfaction that he recalled in 1880, when he dictated to Cosima the final words of *Mein Leben*, his survey of the first fifty years of what the redoubtable biographer Mrs Mary Burrell called 'knocking about':

The perilous path along which my destiny summoned me that day towards the highest goals was never to be free from cares and worries, some of them of a kind I had not known before. But never did my noble friend fail to lift from me the burden of the vulgar cares of everyday life.

The noble friend was King Ludwig II of Bavaria. The miracle Wagner had looked for had come to pass.

CHAPTER SIX
The Royal Miracle

Ludwig II, of the royal house of the Wittelsbachs, succeeded to the throne of Bavaria on the death of his father, King Maximilian II, on 10 March 1864. He was eighteen years old, slim and very tall, strikingly beautiful – to call him handsome would suggest too masculine a quality – and utterly in love with Wagner's work. In the last pages of *Mein Leben* Wagner recalls passing through Munich on his flight from Vienna to Mariafeld a week or so after the old King's death. The city was mourning its dead monarch. Wagner, with no inkling of what was about to happen, caught sight in a shop window of a portrait of the new King, the youth who was to open the royal exchequer to all his hero's demands, and in so doing, almost bring the Bavarian court down in ruins around him.

Throughout the nineteenth century Bavaria enjoyed, as it still does today, the reputation of a resolute Catholic independence, which its opponents tend to regard as conservative obstinacy. In the mid-nineteenth century this independence was exercised above all against Prussia and its 'Iron Chancellor' Bismarck, who achieved his goal of German political unity under Prussian hegemony through three wars – against Denmark in 1864, against Austria in 1866 and against France in 1870-71. Maximilian had been on the throne during the years of confusion that led to the first of these, the years of the problem of Schleswig-Holstein, whose complexities were such, said Palmerston, that only three men had really understood them: one had died, the second was a lunatic and the third, himself, had since forgotten it all. Bavaria refused to align herself with the annexationist aims of Prussia and had no part in the

Austro-Prussian invasion of the Danish province of Schleswig in February 1864, but this could not influence the inexorable march of Bismarck's power. Nor could Bavarian sympathy for Austria, though Bismarck would have preferred complete neutrality, affect his policy of seeking a war that would remove once and for all the rivalry of Austria in the fight for leadership of the Germanies.

With the Franco-Prussian War of 1870 national pan-German sentiment in Bavaria eventually overcame traditional particularism, and the Bavarian government, deciding that the war against France concerned all the German states and was not just a private Prussian adventure, voted to join the cause. But it was the last state to do so, and only then did Bismarck's dream of the unity of North and South Germany become reality.

Maximilian, who ruled for sixteen years, had become King in 1848 on the abdication of his father Ludwig I. The name of Ludwig I may first revive the memory of his affair with the notorious 'Spanish dancer' who called herself Lola Montez, the Irish girl Eliza Gilbert, who had been Liszt's mistress a few years before, but his true memorial lives in the magnificent art collections and public buildings of Munich – the Glyptothek, the two Pinakotheken, the Odeon, the university and many others. Maximilian continued his father's patronage of the humanities and the sciences, and the young Ludwig grew up surrounded by the arts, sharing his time between the Munich Residenz, the summer palace of Nymphenburg, the mountain castle of Hohenschwangau and other properties of the Wittelsbach family.

Sensitive, often unpredictable in behaviour and, like his younger brother Otto, almost pathologically introvert, Ludwig had become Crown Prince of Bavaria when he was three, and from the beginning the restrictions and the isolation inseparable from his status intensified his innate loneliness. His relationship to his mother, a niece of King Friedrich Wilhelm III of Prussia, was proper and respectful rather than affectionate, and the person to whom he felt most closely drawn during his childhood was his governess Baroness Sibylle von Meilhaus, the woman who brought him her first-hand account of the performance of Wagner's *Lohengrin* at Munich in 1859. The walls of the castle of Hohenschwangau were covered with brilliantly-coloured frescoes of scenes from the medieval legends of *Tannhäuser* and *Lohengrin*, commissioned by Maximilian, who had bought and rebuilt the castle; indeed its very name, 'High Swan-Land', together with the nearby lake, the Schwansee, invokes the legend of Lohengrin, Knight of the Swan.

Steeping himself in this Romantic world of Germanic myth that surrounded him, the young Ludwig fell more and more deeply into a day-dreaming world of fantasy, identifying himself with the peerless Lohengrin, emissary from the castle of the Holy Grail. A performance of Wagner's opera in Munich in 1861 overwhelmed him; he began to read Wagner's theoretical works, acquired a copy of *Tristan* and in 1863 was reading the text of *The Ring*, with Wagner's new preface on the establishment of a festival and a special theatre for the realization of his plans.

Scarcely had his father's funeral taken place than Ludwig set in train his plans to bring Wagner to the Bavarian court, plans which culminated in Pfistermeister tracing his elusive quarry to Stuttgart. The same evening Pfistermeister proudly escorted his valuable charge on the train journey from Stuttgart to Munich delivered him to the luxurious Bayerischer Hof hotel, then went to the Residenz to report his success. The King plied him with questions until midnight about how the great man was, what he had talked about, how he now viewed the future and so on. He would receive Wagner, he said, the following afternoon.

The encounter of the two such utterly different men – the

Royal Adonis, eighteen years old, slim and willowy, six foot three in height, secure, with great riches at his command, introvert to the point of melancholia, and the short, stocky composer, now almost fifty-one, laden with debts, facing a desperate future, energetic and totally self-centred – was as impressive and moving for the one as for the other. 'If only you could have seen how his gratitude shamed me,' wrote the King to his cousin, the Archduchess Sophie,

when I extended my hand to him and gave him my sincere word that his great Nibelung work would not only be completed but also performed in the manner he intended. He bent low over my hand and seemed moved by what was really so natural, for he stayed in this position for a long time without saying a word. I felt we had exchanged roles. I stooped down to him and drew him to my heart with a feeling that I was taking a silent oath to be faithful to him till the end of time.

'So fine and intelligent is he,' wrote Wagner to Eliza Wille, 'so glorious and full of feeling, that I fear his life will perish like a fleeting, heavenly dream before the realities of this common, vulgar world.' And to Mathilde Maier, to whom he also sent a picture of the King: 'Our meeting yesterday was like one long love scene. He has the deepest understanding of my nature and my needs; he offers me everything that I want for my life, my creative activity and the production of my works. I am simply to be his friend – no official appointment, no functions. He is the complete fulfilment of my desires.'

It would be a mistake to see in phrases such as these or in the fulsome, high-flown style of the numerous lengthy letters that passed between the two men, any ground for maintaining that Wagner, well known for his ruthlessness when his own personal and artistic interests were at stake, somehow dominated the young King against his will and judgment. For all his introversion, his homosexuality and the desperate sense of guilt associated with it, and other traits compounded into the familiar picture of a 'mad' King, Ludwig had a shrewdness and an awareness of real issues that hardly fit the image of an unworldly and unbalanced dreamer. Bismarck described him in his memoirs as 'a clear-headed ruler with a national German outlook', and Prince Chlodwig von Hohenlohe, one-time Bavarian Foreign Minister and later Imperial Chancellor, noted in his diary for 1865: 'We have the most amiable and engaging monarch I have ever set eyes on. His is a noble and poetic nature. He has plenty of brains, and character to boot.' Far from unsettling Ludwig's mind, Wagner and his works served as an anchor to which the young King clung, time and again, to save himself from being swept away by the tides of responsibility and depression.

Ludwig, for his part, was certainly not blind to the faults and unpleasantnesses in Wagner's character. But he understood his hero like no other man, and like only one woman, letting nothing divert him from the support of his art yet retaining his independent judgment both on the Master's personal conduct and on the effects of his personal attachment on his formal royal responsibilities.

At the moment of their first meeting Wagner had lived in Ludwig's heart and mind for many years, and their meeting crowned the joy of long anticipation. Ludwig, on the other hand, had burst into Wagner's life only the previous day, embodiment of the miracle in which he saw his sole hope of salvation. Their expectations of each other were utterly different. Wagner had before him a practical goal, the need for a Maecenas to take the day-to-day problems of living from his shoulders and give him his artistic freedom. Ludwig, for whom *Tannhäuser* and *Lohengrin* represented an escape world, a refuge from the greyness and ugliness of an intolerable reality, saw before him an ideal, the creator of new spiritual values, the man with the vision of the 'work of art of the future'. *Lohengrin* meant for him not the beauty of music but the significance of myth, not a challenge to the old traditions of opera and the entire contemporary world of musical expression but a means of returning to the past and of worshipping the values of medieval national legend. When the two men discussed who would sing the title role in a performance of *Lohengrin*, Ludwig envisioned a man of inspiring presence, an heroic embodiment of beauty and purity, almost a god in human form; Wagner, however, was looking, not for a handsome hero but for a gifted heroic tenor, a man with the intelligence to understand the spiritual meaning of the opera and the musical ability to convey this meaning to an audience.

Wagner was a practical artist – a practical idealist, one might even say. The remarkably detailed stage directions on his scores, his exegetic articles and programme notes on how to sing, play and produce his works, as well as on how to understand them, and above all his precise image of the architectural, theatrical, musical, organizational and administrative *desiderata* for the establishment of what became the Bayreuth festival – all this shows his intense concern to pursue the realization of his intentions through to the end. Many composers, hearing, perhaps, a kind of 'objective', Platonic performance of a work as they write, give their music to the world as a written score and leave its interpretation to the performers whose task it is to interpret. But Wagner was not one of them.

Having given Wagner 4,000 guilders from the Bavarian treasury to meet at least his most pressing debts in Vienna, Ludwig rented a house, the Villa Pellet, for him near Schloss Berg, the royal residence on the beautiful Starnberger See, some fifteen miles south of Munich. He also made him an annual allowance of 4,000 guilders – one cannot call it a salary, since Wagner had no formal obligations to the court in the way that a servant usually has to his patron. From this Wagner also had to support the ailing Minna in Dresden. Further substantial sums were later made over to him as and when he found specific cause, such as his removal expenses to Berg and the signing of a contract to finish *The Ring* – the third time he had sold this particular item.

Once established in the Villa Pellet, Wagner was collected each day by the royal coachman and driven to Schloss Berg, where the two men discussed, on the King's initiative, how to introduce Wagner's works to the Bavarian public, both in their complete operatic form and in concert selections. Hans von Bülow, Karl Klindworth and the tenor Schnorr von Carolsfeld were among those to be brought to Munich to help in the enterprise. Like Wagner, Ludwig had a deep-seated scorn for the contemporary theatre. Verdi maintained that operatic quality was measured at the box-office: success equals large audiences, the satisfied consumers of the work of art. Wagner, on the other hand, equated popular success with sinking to the level of the philistine masses and betraying the responsibility of art to lead men's minds upwards and outwards, to create an awareness of higher truths, to reveal new moral and spiritual values. That he found in Ludwig one equally committed to a conception of the stage as a 'moral institution', in Schiller's phrase, a place in which mere entertainment gives way to didactic purpose, to catharsis and regeneration, was the long-sought miracle that saved him.

Ludwig, on his side, saw that Wagner's art could flourish only if the pressures of commercial success were removed. Wagner carried this a logical and characteristic step further by positing that his works should not be part of a repertoire that included the compositions of others but should constitute a programme of their own, a closed self-contained world, unified in meaning and expression, in ends and means. Small wonder that envy and resentment spread among those Bavarian artists and intellectuals who had enjoyed the generosity of Maximilian II but now found that his son had turned his back on them in favour of a megalomaniac Saxon upstart of dubious artistic credentials, questionable morals, and with a none too savoury political past.

Yet with all this unexpected security, the sudden freedom to spread himself in luxury, the golden prospect of the fulfilment of his artistic dreams, he lacked one thing – the company of a woman. In June, a month after moving into the Villa Pellet, he wrote to Mathilde Maier, beseeching her to join him and enclosing an assurance to her mother of the strictly proper arrangements he would make for her privacy. Mathilde would hardly have consented, but before she could reply, Wagner wrote again; he could not contemplate plunging them both into an emotional catastrophe, he said, and would soon be able to make other provision for running his household. 'I am, I must confess, egoistic – I want rest and peace, the comfort of being embraced'. 'Farewell, my child', he ends. 'Take care of yourself, and love me in spite of everything.' Behind this sudden change of heart lies, not a reappraisal of the situation, not a change of external circumstances, not even a different attitude towards Mathilde herself, but a new name, that of the most important woman in Wagner's life – Cosima von Bülow.

What made Wagner use the throw-away phrase 'in spite of everything' can be assumed, guessed at or invented. He continued to write to Mathilde long afterwards, and she was in the audience at Bayreuth in 1876. But two weeks earlier he had invited the Bülows to bring their two little daughters and spend the summer with him – this he told Mathilde. On the same day as he finally put Mathilde off, Cosima and the children – without Bülow, who was unwell and felt unfit to travel – arrived from Berlin. Bülow, exhausted and afflicted with attacks of paralysis, came a week later, and the whole family stayed at the Villa Pellet until September. It was in this very week that Cosima von Bülow and Wagner consummated the relationship that was to sustain him, physically and spiritually, until the end of his life.

The second of the three illegitimate children – Blandine, Cosima and Daniel – born to Liszt and the Countess Marie d'Agoult, Cosima was born at Como on Christmas Eve, 1837 and died in Bayreuth in 1930, in her ninety-third year, almost half a century after Wagner. Physically far less attractive than her elder sister, she had the lankiness which brought her the nickname of 'Stork', but as she grew older, she developed an aristocratic bearing, an air of high breeding and a keen intelligence which attracted their own measure of attention. The education of all three children was French and Catholic; when she was thirty-four, two years after marrying Wagner, Cosima formally became a Protestant but in spite of growing progressively more Germanophile after the Franco-Prussian War of 1870, she could never entirely throw off the influence of her upbringing and never lost her French accent when speaking German. When, after a liaison of some ten years, Liszt and the Countess began to drift apart, the children were given into the care of Liszt's mother in Paris, where the Countess, a friend of George Sand and of Chopin, made a new career for herself as a writer of historical novels under the pseudonym of Daniel Stern.

When Liszt finally abandoned Marie d'Agoult, indulged himself in passing with Lola Montez, then, in 1847, took Princess Carolyne von Sayn-Wittgenstein as his mistress, the three children found themselves caught between affection for their mother, who had no legal rights over them, and submission to their father's determination – incited by the Princess – to estrange them from her. They were taken away from Liszt's mother and put in charge of the Princess's old governess, were allowed no friends of their own age and even forbidden to mention their mother's name. This was the time, in October 1853, when Wagner first saw Cosima. When she was seventeen, Cosima, together with Blandine and Daniel, was put in the care of Hans von Bülow's mother in Berlin; two years later, in August 1857, the nineteen-year-old Catholic Cosima married the Protestant Bülow, a nervous, irascible, highly-strung conductor and pianist of twenty-seven, who had been a fanatical admirer of Wagner's music and a faithful disciple of the Master since he was sixteen. He could not withstand the unconscious comparison in Cosima's mind with Liszt who, difficult and intolerable in his own way, was a man of powerful self-assertion and a musician of genius, while Bülow was neither. 'Cosima is a girl of genius, very like her father,' wrote the Countess Marie. 'Her powerful imagination will lead her away from the normal paths. She feels the *démon intérieur* and will always sacrifice to it what it demands of her. Circumstances have pushed her into a marriage in which, I fear, there will be no happiness for anyone.'

And it never was a successful, let alone a happy marriage. Whatever its basis from Cosima's point of view – perhaps an offer of comradeship to a man who found it hard to come to terms with life, perhaps a sense of pity for him, a desire to help him make something of himself – it was certainly not a compelling love or a romantic passion. The conflicts that corroded her family relationships – affection for a mother from whom she was deliberately kept apart, the harshness with which her father's new mistress treated her, the coolness in her relations with a famous father whom she rarely saw – had given her character a certain hardness but at the same time a great capacity for self-sacrifice, a capacity demanded, in their different ways, by her marriages both to Bülow and to Wagner.

But this self-awareness and self-control could also break down and reveal a very different Cosima. During the last intolerable days of Wagner's exile in the Wesendonk Asyl in August 1858, the Bülows, Cosima's mother and Wagner's unhappily married friend Karl Ritter had come by their independent roads to visit him. When the Countess Marie left, Cosima and Karl accompanied her to Geneva, returning to the Wesendonk estate a few days later. While they were on a boat trip on the lake, Cosima suddenly threw her arms round Karl and begged him to kill her; weighed down by his own misery, he told her that he too wanted to die. But this so startled Cosima that she shrank from her desperate impulse, and later she wrote to Karl begging him to forget the whole episode.

Just before the Bülows finally took their leave of Wagner and the Asyl – 'Hans weeping, Cosima silent and sombre', Wagner recalled in *Mein Leben* – she fell at his feet and covered his hands with tears and kisses. 'Astonished and alarmed,' he wrote afterwards to Mathilde Wesendonk, 'I gazed at this mystery without being able to unravel it.'

The mystery did not begin to unravel itself for another four years, during which they met only a few times. Wagner remembered a shyness and hesitancy in her attitude towards him. Then, in 1862, she suddenly changed. In *Mein Leben* Wagner tells of a visit in August of that year to Frankfurt, in the company of the Bülows, to see a performance of Goethe's *Tasso*, with Friederike Meyer as the Princess. Hans was depressed, ill-humoured, near despair, Cosima cheerful and relaxed:

When, in the course of this stay in Frankfurt, I gave a performance of 'Wotan's Farewell' from *The Valkyrie* for my friends in my own fashion, I observed on Cosima's face the same expression that had so amazed me when she said goodbye to me in Zurich, except that now her abandonment had given way to bliss and serenity. We spoke no word, but our silence concealed a secret, and so utterly did I now believe that she belonged to me that my excitement drove me to indulge in the most impetuous behaviour. As I was accompanying her across a square in Frankfurt towards our hotel, I caught sight of an empty wheel-barrow, so I told her to sit in it and I would wheel her over to the hotel. She immediately agreed, which so astonished me that the courage to carry out my crazy idea completely deserted me.

For much of the following twelve months Wagner was travelling across Europe to conduct concerts of his own music – Vienna, Prague, St Petersburg, Budapest and elsewhere. Then, on the morning of 28 November 1863, he visited the Bülows in Berlin, where, to his friends' amusement, his first act was to realize some ready cash by selling a gold snuff box, a present from the Grand Duke of Baden, for sixty thalers. Hans was conducting a concert that evening and needed to study his scores, so he left his wife and friend together. In the afternoon they took a drive in a carriage. 'This time,' he wrote in *Mein Leben*, 'there was no jesting. Silently we looked into each other's eyes and felt ourselves gripped by an irresistible desire to unveil the truth fully and openly, and without uttering a word, to unburden ourselves of the unhappiness that oppressed us. Sobbing and weeping we pledged ourselves to belong to each other alone, and our souls were comforted.' In 1877 Cosima wrote in her diary of this day as 'that on which we found each other and were united in the tragedy of *Liebestod*'.

On 29 June 1864 – they had not met since that November day – Cosima arrived at the Villa Pellet with her little daughters Daniela and Blandine, and the Wagner-Cosima-Bülow triangle, already a spiritual configuration, now also became a physical reality. Tristan and Isolde were joined in an indissoluble union; King Mark submitted to what he was powerless to change. Cosima was a strong woman, strong in the passionate nature she had received from her father, strong in her resolve to sacrifice herself to the man and the cause which now gave her life meaning. Recognizing that Minna, for whom she had a certain plain human sympathy, had never been a fit companion for Wagner, she was also scornful of the 'pale and sickly' Mathilde Wesendonk, who, she said, lacked the courage 'to break her existing ties, surrender herself to love and give her support to her lover'.

Among the summer visitors to the Villa Pellet were the pianist Karl Klindworth, later the guardian of the young Winifred Williams who was to take Wagner's name as his daughter-in-law, the Munich sculptor Caspar von Zumbusch, whose bronze bust of King Ludwig II stands in front of Wahnfried, the Wagner family villa in Bayreuth, and the socialist writer Ferdinand Lassalle, comrade of Karl Marx, partisan of the 1848 Revolution and father of the German working-class movement. Lassalle came on a purely personal errand, seeking Wagner's intercession with Bavarian courtiers and officials to help overcome the refusal of the Bavarian chargé d'affaires in Geneva, Baron von Dönniges, to allow him to marry his daughter. For Lassalle's emotional entanglement Wagner had no sympathy, and in a letter to Eliza Wille he described Lassalle, with dislike rather than with admiration, as an example of 'the type destined to become important, a type I would call Germanic-Jewish'. Wagner had long put the cause of revolution behind him. Cosima, while too young to have experienced the meaning of 1848, had nevertheless moved in French salon circles where socialism, materialism, the social reform of the arts and other radical issues held the floor, but like Wagner, she quickly returned to, or perhaps never really gave up, the proud, aristocratic values with which the world associated her.

Until all the notes and letters of Wagner, Cosima, Bülow and Liszt are revealed – and maybe not even then – we shall not know how long Bülow remained ignorant of the situation, or how he learned of the love between his wife and his friend. During his almost complete paralysis in the late summer of 1864 he chose to stay alone in the Europäischer Hof Hotel in Munich rather than with his wife at the Villa Pellet, and when Cosima brought her father from Karlsruhe, where he was attending a musical festival, to visit him, she must surely have told Hans of her crisis. Letters from Liszt to Bülow later in the year imply that he is fully aware of the situation as he tries to lift his son-in-law out of his depression and encourage him to resume his work. This was the first time in three years that Liszt and Wagner had met, and worried though he was by his son-in-law's physical and psychological condition, Liszt rejoiced at his friend's new-found fortune under royal patronage and marvelled at the parts of *Die Meister-singer* that Wagner showed him.

As soon as Bülow had regained strength, he, Cosima and their children went back to Berlin. But he had long been unhappy there as conductor and as teacher at the Stern Conservatory, largely because of his championship of the 'new music' of Liszt and Wagner against the conservative opposition of the musical establishment. When Wagner persuaded the King to offer him a post as *Vorspieler*, or court pianist, in Munich, he therefore accepted with enthusiasm. So by the end of this *annus mirabilis* of 1864 Wagner not only enjoyed economic security and the uninhibited favour of his new King but had also found a job for his most valued musical assistant – his ideal conductor, as he unhesitatingly conceded – and thus guaranteed the constant presence of his mistress.

The first 'declaration of intent' to issue from the almost daily discussions between Wagner and Ludwig at Schloss Berg was the essay *On State and Religion*, in which Wagner undertook to describe how his views on social and political matters had changed since his revolutionary writings of the 1840s and 1850s. Wagner was by nature verbose, and his prose style is maddeningly prolix. When it is a musical argument that stands in the centre of his attention, his wordiness may irritate without destroying the attention we pay to his exposition. But in his cultural, pseudo-philosophical essays like *On State and Religion* opacity of language often conceals paucity of thought, and the 'explanation' of the piece lies outside the arguments within it.

On State and Religion is a direct response to his new status as the honoured collaborator of a King, whom he must needs present as the guardian of values temporal (state) and eternal (religion). And since he has now left the ranks of the have-nots and joined the privileged company of the haves, he can disclaim his revolutionary past, his captivation by the radical message of Proudhon and Bakunin. He even utters such astonishing disavowals as: 'Anyone who ascribed to me the role of a political revolutionary and really regarded me as belonging in such company, obviously knew nothing about me and only formed his judgment on the basis of outward appearances.' It is as though there had been no warrant for his arrest in 1849; as though he had never associated with Röckel and the other rebel leaders in Dresden; as though he had never had to flee into exile, banished for thirteen years as *persona non grata*. What he writes about Church and State, as about the monarchy, or the press, or the contemporary theatre, or the Jews, is in its origins an extension, a rationalization, of his personal circumstances of the moment, not a detached appraisal of an urgent current issue. This does not necessarily negate the validity of the views he expresses, but it sets a different context for them from that of truly objective cultural and historical studies. Wagner's concern was always with the subject rather than the object.

So it was in his social life also. 'Wagner does not know or understand how exhausting he is,' wrote Peter Cornelius.

Just as an example: The other day we were with Frau von Bülow; Wagner took out Schlack's translation of Firdousi and read some of the stanzas about Rustam and Sohrab. Meanwhile Bülow finished giving a lesson. Ten minutes later they were immersed in *Tristan und Isolde* – they sang the whole of the first act. Then tea was served, but hardly had we drunk half a cup than Wagner was busy telling us about his *Parsifal*. And so it went on all evening. Our great friend simply has to sing, read or talk about himself the whole time, otherwise he is not satisfied.

At about the same time as *On State and Religion* Wagner composed a *Huldigungsmarsch (Homage March)* to honour the King's birthday on 25 August 1864, his first music for a long time. In a letter to his royal friend he wrote: 'I am now resolved to lay aside all other work, however profitable its comparatively easy completion might make it, so as to devote myself entirely to my *Nibelungenring.*' Ludwig's response to opera, whether *Tristan* (now his favourite Wagner work) or, say, Verdi's *Aïda*, which he also enjoyed, was essentially to the spectacle as the realization of his vision of the meaning of the work, the theatrical experience *in toto*; whether he understood or appreciated much of the music seems very questionable. More than once Wagner dubbed him unmusical, with no ear for quality of performance. The Countess of Leiningen-Westerburg, a lady of the Munich court, said the same in her memoirs: 'He was completely unmusical. His piano teacher often maintained to my father that he did not know a Strauss waltz from a Beethoven sonata. What constituted the tremendous attraction of Wagner's works for him was the romantic substance of the poems.'

In the autumn, with the King back at the Residenz, Wagner also returned to Munich, occupying a sumptuous mansion, Briennerstrasse 21, near the palace, which Ludwig had taken for him. He proceeded to deck out the house with lavish furnishings, coloured silks and brocades, frills and lace, exotic perfumes and other baubles of the flamboyant luxury with which he liked to surround himself. The provision of this finery was placed in the hands of his *Putzmacherin*, the Viennese milliner Bertha Goldwag, who had furnished his house in Penzing and was now summoned to Munich to display the ostentatious materials which she knew he loved. His servants, Franz and Anna Mrazeck, and his dog Pohl, also joined him from Penzing.

In Munich he began to fulfil his vow to commit himself to the completion of *The Ring*, turning to the score of *Siegfried*, on which he had done no work for seven years. Three years, he optimistically reckoned, would see *Siegfried* and *Götterdämmerung* finished, and an elaborate contract was drawn up with the King, promising Wagner a total of 30,000 guilders over these three years, together with 'perks' such as the rent-free house on the Briennerstrasse, in return for the four complete scores of *Der Ring des Nibelungen*. In a letter to Wagner from his castle of Hohenschwangau, the King formally declared his intention to have a special theatre built in Munich 'so that the performance of *Der Ring des Nibelungen* shall be perfect', and the architect Gottfried Semper, Wagner's old companion and fellow-revolutionary from Dresden days, was brought to Munich from Zurich, where he had been Professor of Architecture since 1855, to design the building whose principles had already crystallized in Wagner's mind. There were mutterings in certain quarters about the young King's folly in pandering to the excessive demands of this unbridled and dangerous new composer. But with Hans von Bülow, now engaged by the King, having earned an enthusiastic reception on his first public appearance in Munich as a pianist, and with Peter Cornelius there, also as a paid servant of the Court, to help in establishing the Wagnerian empire, the stage seemed set for the consolidation of his fame and the fulfilment of his dreams. Pain from stomach ulcers forced him several times to turn away from his work, but before the end of the year he had begun scoring the second act of *Siegfried*.

A new theatre alone, of course, could not produce the operatic revolution on which Wagner and his monarch had embarked. The next step in his campaign – a campaign waged, like all Wagner's crusades, with relentlessly practical weapons – was a long report to the King *On the Foundation of a German Conservatoire in Munich*, in which he urges the training of actors and singers in an expressly German, i.e. Wagnerian spirit, and the development of performance and production to create an individually German, i.e. Wagnerian art; instruction in instrumental playing matters far less to him. The new *Musikschule*, with Bülow as its director and with the help of Cornelius, Heinrich Porges (one of Wagner's close Jewish friends) and Friedrich Schmitt, a singing teacher from Leipzig, came into being a few years later.

Wagner always affected a thoroughgoing scorn for most opera singers of his day, and took it for granted that the 'singers of the future' would be raised on the sustenance they derived from his 'music of the future'. But he never envisioned a new type of singer totally isolated from the performance of other music, or a 'closed shop' of performers who arrogated to themselves proprietary rights in his music, cultivated a cabbalistic so-called 'Bayreuth style', or who conversely were cast by outsiders as incapable of performing any other music. In this as in other things, Wagnerians, no less than Marxists, Freudians and other disciples of all-consuming creeds, have often shown themselves *plus royaliste que le roi*.

The emphatic, correctly accentuated vocal declamation that lies at the heart of his demands reflects his call for opera-as-drama, an entity far removed from *bel canto* Italian opera, the Grand Opera of Meyerbeer or the works of Mozart. It requires a grasp of dramatic values embodied in a poetic text utterly different in conception and function from the conventional libretto, for out of this text emerges a dramatic, declamatory vocal line, often unlyrical and unvocal to the point where the human voice is treated almost as an instrument of the orchestra. Even faithful admirers of Wagner were sometimes critical of the results this produced. The French composer Saint-Saëns, a convert since the Paris *Tannhäuser* of 1861 but also one who set great store by lyrical beauty, noted after attending the first Bayreuth Festival in 1876: 'Most of those who took part in *Der Ring des Nibelungen* screamed rather than sang.'

Established music teachers and practitioners understandably took offence at the implications of Wagner's tract and joined the lobby of Bavarian politicians and officials who were uneasily watching the command that this intemperate Saxon intruder had already gained over the King's affairs. Not least of these was the King's personal secretary, Franz Pfistermeister, the man who had ferreted Wagner out in Stuttgart and brought him to Munich. The inner circle of Wagner, Cosima, Ludwig, Bülow, Semper and Cornelius was now joined by Wagner's old friend of Paris and Dresden days, the painter Friedrich Pecht, who did a youthfully flattering portrait of the fifty-three-year-old composer for the King, diplomatically incorporating in a corner an idealized bust of Ludwig himself.

But how easy it was to plant suspicions in the sensitive young King's mind, and how quick he was to take offence, showed itself already in February of the following year, 1865. Because Wagner had condescendingly addressed him as 'Mein Junge' ('My boy') in Pfistermeister's presence, he suddenly refused to receive the astonished Wagner at the Residenz after having invited him to come. This particular tantrum was quickly forgotten, but a growing public resentment of Wagner's activities led to a number of satirical cartoons in the Munich magazine *Punsch*, which made it clear that it was out to pillory every flaw in his character and every ineptitude in his behaviour, to the smug delight of courtiers and politicians.

The first item in the programme of activities which the King and Wagner drew up was the première of *Tristan und Isolde*, which had lain in Wagner's drawer, fully completed, for over five years. Rehearsals filled the spring months, and finally, after upsets of one kind and another, this most intense, most hermetic, most autobiographical of his works was performed in the Munich Hoftheater on the evening of 10 June 1865 before an audience of 2,000 people, with King Ludwig II in the royal box. The conductor was Hans von Bülow; the tenor Ludwig Schnorr von Carolsfeld, whom Wagner had always wanted for the part, was loaned from Dresden to sing Tristan, and his wife Malwine sang Isolde; the role of Kurwenal was taken by Anton Mitterwurzer, who had sung Wolfram von Eschenbach in the first performance of *Tannhäuser* twenty years earlier.

Rapturous public applause may not signify profound public understanding, and one may wonder how close those who applauded came to realizing the meaning of the drama they had seen and of the music they had heard. But although there was hissing in some parts of the auditorium at the end of each act, it was drowned by the clapping and cheering. The King was deeply moved. Above all the performance of this allegedly unperformable work, after years of frustration and near-despair, was of an excellence that surpassed anything that Wagner had experienced with his earlier operas. For Schnorr von Carolsfeld, one of the great singers of the day, it was the climax of a career tragically cut short by his sudden death* only a month

---

*After he had caught a chill during the rehearsals of *Tristan* on the draughty Munich stage.

later. 'We are all in a trance at the work's remarkable success,' wrote Bülow to the composer Joachim Raff, 'particularly at the ever-increasing sympathy of the public. It is the greatest success that a new Wagner work has ever had anywhere [Bülow did not know Wagner in the days of *Rienzi*]. The Schnorrs were incredible, the other singers quite tolerable, the orchestra excellent.' Four performances were given over the space of three weeks; the third was seen by Anton Bruckner, who had been completely won over to Wagner by *Tannhäuser* in Linz in 1862 and remained an ardent disciple to the end.

Predictably, the critics ensured that *Tristan und Isolde* also received its fair measure of abuse. Some saw the immorality of the theme as the most offensive aspect of the work, undermining the moral fibre of the nation. 'Not to mince words,' said the prestigious *Allgemeine Musikalische Zeitung*, 'it is a glorification of sensual pleasure, tricked out with every titillating device . . . What Wagner presents here is not life as found in the heroic Nordic sagas, which could uplift and strengthen the German spirit, but heroism on the point of ruin at the hands of sensuality.' The Munich *Der Volksbote* refused to accept that the enthusiasm of the audience could have been spontaneous, and put it down to bribery and behind-the-scenes manoeuvering on the part of the Wagner faction. Eduard Schelle, who had also reported on the Paris *Tannhäuser*, delivered a comprehensive judgment: 'The text is a manifest absurdity in every respect. As to the music, except for a few sections it is the cunningly concocted product of a morbid and decadent imagination.'

The imagery of sickness and disease has often been invoked in characterizations of Wagner's music, and in particular of *Tristan*.

> 'He who hath seen Beauty
> Is already close to Death'

– wrote the nineteenth-century poet August von Platen. Nietzsche, starting from what he called Wagner's 'intemperance and lack of self-control', and conscious, all too conscious of the dangerous attractions of Romantic music, found himself unable to resist the seductiveness of *Tristan*: 'The world is a poor place for the man who has never been sick enough to enjoy this "ecstasy of Hell"' (*Ecce Homo*). Thomas Mann, too, in the little story *Tristan*, with its consumptive hero Detlef Spinell, in *The Magic Mountain* and in many an essay returns to the constellation of *Tristan und Isolde*, Schopenhauer, Romanticism and decay. And there is no more chilling embodiment of sickness in music than the figure of the demonic composer Adrian Leverkühn, hero of Mann's novel *Doktor Faustus*, whose creative life is bought at the price of his sacrifice to the devil and to the goading sufferings of syphilis.

It is above all with the chromaticism of *Tristan* in mind that we can sense what Hanslick meant:

I know very well that Wagner is the greatest living composer of opera, and in a historical sense the only one worth talking about . . . But when art enters a period of luxury, it is already on the decline. Wagner's operatic style recognizes only superlatives, and a superlative has no future. It is an end, not a beginning . . . One could say of this tone poetry: There is music in it – but it is not music.

Wagner's *Tristan* has all the hothouse excitement, all the importunate passion, all the enveloping, crushing intensity that has made Wagnerians of some and anti-Wagnerians of others. It split the musical world on the day of its first performance, and has done so ever since.

After *Tristan und Isolde*, the artistic programme drawn up by Wagner and the King provided for new productions of *Tannhäuser* and *Lohengrin* in the small Residenztheater or the bigger Court Theatre, the complete *Ring* in the as yet unbuilt Festival Theatre, followed by *Die Meistersinger* (still unfinished), *Parsifal* (not even started) and *Die Sieger* (which never got beyond the stage of the prose draft of 1856). But the King also had another request. 'It would give me a quite unbelievable pleasure,' he wrote, in the flowery style characteristic of the correspondence between the two men, 'if you would offer me a detailed description of your intellectual development and also of the outward course of your life. May I cherish the hope that I shall one day find this wish of mine fulfilled?'

So, having before him numerous collected notes and jottings from over the years, together with the *Autobiographical Sketch* of 1843 and the *Communication to my Friends* of 1851, Wagner began the immense task of dictating to Cosima *Mein Leben*, one of the most remarkable autobiographies ever written by a great artist. At the top of the first page of Cosima's manuscript stands the place – Munich; the date – 17 July 1865; and a device composed of the intertwined letters R-C-W, which tells its own story.

That story had moved a stage further in April of the same year with the birth of Cosima's daughter Isolde, her third child. Cosima was Bülow's wife, and Bülow, whatever he may have known or suspected, treated Isolde as his own child. She may have been. But the weight of evidence – the cohabitation of Cosima and Wagner at the crucial moment in the Villa Pellet in June 1864, the physiognomy of Isolde herself, Cosima's own later statements (albeit long after both Wagner and Bülow were dead, and in highly emotive circumstances) – makes Wagner her father, as the way he talked about her to Cosima shows he believed himself to be. In 1914, after a family wrangle over the partition of the Wagner property, Isolde, by then the wife of the conductor Franz Beidler, petitioned to have herself legally declared Wagner's child, not Bülow's. Given the conflicting testimony and the indubitable fact that, during the weeks when she must have conceived the child, Cosima was living in the Villa Pellet with both her husband and Wagner, the court could hardly do other than dismiss the petition. But posterity has believed otherwise.

'In the mornings I write, in the evenings my Friend dictates,' said Cosima in one of her many letters to the King on the progress of *Mein Leben* (*Freund* and *Freundin* were the usual words by which they referred to each other and which others in their intimate circle also used). The fourth and final part was not finished until 1880, but, as befits the circumstances of its royal commission, the story reaches its happy ending in 1864, the year of Wagner's meeting with Ludwig (the so-called *Annals* give us a further four years of autobiography from 1864 to 1868 but they do not form part of *Mein Leben*). Like the *Communication to my Friends*, *Mein Leben* was not intended for the eyes of the public, and when, at the end of 1870, the first volume was ready for printing, Wagner ordered only fifteen copies. After his death Cosima succeeded in reclaiming these copies, and the first public edition, prepared from an extra copy which the printer, Bonfantini of Basle, kept for himself, did not appear until 1911.

The particular circumstances in which *Mein Leben* was written inevitably influenced the way in which Wagner handled some of the episodes in his past. He treats his involvement in the Dresden revolt, for instance, with a detachment and a lightheartedness which might reassure his royal patron as to his political maturity and his loyalty to the monarchy, but which certainly does not tally with the rebellious republicanism that inflamed him at the time. Nor can we take our eyes from the ironical scene of Wagner dictating to his mistress how he had fallen in love with Minna, the pitiful wife to whom he was still legally bound, how he had planned to elope with Jessie Laussot, how he had formed passionate attachments with Mathilde

Wesendonk, with Mathilde Maier, with Friederike Meyer – all this to the woman who had just born him one child and, his faithful handmaid to the end, was to bear him two more.

Some years later, when they were married, he said to Cosima, as she wrote in her diary: 'No one could have been a more appropriate consort for me than you. You are the only one who made me complete. With the others I just delivered monologues.' Maybe – but the nature of his real relations with the 'others', as preserved in letters and in testimony from the time, does not always match such assurances. Yet for all this, *Mein Leben* is a remarkably frank and accurate narrative, entertaining, often witty. And although there are errors of detail and lapses of memory, Wagner is not concerned to draw a veil over embarrassing moments or deliberately to falsify the record for the benefit of his 'image' for posterity.

In September 1864 Wagner had vowed to Ludwig that he would make the completion of *The Ring* his prime task. Now, almost a year later, he had got no further than doing a fair copy of the score of the first act of *Siegfried* and beginning to score the second. However, alongside the dictation of *Mein Leben*, he did produce, to the King's great pleasure, a lengthy prose draft for *Parsifal*, a subject which, linked in legend and in spiritual theme to *Lohengrin*, had lain dormant in his mind for the past twenty years. Thus there were now three entirely separate subjects, in varying stages of evolution, awaiting their musical consummation: the completion of *Siegfried* and the composition of *Götterdämmerung*, to finish *The Ring*; *Die Meistersinger*, of which only the overture, the beginning of Act One and the prelude to Act Three had been written; and *Parsifal*, as yet only a sketch.

Also written specifically with the King in mind was an essay *Was ist deutsch? (What is German?)*, an idealistic statement, with the broad, tendentious, often inaccurate historical sweep typical of Wagner in this pose, of the cultural values that Germany should embrace in order to achieve national greatness. The paradigm of these values, says Wagner, is Johann Sebastian Bach, who proved that greatness lies in the pursuit of the beautiful and the noble innate in the national culture, not in the cultivation of a fashionable success based on the imitation of short-lived foreign attractions. Moreover, this beauty and nobility, witness Bach again, exist for their own sake, not as means for acquiring fame and profit. Lurking at the back of Wagner's mind is the same pseudo-thought as in *Music and the Jews*: greatness can be achieved only through the assertion of indigenous national values, the German *Geist*. Everything alien to this *Geist* – the French cult of ostentation, the infiltration of Jews into positions of influence, the abuse of the concept of 'democracy', misunderstood and turned into something thoroughly un-German, the false gods worshipped by the press – must be eradicated.

Like his essays of the 1840s and 1850s, *What is German?* seeks to rouse his countrymen from their lethargy and make them aware that it is not enough to bask in the comforting knowledge that they have inherited the tradition of Goethe and Schiller, Bach and Beethoven. They must fight to preserve and redefine the meaning of this inheritance, and in so doing, learn what it means to be the German *Volk*. It is the same Wagner who in 1849 had defined *Volk* as 'The epitome of all who feel a collective need.' We have since learned where an idealism expressed in such terms can lead, when it becomes the slogan of a demonic national leader.

In August Wagner spent three weeks at the King's hunting lodge by the Walchensee, in the foothills of the Bavarian Alps, and in November the King invited him to his castle of Hohenschwangau, where a special music room was provided for him. Here the two men spent a blissfully happy week together, walking in the mountains, composing poems of homage to each other, discussing plans for the future artistic life of their kingdom, living an unreal life in a real world. Ludwig made still more funds available for his ever-needy friend to settle old debts which had apparently still not been cleared up. This time it was a matter of what Wagner blithely called a 'loan' of 40,000 guilders. Pfistermeister and Bavarian treasury officials, who already knew that loan and gift meant the same to Wagner, strenuously opposed the transaction but could not prevent it. Cosima, who had now acquired her own personal right of access to the King and was taking the management of Wagner's affairs more and more into her own hands, presented herself at the treasury on his behalf, expecting to be handed the money in notes. 'But to my utter astonishment,' she afterwards wrote to the King, 'I was told that I could not have paper money and would have to take coins.' Cosima was a cool, resourceful woman, quite equal to dealing with this deliberate attempt to embarrass her. She immediately sent for two cabs, had the heavy sacks of silver coins loaded into them and driven to Wagner's house in the Briennerstrasse. A few weeks later he asked for, and was granted, an increase in his annual stipend from 4,000 guilders to 8,000. For the three-and-a-half years from May 1864, when he first came to Munich, till the end of 1867, eighteen months or so after he had been living in Tribschen, he received an impressive total of some 130,000 guilders, according to Ernest Newman's calculations. And this was far from being the end.

It was, however, almost the end of the privileged position he had enjoyed in Munich. Shrugging off the occasional fit of pique on the King's part, the romantic relationship continued in all its extravagance and idealism, but the anti-Wagner campaign was gaining ground. Not only the officials and the politicians were planning his downfall. More and more of the inhabitants of Munich, seeing for themselves the remarkable fixation of their young King and the growing influence of his mentor-cum-protégé, felt provoked to express their irreverent disapproval. Remembering Ludwig I's affair with Lola Montez, they dubbed Wagner 'Lolus' and 'Lolotte', adding overtones of homosexuality and effeminacy to the charge that, like his grandfather, their adolescent ruler was ruining the country in his slavish devotion to a self-seeking adventurer. Nor were they so blind as not to observe that something was afoot between this adventurer and the wife of the recently-appointed Court Kapellmeister.

Earlier in the year an anonymous article had appeared in the *Augsburger Allgemeine Zeitung* under the title 'Richard Wagner and Public Opinion', condemning Wagner's prodigal ways and urging the King to give him up. Shortly after his return to Munich from the week in Hohenschwangau the Munich paper *Der Volksbote* openly accused him of seeking to oust Pfistermeister in order to get his hands on the wealth of the Bavarian treasury. Incensed by this accusation, and failing to sense the trap that had been laid for him, he incautiously published a heated counter-attack against leading Court officials in the *Neueste Nachrichten* three days later, claiming that the King unfailingly supported him in his work for the musical life of Bavaria.

The King, saddened by his protégé's headstrong tactlessness, yet unshakable in his sense of duty and propriety, now had little choice. 'Your Majesty stands at a fateful parting of the ways,' wrote Graf Ludwig von der Pfordten, the Bavarian Prime Minister,

and has to choose between the love and respect of his faithful citizens and the so-called 'friendship' of Richard Wagner. This man . . . is despised by every section of the community, to which alone the throne can turn for support. He is despised not only for his democratic attitudes, which the democrats themselves scorn, but for his ingratitude and treachery towards his friends and benefactors, his wanton extravagance and self-indulgent squandering, and the shamelessness with which he exploits the undeserved favour of Your Majesty.

The cabinet threatened to resign if Wagner were not removed. In December, sorrowfully, assuring him of his eternal loyalty, Ludwig sent a message to him by Johann Lutz, a secretary to the cabinet, banishing him from Bavaria for a period of six months. 'Believe me, my dear friend,' he wrote the following day, 'I had to act as I did. My love for you will never die, and I beg you to retain for ever your friendship for me, for I can say with a clear conscience that I am worthy of it.'

Three days later, early on the dark, cold morning of 10 December, accompanied by Franz Mrazeck, the servant he had brought from Penzing, and his old dog Pohl, Wagner took his leave of Cosima (Bülow was out of town on a concert tour), Porges and Cornelius at the station. 'Wagner looked like a ghost,' wrote Cornelius in his diary: 'pale, distraught, his long, lank hair looking quite grey . . . Cosima had completely broken down.'

He took the train to Switzerland, for his second exile there – first Berne, then Vevey, on Lake Geneva, then near Geneva itself. Here he rented a country villa called Les Artichauts – the King, he knew, would pay – and turned, after an interval of four years, to the first act of *Die Meistersinger*. He seemed to have shed his humiliation and the temporary frustration of his ambitions. Behind him, in Munich, he left a broken man living only for the day when he could return. That day never came.

It was a winter of separations: of Ludwig from Wagner, of Wagner from Cosima, and of Minna from Wagner – for ever. On 25 January 1866, after years of a gradually worsening heart condition, she died of a stroke. They had last seen each other in November 1862. She had clung to her hopelessly broken marriage to the end, knowing that it could never be restored but refusing to accept a divorce. Her ill-health she attributed to the suffering that her husband had inflicted on her, but where another might have washed his hands of the responsibility, Wagner never failed to send money for her upkeep, and as late as 1863 he assured Natalie, her daughter, that he would never divorce her. He continued to write from Munich through 1864 and 1865, and made a quarterly allowance to Natalie herself. As to Wagner the artist, Minna considered he had been great only so long as he had lived with her: he had reached his peak with *Rienzi* and *Die fliegende Holländer*, she maintained, while *Tristan*, which had taken him an age to complete, and *Die Meistersinger*, which looked as though it would never be finished, represented his decline. Her personal arch-enemy had always been 'the Wesendonk woman'; Cosima she called 'common', and Bülow was no better. She was determined to live on her sorrow till the end.

The news of Minna's death was cabled to Wagner by Dr Pusinelli via Cosima in Munich. He could have reached Dresden in time for the funeral but, whatever the reasons, he did not try, and the arrangements were left to Natalie. A few days afterwards his old dog Pohl also died, and he was beside himself with grief. Wrapping the body in a coverlet and ordering a special coffin, he went through a burial ritual bizarre in its pathos, a display of devotion which one is tempted to interpret as a surrogate act of mourning for the wife whose body he had not followed to its last resting-place.

Minna's memory still haunted Wagner long afterwards. Cosima describes in her diary in August 1870 a dream he had. Minna appeared in front of them, making offensive remarks; the only way he could answer back was to shout at her: 'Go away! You're dead!' 'So loud was his shout,' said Cosima, 'that it woke him up.'

Two things now mattered to Wagner above all else, the one inseparable from the other: the peace in which to work on *Die Meistersinger* and *The Ring*; and the constant presence of Cosima. In letter after letter Ludwig poured out his yearning to have his dear friend back in Munich the moment the political agitation had subsided, but the prospect of returning to the atmosphere of animosity and resentment he had just left became more and more disagreeable to Wagner the longer he considered it. His projected Festival Theatre, moreover, could as well be built elsewhere in Bavaria. 'I have not given up hope,' wrote Ludwig, almost in desperation, 'better times will come, everything will quieten down here, my Friend will return and inspire me with his presence, we shall go forward with our artistic plans, the Music School will be founded, the Festival Theatre will rise in unimaginable splendour and pride . . . I implore you, let a few months go by, then a great deal will have changed.' But Wagner was set on his creative independence and had no intention of going back.

Cosima and her eldest daughter Daniela arrived at Les Artichauts in March. On a trip through Switzerland soon afterwards, which took them to Lausanne, Berne and Interlaken, they saw on the lakeside near Lucerne a lonely villa, large, somewhat neglected and uninhabited. It was called Tribschen, and it belonged to a certain Colonel Walter am Rhyn. Wagner found it ideal. Ludwig sent a gift of 5,000 francs to cover the first year's rent, that for subsequent years being met from the proceeds of the sale of his Munich house in the Briennerstrasse, which Ludwig had given into his personal possession. The completion of *Die Meistersinger* and *Siegfried*, Acts One and Two of *Götterdämmerung*, the *Siegfried Idyll*, the essays *Beethoven*, *Über das Dirigieren (On Conducting)*, *Deutsche Kunst und Deutsche Politik (German Art and German Politics)*, *Über die Bestimmung der Oper (On the Destiny of Opera)* – this was the harvest of the six years at Tribschen, years that were among the most settled and contented of Wagner's whole life.

As a structure, Tribschen is a near-square, plain, three-storey house with medium-sized, somewhat low-ceilinged rooms leading one into the other. But its situation, on a raised promontory overlooking the Lake of Lucerne, is breathtakingly beautiful. Tall trees surround the estate, and the windows of the salon, in which Wagner's Erard stood, look north and east to the angular mountains on the other side of the water. 'Wherever I turn when I go out of my house,' he wrote to Ludwig, 'I find myself in a magic world. I know of no more beautiful place on earth, no place where I feel more at ease.' True to his life-style, he engaged a governess for Cosima's children and six domestic servants; equally true to his love of animals he offered asylum to two dogs, a horse, Cosima's two peacocks (called Wotan and Fricka) and a number of sheep and chickens; later a brace of golden pheasants and a cat joined the menagerie.

After making a few internal alterations to the house, with Colonel am Rhyn's consent, Wagner furnished the rooms in his usual Baroque taste, lavish rather than discreet, with pink satins and brocades predominating. He himself dressed in corresponding finery – a shirt of fine linen and lace with a light blue satin cravat, black velvet coat, black satin knee-breeches, black silk stockings and the broad black velvet beret familiar from so many portraits. Rising at seven, he would work on *Die Meistersinger* through the morning; lunch was at one, followed by a walk, sometimes including a call at one of his regular inns in Lucerne. Back at Tribschen, he resumed work at five or six, until a family supper at eight; the rest of the evening he spent either dictating *Mein Leben* to Cosima, reading with her, or playing the piano and singing in his characteristically uninhibited manner.

Cosima joined Wagner at Tribschen with her husband's two daughters – Daniela, aged four, and Blandine, aged three – and the baby Isolde in May, a week or so before his fifty-third birthday. At midday on his birthday itself the servant announced that a gentleman giving his name as 'Walther von Stolzing' had arrived at the door. It was Ludwig. A flurry of telegrams had preceded his arrival, and his aide-de-camp Prince Paul von Thurn and Taxis had already come to Tribschen two days before to prepare the ground, but the climax of this piece of romantic play-acting, the reunion of the two friends after a separation of five months, was a moving moment for both of them.

Ludwig stayed two days and returned to Schloss Berg with Prince Paul, incognito as he had come, strengthened in spirit by the precious hours spent in Wagner's and Cosima's company. The news of his escapade caused great indignation in Munich. How, people demanded, could a ruler indulge in such frivolous behaviour, above all in the house of an overbearing, self-centred bankrupt who had seduced him into underwriting his huge past debts and his grandiose future projects, and of the shameless woman who was living with him in sin? Were these the voices to which a King should be listening, particularly at a moment of political tension?

The tension was real enough. Since the Danish war of 1864 Bismarck's onward march towards making Prussia undisputed leader of Germany had been inexorably leading to a confrontation with Austria. Bavaria, the largest of the remaining states, was geographically contiguous with Austria, was also Catholic and had shared close linguistic and cultural traditions with it since the beginnings of German Christianity. There was no question of Bavaria siding with Prussia – no German state did, in fact, when war broke out in June 1866 – but hope lingered in some quarters that she might remain neutral. In the event she joined the war on the side of Austria and shared in its defeat after a mere four weeks of fighting. More than once the King talked of abdicating and leaving Munich, both before and after the Bavarian defeat at Kissingen, but this was less a political response – he still enjoyed the affection of the common people – than the expression of his loneliness away from Wagner.

In his role as self-appointed advisor to the King, Wagner counselled patience, but proceeding, as he always did, from what the furtherance of his own interests demanded, he displayed a remarkable ambivalence in the face of the conflict of policies between Bismarck and Ludwig. At one moment, knowing that he would never settle in Berlin and that the establishment of his Festival Theatre, wherever it turned out to be, rested on the patronage of his royal friend alone, he would urge an independent political line for Bavaria. Refusing to influence Ludwig to join Bismarck, he wrote to Dr François Wille, his old Zurich friend: 'Ludwig will only learn what is really in Germany's interests when Bismarck and other bad, thoroughly un-German creatures have completely disappeared. Under no circumstances will I, or can I, countenance the implication of the young King of Bavaria in such policies.' Barely a week later, however, seeing that Bismarck's pan-German juggernaut would not be stopped, and deeply conscious of the identity between his art and the florescence of 'Germany' in the fullest sense, he threw his weight behind the Prussian solution: 'If you *must* engage in politics,' he wrote to Röckel, 'follow Bismarck and Prussia. As God is my witness, I can see no alternative.'

Politics and the Austro-Prussian War may have dominated the external framework of Bavarian life, but Munich society continued to wax indignant over what they saw as Wagner's influence over their young King, and to gossip about the scandalous Wagner-Cosima-Bülow triangle in whose existence Ludwig alone, it seemed, refused to believe. Indeed, the King was now induced by the most shameless deception on the part of Wagner and Cosima to issue an extraordinary public declaration in the form of a letter to Bülow affirming his absolute confidence in Cosima's honour. 'As I have been in a position to obtain the most intimate knowledge of the noble character of your honoured lady,' he wrote, 'it only remains for me to discover the inexplicable reasons for these criminal insults, so that, having obtained the clearest insight into this outrageous conduct, I may see that the strictest justice is meted out to the offenders.'

The source of this 'most intimate knowledge', of course, was Wagner. When the citizens of Munich had finished seething at the offensive stupidity of Wagner and Cosima and gaping at the boundless gullibility of Ludwig, they could only start to worry about the sanity of the monarch in whose hands the fate of their country lay.

Bülow was already living with Wagner and Cosima at Tribschen when the King's letter was published. Possibly he thought that this would make the *ménage* look respectable and give credence to Ludwig's declaration, but he must have been a willing party to the whole affair at least by this time, and probably from far earlier. Powerless to influence the relationship between his wife and Wagner, he had an infatuation with Wagner's music which overrode everything and offered him the sublimation of his personal grief. In Munich he enjoyed respect as a musician but not affection. He was fanatically industrious, moody, easily angered and easily tired, with a caustic tongue; his aristocratic Prussian origins, like his Protestantism, also struck a jarring note in many circles, while his promotion of the 'progressive' music of Wagner and Liszt in his capacity as *Kapellmeister* hardly endeared him to the cultural establishment.

At Tribschen Wagner the musical sorcerer again caught Bülow in his spell. Bitter, miserable, anxious to get away from Munich – later in the year he went to Basle as pianist and teacher – Bülow spent two disconsolate months in the summer watching the relationship between his idol and his wife flourish as the dictated pages of *Mein Leben* accumulated. Yet he could not resist the glories of *Die Meistersinger*, to which Wagner was now devoting his full energies. 'All that is ideal and worth preserving in the German spirit lives in this one mind,' he wrote. He was persuaded to return to Munich next year as director of the projected Bavarian Conservatoire which Wagner had urged the King to establish, and it was he who proudly conducted the first performance of *Die Meistersinger* in Munich in 1868.

Another who joined the Wagner 'team' at this time was a young horn player from Vienna called Hans Richter, later to become conductor of the first *Ring* cycle in 1876. Wagner engaged the blonde, curly-haired Richter as a secretary and copyist, installing him in a room at the top of the house and treating him as a member of the family.

As the year 1867 came, work on *Die Meistersinger* was moving slowly but smoothly ahead. By the beginning of March the orchestral sketch of all three acts was complete, leaving only the scoring to be done. Only in the seclusion of Tribschen could he work like this: to return to Munich, though he knew the King desperately desired it, would be fatal, though he dared not say so. The month before, on 17 February, Eva, Wagner's and Cosima's second child, was born. Bülow, who can hardly have believed that the child was his, travelled the short distance from Basle to Lucerne that afternoon and went to the house. Approaching Cosima's bedside, he said to her: 'Je pardonne.' Cosima replied: 'Il ne faut pas pardonner, il faut comprendre.'

Like Isolde, Eva was publicly christened as the daughter of Hans and Cosima von Bülow. But unlike Isolde, she was raised as a Wagner, and it was as Eva Wagner that she married the English, later naturalized German, cultural philosopher Houston Stewart Chamberlain, whose book *Foundations of the Nineteenth Century*, which claimed that all the great cultural figures of history were of Aryan racial stock, became a canonical text in Nazi Germany. Circumstances such as these have since been drawn into the consolidated argument, often peddled with more zeal than discernment, that would make Wagner into a forerunner of Hitler.

In 1911 Eva received, as a present, the diary that her mother kept over the last fourteen years of her life with Wagner, from 1869 to 1883. Clearly intending to keep the contents of this diary secret as long as possible, Eva presented the papers to the Richard-Wagner-Gedenk-stätte in Bayreuth, with instructions that they were to be held sealed until thirty years after her death. She died in 1942. After years of legal wrangles between the Wagner family and the town of Bayreuth, starting long before the thirty years expired, the diaries were finally opened in 1974 and published in 1976 and 1977, one hundred years after the events, the personalities, the arguments and the emotions they record. Cosima does not reveal any skeletons that have been hanging in the Wagner family cupboard for a century, but no story of the life of Richard Wagner can now be written without this evidence, and it is an absorbing, often moving tale that Cosima tells. The circumstances surrounding our one hundred years' wait to see it – indeed, the doubt whether, had the Wagner family at Wahnfried won its case against the Bavarian authorities, we should have been allowed to see it in full, unexpurgated form at all – have the quality of a novel in their colourful intensity. In this, as in so many other episodes of the Bayreuth saga, the larger-than-life hero has ensured the survival of his larger-than-life image into posterity.

* * *

From time to time Wagner went to Munich or Schloss Berg to be received in audience by the King for a discussion of political matters and of the production of his works. Not that the surface of their relationship always remained unruffled. For a performance at the Court Opera of his favourite *Lohengrin*, for instance, prepared at his own ardent request, Ludwig insisted that the faithful Tichatschek, whom Wagner had chosen for the title role, should be replaced by a younger man; Tichatschek was now sixty, and although his voice still had much of its fine ringing quality, he did not look like the dashing young knight of Ludwig's vision. So, going directly against Wagner's wishes, Ludwig discharged Tichatschek and engaged Heinrich Vogl in his place. Wagner thereupon went back to Tribschen in a huff and did not attend the performance. Later in the year the King intervened to prevent the publication in the government-sponsored *Süddeutsche Presse* of any more instalments of Wagner's *German Art and German Politics*, the anti-French tone of which was proving embarrassing to the Bavarian government, and this too roused Wagner's indignation. But a further audience, a pacifying, even apologetic letter from the King, and harmony was restored.

The Wagner-Cosima-Bülow triangle now brought back to the scene a figure who had receded into the background some years earlier and seemed likely to stay there – Cosima's father, Franz Liszt. Liszt, now the Abbé Liszt, a secular priest, had been living in Rome for the past six years. In August 1867 he paid an extended visit to Germany, attending a music festival at Meiningen, conducting his oratorio *The Legend of Saint Elizabeth* at the Wartburg castle, and arriving in Munich the following month with the evident purpose of discussing with his daughter and her husband the whole Wagner question. A few weeks afterwards he went to Tribschen.

'Visit by Liszt: dreaded it, but proved pleasurable,'

noted Wagner in his *Annals*, autobiographical notes covering the years 1864 to 1868. Since 1861, in Weimar, the two men had seen each other only once – at Starnberg in 1864. But at Tribschen much of the old rapport was recaptured, Wagner singing from the newly finished parts of *Die Meistersinger* and Liszt accompanying him from the manuscript of the score. Whatever passed between them on the subject of Cosima, and whatever equivocal arguments she herself may have produced in her defence, could not shake Liszt's loyalty to his daughter. This loyalty, however, implied both tolerance of her adultery and an acceptance of Bülow's degradation, neither of which he could condone. Nor did the fact that both he and his daughter were Catholics make the situation any easier. His estrangement from Wagner in recent years is reflected in the fact that, to judge from the published correspondence, no letters passed between them from 1861 until 1872, when Wagner invited his father-in-law – as he had then become – to the laying of the foundation stone of the Bayreuth Festival Theatre. His visit to Tribschen left little mark on the domestic situation, and the triangle remained as triangular as before. He saw neither his daughter nor Wagner again for another five years.

On 24 October the full score of *Die Meistersinger* was finally finished, and Wagner presented it to the King. The vocal and orchestral scores were engraved by Schott during the spring of 1868, and preparations put in hand for the first performance. Part of his time he spent in Munich attending to these preparations; in Tribschen other activities filled his mind – the dictation of *Mein Leben* during Cosima's stays (she was sometimes there, sometimes at the Bülow house in Munich), a new edition of the pamphlet *Opera and Drama*, first published in 1851, plans for an edition of his complete writings in ten volumes, a memoir on the late Ludwig Schnorr von

Carolsfeld, and the publication in book form of his serialized articles under the title *German Art and German Politics*.

This work, in some ways a kind of political counterpart to *Die Meistersinger*, reveals the increasingly nationalistic tendency of Wagner's thinking, a tendency promoted by the contemporary political theorist Konstantin Frantz, whose federal, pan-Germanic ideal, anti-Semitic slant and rose-hued vision of a Christian Germany great through its recognition of its true spiritual vocation, reinforced many of Wagner's own thoughts and prejudices. Wagner makes liberal play in his book with dangerous, evocative words like *Geist* and *Volk*, appealing to the idealism, the force of regeneration and the sense of vocation and destiny to which Germans over the centuries have enthusiastically, and sometimes disastrously, responded. More specifically, he again links the Germans with the Greeks, as in *Art and Revolution* and other writings of that period, but now also seeks to delineate the German psyche by setting it against the materialism and pragmatism of the French, the Germans' arch-enemies. This leads him to become involved in a confused mass of observations on Church and State, on education, on culture, on the responsibilities of a ruling monarch and other matters on which he could give little useful advice but a great deal of offence. Finally, returning to subjects on which his views are at their most challenging, he again points to the theatre as the ideal medium for the reform of national culture, a theatre pledged to supreme performances of supreme works. For if the theatre is an institution for moral and cultural regeneration, the natural way to achieve its aim lies through the presentation of the highest values of both substance and form; the public will respond as readily to the great as to the mediocre, and should not be fobbed off with the tawdry and the second-rate.

Behind these noble sentiments and plans of action,

never named but ever present, looms the shadow of Bayreuth. Here the pressures of the commercial theatre would no longer apply; here the supreme works would receive their supreme performances; here the new moral and cultural vitality of the German nation would be forged. Wagner's criticisms of the art of his day, and of the society of which that art was the expression, like his presuppositions and his often dubious historical analogies, had changed little since the 1840s. But now, twenty years later, the power to realize his revolutionary vision was almost within his grasp.

The first performance of *Die Meistersinger*, the triumphant expression of the national values that underlie *German Art and German Politics*, was one of the greatest successes of Wagner's whole career. He had been involved in every aspect of the production, demonstrating in rehearsal the gestures and movements he required from his actors, advising Bülow, the conductor, matching stage movements to orchestral score and impressing a sense of drama on his performers and technicians. At the première in the Munich Hoftheater on 21 June 1868 the King took his lonely place in the royal box and in the auditorium were admirers – and enemies – of Wagner's music from many parts of Europe. From his past, still faithful to his genius, came Jessie Laussot and Mathilde Maier, together with the colourful Malwida von Meysenbug, who travelled to Munich from Florence. Spontaneous applause broke out at many points in the performance, and at the end of each act the King beckoned Wagner to come into the royal box and bow to the acclaim from there – 'like Horace at the side of Augustus', Bülow is said to have remarked.

As always, of course, sounds of bewilderment and scorn were heard in certain quarters. The sharp-tongued Hanslick, caricatured in the figure of the pedant Beckmesser, deplored the 'shapeless melodizing' that had been made to take the place of 'independent, articulated melodies', and 'the deliberate dissolution of all fixed forms into a form-less, intoxicating sea of sound'. This is made worse by the 'skinny little plot' that is made to bear the weight of all this music: the result is 'tiresome', 'awkward', 'contrived', 'an abnormality'. In sum: 'The work that has been presented to us is not the creation of a real musical genius but that of an ingenious, chameleonic mind, half-poet, half musi-cian.' It recalls Hanslick's comment on *Tristan*: 'There is music in it – but it is not music'.

Actually *Die Meistersinger* far from 'dissolves all fixed forms', and the famous 'endless melody' is much less endless than in *Tristan*. The work is thoroughly diatonic, a fundamentally 'C-major' opera, and this diatonicism has its formal complement in the two basic musical forms in the work: the march and the song. The march symbolizes order, stability, tradition – the world of the medieval guild of Mastersingers, secure, noble, proud, conscious of tradi-tion and responsibility, but at the same time the world of nineteenth-century Germany, with its aspirations to natio-nal unity and strength. The superb March of the Masters with which the Overture begins is the perfect example. The song symbolizes creative inspiration, lyrical express-ion, the world of art and the emotions – the world of Walther von Stolzing's Prize Song, one of the most famous of all Wagner's melodies.

But all art, however original, rests on principles of order, as Walther is made to discover for himself – so the song moves towards the march. Likewise order and tradition will atrophy, become meaningless if they are not re-lived, re-created by successive generations – so the march absorbs the freshness of the song. This musical synthesis matches the other syntheses in the work – of the medieval and the modern, of art as art and art as craft, of art and life, of originality and discipline, of the love of Walther and Eva as fulfilment and the love of Hans Sachs as renunciation and self-abnegation. The Overture alone, with its rich contrapuntal texture and its radiant scoring, conveys in microcosm all these syntheses and stood for a long while, appropriately, as the only completed part of the opera.

While the psychological nuances conveyed in the orchestral score are as subtle in their different ways as those in *Tristan*, the voice reigns supreme in *Die Meistersinger* as in *Tristan* and *The Ring* it does not – the songs, the quintet in the penultimate scene, and above all the choruses, in the classical operatic tradition, most notably that in praise of 'our noble German art' at the end of the whole work. This assertion of the human over the instrumental, like the diatonic over the chromatic, merges with the genial good-humour that infuses the action to make *Die Meistersinger* the most accessible of Wagner's great music dramas, and the one to which even many in the anti-Wagner camp grant grudging approval.

The remainder of 1868 brought Wagner little musical reward and little personal satisfaction. He still could not bring himself to make a start on the final act of *Siegfried*; *Mein Leben* progressed by fits and starts. Towards the end of the year he wrote a memoir on Rossini, who died in Paris in November, and in a fit of totally irrational and baseless hatred, apparently provoked by a self-induced fantasy of an international Jewish conspiracy against him and his music, prepared a re-issue of *Music and the Jews*, this time in his own name. This only brought him more enemies and put a greater strain on his friends; even Bülow and Cosima – the latter yielded to no-one in her anti-Semitism – disapproved of his action.

He also fell out with two old friends. One was Heinrich Laube, the editor and journalist who had commissioned his *Autobiographical Sketch* of 1842 and helped him over many a financial crisis in Paris. An influential figure in the Viennese dramatic world, Laube had his eye on the directorship of the Munich theatre and expected Wagner to put in a judicious word on his behalf. But Wagner had his reservations, and when Laube translated his grudge into an attack on *Die Meistersinger*, Wagner refused to have any more to do with him. The other was his old revolutionary comrade August Röckel, who had settled in Munich after serving his imprisonment and chose this moment to join in the spicy popular gossip about Wagner and Cosima. In both cases it was personal touchiness that sparked off his anger – the inability to tolerate the slightest criticism and to interpret it as other than an act of unforgivable disloyalty. The cost of total egocentricity is high.

What Röckel, to Wagner's anger, had been repeating about him and Cosima was only what the whole of Munich, except the King, apparently, had known for years. But now Ludwig too began to realize that both his hero and the wife of his Hofkapellmeister had been deceiving him all this time. In September and October the lovers went on holiday in Switzerland and Italy; by the time they returned, Cosima had made her decision. In November, taking Isolde and Eva with her, she left Bülow and went to Tribschen for good. Over eighteen months were to pass before he finally agreed to divorce her and before she and Wagner were formally married.

Even before Cosima's final departure from Munich the King's disillusionment had become evident. He refused Wagner an audience at Hohenschwangau and wrote no letter to him for three months afterwards.

Unsettled by Ludwig's displeasure and offended at being denied a personal meeting, Wagner made an impulsive and unusual decision to visit his family and the scenes of his childhood. Taking the train from Munich, he made for Leipzig, spending a week there with his sister Ottilie, wife of the Orientalist Professor Hermann Brockhaus. Wagner's family ties could not be described as strong, but he did write from time to time to all three of his elder sisters, as well as to his step-sister Cäcilie, especially at moments when the world threatened him with more than his usual share of disillusionment and bitterness. Shortly before, in fact, he had written in just such a tone to his sister Klara Wolfram, and now he found in Ottilie a similar audience.

Only a few close family friends were permitted to know that Wagner was in Leipzig, among them Friedrich Ritschl, Professor of Classical Philology at the university. Ritschl's wife happened to remark one evening after Wagner had played parts of *Die Meistersinger* to the company, that she had already heard this music through one of her husband's students, a young man known as a passionate admirer of Wagner's music. This so intrigued Wagner that he had the young man invited to the house for dinner the following evening. His name was Friedrich Nietzsche.

The next day the twenty-four-year-old Nietzsche described in a letter to his friend and fellow-Classicist Erwin Rohde this first meeting with the man who was first a god, then a devil to him, the man, over thirty years his senior, with whom he established a love-hate relationship which holds the essence of the whole Wagner phenomenon:

I was introduced to Richard [sic!] and murmured a few words of homage. He questioned me very closely about how I had come to know his music, waxed highly abusive about all performances of his operas except the famous ones in Munich, and made fun of those conductors who call out to the orchestra in a languid voice: 'Gentlemen, some passion, please!' Or: 'A little more passion, my fine fellows!' He likes putting on a Saxon accent. Before and after dinner he played the key passages from the *Mastersingers*, singing all the vocal parts with great verve and thoroughly enjoying himself. He is a wonderfully lively, passionate man; he talks very quickly, is very witty and provides splendid entertainment for a private gathering of this kind . . . Afterwards he read to us a part of his autobiography – a delightful episode from his student days in Leipzig which still makes me laugh when I think of it. He writes extremely skilfully and wittily.

Nietzsche, a native of Saxony, like Wagner, was the son of a Protestant pastor who died when Nietzsche was only five, of what doctors diagnosed as 'softening of the brain'. Inheriting this cerebral weakness, Nietzsche suffered already in his schooldays from severe pains in the head and eyes, which forced him at one stage to leave school altogether. Dark-haired, thick-set, disturbingly intense and with a piercing gaze, he studied Classics under Ritschl at the University of Bonn but quickly gave himself over to the joys of Romantic music, above all Beethoven and Schumann. He also began to compose himself. In 1865 he followed Ritschl to Leipzig, where, in the autumn of 1868, he had the great spiritual experience of his life, the shattering experience from whose effects he never recovered – a performance of the Prelude to *Tristan und Isolde*. 'I cannot control my emotions sufficiently to judge this music coolly and critically,' he wrote excitedly to the faithful Erwin Rohde. 'Every nerve in my body trembles. Not for a long while have I experienced such a lasting feeling of bliss and rapture.' Now, six months later, he found himself face to face with the composer of that devastating music.

Wagner was greatly taken by his young admirer and at once sensed that here was someone who spoke his own language. Their minds met, not in any practical musical context but in an area of Schopenhauerian speculation – on the dominance of the cosmos by irrational romantic forces which were apperceived through the experience of music. Nietzsche, young as he was, had already trodden these paths in an essay called *The Daemonic in Music*, written at the age of nineteen. From the spring of the following year, after his appointment as Professor of Classics in Basle, he became a regular visitor to Tribschen, sharing the movements of Wagner's mind, conceiving a mad infatuation for Cosima, and making himself the historian of a spiritual development in which Wagner represented, first the glorious culmination of nineteenth-century musical Romanticism, but ultimately the most dangerous and destructive manifestation of all that this intensely German Romanticism stood for.

In this same spring 1869, Wagner finished scoring the first two acts of *Siegfried* and at last began the composition sketch of the third act. 'Towards midday,' wrote Cosima in her diary on 23 February, 'R. brought me the manuscript of the two acts of *Siegfried*. Indescribable happiness! I thanked him, but he said: "Everything is yours, even before I write it."' Cosima did, indeed, influence the course of Wagner's operas on more than one occasion. At the conclusion of *Die Meistersinger*, for instance, against his original intention to end with the Prize Song and its triumphant reception by the assembly, she urged him to retain Hans Sachs's final speech ('Verachtet mir die Meister nicht').

In June Wagner's and Cosima's third child, Siegfried, was born. 'The sun had just risen behind the Rigi mountain,' wrote Cosima, 'and cast its first rays into the room, proclaiming the most radiant of Sundays. Towards six o'clock R. was allowed in to see me and told me how profoundly moved he was. I was filled with a feeling of joy and happiness, and that fate had now presented us with a son gave us a sense of the most profound comfort.'

A week after the birth of Siegfried Cosima made her formal, long inevitable decision. In a long letter to the sick, unhappy Bülow, whose personal life lay in ruins and whose position as a centre of gossip and criticism in Munich had become so unbearable that he had submitted his resignation as Kapellmeister, she begged him to agree to a divorce. Two days later, with dignity, yet close to desperation, he granted her wish. Calling Cosima and Wagner the two inspirations of his life – 'I might also name your father,' he added – he preserved his dignity in the midst of his shame and suffering: 'You have preferred to devote your life and your incomparable mind and affection to one who is my superior, and far from blaming you, I approve of your action from every point of view and admit that you are perfectly right.' He concluded: 'May God protect and bless the mother of the happy children to whom she will continue to devote herself.' The divorce was legalized in Berlin a little over a year later.

The marriage of Hans and Cosima von Bülow had been as impossible, though in a different way, as that of Richard and Minna Wagner; indeed, it had been a shared unhappiness in their marriages that had first drawn Wagner and Cosima together. Bülow, for both physical and psychological reasons, was a difficult man, and he knew it; he had a weak constitution, suffered from a variety of nervous ailments, was pathologically sensitive and easily upset. His gratitude for Cosima's forbearance was genuine, and however great the suffering and humiliation that she and the idol of his musical world had caused him, he had no thought of laying the sole responsibility for the tragedy at their door. That he could never make Cosima happy, or she him, was no reason in his eyes to deny her the company of the genius who could. His whole life seemed like that of a man born to be unhappy.

Bülow and Cosima did not see each other again for eleven years. In 1882, at the age of fifty-two, he married again. His loyalty to Wagner's music never faltered; he even donated 40,000 marks, the proceeds of a concert-tour, to the fund set up to cover the deficit after the first Bayreuth Festival of 1876. The news of the Master's death in 1883 shattered him. When, a few days later, he heard that Cosima herself was close to death as she mourned her husband, refusing to eat or to be comforted, he sent her a telegram that has become famous. It said, simply and nobly: 'Soeur, il faut vivre.'

Bülow died in 1894, eleven years after his Master. Cosima, she of the iron will and single-minded devotion to the cause of her husband's music, lived until 1930.

While Wagner was working on the completion of *Siegfried*, preparations were under way in Munich, on the King's orders, for the staging of *Das Rheingold*. A production of this first part of *The Ring*, together with the second part, *Die Walküre*, had formed part of the artistic programme drawn up by Wagner and Ludwig during the early days of their association, but it depended, like all such productions, on the collaboration of Wagner's hand-picked assistants, paramount among them Bülow. For Wagner himself the Cosima-Bülow scandal had soured the atmosphere in Munich, and he had no wish to involve himself with anything that went on there. Bülow's resignation also meant the virtual end of his dream of a festival theatre in Munich, built to his own specifications, a model of which had been made by Gottfried Semper. (By a strange coincidence, Semper's Court Theatre in Dresden, scene of the première of *Rienzi* and *Der fliegende Holländer*, was burned down on the day that *Das Rheingold* was first performed in Munich.)

With Bülow's departure young Hans Richter, who had left Tribschen to become chief coach at the Court Theatre two years earlier, was entrusted with conducting *Das Rheingold*. Wagner had ostentatiously refused to take any part in the preparations, but the King had set his mind on the performance and refused to be put off by the Master's prevarications. After the dress rehearsal on 27 August, attended by the King and a specially invited audience of some five hundred, including Liszt, Richter sent a telegram to Tribschen, telling Wagner that the décor and the various mechanical contrivances, such as the system of trolleys by which the swimming of the Rhine Maidens was to be simulated, had proved so ludicrously inefficient that the performance had turned into sheer chaos. The baritone Franz Betz, chosen to sing the part of Wotan, wrote to Wagner in the same vein, and Richter and Betz, incited by Wagner, together threatened to withdraw their services unless matters were put right.

This brazen attempt by Wagner and his circle to prevent *Das Rheingold* being given aroused the King's indignation and brought about Richter's summary dismissal. 'The employees of the theatre are to obey my orders,' he wrote angrily to the court secretary Lorenz von Düfflipp on 30 August, 'and not Wagner's whims. I have never experienced such affrontery in my life.'

On 1 September Wagner arrived in Munich in order either to supervise the rehearsals himself or to thwart the performance. He succeeded in neither. The King refused even to answer his letters, had a new conductor and a new Wotan engaged, and took his place in the royal box for the première on 22 September. Wagner was arrogantly and conspicuously absent. His final outburst had been directed at Franz Wüllner, the conductor: 'I warn you, Sir – keep your hands off my score, or the Devil take you!' The following year Wüllner laid his hands on *Die Walküre* also, again in spite of Wagner's protests, and again in his absence. The King had shown him who was master, and Munich society rejoiced to see him humbled.

But, as Wagner knew and exploited to his full advantage, the King could not bear to live on his anger for long. *Das Rheingold*, the mechanical problems of its staging solved with dazzling ingenuity by one Carl Brandt, whom Wagner later engaged for Bayreuth, was a *succès d'estime*. *Die Walküre*, on the other hand, which followed in June 1870, received a rapturous welcome from an audience that included Saint-Säens, Joachim and Brahms, though

Wagner tried to dissuade his friends from attending an occasion that had not been granted his seal of approval. As the vision of his artistic ideal returned, and with it the memory of those blissful meetings in Schloss Berg, when they had mapped out the Bavarian 'art of the future', the King could bear Wagner's resentment no longer. 'Your ideals are mine,' he wrote in a letter sent to Tribschen: 'my mission in life is to serve you. No man is capable of hurting me, but when you are angry with me, you deal me a death-blow . . . What is the dazzling possession of a throne compared to a friendly letter from you? Believe me, Parzival knows his duty and, once purified, will endure any test.' The master had become the servant again.

With his frustrations behind him and his dominance re-established, Wagner worked steadily on in the tranquillity of Tribschen. He played four-hand arrangements of Hadyn and Mozart symphonies with Cosima, who occupied much of her day with her children, sometimes to Wagner's jealous irritation. But such discords were quickly resolved, and their perfect bliss was restored. 'In the evening Richard and I talked about the secret inner nature of our relationship,' wrote Cosima in her diary, 'how shy yet overwhelming our first meetings had been, how unplanned our first union, how we had both silently thought only of renunciation, and how circumstances and people forced us to realize that our love was truly real and that we could not do without each other.'

In August 1869, to Wagner's great joy, his favourite sister Cäcilie visited Tribschen. It was the first time they had seen each other for twenty-one years, and as they looked together at some old letters of Geyer's to their mother, which had recently come into Cäcilie's hands, Wagner found himself wondering, as so many have done since, whether Geyer was his father. He never seems to have been sure, one way or the other. Nor shall we be.

The orchestral sketch of Act Three of *Siegfried* was finished in the same month as Cäcilie's visit. Then, putting this on one side instead of starting to score it, he turned to *Götterdämmerung*, made the composition sketch for Act One in June 1870 and the orchestral sketch the next month, leaving the instrumentation of *Siegfried* till the following year. The first performance of *Die Meistersinger* in Berlin in April 1870 provoked more hostility than enthusiasm, but in Vienna it was well received, as was *Lohengrin* in Brussels the same year, conducted by Hans Richter.

The art of conducting had exercised the mind of Wagner, the practical musician, since his earliest orchestral compositions and his first professional appointment as chorus master in Würzburg back in 1833. Even if he had never composed a note, his critical essays on composers and their works, on matters of theoretical and practical principle, on interpretation and technique, all products of experience 'in the field', would command our attention. One of the most significant and fascinating of these essays, published in successive weekly issues of the *Neue Zeitschrift für Musik* between November 1869 and January 1870, is *Über das Dirigieren (On Conducting)*. On the one hand it offers a host of insights into contemporary conditions in the world of music – the style and standard of orchestral playing in Germany, France and England, where he had conducted, the training and attitudes of the musicians, fashions and practices in conducting (he disapproved of Mendelssohn's uniformly brisk tempi and almost unrelieved, undramatic *mezzo forte*) and styles of orchestral and operatic performance in general.

At the same time, it shows us how Wagner himself conducted, how he sought the *melos*, the melodic essence, of each theme, each phrase, making the orchestra *sing*, as he himself had learned the art of musical phrasing from listening to the great soprano Wilhelmine Schröder-

Devrient, and how he thereby revealed the inner soul of, say, an Allegro by Mozart, natural, direct, chaste, and an Allegro by Beethoven, powerful, deliberate, passionate. For Allegro is not a fixed, unchanging value but a concept whose meaning is determined by the *melos* of the piece in question. So as the *melos* of a symphonic Allegro by Mozart is different from that of a symphonic Allegro by Beethoven, so the tempo, the dynamics and everything else that the conductor has to decide must necessarily also be different when he comes to interpret the two movements. If he does not feel the *melos*, he will set a wrong tempo and the performance will be ruined. When Wagner conducted the overture to *Tannhäuser* in Dresden, it took twelve minutes; it is not difficult to imagine his reaction when told that a recent performance in Munich had taken twenty. Distinguished modern conductors like Sir Adrian Boult, who takes a little over fourteen minutes, Klemperer (of whose *Fidelio* in 1961 Stravinsky said 'the main tension was in seeing how slow it is possible to conduct without actually stopping'), who takes fourteen-and-a-half, and Hans Knappertsbusch ('He does not beat time, he beats eternity'), who takes fifteen, would have needed to justify themselves to the Master.

The one dissonant element in the harmony of Tribschen was Cosima's feeling of responsibility – not shared by Wagner – for the misery of Hans von Bülow. 'Nowhere can there be such a wretched creature as poor Hans,' she wrote in her diary. 'He feels miserable because I have left him, yet never was I able to give him pleasure, let alone make him happy . . . Our marriage was based on a complete misunderstanding. Yet he would never have lost me if Fate had not brought into my life the man whom it became my unquestionable vocation to live and die for. There is not a single thing for which I can blame him, though the burden of these past years has been almost beyond endurance.'

Bülow himself had by this time settled in Florence and overcome much of his grief, finding solace in the company, among others, of an earlier victim of Wagner's ruthless egocentricity – Jessie Laussot, whom Bülow had known from the days in Dresden when they were pupils of the same piano teacher. He now found the strength to initiate the formalities for his divorce from Cosima, and in July 1870 the marriage was dissolved. On 25 August, at eight o'clock in the morning, Cosima and Wagner were married in the Protestant Matthäus-Kirche in Lucerne, with Hans Richter and Malwida von Meysenbug as witnesses. 'I pray for two things,' said Cosima: 'that I shall always be able to help Richard achieve success and happiness, and that Hans, however far he may be from me, may find peace and contentment.'

Although isolated, by living in Switzerland, from the day-to-day political tensions in Germany, Wagner could not but declare an attitude towards the conflict between France and Prussia which Bismarck had deliberately provoked as the final step to German unification. Political progress in nineteenth-century Germany offered a choice between the idea of liberalism and the idea of nationalism. Some idealists thought they could have both, but if the events of 1848 had not made it clear that they could not, those of 1870 certainly did. Equally clear, even among those sections of the population who would have dearly thought otherwise, such as the Catholics and the working classes, was the realization that the liberal idea would be sacrificed to the nationalist idea, not vice versa. Catholic Bavaria had no wish to throw in its lot with Protestant Prussia, and King Ludwig desperately hoped, up to within a few days of the outbreak of fighting, that he might preserve Bavarian neutrality. But France's declaration of war in July 1870 – announced, ironically, by Emile Ollivier, husband of Cosima's sister Blandine, who had recently been appointed by Napoleon III to head a

Ministry responsible to the French Parliament as well as to the Emperor – closed the issue. The French armies were defeated; an armistice was signed in January 1871, and in the same month the foundation of the Second Reich, Bismarck's memorial to himself, was celebrated in the Hall of Mirrors at Versailles.

Wagner's contribution to the German cause included two embarrassingly trite poems, one in appreciation of King Ludwig's entry into the war by the side of Prussia, the other, 'To the German Army before Paris', a patriotic ode which he sent to Bismarck, who replied with a warm personal note of thanks. To the new Kaiser, William I, King of Prussia, he dedicated an Imperial March (*Kaisermarsch*) with choral finale, written first for military band, then for full orchestra, which caught the mood of pride and confidence appropriate to the early years of the brave new empire.

The patriotic urge that stimulated these ephemera, like his various utterances on the *Volk* and its qualities, did at least have its origin in an ideal conception of new spiritual values for the German nation. But the Franco-Prussian War also provoked him to violent anti-French outbursts, of the kind in which he had already thundered against the Jews – in both cases, be it said, ably seconded by Cosima. He even hoped that Paris would be totally destroyed by the German army: 'If Paris were burned to the ground, it would symbolize the ultimate liberation of the world from the pressure of what is bad.' At the same time – again the parallel of the Jews comes to mind – he had many French friends. Indeed, the writer Catulle Mendès, his wife Judith, Villiers de l'Isle Adam, Saint-Saëns and Duparc, all of them admirers of Wagner's music, were on a visit to Tribschen at the time war was declared, and found themselves subjected to a tirade of abuse about the inadequacies of French culture and the poverty of the French spirit. Yet, embarrassed and offended though they were, none of them deserted him: his genius was too great to abandon because of resentment of his personal behaviour. And the same evening Saint-Saëns accompanied him at the piano as he sang parts of *The Ring* to his sorely tried but deeply impressed audience.

Two works emerged from the confusions, personal and political, of the latter half of the year 1870. One was the beautiful little *Siegfried Idyll*, a perfect gem of Romantic music born in perfect Romantic circumstances. Entirely without her knowledge Wagner quietly elaborated two themes which he had intended some years earlier to use in a string quartet for Cosima, and which had subsequently found their way into Brünnhilde's part in the duet with Siegfried at the end of Act Three of *Siegfried*. Scoring the material for small orchestra – flute, oboe, two clarinets, bassoon, two horns, trumpet and strings – he gave it to Richter to rehearse secretly with a group of musicians in Lucerne (Richter himself took the small trumpet part).

On Christmas morning 1870, Cosima's thirty-third birthday, the players came to Tribschen and silently took up their positions on the stairs and in the hall. Then, to an audience consisting of the spellbound Cosima, her astonished children and Nietzsche, Tribschen's most frequent house guest, Wagner conducted the first performance of his birthday serenade to his wife. In the afternoon the performers played it twice more. The dedication reads: 'Tribschen-Idyll, with Fidi's [i.e. their son Siegfried's] Bird Call and Orange Sunrise [a reference to Cosima's description of the moment when Siegfried was born]. Presented as a Symphonic Birthday Greeting to his Cosima by her Richard, 1870.' It was a sad moment when, in 1877, his financial situation forced him to sell to Schott this intimate family document, so intensely expressive of the relationship between him and Cosima.

Musical greetings of this kind had already become something of a tradition at Tribschen. The previous year,

1869, Hans Richter had come especially from Munich at Cosima's behest just to wake Wagner on his birthday with Siegfried's horn-call at six o'clock in the morning. And for his birthday in 1870 she organized a military band of forty-five musicians to come at eight o'clock in the morning and play his *Huldigungsmarsch* in the grounds of Tribschen. But the occasion of the *Siegfried Idyll* takes pride of place.

The other work was the essay *Beethoven*, on the surface a contribution to the centennial celebrations of Beethoven's birth, in its deeper significance the most profound of Wagner's mature utterances on the philosophy of music and in particular on the relationship between words and melody. The *Gesamtkunstwerk* and the 'work of art of the future', in their original conceptual form, together with the principles laid down in *Opera and Drama*, are now left behind: poetry becomes subordinate, drama becomes the visible counterpart of music, and music, expounded by Wagner in the terminology of Schopenhauer, stands supreme with its unique powers of revelation as the perfect embodiment of cosmic purpose – what Schopenhauer called 'the objectification of the Will'. The world of vision, says Wagner, is fraught with illusion, but the world of sound, directly expressive of nature, embraces true meaning, meaning intuited in the sublime ecstasy of heightened awareness that music induces.

All this is, in effect, a new *apologia pro vita sua* by the Wagner who, having composed *Tristan, Die Meistersinger* and the first three parts of *The Ring*, now sees that, whatever he may have postulated in his theoretical writings of the 1840s and 1850s, it is music that dominates, music by which his artistic achievement stands or falls. He now draws the theoretical consequences of his creative practice: Beethoven, the greatest of composers, merely serves in the essay as a convenient exemplar, a figure with whom he can reveal his profound empathy and in whose line of succession he can set his own music. And as in his youth, in the distant days of *Leubald und Adelaïde* and similar passionate excesses, he now again ranges the giant of music, Beethoven, alongside the giant of drama, Shakespeare, the latter giving visible form, through the power of drama and the word, to the dream-like mysteries enshrined in the sound-world of Beethoven's music.

As a contribution to the Romantic philosophy of music, Wagner's *Beethoven* is on the one hand an idiosyncratic derivative of Schopenhauer's metaphysic, on the other a high-flown rhapsodical allegory of the creative artistic process. It offers nothing new to our understanding of the nature of music, and the notion that there is a mysterious relationship between cosmic meaning and the mathematical proportions inherent in musical sounds goes back to Ptolemy and the Music of the Spheres. But as a psychological document it is highly revealing. Most of Wagner's theories, whether on music, on culture in general or on political and social matters, do not emerge from dispassionate analysis or true philosophical speculation but are extrapolations from his personal circumstances and predispositions of the moment. A change of circumstances brought a change in personal perspective, and with it, through the process of self-discovery, a change of values, accompanied by a theoretical justification of the new values.

Through the creation of his own operas, above all *Tristan* and *Die Meistersinger*, he had been made to experience the domination of music, a domination as unmistakable – though Wagner could hardly have endured the thought – in Meyerbeer and Grand Opera as in Mozart, Beethoven, Weber and now himself. He thus externalized this realization in the form of an intellectual sub-structure based on old metaphysical thought – patterns which portrayed music as the mystical reflection of World Spirit and World Purpose. In so doing, he made himself a high priest of this mystical philosophy and linked his own artistic creativity to the processes of the cosmos. Whatever the means, Wagner always retained his position at the centre of a world of his own creation.

Just before Christmas the first volume of *Mein Leben*, which Wagner had been dictating to Cosima on and off since 1865, was printed in Basle in a private edition of fifteen copies. To Nietzsche's delight, Wagner asked him to read the proofs. The first copy went to King Ludwig; one was sent to Liszt in Rome, and another to Countess Marie von Schleinitz, a friend of Cosima's and one of Wagner's aristocratic benefactors.

In February 1871 the score of *Siegfried* was at last finished, after a gestation of almost fifteen years. By right it should have been delivered to the King, who had already paid for the entire *Ring*. But knowing that Ludwig would then have it performed in Munich without his cooperation, like *Das Rheingold* and *Die Walküre*, Wagner continued for months to deceive the King into believing that it was not yet finished, even during the time when Richter was making a copy of the full score and Klindworth was preparing the piano version. His own interests brooked no interference.

Work on Act Two of *Götterdämmerung* continued sporadically through the year. He wrote an essay *Über die Bestimmung der Oper (On the Destiny of Opera)*, a kind of sequel to *Beethoven*, and a pamphlet *Über die Aufführung des Bühnenfestspiels 'Der Ring des Nibelungen' (On Performing the Festival Drama 'The Ring of the Nibelung')*. He also conducted two concerts in Berlin, the first of them in the presence of the Emperor Wilhelm I, the Empress Augusta and the entire Prussian court. The programme consisted of his newly composed *Kaisermarsch*, Beethoven's Fifth Symphony and excerpts from *Lohengrin*.

Crowds now gathered wherever he appeared, and his

presence in the Prussian capital was a major event. Success and influence in Berlin had long been the dream of German playwrights, actors and musicians, doubly so now that it was the capital of the new Empire, and whatever his obligations to Ludwig, Wagner calculated on gaining support there for his festival idea.

A special personal pleasure came when he saw his niece Johanna again, daughter of his brother Albert. Johanna had come a long way since she sang Elisabeth in the first performance of *Tannhäuser* in Dresden back in 1845. For the past twenty years she had been one of the stars of the Berlin theatrical and operatic scene, and more than once her uncle had looked to her to further his cause in the Prussian capital. At a particularly desperate moment in 1854 he had even tried to borrow 1,000 thalers from her in anticipation of royalties from a production of *Tannhäuser* which he hoped – in vain – she would negotiate; her father, however, was more interested in promoting his daughter's financial interests than in helping his headstrong brother, whose talent, he said openly, he esteemed but whose character he did not. Johanna had married in 1859, and by the time when, in April 1871, she sought out her now famous uncle and future aunt in the Tiergarten Hotel in Berlin, the old affection between them was restored.

But it was not the name Berlin that dominated this year and every year of Wagner's life from now on. Nor, in spite of King Ludwig II, was it Munich. It was a sleepy little South German town of some 12,000 inhabitants, formerly belonging to Prussia but since 1810 assigned to Bavaria, called Bayreuth.

Attractively situated on the Red Main River some sixty miles north of Nuremberg, between the plateau of the Fichtelgebirge to the north-east and so-called Franconian Switzerland to the south-west, Bayreuth grew up as a communication and distribution centre, principally for the products of farming industries, subsequently also for locally manufactured textiles. Medieval in its origins, it became the residence of the Margraves of Brandenburg-Kulmbach in 1603, and most of the surviving buildings of interest, including the Neues Schloss and the opera house, owe their existence to the Margraves.

Wagner's first, pleasant memories of the place, quite innocent of what it was later to mean to him, went back to 1835 and a journey from Karlsbad to Nuremberg. The conception of a closed performance of *The Ring* on four successive evenings, in a festival setting especially designed for the purpose, had already been made explicit in his *Communication to my Friends* of 1851 and recently reiterated in his essay *On Performing the Festival Drama, 'The Ring of the Nibelung'*. The union of the festival idea with the town of Bayreuth was forming in his mind in the spring of 1870. At Cosima's suggestion, he consulted the Brockhaus encyclopedia about the history and nature of the town, and must have made his final decision at this moment, for that day – 5 March – became for them the 'birthday' of Bayreuth.

That the town was not swamped by summer visitors, and that it lay in the centre of Germany yet was still within Ludwig's Bavarian Kingdom – Wagner gave these as further reasons for his choice. A number of visitors to Tribschen were told of the plan in the course of the year – Catulle and Judith Mendès, Karl Klindworth, Nietzsche and his friend Erwin Rohde, Marie von Mouchanov-Kalergis and others. But not Ludwig, lest he discover the real reason why Wagner pretended to have not yet finished scoring *Siegfried*. Not until March 1871 did he put his scheme before the King.

'I do not like Wagner's plan in the slightest,' retorted Ludwig to his secretary Düfflipp. It is a reaction remarkable only for its mildness. Wagner had openly broken his contract, and the motives behind his lies over *Siegfried* were now obvious; no festival theatre was ever going to be built in Munich, nor was *The Ring* going to be performed there. The King would never desert the cause of Wagner's music, but he could no longer blind himself to the reality – one suspects he had been desperately deceiving himself for years – that Wagner the man would always sacrifice honour, friendship, even love, to his fanatical idealism and the relentless pursuit of his practical aims. Later the artist in Ludwig sought expression in architecture, as he set out to enact his romantic fantasies of medieval kingship in the fairy-tale mountain fastness of Neuschwanstein and the extravagant splendour of the palace of Herrenchiemsee. But nothing could take the place of Wagner. In this world of unreality, lonely, suspicious, fighting his latent homosexuality, aware for the last seven years of his life that he was going mad, this tragically unhappy creature drowned himself in the Starnberger See in 1886, three years after the death of his hero, the only human being he had truly loved.

A few days after Easter 1871 Wagner and Cosima travelled to Bayreuth. 'The people of the town are in great agitation at his presence here,' wrote Cosima in her diary, 'but the opera house is quite unsuited to our purpose. We shall have to build one. So much the better.' The stage of the sumptuous rococo opera house built in the 1740s by the Margrave Friedrich, though large by contemporary standards, was too small for *The Ring*. Wagner found the atmosphere of the town congenial, however, and made a firm decision to establish himself and his festival here. The town's almost complete lack of literary or musical tradition – its only famous literary resident had been the novelist Jean Paul Richter, who died there in 1825 – made it doubly desirable. So also did its smallness and its unpretentiousness, bordering on insignificance. Offers to provide facilities for the new theatre in Darmstadt,

Baden-Baden and Bad Reichenhall, all places which would have provided the fashionable, spa-loving audiences that Wagner detested, fell on deaf ears.

For the rest of the year Wagner devoted most of his energy to preparing his Festival – calculating costs and the ways of meeting them, publicizing his intentions in as many places and as many ways as possible, negotiating with the Bayreuth civic authorities over suitable sites for his theatre and his private house. In May he made a public announcement that his Stage Festival *Der Ring des Nibelungen* would take place in the summer of 1873. That to prepare such a mammoth undertaking in two years was hopelessly unrealistic, when not a spade had been lifted or a penny collected towards the cost, did not seem to cross his mind.

The finance – Wagner aimed at a remarkably modest figure of 300,000 thalers – was to be raised in the first instance by the sale of 1,000 'Patronage Certificates' (*Patronatscheine*) at 300 thalers each, the holder of a certificate having the right to attend the Festival performances. Wagner's young Jewish friend and admirer from Zurich days, Karl Tausig, undertook to launch the appeal; when, barely thirty years old, Tausig died of typhoid only a few weeks later, the financial organization passed to the banker Friedrich Feustel, chairman of the Bayreuth town council, Theodor Muncker, Bürgermeister of Bayreuth, and Emil Heckel, a music dealer from Mannheim. In order to capture those unable to afford a 300-thaler Patronage Certificate, Heckel had the ingenious idea of founding a chain of Richard Wagner Societies throughout the country, each Society becoming the corporate owner of a Patronage Certificate through the subscription of its members, who would share among themselves the entitlement to be present at the festival.

Negotiations for the first chosen site fell through because one of the owners refused to sell his land. A second site, some 54,000 square metres in area, on the Bürgerreuth hill to the north of the town, was agreed upon and bought by the Bayreuth council in January 1872. The following month Wagner acquired a lot adjoining the garden of the Neues Schloss in the town for his private villa, at a cost of 12,000 guilders. At the same time the administration of the practical and financial preparations for the festival was given into the hands of a committee consisting of Feustel, Muncker and a lawyer called Käfferlein, and the first Patronage Certificates were issued, the majority of them to his wealthy supporters in Berlin.

Between his visits to Bayreuth and elsewhere in the cause of the festival, Wagner wrote, discussed and composed steadily in the domestic tranquillity of Tribschen. He made the composition and orchestral sketches of the second act of *Götterdämmerung*, wrote the preface to a planned edition of his collected prose and poetry, to include the libretti of his operas, and contributed an article on the French composer Auber to the *Musikalisches Wochenblatt* in Leipzig, not to mention innumerable private and professional letters (over 5,000 letters written by Wagner have survived). In the evenings he would often read to Cosima or she to him – the *Edda*, Gibbon's *Decline and Fall*, Carlyle, Jakob Grimm, stories by Gottfried Keller. The stream of visitors continued – Carl Brandt, the technical wizard who had managed the stage effects for the première of *Das Rheingold*, the publisher Franz Schott and his wife, *Kapellmeister* Karl Eckert from Stuttgart, Gräfin Marie von Schleinitz and her husband, scholars, neighbours and well-wishers.

The most welcome visitor, however – he stayed at the house no fewer than twenty-three times between 1869 and 1872 – was the young Professor of Classical Philology at the University of Basle, Friedrich Nietzsche. The spiritual affinity between them, the fifty-six-year-old Wagner and the twenty-five-year-old Nietzsche, continued to be felt by both men. Little sources of annoyance and scorn, like Nietzsche's earnest ethic of vegetarianism – Wagner had an unpleasant gift of mocking, and himself taking offence at, the most unimportant of things – were not allowed to cloud their relationship. 'Professor Nietzsche is a very pleasant man and feels at home in Tribschen' – there are many such entries in Cosima's diary.

Wagner, inevitably, set the pace, and Nietzsche, struggle though he might, never escaped from his dependency. 'Everything considered,' he wrote in *Ecce Homo*, five years after Wagner's death, 'I could not have survived in my younger days without Wagner's music.' And elsewhere: 'I am still searching for a work of such dangerous fascination, of such sweet and terrible immortality, as *Tristan* – I have searched all the arts in vain.' Not that Wagner's expectations of his new friend were always fulfilled. Wagner's humour, for example, as self-centred as any other side of his personality, apparently aroused no response. 'Your brother is just like Liszt,' he once complained to Nietzsche's sister: 'he doesn't like my jokes either.'

From the beginning Wagner felt in the presence of Nietzsche not only that he was adored but also, as the young Classicist rhapsodized about Greek tragedy and the culture of Antiquity, that he was understood. In Nietzsche's famous early work, *The Birth of Tragedy from the Spirit of Music*, an early copy of which he sent to Tribschen in January 1872, Wagner is cast as the Greek dramatist reborn, the genius whose union of the arts under the supreme power of music proves that the joyous, serene, heroic spirit of Greece still lives. This was just what Wagner wanted to hear, a restatement from a completely different starting point of the historical role which he had claimed for himself in *The Work of Art of the Future* and his other Zurich essays of 1849 and after. But in the course of writing his book Nietzsche had allowed his hero-worship to warp his intellectual judgment. For the plain fact is that there is no connection between Wagner and Greek tragedy, and tragedy was *not* born from the spirit of music. Whatever the interest of *The Birth of Tragedy* – an interest that centres less on Wagner, and far less on Greek tragedy, than on the predilections of Nietzsche himself – its fanciful excursion into Wagner's music at the end has neither critical nor historical validity. Scholars were not slow to tell him so, and the following year his students at Basle deserted his lectures.

Nietzsche's central work on Wagner, *Richard Wagner in Bayreuth*, written between 1875 and 1876, is at once one of the most penetrating studies ever written of the psychology and inner meaning of Wagner's music, and, in biographical terms, the watershed in the relationship between the two men. Philosophically it is a deeply ambiguous work. Approached in the spirit of *The Birth of Tragedy*, it reads like a deeply perceptive tribute to the Master: Wagner himself, filled with the excitement of the coming Festival, took it as such. But it is also a valedictory tribute, to be read between the lines rather than on them, the testimony to a friendship and an inspiration not merely past but now resented, even reviled. Nietzsche was already suffering from the excruciating attacks of migraine which, accompanied by vomiting and fits, sometimes brought him near to paralysis and were the physical cause of his later madness. Even as Wagner was directing the final rehearsals in the Festspielhaus in 1876, Nietzsche crept away from the scene and began to chronicle his growing hatred of everything that Wagner, Bayreuth, the German romantic spirit and the nationalistic Second Reich stood for. The two men met only once again.

For the violently anti-Christian Nietzsche the news in 1877 that Wagner was absorbed in the story of Parzival, with its heavily Christian message of purification and redemption, came as an intellectual *coup de grâce*. For

Nietzsche worshipped Wagner not for what he was but for what he took him to be, and his adulation represented a self-deception that could only find tragic resolution. When Wagner wrote of the culture of Antiquity, of the German *Volk*, of Beethoven, of 'the art of the future', he was really writing of himself. And when Nietzsche wrote about Wagner, or about Schopenhauer, he too was writing about himself. Wagner's friendship, he said later, had given him the only real happiness he had known: he had wittingly sacrificed it to regain his intellectual integrity. But Wagner's music, about which no one, not even Thomas Mann, has written more profoundly, wrenched his consciousness apart and destroyed his spiritual equilibrium. It was a condition defined by Tolstoy – who wrote scathingly in *What is Art?* about the 'nonsensical rubbish' of *The Ring* and called it 'counterfeit art' – as one of hypnosis.

After Wagner's death Nietzsche conceived a mad spiritual passion for Cosima – a re-expression of the Tribschen idyll of twenty years earlier – addressing her as Ariadne, signing his letters Dionysus and casting Wagner in the role of Theseus. In the mental asylum at Jena he said to his doctor: 'My wife Cosima Wagner brought me here.' For Wagner the eight years of Nietzsche's passionate attachment formed a gratifying episode which was quickly forgotten in the euphoric fulfilment of the Bayreuth dream. For Nietzsche they were an experience that pierced the core of his being, an experience that left a scar which identified him for the rest of his life.

As 1871 and the early months of 1872 slipped away at Tribschen in work on *Götterdämmerung*, in negotiations with the authorities in Bayreuth and in discussions on the financing of the Festival, Wagner realized that his theatre could not possibly open in 1873. Quite apart from the construction of the building itself, he needed time to find suitable singers, recruit orchestral players and stage technicians, and direct the artistic preparations. Hans Richter, already chosen to conduct the performances, would then need months of discussion and rehearsal with the personnel. And there was also the little matter of the score of *Götterdämmerung*, which was itself still under construction, and remained so almost until the end of 1874.

But whether it was to be 1873, 1874 or whatever – in the end it became 1876 – Wagner now lived, and knew that he lived, for one thing alone. His Mecca would be built in Bayreuth, and here the prophet must preside. In April 1872, after six years which, for all their times of anger and exasperation, had been among the most contented and most productive he had known, he finally left Tribschen. Two days later he reached Bayreuth and established himself in the Hotel Fantaisie, adjoining the Schloss Fantaisie and its magnificent park.

Cosima and her children joined him the following week. For them the end of the Tribschen idyll was in many ways a sadder moment than for him. The rooms stripped and the family's possessions packed into boxes, Cosima wandered through the empty house again and again on her last evening. 'I am filled with gratitude to the God who granted me such happiness here,' she wrote in her diary for that day. 'All things were wonderful in this place, even those things that were hard.' In 1931 the town of Lucerne acquired the house and turned it into a Richard Wagner Museum, restoring the interior in accordance with contemporary descriptions, and exhibiting items of historical and personal interest, including Wagner's favourite Erard grand piano.

Wagner laid the foundation-stone of his Festival Theatre at eleven o'clock in the morning on his fifty-ninth birthday, 22 May 1872. Countess Marie von Schleinitz, Marie von Mouchanov-Kalergis, Nietzsche, Rohde, Peter Cornelius, Malwida von Meysenbug and a host of other aristocrats and friends were present at Wagner's invitation. Liszt, at this time back in Weimar, was not, to Wagner's irritation. King Ludwig sent a telegram of congratulation.

The rain poured down throughout the ceremony, and after the stone had been formally laid and a military band had played Wagner's *Kaisermarsch*, the guests were forced to retreat to the old opera house in the town for the remainder of the ceremony. Here Wagner delivered the festive oration planned for the moment of the stone-laying itself. Describing to his audience the sharply-raked auditorium, the hidden orchestra pit (originally designed by Semper) and other outstanding features of the building, he dedicated his enterprise to the spirit of Germany: 'It is in the nature of the German spirit to build from within, and our temple will stand as an outward symbol of this inner spirit.'

Later the same day he conducted a special performance of Beethoven's Ninth Symphony before an invited audience in the opera house, with Marie Lehmann (sister of the more famous Lili), Wagner's niece Johanna, Albert Niemann (the Paris Tannhäuser and the first Bayreuth Siegmund in *Die Walküre*, and Franz Betz (creator of the role of Hans Sachs in *Die Meistersinger*, and of Wotan in the Bayreuth *Ring*) as the solo quartet.

After the concert a banquet was held in the Hotel zur Sonne. With dignity and sincerity Wagner expressed his gratitude to the people of Bayreuth for their cooperation and linked the King's name with his own in a restatement of the national cultural purpose that had led up to this happy moment. Nor did his speech lack wit:

Gentlemen, jokes have been bandied about because our theatre is to be built near the mental asylum. All of you know the reasons that led me to choose this town, but I confess I did not realize that the air in Bayreuth is so fresh that it can restore the mentally sick, and that patients who have gone out of their minds can be healed here by wise physicians. It would be no bad idea to erect near this asylum an institution for the benefit of all those who have lost their senses, above all the sense of being German – an institution where such sufferers can be cured of all those perversions and disfigurements in art which they have contracted from foreigners, to whom they have become an object of derision.

'This day,' wrote Nietzsche in his essay *Richard Wagner in Bayreuth*, 'marked the beginning of his sixtieth year. Everything heretofore had been a preparation for this moment.' The unique and wonderful institution Wagner had founded was a far cry from the utopian popular celebration of art à la Classical Greece which he had dreamt of and preached in his thirties. As kings and courtiers, aristocrats, statesmen and artists gathered round him, the élitist reality of his ideal became clearer than ever, both to him and to the world. What Wagner said he would do, and what he actually did, were often poles apart. In the name of great music let us thank the gods that it was so.

CHAPTER SEVEN
Bayreuth

When Kaiser Wilhelm I arrived for the Bayreuth Festival in August 1876, his first words to Wagner, who headed a receptior. party at the railroad station, were: 'I never thought you would bring your plan to fruition, but now the sun has bathed your achievement in radiance.' But the sun did not shed its radiance, literally or metaphorically, on that rain-soaked day in May 1872 when Wagner laid the foundation stone of his theatre and announced the principles of his grand cultural design.

The 300-thaler Patronage Certificates, confidently expected to solve the financial problem, attracted few subscribers. Over a year after the scheme was launched, only some two hundred had been sold, whereas even on Wagner's own over-conservative calculation of the building costs, at least a thousand would have been needed. He had always had a poor opinion of the German princès; the lack of support for Bayreuth now showed him how right he had been. 'I have reached the point,' he wrote to Nietzsche in October 1872, 'where I am not going to mince matters. If the Empress Augusta herself were to cross my path, I would tell her what I thought of her.'

Meanwhile he finished the orchestral sketch of Act Three of *Götterdämmerung* and resumed the dictation of his autobiography to Cosima. At the end of September 1872 they and their children left the Hotel Fantaisie outside Bayreuth and moved to a house in the town, No. 7 Dammallee, where they stayed until their new villa was finished a year and a half later. Much of Wagner's day was spent in the company of Cosima, sometimes together with the children. At midday he would on occasion join the locals in Angermann's beer parlour, taking his dog Russ with him, the great Newfoundland he had brought with him from Tribschen. In the evenings he and Cosima reminisced or read together. Scarcely a day went by without neighbours or friends calling at the house.

In October Liszt paid his first visit to Bayreuth. Ever since he had learned of the liaison between Wagner and Cosima, which had brought a new worry into his unstable, care-worn life, a muted disapproval, an air of injury had hung over his relationship with his daughter and with his once intimate friend. Cosima had not written to him for almost a year before her divorce from Hans von Bülow, for whose well-being Liszt seemed at times more concerned than for hers or Wagner's, and he learned of her marriage to Wagner from a newspaper report a week after the event. Wagner had not seen him since his visit to Tribschen in 1867.

Before inviting him to Bayreuth they had visited Liszt in Weimar, where he now lived for several months each year. On the one hand, Liszt still submitted to the will of Princess Carolyne von Sayn-Wittgenstein, a convert to the allurements of mystical experience and an implacable enemy of Wagner the man and Wagner the musician. But he had also fallen under the influence of the young Baroness Olga von Meyendorff, wife of the Russian Ambassador in Weimar, who belonged to the formidable group of influential women – Countess Marie von Schleinitz, Malwida von Meysenbug, Maria von Mouchanov-Kalergis, Baroness Loën and others – who agitated tirelessly on Wagner's behalf. Liszt was suffering the consequences, physical and psychological, of the excesses of his earlier life, his nerves undermined by years of addiction to alcohol and tobacco, beset by conflicting uncertainties as to where he belonged and what he should do with his life. 'My father's weariness of heart has given me a terrible shock,' wrote Cosima in her diary: 'I cried a

great deal in the night.' He gave a few desultory performances on the piano – Chopin Preludes, some Beethoven,
his own Mephisto Waltz – but when he started to play
from *Götterdämmerung* everything went wrong. At dinner
he was morose and talked only to the Baroness Olga,
ignoring Cosima and the rest of the company.

During his week's stay in Bayreuth Liszt unburdened
himself to Cosima of his unhappiness – how Princess
Carolyne was pressing him to have nothing to do with his
daughter and her immoral husband, bitterly insisting what
a pernicious effect Wagner's music had; that he and
Cosima had totally destroyed poor Bülow; and so on.
Cosima's decision to renounce her Catholic birthright and
enter the Protestant Church, which she did two weeks
later, saddened him still more. Characteristically, this
long tête-à-tête between father and daughter made
Wagner jealous, and he sulked for most of the following
day. The once proud Liszt, now joyless and weary, found
Bayreuth a pleasant place, but he left behind him a mood
of dejection and pity. 'Everything he said about the
world,' wrote Cosima, ' – to which, after all, he belongs,
like us – was terrible.'

Towards the end of the year, unabashed by the depressing state of the festival finances, Wagner took Cosima
with him on a tour of German opera houses to recruit
singers for Bayreuth, visiting Frankfurt, Mannheim,
Stuttgart, Cologne, Leipzig, and several other cities,
including Magdeburg. Here he showed Cosima the scene
of the then tragic, now comic episode of his opera *Das
Liebesverbot* almost forty years ago. The tour, as reported
in his article *Ein Einblick in das heutige deutsche Opern-
wesen (An Impression of the Contemporary Operatic
Scene in Germany)*, produced a string of negative impressions of producers, conductors, singers and audiences,
confirming what he had always scathingly maintained –
that hardly anyone, either behind the footlights or in front

of them, could conceive of the fusion of singing and dramatic acting demanded by the sustained dramatic pressure and the continuous musical texture of his works. Yet only a few years later Bayreuth itself was to prove the opposite.

Apart from praying, not always without success, for a miracle, there had been at Wagner's disposal a ready means for improving his financial situation ever since the days of his exile in Switzerland. This – though he was reluctant to make use of it, now, of all times – was to go on tour as a guest conductor. In the 1850s and 1860s Vienna, London, St Petersburg, Paris, Brussels, besides many German cities, had heard his dynamic performances of the classics and excerpts from his own works. Now a far more famous figure than at that time, he commanded the sort of following enjoyed today by men like Karajan and Solti. As Friedrich Feustel, shrewd chairman of the Festival Committee, pointed out, each stage on such a fund-raising tour would sell more Patronage Certificates and be followed by the foundation of new Wagner Societies. The arrival of some unpaid bills from Lucerne, including one for 3,000 francs from Colonel am Rhyn, the owner of Tribschen, was a further irritating reminder of the claims of financial reality. He was also beginning to suffer from the heart pains which became progressively worse throughout the remainder of his life.

But if the Festival were to materialize, he could hardly do other than Feustel urged. After seeing a miserable performance of *Rienzi* in Dresden in the company of the Wesendonks, Dr Pusinelli and the tenor Joseph Tichatschek, he and Cosima went to Berlin. Here, in the house of Count Alexander von Schleinitz and before a select audience that included Prince George of Prussia, Field-Marshall Helmuth von Moltke, the scientist Helmholtz and the painter Adolf Menzel, he gave a reading of *Götterdämmerung*. Then came concerts in Hamburg,

Berlin and Cologne, all of which attracted moral support, or assurances of moral support, and money, or promises of money. Further such concerts were needed two years later.

Despite these efforts all the money so far collected had been spent before the end of 1873, by which time only the outer shell of the theatre had been erected. In a circular letter to the patrons Wagner was forced to announce that the Festival could not possibly open before summer 1875, and he called a meeting to discuss the form of a further appeal to the music-loving public at large. A pleasurable interlude in his worries was a visit from the composer Anton Bruckner, long a worshipper at the shrine of Wagner's music, who came to ask the Master's permission to dedicate one of his symphonies to him – 'but only', wrote Bruckner in his account of the meeting, 'if the Master were more-or-less satisfied, since I did not wish to profane his glorious name.' Of the three scores Bruckner brought with him, Wagner chose that of the Third Symphony, and summoned the delighted Bruckner to his new villa where the dedication was celebrated with tankards of beer. So intoxicated did Bruckner become with a mixture of beer and exaltation that the next day he could not remember for sure which symphony Wagner had accepted, and had to write to him to confirm that it was indeed the No. 3 in D minor – 'the one where the trumpet begins the theme', as he described it.

Religious matters, especially the concept of Christ the Redeemer, frequently arose in conversation at this time, according to Cosima's diary. Wagner also returned to his interest in Oriental religions and asked to have the standard works of Indian literature sent to him. But despondency returned with the failure of the new appeal for subscriptions.

The situation soon became even gloomier. After much embarrassed hesitation Wagner travelled to Munich to ask the King to underwrite the expenses of the opera house until the actual money from the sale of Patronage Certificates was received – in Wagner's eyes a mere matter of weeks, if not days. The King, still piqued that Wagner had taken his Festival Theatre away from Munich, and perhaps irritated by his protégé's earlier direct approach to the Kaiser, refused. An appeal to the Grand Duke of Baden, with whom Wagner had always had friendly relations, in the hope that he could get the Kaiser to support the festival as a contribution to the new spirit of German unity, also fell on deaf ears. The whole great project faced bankruptcy and ruin.

Suddenly everything changed. Exactly why, less than three weeks after saying No, the King found himself unable to resist his 'dearest Friend's' desperate plea, we do not know. But in January 1874, in a letter from Hohenschwangau full of the romantic affection and fulsome phraseology that characterized their exchanges he took Wagner completely by surprise. 'From the depths of my heart,' he wrote, 'I beg you to forgive me for my dilatoriness in writing to you. Do not be angry with me, dearest Friend. No, No, a thousand times No! The matter cannot end like this. We must find help. Our plan cannot be allowed to fail!'

Maybe it was the '*our* plan', a sudden surge of ambition and pride in his involvement in the whole glorious concept, that brought about the King's remarkable volte-face. Again the young King of Bavaria, 'mad' or merely farsighted, had shown Wagner that he was the only ruler with a true sense of German values. 'O my gracious King,' he joyfully cried, 'if you but cast your eye over all the German princes, you must realize that you are the only one among them to whom the spirit of Germany can look with hope!' In February a detailed agreement was drawn up between the Court Secretariat and the Festival Committee (Wagner, Feustel, Bürgermeister Muncker and the lawyer Käfferlein) for a loan of 100,000 thalers from the King's privy purse to cover the interior fittings of the theatre, the gas installation and the scenery. Half the proceeds of any concerts by which Wagner sought to raise funds for the Festival, together with all the future income from the sale of Patronage Certificates, was to be made over to the King, and the full loan was repayable in a year-and-a-half. It was a formal business document, legally binding, a far cry from the gifts and pseudo-loans that Ludwig had almost casually showered on Wagner in their early days.

The contracts for the outstanding work on the theatre could not be placed, and when Hans Richter arrived in Bayreuth in May, he and Wagner began to draw up provisional casts of singers: Richter even took some of the chosen soloists through parts of their roles. Wagner told the King that the final rehearsals would now be held in the early summer of 1876 and that the often-postponed opening performance would take place in August, which it did. More than once Wagner had to ask the King to waive repayments due under the contract, because at the time the agreement was made the Festival had been announced for the summer of 1875 and was thus expected to have covered the remainder of the debt by then. Each time Wagner asked, the King, the saviour of Bayreuth, agreed.

Also to Ludwig's generosity Wagner owed the fine new private villa which he, Cosima and their children had moved into in April 1874. He gave it the cryptic name 'Wahnfried' ('Dream Fulfilment'), which he interpreted in a two-part rhymed inscription on the front of the house:

Hier wo mein Wähnen Frieden fand
Sei dieses Hause von mir benannt: Wahnfried

(This place, where my longings found peace and rest,
Shall receive this name and ever be blest.)

A large allegorical graffito above the portal depicts the 'Work of Art of the Future', with the figures of Wotan, Greek Tragedy and Music bearing the heads, respectively, of Wagner's two ideal opera singers, Ludwig Schnorr von Carolsfeld and Wilhelmine Schröder-Devrient, and Cosima, beside whom stands a little boy armed like Siegfried, with the features of the four-year-old son who bore the hero's name. There was a summer-house in the garden where the family took breakfast in warm weather. In front of the house stands a granite plinth surmounted by a double-life-size bust of King Ludwig in bronze, made by Caspar Zumbusch. The idea for the bust came from Wagner; the money, inevitably, came from the King.

The interior of the substantial, somewhat squat house, and the pattern of life of the family that lived in it, are described both by Wagner himself and by one Fräulein Susanne Weinert, who worked as a governess there for nine months between 1875 and 1876. First came a lofty rectangular hall on the ground floor, with black leather sofas, a grand piano and various marble busts – Wagner, Cosima, Liszt, Ludwig II and statuettes of Wagnerian characters. From the hall folding doors led to three adjacent rooms – the 'modest dining room', as Wagner called it, Cosima's reception room and the superb salon with a large rotunda, focal point of the whole house, which served as the family living and reception room, the library, the music room and at times also as Wagner's study.

Glass doors led from the rotunda into the garden at the back of the house; there were rich rugs and carpets on the floor and thick velvet curtains, luxuriously covered armchairs and sofas, and numerous elegant little tables and chairs. Around the ceiling were the crests of the towns in which the first Wagner Associations were established. The bookshelves carried over two thousand sumptuously bound volumes, predominantly German literature and history, but also the Classics, Racine, Caderón, Victor Hugo and other standard authors, and there were many pictures – portraits of Wagner, Cosima, King Ludwig, Schopenhauer and others and objets d'art. Opposite Wagner's large writing desk stood his Erard grand piano, with a smaller desk for Cosima. Later a Steinway concert grand, presented to Wagner by the New York firm in 1876, also stood in the salon. Larger and more resonant than the Erard, the Steinway was frequently played by Liszt; it is the instrument at which he is sitting in the well-known scene reproduced in the photo engraving by Papperitz. Hanging from the ceiling in the centre of the room was a magnificent chandelier. Bedrooms, changing rooms and the children's playroom were on the mezzanine and first floors, and led off the four sides of a gallery above the hall. The satins and silks worn by Wagner, and especially Cosima's robes and gowns, were the perfect counterpart to the extravagant but not always impeccable taste of the house.

Wahnfried, surrounded by trees and lawns adjoins the beautiful park belonging to the Neues Schloss. Wagner, who knew just what he wanted, made the basic plan himself. It is grander, weightier than Tribschen, but it cannot match the magnificent natural setting of the villa on the shores of Lake Lucerne. The idyll in Wagner's life that was Tribschen is perfectly symbolized by the frank, open serenity of that house; Wahnfried is the residence of the man who has 'arrived', and it radiates the atmosphere of rich formality and self-assurance that surrounded the Master like a halo during the nine years – the last years of his life – that he lived there. Since his death successive generations of the family have striven to ensure that the name Wahnfried should be synonymous with the true worship of Wagner's art.

In 1945 a bomb destroyed part of the house, including the salon. Wieland Wagner, the composer's grandson, repaired the habitable parts and lived there with his family until 1966. In 1973, when the future of the festival, of the archives and all the other aspects of the Wagner industry was finally settled by the establishment of the Richard Wagner Foundation, Wahnfried became the property of the town of Bayreuth, which restored the house, as far as possible, to its former condition. In 1976, the centenary of the Bayreuth Festival, it was opened as a museum with hundreds of items of Wagneriana and 'Wahnfriediana' from the past century and a half.

Between ten and one each morning, Wagner told the King, he worked in the salon – this meant, in the first instance, at the score of *Götterdämmerung* and at the manuscript of Volume Three of *Mein Leben*, shortly to be sent to the printers. After lunch with Cosima and the children he would look through the local newspaper and talk to Cosima about art, philosophy and the affairs of the world; a short nap, then back to the salon with Cosima to attend to correspondence. In the late afternoon he went for a walk, or took a drive with the children in the chaise; he tended to avoid visiting the festival site because of the crowds of sightseers. Then came the evening meal, again with the children. From eight o'clock onwards he and Cosima would sit in the salon and read together or receive callers. Sometimes they played whist, especially when Liszt came.

A number of the visitors wanted just to discuss the problems of art and life with the Master, others urged him to play to them and joined him in impromptu music-making. Among these latter were the members of what came to be known as the 'Nibelung Bureau' – a group of young musicians employed to copy orchestral parts, read proofs and do other practical jobs while learning from the inside, with the guidance of the Master himself, how to interpret and perform his music. Later well-known Wagnerian conductors like Hermann Zumpe, Anton Seidl and Felix Mottl worked in the 'Nibelung Bureau' at one time or another, as did the Jewish-Russian pianist Joseph Rubinstein, who later became a member of the family circle.

Wagner and Cosima both slept fitfully, and their restless imagination made them prey to dreams which frequently bordered on nightmares. Time and again the worried Cosima began a day's entry in her diary with 'R. spent a very bad night'; 'R. barely slept and was tortured by violent dreams'; 'R. dreamt that he was enraged by having made a huge blot on a page he was scoring, but the score turned out to be someone else's'; and similar visions. On one occasion, to Cosima's amusement, he dreamt that the Queen of Prussia had come to him and said she was his mother. From the nervous irritability caused by sleeplessness and strain came a series of unpleasant physical ailments and disorders. He was plagued with a painful rash on his fingers, had chills and fits of sweating which he tried to cure with leeches, abscesses developed in his mouth, and he was often in a state of lassitude and depression.

The governess Susanne Weinert shows Wagner as the most amiable of fathers, always happy to play with the children, who were devoted to him – Bülow's daughters Daniela and Blandine as totally as his own three children – and always courteous and affectionate in his behaviour towards Cosima (Cosima's diaries also show that he could destroy this amiability with fits of moodiness and spite which, though she had not provoked them, she was forced to endure). Also belonging to the household were a half-dozen or so servants, all proud to be at the disposal of their master and mistress. Finally came the four dogs: Wagner's Newfoundland, Russ (who has his own little gravestone in the garden of Wahnfried close to his master), a Spitz called Putzi and two more Newfoundlands, with names taken from *Tristan* – Brange (derived from Brangäne) and Marke – who belonged to the children.

Wahnfried was a real family house for a real family. It was not a retreat in which a great composer cloistered himself in the hallowed name of art, reluctantly tolerating the occasional intrusion of domestic matters into his private world. The big wooden swing in the garden belonged as much to the household as the grand piano in the salon, and the birthday parties and firework displays as much as the musical evenings with friends and disciples.

The sometimes startling directness of the relationship between the children and their parents is revealed by a simple episode told by Susanne Weinert. In a little grove in the middle of the large garden at the rear of the house, surrounded by trees and shrubs, was an area chosen by Wagner as his and Cosima's last resting-place. Taking their governess to the spot, the children showed her the plain grey terrazzo slab – it still bears no inscription – and said: 'This is Papa's and Mama's grave.'

The artist, living by and for his vision, fighting to create the expressive form that shall be its finite realization, is, *qua* artist, a lonely man. The prophet, in the grip of his message and of his impulse to proclaim it, may have his young disciples but in the end, as in the beginning, he is a voice crying in the wilderness. The creator of the 'work of art of the future' was by definition both artist and prophet. Yet his dream was about to become an incredible reality; the inspiration of Cosima, the security of his family life, the devotion and cooperation of friends and colleagues – all this made for a condition the very opposite of loneliness.

But not a few of those, friends and relatives, who had watched him struggle through his days of failure and rejection and had refused to doubt his ultimate victory, now suddenly left the scene, just before his moment of supreme triumph. In May 1874 his publisher Franz Schott and Marie von Mouchanov-Kalergis, one of his most generous benefactors and loyal supporters, both died; in October his brother Albert, the eldest of the Wagner family, also died, together with Heinrich Wolfram, his sister Klara's husband. (Klara died the following March; Luise had died in 1872 and now only Wagner and Ottilie, the youngest of his sisters, were left.) Another loss was that of the fifty-year-old Peter Cornelius, an attractive figure who had been a true, though not uncritical friend of the Wagnerian cause since the days of Wagner's Swiss exile. At sixty-one, Wagner found himself surrounded by younger generations: his wife was thirty-seven, Nietzsche thirty, King Ludwig only twenty-nine, the first generation of Wagnerian conductors – Richter, Seidl, Zumpe, Franz Fischer, Hermann Levi – were in their twenties and thirties. Wagner knew, and revelled in the knowledge, that it was his task to transmit an understanding of his art, both conceptual and practical, to those on whom its survival depended.

Nietzsche, though already beginning to sense in Wagner's music and the whole Festival concept the sinister influence which soon turned him into the bitterest opponent of all that Wagner stood for, still came regularly to Bayreuth. He had been at the foundation-stone ceremony in 1872 and had delivered a formal address to the meeting of the Patrons in 1873 at which the fresh appeal for funds had been made. Earlier in 1873, in the company of his friend Erwin Rohde, now a professor at the University of Kiel, he had shown Wagner some of his own musical compositions; one of them, a piece for piano, four hands, he and Wagner even played together. In the summer of 1874, unhappy with his life in Basle and in a poor physical and mental state, he arrived for a ten-day visit to Wahnfried, proudly bearing the piano score of Brahms' recent *Triumphlied* for choir and orchestra.

Wagner liked neither Brahms the man nor Brahms the

composer (though many of Brahms' greatest works were yet to come – the four symphonies, the violin concerto, the B-flat major piano concerto, the clarinet quintet – they would hardly have changed Wagner's opinion). Together with Tausig, Peter Cornelius and Weissheimer, Brahms had corrected the orchestral parts for Wagner's concerts in Vienna in 1862-3, but this counted for little. The two men had met only once, in February 1864, when Dr Standhartner brought Brahms to Wagner's house in Penzing. Musically there was hardly a single point of contact between them. Brahms had gone to *Das Rheingold* and *Die Walküre* in Munich in 1870 but later was known to dissuade his pupils from concerning themselves with Wagner's music. In 1875 there was to be an unpleasant contretemps between them when Brahms, who, back in the 1860s, had received as a present from Tausig the manuscript of Wagner's new Venusberg scene for the Paris *Tannhäuser* of 1861, refused to return it for Wagner to publish. Eventually he did, but only in return for a copy of the de luxe edition of *Das Rheingold*. In her diary Cosima makes no effort to disguise her and Wagner's scorn for the 'crude, boorish' man and his 'mediocre' music.

Confronted with Brahms's *Triumphlied*, Wagner waxed contemptuous. Cosima's diary – though whether the words are hers or Wagner's is not clear – calls it 'Handel, Mendelssohn and Schumann all wrapped up in leather'. But Wagner's trust in Nietzsche's loyalty was still unblemished. According to Elisabeth Förster-Nietzsche, Nietzsche's sister, it was Wagner's wish that in the event of his death his little son Siegfried should be placed in the care of Nietzsche as his ward and mentor.

In November 1874 came one of the great moments in Wagner's creative life, the culmination of an immense plan whose beginnings lay twenty-six years back in the revolutionary year of 1848 – the completion of the orchestration of *Götterdämmerung*, and thus of the entire

Ring cycle. At the bottom of the final page of the score he wrote: 'Completed at Wahnfried on 21 November 1874. I have nothing more to say. RW.'

The precision and the sentiment both reflect attitudes of mind that lie deep in Wagner's personality. The orchestral sketches and full scores of his operas are meticulously executed, points of detail being recorded from the earliest stages of the composition. The whole activity reflects his determination to make every nuance of his meaning explicit, to register every movement in his emotional and intellectual world, and to create a moment of artistic beauty out of every such movement. When a work was completed, he had to proclaim and perpetuate the triumphant moment of completion. Even more precise than the inscription at the end of *Götterdämmerung* is that on the score of *Die Meistersinger*: 'Tribschen, Thursday, 24 October 1867, at eight o'clock in the evening.' The same extrovert pride and sense of personal perfection lie behind his taste for expensive clothes and lavish furnishings.

So the whole epic of *The Ring* – four days of music and drama, of revolution and murder, of love and violence, of fate and morality and a thousand other things – reaches its devastating climax. The age of gods and heroes passes as the flames of the fire kindled by Brünnhilde engulf Walhalla. The cursed ring itself, symbol, in various forms, of the destructiveness of power and the assertion of the self, comes back into the rightful possession of the Rhinemaidens after passing, like Brünnhilde, through the ordeal by fire and water. At the end of *Götterdämmerung* the ring of the Nibelung, the curse finally broken, has come full circle, the ring as symbol of union, enclosing, embracing, compelling. The last leitmotif to be heard is the motif of Redemption.* The final D-flat major chord

___
*

swells to fortissimo, then diminishes to piano: triumph and fulfilment, but also reconciliation and assurance of peace. The world of the gods does not end with a bang, but neither does it end with a whimper.

Wagner's original ideal conception – he later retreated from its absolute validity – demanded that *The Ring* should only be performed as a complete cycle. *Das Rheingold* and *Die Walküre* had already been given separately in Munich at King Ludwig's behest but against Wagner's wishes; *Siegfried*, together with *Götterdämmerung* he succeeded in saving for the first performance of the complete *Ring* at Bayreuth.

The longest and most significant break in the composition of *The Ring* comes between the orchestral sketch of Act Two of *Siegfried* in 1857 and the composition sketch of Act Three in 1869. Wagner seemed by 1857 to have worked himself into an exhausted musical silence over his world myth of *The Ring*, and to have needed for his development the stimulus of a totally different world – the world of Schopenhauer, of Mathilde Wesendonk, of *Tristan und Isolde*. Perhaps too, having brought his young hero to 'the wonderful solitude of the forest', as he described the end of Act Two to Liszt, he contemplated with uncertainty, even unease, the confrontation between Wotan, tragic embodiment of the old order, at the end of his power, struggling against the irrevocability of a fate he has himself willed, and Siegfried, the Brave New Man, who splinters Wotan's spear with his sword and climbs the mountain to claim the sleeping Brünnhilde. The whole story of the Siegfried music, indeed, is one of delay and postponement. As early as 1851, immediately after writing the poem of *Siegfried* (then still called *Der junge Siegfried*), he told Liszt he would start on the music at once, yet instead he turned to the texts of *Das Rheingold* and *Die Walküre*, and began the composition sketch of *Siegfried* only after its two predecessors were complete in full score.

The first and third scenes of Act Three of *Siegfried* are governed by love, by the life-giving opposition of the masculine and feminine principles, embodied in the representations of the old order (Wotan and Erda) and the new (Siegfried and Brünnhilde). In between stands the scene between Wotan and Siegfried, between the world of the past and the world of the future, in which the newly-forged sword of the New Man, the man of action, shatters the spear and the authority of the old law and its custodian. As Siegfried presses his kiss on her lips, Brünnhilde wakes; the future belongs to the two lovers, and their love is what takes the world forward, as love took the lives of Wagner and Cosima forward, and with them the Wagnerian work of art that was to belong to the future.

In its ultimate form, adopted only at the time when the music came to be written, the text of the end of *Götterdämmerung* returns to the same theme. Siegfried and Brünnhilde, destined for each other from the beginning, are drawn apart by the illusoriness and the treachery of the world of appearances but find the eternal consummation of their love in death. Brünnhilde rides on Siegfried's horse into the flames that sweep over the body of her murdered lover and eventually consume the hall of the gods themselves. Love is absolute, its demands and its rights unconditional, its final victory ineluctable. In this dimension of his meaning it is not an idea, a philosophy, or even a conviction that Wagner leaves us with: it is a demonstration.

A demonstration – the stage carries the symbolic actions that bear Wagner's meaning. But above all, like everything from *Tristan* onwards, an exposition through music. The very fact that, *pace* later emendations of detail, the book of *The Ring* had been complete since 1852, means that Wagner the composer looked back at Wagner the dramatic librettist over a span of twenty years. His last words on the subject are, so to speak, in the notes. The events of the myth were set, likewise the roles of the characters within the myth; what was now infused into the events and roles was psychological intensification, the passionate expressiveness which it is in the power of music to convey, and with which the music of Wagner throbs like that of no other composer.

Leitmotifs from *Das Rheingold, Die Walküre* and the first two acts of *Siegfried* – the Wanderer motif, the Sword and Spear motifs, the Valkyries motif and so on – lay ready to be re-exploited when Wagner took up the composition of *Siegfried* again in 1869. (Wolzogen's *Thematic Guide*, which was on sale in Bayreuth at the first Festival, contains no fewer than ninety motifs.) The leitmotif is in essence a device of reminiscence, a link with the past, or a symbol of presentiment. As such, it works cumulatively, the musical equivalent to the narrative recapitulation characteristic of the whole *Ring*: the events of *Das Rheingold* are retold in *Die Walküre*, those of *Das Rheingold* and *Die Walküre* in *Siegfried*, and those of all three in *Götterdämmerung*. But the composer of 1869 was not the composer of 1857. The external links with the earlier material are still there, but the pattern of recurrent leitmotifs, whether old or newly-invented, no longer produces of its own accord the unified musico-dramatic form which embodied Wagner's ideal, and which, as he so confidently expounded in his treatise *Opera and Drama*, would emerge spontaneously from his chosen method of composition. Act Three of *Siegfried* has a broad sweep which embraces the individual motifs in a series of expansive musical gestures, absorbing them into a grand harmonic and melodic structure governed by a single musico-dramatic principle. Formerly the individual motifs and emotions had themselves directed the course that the action took, one impulse leading to another; now a central will directs events, striving towards a known and defined goal. The rhythmic vitality of this act, more marked even than that of *Die Walküre*, symbolizes this movement. The orchestral colours glow more warmly; new, richer leitmotifs are introduced; the drama has lost none of its intensity, but the 'feel' has become grander, more 'operatic', as the nineteenth century understood the genre. Yet the unity of the whole work, the sense that the third act, above all the love duet between Siegfried and Brünnhilde, is the goal towards which the first two acts have been striving, both musically and conceptually, is as unmistakable as it is remarkable. *Götterdämmerung*, in which the march scenes and march rhythms of *Siegfried* become still more insistent, makes this unity still firmer, both summarizing and consolidating the four days of epic drama.

Götterdämmerung, the depiction of the passing of an era, is the perfect symbol of Wagner's position in the history of music. He is an epitome, the culmination of a tradition, the tradition of nineteenth-century German romantic music. He is an end, in the way that Bach is an end, and Mozart. So all-enveloping, suffocating did his massive presence feel to many composers of later generations, so utterly did he seem to have drained the common reservoir of musical thought and expressiveness, that the only hope for survival appeared to lie in discovering totally new sources of vocabulary, totally new idioms of expression – whole-tone scales, atonality, dodecaphony, non-European musics, jazz. Much of the late nineteenth- and early twentieth-century opposition to Wagner and his influence, especially among 'progressive' musicians like Debussy and Stravinsky, stemmed from such an interpretation of the situation.

As in all Wagner's works after *Lohengrin* (except *Die Meistersinger*, the exception to all Wagnerian rules), the musical weight in *Siegfried* and *Götterdämmerung*, the gravamen of the symbolic and spiritual meaning, rests on harmony. 'Among the artistic faculties of man,' he had said in *Opera and Drama*, 'harmony has no equal. It is a natural force which one can be aware of but which one cannot understand.' And as the basic force is harmony, so modulation is the motion of harmony. Modulation rests on chromaticism, and the insistent chromaticism of Wagner's musical language makes for restless motion, the ever-threatening fluctuations of modulation – the counterpart of his rhapsodical 'endless melody'.

Siegfried, above all Acts One and Two, is heroic music-drama; *Götterdämmerung* – Wagner started on the composition sketch while still occupied with the scoring of *Siegfried* – is opera, Grand Opera. Its ensembles, the set trio (Brünnhilde, Gunther and Hagen) at the end of Act Two – how rare in Wagner for principal characters actually to sing together! – the profusion of purely picturesque effects and orchestral scene-painting (the dances of the Rhine Maidens, the depiction of sunrise and sunset, of the landscape in which Siegfried is murdered, of the funeral pyre, of the Rhine in flood, of Valhalla engulfed by the fire), the dense air of theatricality and lavish display that hangs over the whole work: this is the stuff of opera. The orchestra is at its most dominant, sweeping the action along in a torrent of glorious sound. Brünnhilde is swallowed up by the flames that she herself has kindled, but musically, symbolically, as the work surges on towards its triumphant end, it is the orchestra that engulfs her. Similarly it is the orchestra, in the superb last pages of the score with their review of the leitmotifs which have threaded their paths through the massive four-day spectacle, that pronounces final judgment on the shattering events we have experienced. Hanslick was being deliberately offensive when he remarked: 'Given the text and the orchestral accompaniment, a good musician versed in Wagner's music would be able to insert suitable vocal parts in the vacant spaces.' But the observation that the voices have become merged – 'swallowed up', Hanslick would have wanted to say – in the orchestral texture like instruments is accurate enough.

The orchestra needed for *The Ring* is large – triple wood-wind, plus cor anglais and bass clarinet, eight horns (four of them sometimes replaced by so-called Wagner tubas, modified horns which produce a warm tone colour lying between that of the horn and the tuba), three trumpets, four trombones, plus contrabass tuba, bass trumpet and contrabass trombone, six harps and percussion. At Bayreuth the orchestra consisted of one hundred and fifteen players, including sixty-four strings (the present Covent Garden orchestra, for comparison, numbers ninety; the orchestra at Glyndebourne has a similar number – in both cases with forty-eight strings). Their particular disposition in the sunken pit – different from that in the conventional orchestra pit – produced that blend of rich, velvet tone and sumptuous harmony which constitutes the characteristic 'Wagner sound'. (Wagner once told Uhlig that harmony and instrumentation were inseparable in his music. The only orchestral instrument with whose technique he was not conversant was the harp.)

Conceptually *Der Ring des Nibelungen* is a unity. Stylistically, composed over a period of twenty-five agitated years, repeatedly interrupted by personal, psychological, political and artistic contingencies, its music cannot be so in the ordinary sense. But as the symphonic panorama unfolds, as one powerful movement, one profound experience is followed by another, so we confront a oneness like that which embraces the work of Beethoven, the spiritual reality that unifies the twenty years which separate the First from the Ninth Symphony. Indeed, the link with Beethoven is one that Wagner himself claimed, and it is hardly a coincidence that he should have written his long essay on his great spiritual progenitor at the time (1870) when his mind was occupied with *Götterdämmerung* and the *Siegfried Idyll*.

To wonder whether, had external circumstances been

different, Wagner could have continued work on *Siegfried* in 1857 and finished *The Ring* in a single sustained effort, is an idle thought. It requires us to imagine that he was never forced to flee from Dresden, that he never went to Switzerland, that he never met Mathilde Wesendonk – in short, that he was not Richard Wagner at all. Little can be gained from asking whether Berlioz would have written the *Symphonie fantastique* if he had not met Harriet Smithson, or whether Schubert would have composed his six hundred Lieder if he had lived a comfortable and ordered existence. Pointless questions provoke pointless answers. The historical record shows that between the world of *Das Rheingold, Die Walküre* and the first two acts of *Siegfried* on the one hand, and the world of Act Three of *Siegfried* and *Götterdämmerung* on the other, lie the two totally contrasted masterpieces *Tristan und Isolde* and *Die Meistersinger*, vital moments in the organic development of Wagner's musical personality. Without them *Siegfried* and *Götterdämmerung* would not be what they are.

No concern with *The Ring* that makes its object of attention the subject-matter, the symbolism of the epic narrative or the dramatic structure, can reach the heart of the work, nor can an approach launched from material, Wagnerian or otherwise, extraneous to the work itself. There is no reason to deny the interest in relating the content of Wagner's poem to its medieval source material; or in probing it in psychoanalytical terms, Freudian, Jungian or whatever; or in pressing its significance as a document of socio-political protest; or in seeing it as a call for the supersession of old values and the regeneration of man; and so on and so on. *The Ring*, mighty work of art that it is, can take all this and more. And why should one not set the theories of *Opera and Drama* and *The Work of Art of the Future* against the tetralogy of *The Ring* itself, and discover that in practice it is not drama but epic; that, fortunately, music is not made the servant of a dramatic or any other purpose and that, equally fortunately, the finished product is not at all like the 'work of art of the future'. But none of this brings us to the living heart of the work. Only the music can do this.

Wagner once described his works as 'acts of music made visible'. There the matter can rest.

King Ludwig had saved the Bayreuth Festival from collapse. He had also made it possible for its creator to live in the luxury to which he considered himself entitled. But an immense gulf still separated vision from reality. The construction of the interior of the theatre itself, to the unusual specifications and demands of Wagner and his architect, had a long way to go, while in the planning, musical, theatrical and otherwise, of auditions, rehearsals and performances, he had barely got beyond preliminaries.

In February 1875, at the renewed prompting of Feustel and the Festival Committee, Wagner went to Vienna to conduct a concert of excerpts from *The Ring*. Cosima went with him, leaving the children in the care of Nietzsche's sister, later Elisabeth Förster-Nietzsche, who has given her own idiosyncratic description of the Wagner household in Bayreuth and of her brother's relationship to Wagner. Elisabeth Nietzsche took particular pride in her intimacy with the Wagner family and was on *Du* terms with Cosima, but her principal concern in life was her brother and the furtherance of his interests. It was to her that he confided all his life, in conversation and in letters, his innermost thoughts and fears. The anti-Semitic sentiments, however, that she shared with Wagner and, especially, Cosima, disgusted him – the anti-Semitism at Wahnfried played its part in estranging him from Wagner – as did her marriage in 1885 to a teacher called Bernhard Förster, whose anti-Jewish agitation had led a few years before to his dismissal from his post in Berlin. Cosima last mentions her in 1879.

As her brother's literary executrix, Elisabeth Nietzsche suppressed, censored and otherwise manipulated his correspondence and posthumous writings to produce the image she wanted posterity to have. In this she is the perfect companion to Cosima, who similarly controlled after Wagner's death what use, if any, should be made of the archive material at Bayreuth, and threatened legal action against anyone – like Uhlig's daughter Elsa, who planned to publish in full Wagner's often outspoken letters to her father, his close friend – who was reluctant to bow to her authority.

After the concert in Vienna came one in Budapest, in which Liszt also took part: he conducted his latest work, the cantata *The Bells of Strassburg*, and played the solo part in Beethoven's Emperor Concerto, with Richter conducting. Wagner conducted selections from *Siegfried* and *Götterdämmerung*. Four days later he went back to Vienna and repeated his first programme there. The three concerts brought in some 15,000 guilders.

After a brief return to Bayreuth he set out in April for Leipzig, Hanover and Brunswick in search of soloists for *The Ring*, then gave two concerts in Berlin, which left him with 4,000 guilders. There followed a third concert in Vienna, then a final return to Bayreuth in July for preliminary rehearsals with the singers so far engaged, with the orchestra and with technical experts – this a whole year before the opening performances.

The sense of community among the artists, the awareness of being involved in some extraordinary new creative venture, showed itself in a remarkable loyalty and selflessness. The members of the orchestra, drawn from various opera houses in Germany, who had given up part of their summer to come to Bayreuth, asked only for their expenses; some of the singers did the same. The orchestral and choral run-throughs took place in the still unfinished theatre; Richter conducted, with Wagner following the score from a little table at the side of the stage and interrupting proceedings from time to time in order to make his intentions clear. The soloists generally rehearsed in the resonant central hall in the Villa Wahnfried, accompanied at the piano by one or other of the factotums in the 'Nibelung Bureau'.

Personal tensions and frustrations occasionally ruffled the surface of this harmonious cooperation. Prima donnas and *Heldentenore* have a reputation for volatility, while Wagner was neither the easiest of masters to serve nor the easiest of friends to love. 'It is very hard to follow Wagner when he talks,' wrote Richard Fricke, the choreographer who worked with Wagner throughout the rehearsals.

At one moment he seems to be speaking to himself, at the next he thunders out in such a way that one only has a vague idea of what he is talking about. He bursts out laughing, then he becomes irritated and waxes scornful and sarcastic over what has annoyed him. . . . It is hard to work with him because he jumps from one subject to another and never concentrates long enough on one thing to bring it to a satisfactory conclusion. He wants to be his own producer but he lacks the ability to concern himself with details, because his mind is always centred on the whole, so that by tomorrow he will have forgotten the instructions and arrangements that he made today.

But all around him sensed that they were in the presence of a genius with an unshakable vision, a practical genius who knew exactly what he wanted and had all the professional skills, in music, in acting, in stagecraft, in production, to achieve it.

In return for releasing some of his star singers, among them Amalie Materna (the first Brünnhilde of *The Ring*), for the Bayreuth rehearsals, the Director of the Vienna opera, Franz Jauner, insisted on Wagner's cooperation in new productions there of *Tannhäuser* and *Lohengrin*, which Richter was to conduct. Wagner had always had a particular affection for the Viennese public, and they received him as warmly as ever, enthusiastically applauding the two works. The press was equally consistent in its hostility, although, faced with the growing public acceptance of Wagner's music, less sure of itself than a few years earlier. Much of his free time Wagner spent in the company of old friends, like Semper and Dr Standhartner, and of more recent acquaintances, among them the painter Hans Makart.

In the excited audience at the first of the Vienna performances of *Tannhäuser* in November sat a fifteen-year-old boy called Hugo Wolf. A day or so later the young Wolf managed to smuggle himself into the Hotel Imperial where Wagner and Cosima were staying, and present his first compositions, some piano pieces, to the great man. 'I walked towards him,' he wrote to his parents, 'and greeted him with reverence, whereupon he thanked me kindly . . . I am completely beside myself at the sound of the music of the great master, and have become a Wagnerian.' Wolf, one of the greatest of all song writers, based his art on Wagner and remained a Wagnerian to the end of his life. In 1882 he tried to see Wagner at a performance of *Parsifal* in Bayreuth, but the two men did not meet again. By a pleasant turn of history, Wolf played some of his early songs to Liszt a year later and owed to Liszt's enthusiasm the inception of his real career.

At the beginning of 1876 Wagner started to dictate the last part of *Mein Leben* to Cosima. The first three parts of the private edition, covering the years down to the Paris *Tannhäuser* of 1861, he had sent as a Christmas present to King Ludwig the previous month. The final part, which, as he had promised Ludwig it would, took the story to the climax of his meeting with him in 1864, was eventually completed in March 1880.

In the middle of work on *Mein Leben* and his activity for the organization of the Festival there arrived a letter from America that was to bring an unexpected windfall to his financial resources. *Lohengrin* had been given in Boston the previous year to tumultuous applause. Now came a request from Philadelphia for a Grand March to celebrate the opening of the World Fair and the centenary of the Declaration of Independence, 4 July 1876. Wagner demanded, and received, a fee of 5,000 dollars, to which were added a further 3,000 thalers from Schott for the publishing rights. His *Kaisermarsch* to salute the German Reich of 1871 and the American Centennial March would vie with each other for pride of place in a demonstration that the noblest of causes does not necessarily inspire the greatest of music.

A further contribution to the Bayreuth funds followed the performance of *Tristan* in Berlin in March. Wagner supervised the rehearsals for this performance, and the general administrator of the Berlin opera house, one Botho von Hülsen, anxious that Wagner's great project should not founder for lack of money, requested of the Kaiser that the proceeds of the performance be transferred to the Festival fund. The seat prices were increased yet the house was still packed, and almost 5,000 thalers found their way into the Bayreuth coffers. A few months later the Bavarian authorities made their own financial gesture by temporarily waiving repayment of the loan which had saved the whole enterprise.

From the beginning of May singers, conductors, coaches, repetiteurs and technicians began to arrive in Bayreuth, some in eager confidence, others still in uncertainty, even confusion, over what was expected of them. The first round of rehearsals lasted six weeks; after a break of two days the second round started and lasted two weeks; a three-day intermission, and the final round was concentrated into a mere six days, from 29 July until 4 August.

Of the four final dress rehearsals (6-9 August) three took place in the presence of an audience, so that sound-balance and the other acoustical problems of a new, untried hall could be checked. At the rehearsal of *Das Rheingold* there was just one figure in the auditorium – King Ludwig II of Bavaria. He had long cherished a desire to hear *The Ring* alone, free of the protocol, the ceremony and the public gestures that always accompanied his appearances. Once it became known that he was coming, the town naturally prepared a suitable display in welcome. But Ludwig knew what he wanted. He arrived by train at one o'clock in the morning, was met by Wagner and driven to the Eremitage, the Margrave's country seat outside the town. The two men had not met since the first performance of *Die Meistersinger* eight years ago. In the evening, avoiding the crowds, the King drove up to the opera house by a roundabout route without being noticed and watched *Das Rheingold* from the royal box, alone except for Wagner. At the other three performances the select audience was not allowed to intrude on the King's private pleasure and after *Götterdämmerung* he returned to Hohenschwangau as he had come, in the night and unnoticed.

This was the supreme moment in Ludwig's life, the triumphant justification of his trust in Wagner's vision after years of opposition, of doubt, of resentment, sometimes even of distrust and hidden anger. 'I came with high expectations but what I saw far, far exceeded them,' he joyfully exclaimed in a letter to his hero. 'How happy is the century that has seen such a spirit arise in its midst! How envious future generations will be of those who have known the immeasurable happiness of living in the same age as you! It is my desire to serve you as long as I live and breathe!' He returned to Bayreuth for the third cycle of *The Ring* a little over two weeks later, this time publicly.

Production difficulties of one kind or another continued

right up to the last minute. Singers dropped out and had to be replaced; there were demarcation disputes between Brandt, the choreographer Richard Fricke – who had to stage such moments as the swimming of the Rhine Maidens and the toiling of the Nibelungs under Alberich's whip – and Carl Doepler, the costume designer; some of the mechanical devices, like the Rhine Maidens' swimming machines, struck terror into the hearts of the none-too-athletic singers expected to submit to them; and the dragon that Siegfried was to fight, ordered from a London firm, arrived belatedly in sections, the neck never arriving at all, having been sent in error, it was later said, to Beirut instead of Bayreuth.

The Festival opened on 13 August. Between then and the 30th three cycles of the complete *Ring* were given, with intervals of four days between the cycles. Among the guests were two emperors – Kaiser Wilhelm and the Emperor Don Pedro II of Brazil – the King of Württemberg, the Grand Duke Carl Alexander of Weimar, the Grand Duke of Schwerin and other German princes, many lesser aristocracy and the subscribers to the Patronage Certificates; Tchaikovsky was there, so were Bruckner, Grieg and Saint-Saëns, writers like Karl Hillebrand and Catulle Mendès, with his former wife Judith Gautier, and the painters Makart and Menzel. Also present were many of the close friends and benefactors who had watched, and often suffered, as Wagner carved out the path that led to this moment of fulfilment – Otto and Mathilde Wesendonk, Liszt, Mathilde Maier, Malwida von Meysenbug, Marie von Schleinitz, Countess Hildegard von Usedom and others. Cosima noticed that among the considerable number of foreigners present there was a large proportion of Englishmen. Among them was the naturalized Charles Hallé, whom Wagner remembered from their meeting in very different circumstances in Paris in 1840. Hallé later wrote in his autobiography:

At Bayreuth, in 1876, during one of the welcome entr'actes, we met in the open air, he [Wagner] being surrounded by a crowd of admirers. It was then that he alluded to the pleasant evenings in Paris, expressed how gratified he was that I, too, had come all the way from England to hear his works, and ended by saying emphatically: 'You see, my dear Hallé, I shall make Bayreuth the centre of civilization.' 'A noble aim, my dear master,' was my answer. We never met again.

Also in the British contingent that came to Bayreuth for one or other of the three *Ring* cycles were the pianist Edward Dannreuther, founder of the London Wagner Society and a well-known teacher, and the young composers Charles Villiers Stanford and Hubert Parry. Stanford had a characteristically unsentimental memory of the occasion. '"He that is not with me is against me", was the motto of the whole Festival,' he noted drily in his *Pages from an Unwritten Diary*. Parry, on the other hand, the quintessential upper-class Englishman, had been swept off his feet by the time the end of *Götterdämmerung* was reached. 'I was in a whirl of excitement over it,' he exclaimed, 'and quite drunk with delight.'

Looking back two years later, Wagner wrote: 'It truly seemed that no artist had been honoured in such a way. It had been known for an artist to be summoned to an emperor or a prince, but nobody could recall that emperors and princes had ever come to an artist.' And as he surveyed the assembled wealth and elegance that had made its way from all over the world to this insignificant little south German town, he could see that what he had created was a far cry from the instrument of popular education which he had so enthusiastically fashioned for his purpose in the revolutionary, vision-filled days of his Swiss exile. It was, and remains – how could it be otherwise? – an entertainment for a privileged élite. Or, in its most extreme form, a religious rite attended by devoted, well-shod pilgrims from the more prosperous parts of the globe.

The Bayreuth theatre on the Green Hill above the town seats 1,900 – an immense number by nineteenth-century standards – and is a light construction of brick and wood. The only addition to the original structure is the rectangular entrance foyer, the so-called *Königsbau*, built in 1882, which incorporates the balcony from which trumpeters sound the fanfares that summon the audience for the beginning of each act.

The auditorium is almost entirely wood – lath and plaster walls, hollow, uncarpeted wooden floor, hollow wooden side pillars rendered with plaster, an unsupported ceiling of canvas stretched over wooden struts, and plain wooden seats (the original ones were of bast stretched over wooden frames) with neither arm-rests nor upholstery, which have taxed the endurance of many a listener. These features, together with the sunken orchestra pit, and the shell that makes the orchestra invisible to the audience – an idea first proposed by Wagner in a preface to the poem of *The Ring* in 1863 – create the inimitable acoustic of the hall. Everything reflects the sound, nothing absorbs it; the structure is part of the process of musical creation, and every precious particle of sound is transmitted to the listener's ear.

Wagner saw a two-fold advantage in an invisible orchestra, the one aspect visual, the other aural. With no distracting movements and lights, in particular no gesticulating conductor, to disturb the audience's view of the stage, the eye could concentrate on the action. At the same time the shell-like canopy that concealed the orchestra, some of whom sat virtually underneath the stage, promoted the luxuriant warmth of orchestral tone and colour in which Wagner sought to envelop his listeners. For the players themselves the sharply-stepped levels on which they are arranged – the strings at the front, the brass at the farthest and deepest point – make for cramped conditions that become the more unpleasant through the heat generated in their almost completely sealed enclosure. Since the audience cannot see them, however, they can permit themselves the luxury of playing in their shirtsleeves.

Wagner had from the beginning insisted that his wooden theatre should be regarded only as a provisional structure, the nation being left, as he put it in a letter to Feustel in 1872, 'to build it in monumental permanence'. In the name of glorious musical sound we may be grateful, a hundred years later, that it is still as 'provisional' as ever.

For so revolutionary and incredibly complex an undertaking, the first cycle of *The Ring* passed off with remarkably few mishaps. In *Das Rheingold* Wotan dropped the ring, the gas lighting repeatedly failed, and one of the stage-hands hauled up a backcloth too early, revealing the rear wall of the theatre and a group of scene-shifters in their shirtsleeves, but the other three works generally went off well, Cosima noted in her diary. The day after *Götterdämmerung* Wagner gave a banquet in the Festival restaurant to show his gratitude to his artists and technicians and the following day he and Cosima entertained over 200 guests at a reception in Wahnfried.

After the final *Götterdämmerung* Wagner, who later became very depressed at the inadequacies of the performances, came on to the stage to receive the applause, which was led by King Ludwig from his box. Moved and elated, yet as self-assured, almost arrogant, as ever, he said to his exhilarated audience:

It is to your patronage and to the immense efforts of my performers and musicians that you owe this achievement. All the other things I might wish to say to you can be summarized in a few words – indeed, in a single statement. You have seen what we are capable of doing; it is now up to you to *will* us to do it. And if you so will us, then we shall have an Art!

The typically self-centred implication that there had

hitherto been no real art – no real dramatic musical art, that is – provoked incredulous derision in some quarters and indignation in others. But then, as Saint-Saëns, who was present to hear Wagner's words, wrote: 'Wagner's admirers have long known that his tactlessness is as great as his talent, and they pay no attention to such remarks.'

All this makes the first Bayreuth Festival sound an unqualified financial and artistic success like the festivals of modern times, its artistic quality acknowledged by the entire musical world. Nothing of the kind. The three cycles of *The Ring* ended with a huge deficit of some 150,000 marks, hardly the basis on which to make the Festival an annual event. Wagner's suggestion that the State should take over the opera house, then provide funds for the town of Bayreuth to organize an annual festival, produced a cold silence. Although in 1878 the Bavarian court authorities granted a loan in exchange for the right to perform *Parsifal*, and also agreed to pay Wagner royalties on performances of his works in Munich, further public assistance was out of the question. The interest on unpaid debts continued to mount even after Wagner's death. In 1900 the King's Secretary Ludwig Bürkel, successor to Düfflip, noted: 'Bayreuth Festival debt: the Wagner family is still paying the deficit. 120,000 marks have now been collected through annual payments. 100,000 marks remain to be paid.'

The press, spurred on by the indefatigable Hanslick, picked on the imperfections of the first performances in 1876 to deflate the whole gigantic concept, and although the first cycle was sold out, there were many empty seats at the other two. Those who attended were credited with stamina rather than taste, and since the theatre was over a mile outside the town, the long ascent to it not properly surfaced, and the available hostelries quite unable to cope with the sudden influx of affluent visitors, a certain power of endurance was indeed called for. Tchaikovsky, after granting Wagner's powerful technique and industry, and acknowledging the grandeur of the whole Festival enterprise, devoted a good deal of his rather sardonic memoir on the occasion to complaining about the banal conversation of the audience during the intermissions and grumbling at the poor catering:

Every piece of bread and every glass of beer had to be fought for; it was an incredible strain, and needed cunning as well as infinite patience. The guests were in a state of confusion and chaos, all shouting at the same time. At the side of the theatre two large marquees had been put up which announced on big placards that a good lunch would be served at two o'clock, but it needed an act of the sheerest heroism to fight one's way through the hungry masses. . . .

While admitting that many well-known musicians had in fact come to Bayreuth, Tchaikovsky pointedly observes that 'those of the first rank' – he names Gounod, Verdi, Ambroise Thomas, Brahms, Joachim, Anton Rubinstein and Bülow – had not.

More and more people, however, were beginning to admit that, although they did not fully understand what they had experienced in Wagner's theatre, and found certain aspects of it disturbing, even unpleasant, here was something too great to ignore. In particular they began to identify the power of *The Ring* as residing in the music, whatever Wagner might have earlier said about music being merely a means to a dramatic end. 'He has won the battle,' wrote the critic Wilhelm Mohr in 1876, in his brochure on the Festival,

and curiously enough he has done so in the one area where he was not trying to win it – in fact, where he had to struggle hardest for victory, namely in the field of *music*. He has not enhanced his reputation as a poet, his old dramatic cunning has nothing to offer that we have not already seen in *Tannhäuser* and *Lohengrin*, and his new theatrical miracles not only conflict with what modern stage machinery and technicians can do but, far worse, are at odds with the nature of art itself. The victory has gone to Wagner the *musician*. Because of his principles, irrespective of his principles, and contrary to his principles, he has created beauty, life in its fullness, and has brought into being musico-dramatic creations of a totally new kind. The old form has not been destroyed in this new beauty but has undergone a transformation like that of Siegfried's sword Nothung, which was filed down, melted, recast and forged. . . . He is victorious, even though his 'Work of Art of the Future' may have been defeated and now be seen as an exaggeration or a premature idea.

The aesthetician Conrad Fiedler wrote in a similar spirit to the sculptor Adolf von Hildebrand in September 1876: 'In Wagner the dramatic action and the music are not separate components; rather, it is only in the music that the dramatic action comes into being. The music is never independent of the action but also, so to speak, never lets go of the action, and is never let go by it, so that the expression of the action becomes steadily more intense.' In an interesting comment on Hildebrand's doubts – many have since shared them – whether Wagner's appeal is artistic or anti-artistic, Fiedler adds: 'As to what you say about the effect of Wagner's music, namely that it does not derive from its artistic qualities, that is quite true for a large section of the population. But it does not prove that Wagner's works do not possess artistic qualities.'

To feel pride in a German art – Bach, Beethoven, Weber, Schumann – was an appropriate emotion in these years of the consolidation of the Second Reich. But for Wagner to usurp the exclusive right to represent this German-ness bordered on a total distortion of the true ethos of the nation. Writing in the influential Berlin journal, the *Vossische Zeitung*, in September 1878, the critic Gustav Engel, approved of Wagner's demand for a solemn, almost reverential attitude to art on the part of his listeners, groaned at the often appalling *longueurs* of his works and then concluded:

Wagner's fundamental German-ness is un-German. He is representative of only one facet of the life of the nation – the obstinate, German-at-all-costs side, the striving for depth without clarity, for truth without beauty, absolute subjectivity with no objective restraints. In a word, Wagner's work has about it something Gothic, something barbarian, in the sense that Goethe used the words, and we must seek to rid ourselves of this Gothic-ness and barbarism.

Thirty-five years later Thomas Mann put the same antithesis, fearing that humanistic values would be sacrificed to the irrational, daemonic powers of darkness. 'The Germans,' he wrote in 1911, 'should be made to decide between Goethe and Wagner. They cannot have both. But I fear they would choose Wagner.' The course of German history since that time has hardly proven his fears to be groundless.

It was fears like these, coupled with a distrust of the grandiose and a contempt for the sort of clientèle that he saw making their way to the Master's shrine on the 'Green Hill' in Bayreuth, that filled the mind of a man who came to Bayreuth for the dress rehearsals but fled from the scene before they started; who returned to Bayreuth ten days later, reluctantly and full of foreboding, for the opening of the festival; who endured *Das Rheingold* but gave away his tickets for the remaining evenings; at one time Wagner's most ardent disciple, later the most famous defector from his cause – Friedrich Nietzsche.

Nietzsche was already tortured by the attacks of migraine which later drove him out of his mind, and his weak eyes, overstrained by concentrating on the stage spectacle and by peering at his score in the semi-darkness of the theatre, were so painful that he could neither read nor write. His fellow-philosopher Dr Paul Rée, one of the friends, like Erwin Rohde, Carl von Gersdorff and Franz Overbeck, whom he had converted to Wagner, read aloud to him; at other times the young composer Peter Gast, alias Heinrich Köselitz, who became his faithful companion and amanuensis, took down parts of *Human, All Too Human* from his hesitant dictation. This is the work, published two years later, that reveals Nietzsche's irreversible estrangement from Wagner the man and Wagner the musician, but signs of his inner alienation had become apparent in private contexts long before this.

Nietzsche's contribution to the Festival year of 1876, however – *Richard Wagner in Bayreuth*, the fourth of his studies under the title *Thoughts out of Season* – is a Janus-like work. Taken in one way, it reads like a hymn of praise. 'Friend, your book is amazing. However did you come to know me so well?' exclaimed Wagner in his joy at being understood – so he thought – as he ought to be understood. Nietzsche wrote the first eight of the eleven chapters during the autumn of 1875, in the full flush of that reverence for Wagner's art that had dominated the past sixteen years of his life and given him countless hours of happiness at Tribschen. But some inner doubt then made him put the work aside, and although he completed it a few months later, he knew that he had lost his way, defaulting on his earlier conviction. 'I am not master of my task, and I know that I am not entirely sure of my own direction, let alone of any help to others,' he wrote to Rohde. Seen in its full context, *Richard Wagner in Bayreuth* has the appearance as much of a farewell as of a hail.

What Nietzsche saw of the Festival itself, both the theatrical experience of the operas and the atmosphere generated by their pretentious patrons, with their uncritical fawning, their noisy nationalism and their incipient anti-Semitism, alienated him still further. Above all he despised the substitution of art for morality, the conversion of ethical issues into matters of aesthetic judgment – an article of faith to the whole German Romantic movement of the nineteenth century. Nietzsche was a moralist, in art as in everything else. At the heart of a work of art must lie an ethical reality. 'Everyone who has not lost the power to ponder such things,' he said in his address to the Patrons of Bayreuth in 1873, 'must experience an artistic undertaking as an *ethical* phenomenon and must give his approval as such.' For Nietzsche art was the servant of life, a new and truer life. For Wagner art *was* life. Nietzsche had to ask himself whether an activity in art served the aims of the new life; his instinct, his disillusionment, his apprehension told him that the Bayreuth Festival did not.

From that moment on the arch-priest became the arch-fiend. Two years later, in *Human, All Too Human*, Nietzsche called Wagner 'a Romantic in despair, decaying and rotten', adding, with Romantic music, the supremely Romantic music of Wagner, in his thoughts: '"Beware of Music!" This is still my advice to all those who have the mettle to preserve their integrity of mind.' The future now lay, not with music but with poetry, for music is an end, is death: 'All true, all original music is a swan song.' When, after *The Ring*, Wagner turned towards the values of Christianity, his mind occupied with the ethic of *Parsifal*, their incompatibility became even more evident, for Nietzsche's anti-Christian attitudes, expressed in philippics as violent as his anti-Wagner writings, had already begun to harden.

It was Nietzsche who turned his back on Wagner, not *vice versa*, but by the time of *Human, All Too Human* the savage hostility between the two men had become mutual. In August of that year, three months after receiving Nietzsche's book, Wagner suddenly said to Cosima, in a conversation about entirely different things: 'Everything that wicked man has, comes from me, even the weapons he uses against me. How perverse he is, how cunning, yet how shallow!'

The virulent climax of Nietzsche's anti-Wagnerianism

came five years after Wagner's death in *The Case of Wagner* and the autobiographical *Ecce Homo*, both the outpourings of a man in physical distress and psychological unbalance. The hatred that Nietzsche exuded has itself the pathological tone that he now attributes to the 'hysterical, convulsive, distorted' works that Wagner had brought on to the stage. And when we confront his *facit* on the Wagnerian *oeuvre* – 'The whole thing presents a picture of sickness. Wagner is a neurosis' – we cannot but think of the state of mind of the sick man who uttered it. The violence of Nietzsche's hatred only shows, in fact, how impossible it was for him to cure himself of the Wagnerian 'sickness'. He described the agony of his dilemma in a letter to Peter Gast in 1880: 'I suffer terribly when people lose their sympathy for me, and nothing can console me for the loss of Wagner's sympathy in these last few years. How often I dream of him – always in the spirit of when we were together . . . But all this is now past, and what help is it to have sometimes been right to oppose him?'

Looking back on the happy years of his friendship with Wagner, Nietzsche summed up their relationship in moving words:

We were once friends and have now grown apart. But that is as it should be, so let us not draw a veil over it or disguise it, as though we had something to be ashamed of. We are two ships, each with its own course and its own destination. Our paths may cross, and we may celebrate an occasion together, as we have done: at such a moment the two fine ships lie so peacefully alongside each other in one harbour and under one sun, that it seems as if they had had one goal, and had reached it. But then the mighty pressure of our different tasks forced us apart again, driving us into different seas and climes, and perhaps we shall never see each other again. Or rather, perhaps we *shall* see each other again but not recognize each other, such will be the change wrought in us by these seas and climes. It was a law above us that decreed that we should grow apart. For this very reason we should esteem each other more; for this very reason the memory of our former friendship should become the more hallowed . . . So let us hold to our celestial friendship, even though on earth we may have to be mortal enemies.

Whatever the psychological factors at work, whatever the influence of Wagner's overbearing egoism and Nietzsche's desperate physical suffering, the love-hate relationship between these two men has a representative quality that illuminates a vital spiritual conflict in Western culture. A hundred years later there is still no more trenchant, more painfully perceptive, more profoundly disturbing critique of all that Wagner stands for than the analyses that Nietzsche tore from his agonized mind.

One does not readily think of Wagner and Goethe as kindred spirits – rather, with Thomas Mann, as opposite poles of the German character, paradigms of the dichotomy of mind and nature, humanism and barbarism, nationalism and romanticism, classicism and Christianity that runs through the German national consciousness and German history. But one thing they share: an attachment to '*das Ewig-Weibliche*', the feminine principle, and a capacity, preserved into advanced years, for the renewal of erotic experience. The sixty-year-old Goethe fell in love with Marianne Willemer, inspiration of the love songs of the *West-östlicher Divan*; at seventy-three he met the nineteen-year-old Ulrike von Levetzow, who aroused in him the emotion that found expression in the 'Marienbad Elegy' and the *Trilogie der Leidenschaft*. Wagner, sixty-three in the year of the Bayreuth Festival, with less than seven years to live, was now seized with the last passion of his dotage, a passion for the lovely Judith Gautier, thirty-three years his junior.

Judith Gautier, daughter of the French poet Théophile Gautier, who was an early champion of Wagner's music, had visited Tribschen from Paris a number of times in the company of her husband Catulle Mendès, writer, literary editor, and a prominent figure in circles of late nineteenth-century French *décadence*, and of the poet Villiers de l'Isle Adam. She had jet black hair, 'with a white complexion faintly tinged with pink,' wrote Edmond de Goncourt in his *Journal*, 'her mouth standing out like the mouth of a Primitive against the ivory of her broad teeth, her firm and, as it were, drowsy features, her big eyes, animal lashes, stiff lashes like little black pins, which did not soften their gaze with a veil of shadow – all this gave the lethargic creature the mysterious indefinable air of a sphinx.'

The first time she came to Tribschen, in the summer of 1869, she completely swept Wagner off his feet. Excitedly he showed her and her companions the beauties of Lucerne and the lakeside, played them the newest parts of *Siegfried*, worked himself up to a dangerous height on the children's swing in the garden, clambered up the side of the house to the first-floor balcony by means of ledges, mouldings and shutters, and indulged in other frolics better suited to an infatuated teenager than to a public figure of fifty-six. They also played Wagner's *Huldigungsmarsch* together as a piano duet. Both Judith and her husband later recalled being struck, like many others, by the frankness and penetration of his eyes.

Wagner was only one of many captivated by Judith Gautier's beauty and intelligence, and her association with Victor Hugo in particular gives her a place in every biography of that greatest of French Romantic poets. Herself a writer, she campaigned together with her husband for the cause of Wagner's music in France and was at Bayreuth in 1876 to share his triumph. As the strains and tensions he had endured at the festival met the sympathy and charm of his beautiful young admirer, Wagner suddenly found himself passionately drawn to her, as he had once been drawn to Jessie Laussot and to Mathilde

Wesendonk. Like them, Judith fulfilled a need of the moment. He had needed Mathilde for the sake of *Tristan*; now, over the two years of their intimate correspondence, he needed Judith for the sake of *Parsifal*. There is vanity, self-indulgence, self-delusion in the relationship that his letters to her in Paris, written in a quaint and often ungrammatical French, reveal. But there is also a direct and unconcealed passion. 'When I kissed you this morning,' he wrote to her on the day she left Bayreuth after the Festival of 1876, 'was it for the last time? No! I shall see you again! I intend to – because I love you!' A year later his ardour was still as intense: 'The memory of your embraces fills me with the wildest intoxication; they were the crowning glory of my life. In my supreme moments I feel a sweet, blissful yearning to embrace you and never to escape from your love. You are mine – is it not so?'

After Wagner's death Judith maintained that she and Wagner had not been lovers. His letters do suggest at times that she did not respond as enthusiastically as he would have liked (her letters to him have never been uncovered), and on one occasion he makes intriguing reference to having been thrown out of her room in Bayreuth. Much of the affair may have been a self-induced fantasy in Wagner's mind, but all of it certainly was not. As with so many of his relationships, we do not know the full truth, and probably never shall. Nor can we tell how much Cosima, who had an affection for Judith and addressed her by her Christian name, knew about it. She could hardly have been entirely ignorant of it, but her strength of will would have forbidden her to betray what she might have felt. Her sense of mission, of being the one, the happy one, chosen by destiny to sacrifice herself to the whims and fancies of genius, sustained her acceptance of whatever he said and did, whatever he claimed to need, even though it sometimes brought her suffering and embarrassment. This is the context of Nietzsche's remark:

'Bayreuth is Cosima's work. Without her this highest dream of Wagner's would never have become reality.'

It was Judith Gautier who sent Wagner at this time the expensive silks, satins, furs and perfumes which he craved as a kind of aesthetic insulation against the coarseness of the outside world. Although his sensitive skin and his proneness to rashes and allergies were reason enough for him to wear the softest of silks next to the skin, his cultivation of fancy gowns, sashes and headwear went far beyond the cutaneous. As in his letters of the 1860s to the milliner Bertha Goldwag in Vienna, he specifies to Judith the exact texture, the exact shade, the exact shimmer he wants, adding instructions as to the powerful perfumes and bath essences – his sense of smell was weak, he said – that should complement the luxurious fabrics. 'At my age,' he wrote light-heartedly to his '*douce amie*', as he called her, 'one can indulge oneself in childish things.'

Wagner's choice of Bayreuth as the location for his Festival and as the place where he would spend the remainder of his life justified itself in all respects but one – the climate. The raw, damp winters and the unpredictable summers aggravated his respiratory troubles, his skin complaints and his other nervous disorders. Exhausted by the strains of the Festival, he decided to go to Italy with Cosima and the children, both for relaxation and for his health. From Bayreuth he travelled via Munich to Verona, then via Venice, Bologna and Naples to Sorrento, where he stayed for a month in the Hotel Vittoria (now the Excelsior Vittoria).

At Malwida von Meysenbug's villa in Sorrento Wagner and Nietzsche saw each other for the last time. Wagner was preoccupied with thoughts of *Parsifal*, with the concept of redemption, with the Christian symbols of the Last Supper. The depressing news had just reached him of the huge deficit left by the Festival. Nietzsche, already with an uneasy conscience over his behaviour at Bayreuth, dared not now mention *The Ring* and music drama at all, the subject which only a year earlier had linked him to Wagner in the closest of relationships. Moreover his own philosophy was that of the positive will, of one who said 'Yea' to life, like Siegfried, not of an apologetic, self-denying agent of Christian redemption, like Parsifal. 'Where ye see ideals,' wrote Nietzsche, 'I see human, alas, all-too human realities.' There was little left for the two men to talk about.

When he received a copy of the poem of *Parsifal* at the beginning of 1878, Nietzsche observed: 'There is more Liszt in it than Wagner – the spirit of the Counter-Reformation. For me, a person too accustomed to Classical and general humanist values, it is all too Christian, too restricted in time. . . . And the language sounds like a translation from a foreign tongue.' Yet when he first heard the Prelude to *Parsifal* in 1887, he could scarcely contain his emotion. He wrote to his friend Peter Gast:

. . . a sublime, extraordinary feeling and spiritual experience in music at its most fundamental . . . a synthesis of spiritual states which many, including so-called superior minds, will consider irreconcilable . . . an intellectual and psychological penetration which cuts through the soul like a knife. The only thing like it is in Dante – nowhere else.

The paradox cannot be resolved. The admiration-distrust, the exaltation-despair, the love-hate – it is all integral. Such is the power of music – Wagner's music – over the keenest of minds and the bitterest of opponents.

Back in Bayreuth at the end of 1876, Wagner worked at the text of *Parsifal* and continued to explore ways of preserving the festival concept with public aid of one kind or another. The question of performances of *The Ring* elsewhere – Munich clearly had first claim, while Leipzig and Vienna made their own approaches – also had to be considered as a way of helping to meet the outstanding debt.

In March 1877 Wagner signed a contract to conduct six concerts of his music at the Albert Hall in London the following May – excerpts from his operas, together with the *Kaisermarsch* and other marches. He was seasick the whole crossing from Ostend to Dover, 'which made me somewhat ashamed,' wrote Cosima in her diary, 'that I myself felt no discomfort and rather enjoyed the unusual journey.' In London they stayed with Edward Dannreuther in Bayswater. In a hectic round of social engagements he made the acquaintance of Browning, George Eliot and her husband George Henry Lewes – both of whom, connoisseurs of things German, went to Wagner's Albert Hall concerts – the painter Millais and others; Prosper Sainton and Karl Lüders, friends from the days of his Philharmonic Society concerts in 1855, also came to greet him. The seal of his public recognition was fixed with an invitation to an audience with Queen Victoria at Windsor Castle. At the Albert Hall he was also introduced to the Prince of Wales, later King Edward VII, who told Wagner that he still remembered his Philharmonic concerts of twenty years before. Wagner was frequently unwell and tired, but Cosima carried out her strenuous social calendar with enthusiasm. During the last days of her stay she sat for a portrait by Edward Burne-Jones, which has, however, never been found. 'If I had to choose a big city,' she said, 'it would be London.'

The aristocratic grace and bearing of the tall, slim, forty-year-old Cosima made her completely at ease in cultured metropolitan circles and, like other features of her elegant French upbringing, were always something of a contrast to the impulsive, often aggressive and far from aristocratic manner of the short, stocky, provincial husband twenty-four years her senior. The contrast between their social personalities elicited from George Eliot the tart observation: '*She* is a genius. *He* is an *épicier!*'

The concerts themselves, conducted partly by Wagner, partly by Hans Richter, with eight specially engaged soloists (most of them from the Bayreuth *Ring*) and an immense orchestra of 170 players, were an artistic triumph. But because of the huge expenses they produced a profit of a mere £700, about one tenth of the Bayreuth deficit. The soloists each pocketed a fat fee plus expenses, the specially assembled orchestra had to be paid, and although the Albert Hall held an audience of 10,000, a third of the seats were private property and thus brought no benefit to the box office. Cosima, however, regarded the £700 as most acceptable: 'I was prepared for the worst,' she wrote in her diary. 'But R. is very depressed.'

Back in Germany Wagner went for an extended rest-cure to Bad Ems in order to regain his strength, then returned to face the problems of Bayreuth and to work on *Parsifal*. The text had already been finished before his London visit, and as was his custom, he had eagerly read it to groups of friends in search of their approval. In July he sent a copy, written by Cosima, to King Ludwig with the inscription '*Erlösung dem Erlöser!*' – 'Salvation to the Saviour!'

And a saviour Ludwig once more turned out to be. At a meeting of the Patrons of the Bayreuth Festival in September 1877, at which he also read his *Parsifal*, Wagner lamented: 'We are in a terrible state. Nor is there any hope of help from the Reichstag, where not a single man knows what we really need.' Yet his optimism still gave him the confidence to announce plans for the establishment in Bayreuth of a conservatoire in which to train the singers and conductors required to perform his own and other works of a 'truly German spirit'. It was a project reminiscent of that which he had put before the King of Saxony over thirty years earlier – and it met the same fate.

Apart from the official refusal to countenance any financial investment in such a scheme, Wagner's appeal to young musicians to join the conservatoire produced the enrolment of one solitary student.

Suddenly the situation changed yet again. The King, approached both by Wagner and by Cosima, could help no further out of his own resources, but he urged the Court secretariat to enter into an agreement with Wagner and the Festival Committee for a formal loan to save the whole Bayreuth idea from final collapse. So in March 1878, by which time Wagner was well advanced with the music of the second act of *Parsifal*, a contract was drawn up offering an immediate loan of some 98,000 marks at 4½ per cent interest to liquidate the outstanding debt from the first festival. The money was to be repaid from a 10 per cent royalty allowed to Wagner on all performances of his works in the Munich Court Theatre. The agreement, largely the work of Feustel and Muncker on the one hand and the King's new secretary, Ludwig Bürkel, on the other, also stipulated that Munich should receive the performing rights of *Parsifal*.

Nietzsche said that without Cosima there would have been no Bayreuth. There are also many lesser men and women without whom there would have been no Bayreuth. But from the beginning to the end, from the kindling of the youthful fire of idealism to the unwavering determination that the ideal should become reality, and that the greatest composer of the age should be set free to achieve his life's work *ad majorem Germaniae gloriam*, the glory that is Bayreuth stands as the indestructible tribute to the vision of the 'mad' King Ludwig II of Bavaria, perhaps the only man who ever understood what Wagner really needed.

As a kind of compensation for the abortive attempt to establish his conservatoire, Wagner now founded a journal, financed by the Society of Patrons of Bayreuth, in which to give publicity to his principles and their implications. It was called *Bayreuther Blätter*. As editor – originally he had thought of Nietzsche – Wagner chose a rich young man called Hans von Wolzogen, whose devotion to the Wagnerian cause was as energetic as it was sycophantic, and who continued to edit the journal right down to his death in 1938· at the age of ninety. To some the *Bayreuther Blätter* has been a mixture of shameless propaganda and appeals to a deplorable irrationalism: it certainly had its share of anti-Semitic sentiment and chauvinistic emotionalism, in articles both by Wagner and others. At the same time it was the organ in which Wagner published a number of his last statements – some predictable, some preposterous, but all psychologically revealing – on life and art. It was also one of the main vehicles for the propagation of orthodox Wagnerianism in the Cosima era and up to the Second World War. As such it has a special importance for our understanding of what Wagner stood for – or could be made to stand for.

Some of these late essays of Wagner's reveal the old convictions, not to say prejudices, others show significant changes of emphasis since his revolutionary journalistic days in the 1850s. *Modern* (1878), for instance, has the same sneering anti-Jewish tone as *Music and the Jews*, intensified by scorn of the Young German movement, led by the Jews Heine and Boerne, whose materialism and iconoclastic modernism had once held him in its sway.

In *Publikum und Popularität (Public and Popularity*, also 1878) he mounts his familiar hobby-horse of the ignorant public to whose level no self-respecting artist would descend, since no art can be good 'which is from the beginning designed to be put before the public'. The latter part of the essay degenerates into a veiled counter-attack on Nietzsche as a retort to the latter's *Human, All Too Human*. But there is still interest to be found, and a case to be answered, in Wagner's claim that the purity of the work of art as it leaves the mind of its creator is lost if the public that receives it has itself, under the pressures of commercialism and other evils of the culture industry, lost its sense of what is pure. Things being what they are, good art can penetrate the consciousness of the public only in the form of mediocrity, and as long as the public is as it is, the wider dissemination of art can only lead to further debasement. Far from welcoming the prospect of *The Ring* being performed all over Germany and thus reaching people who would never find their way to Bayreuth, Wagner recoils from the thought in horror: 'Only a complete purity of relationship between the work of art and its public can constitute the foundation of a truly noble popularity.' One is reminded of Wagner's remark to Ferdinand Heine back in 1852: 'I am not in the slightest concerned whether people perform my works or not: I am only concerned that they perform them in the manner I intended. If they cannot, or will not, then let them desist altogether.'

At the head of *Public and Popularity* stands an Indian proverb:

It is not the bad that is bad, for the bad rarely deceives us;
The mediocre is bad, because it can seem to be good.

Wagner makes his own use of this Oriental wisdom in a European context. He is sometimes perverse in his attitudes, often inaccurate in his argumentation and always prejudiced and intolerant in his judgments. But here, as in almost everything else he wrote, flashes of insight light up the pages of his ornate, though not humourless Baroque style, compelling the reader to consider sometimes uncomfortable views which many would prefer not to hear.

The essay *Wollen wir hoffen? (Shall We Hope?)*, printed in the *Bayreuther Blätter* in May 1877, shows what he thought of the new German Reich and its abject failure to fulfil its destiny. This, like all his utterances on political and social matters, springs less from sustained critical study than from a subjective assessment of the relationship between external circumstances and his own situation. A discrepancy between his personal interests and the economic and social realities of the day provoked him to criticize these realities, not as the undesirable products of historical pressures but as impediments to the fruition of his artistic ambitions. His periodic outbursts against the Jews exhibit this trait at its most blatant.

But in spite of this, or even because of it, the spontaneity and unconsidered obstinacy of his attitudes can convey something of the spirit of the age, something of its social, economic and cultural pressures, in a way that reflective analysis can not. The 1870s in Germany mark the transformation of a predominantly agrarian national state into an industrial power. The people of *Dichter und Denker (poets and thinkers)* gives way to a nation pledged to technological and material progress, to commercialism and the establishment of new urban and industrial structures in society, and the philosophy of idealism recedes before the pursuit of prosperity and the idolization of material success. One counterpoint to this expansion is the rise of aggressive nationalism, the ruthless cult of political power in international affairs, to which the rulers of Germany appealed with triumphant and tragic success in the prelude to two world wars. Another is the growth of organized proletarianism – the spread of socialist doctrines, the emergence of trade unions, the development of the language of class-warfare and other manifestations of a rampant radicalism.

The materialistic, anti-cultural values of the new German state, especially of Prussia, wrote Wagner to King Ludwig in July 1878, would soon lead it back to barbarism: 'This new Germany utterly disgusts me! Is this what they call an Empire? A Berlin as capital of the

Reich?! We are being mocked from above, and the mocking will soon be echoed from below.' The same scorn of public institutions, above all – with unwavering consistency – the press, finds expression in *Shall We Hope?*, together with Wagner's faith in individual genius and the spirit of the *Volk*. To the question posed in the title of his essay he gives a characteristic answer in self-centred terms: 'As testimony that I, for my part, have not given up hope, I can adduce the fact that in the last few days I have succeeded in finishing the music to my *Parsifal*.'

As to the emergent radicalism of the 1870s and Bismarck's attempt to suppress it through his anti-socialist law of 1878, Wagner, although he had long since lost all revolutionary zeal, still saw the development towards socialism as an historical necessity, and the anti-socialist legislation as retrogressive. Reflecting on his letters of the 1840s to Theodor Uhlig, friend of his Dresden years, he assured Cosima he still believed that socialism would eventually come, although it would not be in the near future.

The operas of *Der Ring des Nibelungen* gradually began to establish themselves in German theatres during the years after the Bayreuth Festival of 1876. *Die Walküre* was given in Vienna at the end of 1877, followed by *Das Rheingold* early in 1878, and the complete *Ring* in the summer of 1879; Munich gave its first performances of *Siegfried* and *Götterdämmerung* in the summer of 1878, and its first complete *Ring* the following November (King Ludwig also had a number of performances of the cycle put on for his private pleasure); Cologne, Weimar, Schwerin, Hamburg and other theatres mounted parts of the cycle in 1878 and 1879.

The first complete performance of all four parts of *The Ring* outside Bayreuth took place in Leipzig. *Das Rheingold* and *Die Walküre* were performed on 28 and 29 April

1878. *Siegfried* and *Götterdämmerung* five months later, on 21 and 22 September; in January 1879 a true 'close' performance of the cycle followed, with a number of singers who were later to join the company of the greatest Wagnerian interpreters.

The man behind these Leipzig performances was the remarkable Angelo Neumann, tenor turned impresario, and joint director of the Leipzig theatre, whose determination to produce Wagner's works had been fired by the Vienna *Lohengrin* of 1875. Neumann had gained Wagner's confidence to the extent of being granted permission to mount these productions, which were a huge success. Wagner received a ten per cent royalty on the proceeds and an advance of 10,000 marks. Neumann put on the first production of *The Ring* in Berlin in 1881, when Wagner himself was present; he also brought *The Ring* to His Majesty's Theatre in London in 1882. With his travelling company of thirty-one singers, sixty-six orchestral players and twenty technicians he gave one hundred and thirty-five performances of *The Ring* operas and fifty-eight Wagner concerts all over Europe in the nine months between September 1882 and June 1883. His regular conductor was Anton Seidl, who had conducted the premières in Leipzig, Berlin and London. Wagner had never disguised that his ideal of a conductor, both of his own works and of the classical repertoire, was Hans von Bülow, whose sensitivity and nervous energy produced playing of the dramatic intensity which Wagner demanded. Bülow's loss to the cause of his music was the price Wagner had had to pay for the love of Cosima. But he saw in Seidl the best interpreter of his works that he had heard – not excepting Hans Richter.

The composition sketch of *Parsifal*, accompanied by intensive study of the works of Beethoven, Mozart, Weber and – for the first time in such detail – Bach, was finished by October 1878, the orchestral sketch by April

1879. Unpleasant summer weather and his general state of debilitation led to further outbreaks of skin diseases and internal disorders which deprived Wagner of the strength, even the desire, to set about the orchestration, and a year went by before the first act alone was fully scored. Further essays appeared in 1879 – on the relationship of words to music, on opera, on music and drama, a passionate attack on vivisection, yet another *lamentatio* on the Philistinism of the age. In August Liszt came to Bayreuth and stayed for ten days. But the climate and his state of health continued to depress him, and at the end of the year, after celebrating New Year 1880 in Munich in the company of Hermann Levi, the painter Franz von Lenbach and Court Secretary Bürkel, he and Cosima, with their children, went to Italy.

For seven months they lived in the splendid Villa Angri on the Posilippe promontory, near Naples, where they entertained a succession of visitors – the rich young Russian painter Paul von Joukovsky, Wagner's latest sympathetic friend, the pianist Joseph Rubinstein, Engelbert Humperdinck, composer of the opera *Hänsel und Gretel*, young Siegfried's tutor Heinrich von Stein, above all the faithful Liszt and the equally faithful Malwida von Meysenbug. Wagner began the dictation to Cosima of the last sections of *Mein Leben* but made little progress with *Parsifal*; his general lassitude and his dejection over the prospects for his operas and the state of culture – or unculture – in Germany, even made him seriously consider emigrating to America.

He did, however, find the strength to finish the rambling essay *Religion und Kunst (Religion and Art)*, the principal statement of his old age on the persistent leitmotifs of the rottenness of the world, the shortcomings of the Reich, the baneful influence of the Jews and other *idées fixes*. The theories of Count Arthur Gobineau, prophet of racial purity and Aryan supremacy, with whom Wagner spent many hours at Wahnfried in 1881, are reflected in this essay, together with an extraordinary assemblage of dogmatic assertions on vegetarianism (which he now advocates as a means of returning to human purity and dignity), vivisection (which he violently attacks for the same reasons), mystical Christianity, Schopenhauer, redemption through love – perhaps the Wagnerian leitmotif *par excellence* – socialism, Judaism and a mass of other things.

The preposterousness of some of these views becomes sadly comical at times. What, for example, are we to make of the following extraordinary message:

There are strong internal grounds for regarding contemporary socialism as worthy of close attention from a social and national point of view, if it were to be firmly and meaningfully combined with vegetarianism, anti-vivisectionism and temperance.

Wagner's vegetarianism proved to be just one more of his passing humours. He had a healthy appetite, and one day, after a few weeks of vegetarian cooking at Wahnfried, he suddenly burst out: 'How can I produce any decent ideas as long as I'm only stuffing myself with grass?' His love of animals was genuine enough, but if the principle of respect for animal life got in the way of his own physical well-being, so much the worse for the principle.

In *Religion and Art* Wagner's call, couched in the infuriatingly pretentious language which he reserved for his higher philosophical flights, is for the reversal of the processes of human degradation and the regeneration of true national and spiritual values through a return to religion in its highest and noblest form. Moreover this is a regeneration in which art, above all German art, i.e. the art of Richard Wagner, shall be the vital mediator.

At the end of *Was nützt diese Erkenntnis? (What Use is this Knowledge?)*, one of a series of appendices to *Reli-*

gion and Art, Wagner formulated the vague moral creed which now guided his thoughts:

We recognize the cause of the historical decay of mankind, as well as the necessity for mankind's regeneration. We believe in the possibility of this regeneration and we dedicate ourselves to its achievement in every respect.

It is not the kind of passionate declaration that people would rush to sign, and it commits no one, not even Wagner, to doing anything in particular. Just for this reason it reveals the mystical, other-worldly frame of mind in which Wagner wrote these last essays and in which, far more importantly, he composed *Parsifal*.

A particularly painful attack of erysipelas drove him away from the oppressive heat of Naples in August. Via Rome, Florence and Sienna – the interior of Sienna Cathedral inspired the setting of the Grail Temple in *Parsifal* – he went to Venice, where he took up quarters in the Palazzo Contarini dalle Figure, on the Grand Canal. At the end of October he went back to Munich, where he saw *Der fliegende Holländer* and *Tristan* in the Hoftheater, together with a private performance of *Lohengrin* for King Ludwig and a few other friends. Two days later he conducted the Prelude to *Parsifal*, again especially for the King. It was the last time the two men met.

When he returned to Bayreuth, Wagner announced to the body of Festival patrons that the next Festival – to consist solely of performances of *Parsifal* – would definitely take place in 1882, although he was still only at the stage of scoring Act One. The King put the orchestra and chorus of the Court Opera at his disposal, and agreed to forgo the right, laid down in the contract with the Festival Committee in 1878, to claim *Parsifal* for Munich, consenting instead to its being performed exclusively in Bayreuth. Hermann Levi, the Munich Kapellmeister, had already been promised the honour of conducting, and came to Wahnfried from time to time in 1881 to discuss matters with the Master.

His health weakened, his energy diminished – the doctors failed to ascribe his frequent chest pains to a heart condition – Wagner now worked more slowly. Cosima, who begins almost every entry in her diary with a sentence on how her husband had slept, still records a large number of nights disturbed by pains and discomforts of one kind or another, or by strange and often unpleasant dreams. But his will lost none of its power, and he still dominated the social evenings at Wahnfried. Old friends came – Carl Brandt, who was to control the stage machinery for *Parsifal* but who died before seeing his work accomplished; the Munich painter Franz von Lenbach, who made a number of famous portraits of Wagner and his circle; Karl Ritter, from his Dresden days; Dr Standhartner from Vienna; the Countess Marie von Schleinitz and her husband; Liszt, of course, who stayed at the house for a number of days each time, and Malwida von Meysenbug. In the autumn of 1881, over three years after the end of her romantic attachment to Wagner, and during one of Liszt's visits, Judith Gautier also came to Wahnfried.

This lavish hospitality cost a great deal of money, as did the servants, the education of the children, and the whole life-style of Wahnfried. Wagner had never been the man to economize whatever the state of his finances, and the more he had, the more he seemed to need. He had his regular monthly allowance from the King, there were now substantial royalties from performances of his works all over the world, and Ludwig even made him an extra grant in 1880 to enable him 'to prolong the stay in Italy that is essential for his health', as the King instructed Bürkel. Yet all this still only sufficed, in his eyes, to cover his basic and entirely reasonable needs.

Newer acquaintances also came – Angelo Neumann,

Engelbert Humperdinck, Paul von Joukovsky, who designed the sets for *Parsifal* and painted pictures of the Wahnfried scene, Heinrich von Stein and Arthur Gobineau, philosopher of racial Darwinism. Berthold Kellermann, a young pupil of Liszt's, who had joined the Bayreuth staff of copyists and musical assistants in 1878 and also gave piano lessons to the children, recalled the evenings at Wahnfried:

Generally there were just one or two friends present. Wagner would read aloud in a wonderfully expressive way, without a trace of a Saxon accent (contrary to what people said). He read the most varied pieces of literature, recently published works as well as older philosophical and historical studies . . . On occasion he would take out the score of an opera from his library shelves, like Marschner's *The Vampire* or Lortzing's *Czar and Carpenter*. Although he was a bad pianist and had no technique, he had a marvellous way of conveying both the action and the music of the opera: he sang all the vocal parts – technically far from perfect but with great vivacity and expressiveness – giving an impression of the work that was far superior to that achieved by any performance of the day. From time to time he got up from the piano and walked excitedly round the room, waving his arms and gesticulating with his hands

This unashamedly demonstrative behaviour matches the emotional and extrovert spirit in which Wagner dealt with his fellow human beings, and which he looked to receive from them in return. His letters too, whether to intimate friends, to publishers or to court officials, convey a sense of personal urgency and intensity that often approaches the importunate, even the excessive. If the members of his own family, in particular, did not show equal ardour, he was disappointed, sometimes disapproving. When the twelve-year-old Eva was reunited with the other children after being isolated for four weeks with scarlet fever, he expected to see them jump for joy. But Cosima had to write in her diary: 'R. was not pleased with the emotional response of the other children. He found them too cool when they saw Eva again.'

Like the governess Susanne Weinert, Kellermann too enjoyed the warmth of the family atmosphere at Wahnfried. Wagner was always affable in his dealings with the servants, he adds, and in fact appeared very much at his ease in the company of the lower classes in general. His impulsive generosity – almost any hard-luck story seemed bound to succeed – led Kellermann to describe him as 'a big child' in money matters.

In September 1881 he wrote an essay called *Heldentum und Christentum (Heroism and Christianity)* for the *Bayreuther Blätter*, a further bizarre supplement to *Religion and Art*, compounded of the racial theories of Gobineau and a concept of salvation that shall save mankind from the total degeneration which, Gobineau claimed, threatened civilization as a result of rampant miscegenation. After visits to Dresden and Leipzig later the same month, partly to discuss the touring Wagner company that Angelo Neumann was to set up, his chest pains and abdominal cramp returned with the onset of cold autumn weather in Bayreuth. The doctors suggested a change of climate, and at the beginning of November he left again for Italy, taking *Parsifal* with him. With Cosima, the five children, their tutor and a servant, he travelled via Munich, Bolzano and Verona to Naples, then took the boat to Palermo, in Sicily. First they occupied three rooms in the suitably luxurious Hôtel des Palmes; three months later they settled with the family into a vacant villa on the Piazza dei Porazzi, belonging to one Prince Gangi.

Here in Palermo Wagner soon settled into a regular pattern of life. The day often began with a walk before breakfast, followed by a morning's work on the score of *Parsifal*, for which he used a striking violet-coloured ink. In the afternoons he and Cosima made trips to other places on the island or visited their new acquaintances in the vicinity.

Joseph Rubinstein, who was to prepare the piano reduction of *Parsifal*, had already arrived from Bayreuth, and Paul von Joukovsky came shortly before Christmas. Wagner and Cosima also read a good deal of Shakespeare together in German translation, while the associations of the island reminded him of *Die Sarazenin*, the opera on the Hohenstaufen hero Manfred which he had planned after finishing *Der fliegende Holländer* but never composed.

Until December his health was tolerable, but from then on Cosima refers almost every day in her diaries to the sudden chest pains that continually interrupted his work – 'R. spent a good night but had violent spasms when he got up' . . . 'Bad, restless night. He finished reading Wolzogen's essay [an essay on Kleist for the *Bayreuther Blätter*] and went back to bed but in the morning his chest convulsions returned' – and many similar descriptions. As to the origin of these pains: 'We discussed the possible causes and came to the conclusion that his work strained him so much that it upset his entire system.'

At last, during a party to celebrate Joukovsky's birthday on 13 January 1882, Wagner scored the final bars of *Parsifal*. A musical item was being played in Joukovsky's honour, when he slipped away to a table at the side of the room. Cosima saw that he was busy with his score. 'It left me no peace,' he said. As the pianist was playing the march from *Tannhäuser*, Wagner got up and came back to rejoin the party. *Parsifal* was finished. 'Later we sat round the table at supper,' Cosima wrote in her diary, 'and he told us that with this, as with all his works, he had lived in perpetual fear that death would prevent him from completing it.'

The next day the painter Renoir, who was also in Palermo, called to seek Wagner's permission to paint his portrait: 'I heard muffled steps approaching across the thick carpets. It was the Master, in his velvet gown with wide sleeves faced with black satin. He is very handsome and kind and shook my hand, invited me to sit down, and we launched into a bizarre conversation, half in French, half in German, interspersed with er's and um's.' They moved from one subject to another, Renoir remembering especially Wagner's sarcastic comments on the German Jews. The following afternoon Wagner granted Renoir a sitting of thirty-five minutes, during which the artist made a rapid pencil sketch. When Renoir showed it to him, Wagner said: 'I look like a Protestant clergyman.' 'Which is perfectly true,' admitted Renoir. 'But at least I was glad that I did not make a complete fiasco of it.' Renoir's finished portrait from this sketch, done in 1893, now hangs in the Paris Opéra.

Wagner stayed in Italy till the end of April, pondering practical matters concerning the *Parsifal* Festival in July, which he now intended to make an entirely public affair, no longer dependent on the Patrons Association. Similarly the *Bayreuther Blätter*, hitherto virtually the organ of the Patrons Association alone, was to become a journal to further the interests of a broader German culture. Together with Cosima and the children he left Palermo in March, making his leisurely progress north by way of Messina and Naples to Venice, where he spent two weeks. On May 1 he was back in Bayreuth, in very poor health and extremely tired, discussing questions of production and rehearsal, above all with Hermann Levi.

Levi had been a close friend of Brahms in the 1860s – he was also a friend of Clara Schumann and the violinist Joachim – and as Kapellmeister in Karlsruhe had devoted a great deal of energy to getting Brahms' work performed. But in 1872 he was appointed to the opera in Munich, and his devotion to Brahms could not withstand the impact of the works of Wagner. Brahms, for his part, took Levi for a turncoat and, in the uncouth, offensive manner which cost him many a friendship, alienated him beyond recall. As Levi transferred his allegiance from Brahms to Wagner, so Hans von Bülow, at one time so close to Wagner and so perfect an interpreter of his works, was to become a passionate advocate of the music of Brahms. There seems something almost fatalistic about the power of Wagner and Brahms, the two greatest German composers of their age, to polarize reaction to their music.

During one of Levi's visits to Wahnfried, Wagner received an anonymous letter accusing Levi of having an affair with Cosima and demanding that he, Wagner, should 'preserve the purity of his work by not allowing it to be conducted by a Jew'. With a tactlessness not untypical of him, Wagner, who did not believe the accusation for a moment, showed the letter to Levi, who, mortally offended, left Wahnfried immediately. It took an imploring letter from Wagner, with assurances of his utter confidence in Levi's integrity as a man and distinction as a conductor, to bring him back.

This is just one more example of the dichotomy in Wagner between public utterance and private behaviour, between theories based on generalized prejudices and a practice governed by personal disposition and self-interest, between the tiresome preceptor of anti-Semitic curses and the man with close Jewish friends and associates. Levi had to endure many intemperate insults to his race from the man he had chosen to serve, but he could still unashamedly write in a letter to his father:

Wagner is the best and noblest of men. That the world misunderstands him and slanders him, is natural: people habitually seek to blacken what is bright. Goethe did not fare any better. But posterity will come to recognize that Wagner was as great a man as he was an artist, as those close to him already know. Even his antagonism towards what he calls the 'Jewish elements' in music and in modern literature springs from the noblest of motives. That he bears no petty animosity, like a Junker or a sanctimonious Protestant, is proven by his behaviour towards me and Joseph Rubinstein, as well as by his earlier attachment to Karl Tausig, for whom he had the most tender affection.

Those – and there are many – who lose no opportunity of using Wagner's public anti-Semitic statements to try and make a proto-Nazi monster out of both the man and the artist might well reflect on the personal testimony of Levi, Rubinstein, Tausig, Lehrs, Porges, Angelo Neumann and other Jews that the psychological reality is more subtle than they believe. Perhaps it is a case of 'blackening what is bright', as Levi put it. Yet at the dress rehearsal of *Parsifal*, irritated and sarcastic in mood because Liszt, purely to fulfil a social obligation, had left the theatre before the end, Wagner was capable of saying to Cosima: 'If I were an orchestral player, I wouldn't like to be conducted by a Jew.'

Hans Keller, who is himself a Jewish refugee from Nazi Germany, recently drew a humane and realistic conclusion in the spirit of Levi's words: 'We desperately cling to Wagner's weaknesses, such as his anti-Semitism . . . or his anti-French posture, both of which turn out to be so silly and boring, such thoughtless generalizations of unpleasant personal experiences, that they don't cause the present writer, a pretty conscious Jew, more than a yawn. They are, in fact, out of character – Wagner's otherwise extremely well-integrated character – and obtrude, like lifeless desert islands, from the boiling sea of his ever restless imagination.'

There was something about Wagner's condition, psychological as well as physical, during these three months of preparation for *Parsifal* that gave many the uneasy feeling that he had not long to live. At his birthday party on 22 May 1882, Cosima's daughter Blandine, now nineteen, covered her face with her hands and sobbed, haunted by a premonition that this would be the last birthday of the man she had come to regard as her father. The previous day he had played the Funeral March from Beethoven's Eroica Symphony and declared that Gobineau, Schopenhauer and himself were the only authors he still read. Urged by King Ludwig to take up *Die Sieger* again, the opera on a Buddhist theme which he had planned in 1856 and which bore a certain conceptual relationship to *Parsifal*, he wrote to the King in July that *Parsifal* would be his last work: 'My utter exhaustion, which only leaves me strength to write these few lines, tells me that my powers are at an end. *Nothing* more can be expected of me.' That the King declined to expose himself to the curiosity of the common crowd at the Festival, choosing to wait for a performance of *Parsifal* given for himself alone, also grieved Wagner. It would have been their last meeting. The same foreboding, a mingled atmosphere of anxiety and resignation, hangs over the entries in Cosima's diary for these last months.

Ten days before the Festival opened, the seventy-year-old Liszt arrived in Bayreuth, to Wagner's joy, and stayed three weeks at Wahnfried. The one only two years older than the other, yet always seeming so much the senior, the at times distant, almost frigid relationship between father-in-law and son-in-law now regained much of the warmth of their Weimar days. For so long Liszt had had to endure the frenzied efforts of his Princess Carolyne, first to estrange his children from their mother, then to force him away from the man whom he had always known to be the greatest composer of the age. Now, only a short time remaining for them both, Liszt returned to Bayreuth to reassert his loyalty to Wagner the man and his faith in Wagner the artist.

Nor had Wagner forgotten his long-standing debt to the first conductor of *Lohengrin*, the first man of influence to fight for the recognition of his works at the time of incredulity or hostility. On the eve of the opening night of the Festival Wagner gave a banquet in the Festival restaurant for his performers. When the Bürgermeister of Bayreuth proposed a toast to Franz Liszt, Wagner sprang to his feet and paid a moving tribute to what Liszt's sympathy and support had meant to him over the past thirty years.

When the two men first met in Paris over forty years earlier, Liszt had been the rich, lionized hero, the greatest virtuoso pianist in Europe, Wagner a struggling, unknown figure, living from hand to mouth. When Wagner died, there was immense public sorrow and mourning, his funeral a state occasion of pomp and circumstance. Three years later, in 1886, Liszt came to Bayreuth for the Wagner Festival. He had caught a cold on the train journey, and ten days afterwards, in a lonely room in the town, he died of pneumonia. His daughter had not invited him to stay at Wahnfried; indeed, so occupied was she with the administration of the Festival that she barely met him. Bayreuth, busy celebrating Wagner, paid merely perfunctory respect as his great friend and advocate was laid to rest.

For the full rehearsals of *The Ring* Wagner had sat at a little table by the side of the stage. For *Parsifal* he took up his position in the front row of the auditorium, communicating with the conductor by means of a little hatch cut in the canopy that concealed the orchestra from the audience. From this position he was able to satisfy himself above all over the tonal balance between singers and orchestra, a sensitive matter in Wagnerian opera, with its massive orchestral forces. A conductor ignores at his peril what Wagner once said to his players: 'Gentlemen, please do not take *fortissimo* too literally, but where I have marked it, turn it into *forte-piano* and *piano* into *pianissimo*. Please remember that there are so many of you down there but only one solitary human throat up here.' A drawing of the pit by a member of the orchestra shows Wagner peering through the hatch as Levi conducts.

As the final rehearsals of *Parsifal* were being held,

friends and admirers gathered in Bayreuth – familiar names from the past like Mathilde Maier, Countess Marie von Schleinitz and Malwida von Meysenbug; Nietzsche's sister Elisabeth and, under Malwida's wing, the fascinating, twenty-one-year-old Lou von Salomé, who later inspired the love of Nietzsche and of Rilke; the teacher and music critic Ferdinand Praeger (an acquaintance from Wagner's London concerts in 1855) and Edward Dannreuther from London. Among the composers present were Saint-Saëns, Delibes, Bruckner and Mahler. Bruckner had visited Wagner, the 'Master of all Masters', as he called him, in 1873 and dedicated his Third Symphony to him; Wagner now promised to perform his symphonies at Bayreuth, adding to Wolzogen: 'I know only one composer who approaches Beethoven – and that is Bruckner.' The young Gustav Mahler, twenty-two when he saw *Parsifal*, wrote a year later: 'When I came out of the Festspielhaus, unable to speak a word, I knew that I had experienced supreme greatness and supreme suffering, and that this experience, hallowed and unsullied, would stay with me for the rest of my life.' In the last decade of the nineteenth century and first decade of the twentieth Mahler became one of the great Wagnerian conductors, but he never conducted at Bayreuth.

Parsifal was first given in the Bayreuth Festival Theatre on 26 July 1882 – the first music heard there since the Festival of 1876. The première was followed by fifteen more performances, the one work constituting the entire Festival, as it did also those of 1883 and 1884.

Preparations had been far less complicated than for the four operas of *The Ring* six years earlier, and under the coaching of Porges, Humperdinck and others the singers realized much more quickly what was required of them. Unlike *The Ring*, where Wagner had chosen one singer for each principal role in all the cycles, for *Parsifal* he used double and sometimes treble casting. King Ludwig had already promised him the Munich orchestra and chorus for the two months needed for rehearsals and performances; Franz Fischer acted as assistant conductor to Levi, and Fritz Brandt, son of the late Carl, took over the management of the stage machinery. This aspect of the production turned out to present the greatest problems, especially in the scene-changes, for which Wagner had not left enough time in his musical interludes. Since the 1876 Festival the so-called Königsbau had been added to the bowed front of the theatre, the Festival restaurant on the left of the building (the opposite side to the present restaurant) enlarged to take 1,500 people – almost the entire audience – and the avenue leading up the hill from the town provided with a firm cinder surface and better gas lighting. But the theatre itself had been shut throughout these six years.

The first two performances of *Parsifal* were reserved for the members of the Patrons Association – a kind of farewell gesture before the Association was dissolved and Bayreuth made a public institution. With the first public performance emerged a practice which quickly developed into a Bayreuth convention, *viz.* that the first act, culminating in Amfortas's uncovering of the Grail, is received in silence, with the applause which Wagner always insisted that his performers should receive being given at the end of the second and third acts.

At the final performance on 29 August Wagner went down into the orchestra pit, took the baton from Levi and, invisible to the audience behind and above him, conducted the work from the end of the Transformation music in Act Three to the last bar. Levi described the scene in a moving letter to his father:

At the end of the work the audience broke into frenzied applause. The scene defied description. But the Master refused to show himself. Instead he sat there in the pit with us musicians, making irreverent remarks. After ten minutes there was still no sign that the audience would stop cheering, so I shouted at the top of my voice, 'Quiet! Quiet!' This was heard in the auditorium, and they really did calm down. Then, still sitting at the conductor's desk, the Master began to speak, first to me and the orchestra, then the curtain was raised to reveal all the performers and technicians assembled on the stage, and he addressed us with a deep sincerity that brought tears to everybody's eyes. It was an unforgettable moment.

'Not much of what he said could be heard in the auditorium', wrote Cosima, 'and he told me that he never remembered what he said on such occasions.' Back in Wahnfried after the performance Cosima and the children remarked on how different the orchestra had sounded when their father took over from Levi. It would not be the first time that the atmosphere of a uniquely moving occasion evoked from players a performance of exceptional beauty.

Not for an hour-and-a-half after the end of the five-hour opera did the audience finally leave the theatre. But they had still not seen the composer.

Wagner had called *Der Ring des Nibelungen* a *Bühnenfestspiel*, a 'Stage Festival'; *Parsifal* he called a *Bühnenweihfestspiel*, a 'Devotional Stage Festival'. This devotional character hovers over the beginning and the end of any discussion of the work – the experience of art as religion, as a mystical rite, the experience behind Liszt's words to Wolzogen the day after the first performance: 'The general feeling was that there is nothing that can be said about this miraculous work. Silence is surely the only possible response.'

Not only Wagnerians received *Parsifal* on this level. At dinner in the Hotel Fantaisie after the first night Angelo Neumann found himself sitting next to a man who had set himself at the head of the anti-Wagner forces, the much-feared Viennese critic Eduard Hanslick. *'Parsifal,'*

Neumann remembered, 'made a direct and powerful impact on Hanslick, who said remarkably little and had become a great deal more tolerant.' And in his critique of the work, reiterating his opposition to what he considered Wagner stood for, Hanslick could not but concede its power: 'The whole time we feel ourselves in the grip of a unique, dynamic personality unshakable in its conviction and determination. The forcefulness that emanates from a powerful will, undisturbed by doubt, will always be impressive, in art as in life.' Though Hanslick adds, to maintain the image of his critical independence: 'It commands admiration and respect, if not always sympathy.' After a concert performance of *Parsifal* in Paris in 1903 the often sharp-tongued Debussy found himself saying: 'This is one of the most beautiful monuments that have ever been erected to the eternal glory of music.'

The origins of *Parsifal*, like those of *Lohengrin* and *Die Meistersinger*, lie in Wagner's stay in Marienbad with Minna in July and August 1845. Here he immersed himself in Wolfram von Eschenbach's *Parzival*, written shortly after 1200, and the anonymous thirteenth-century epic poem known as *Lohengrin*. Later, at the time of his sketch of 1856 for *Die Sieger*, he linked the figures of the Grail King Parzival and Lohengrin, Knight of the Swan, father and son, in a relationship of rebirth. Lohengrin's purity derived from his being the reincarnation of Parzival, who had won that purity for himself.

In Wolfram's epic, as in his principal source, *Pereval ou li contes del graal* (c. 1180) by Chrestien de Troyes, most famous of French medieval poets, the originally independent stories of Parzival and the Grail are combined and brought into the context of Arthurian legend. Wolfram preaches a moral gospel of other-worldly values through which the demands of God and the world are fused in a single ethico-religious principle, and the figure of Parzival – the innocent abroad – symbolizes the return to God after the reconciliation of the warring claims of the flesh and the spirit. In *Mein Leben* Wagner writes that, setting out from the thought of Good Friday, he sketched a whole three-act drama on the subject of Parzival on Good Friday 1857, just before he and Minna moved into the *Asyl* on the Wesendonk estate. 'If there is any purpose in all this suffering,' he wrote in his diary for Mathilde Wesendonk in 1858, 'it can only be the awakening of compassion in man, who, by perceiving the error of existence, becomes the redeemer of the world. The interpretation will become clearer to you one day from the third act of *Parsifal*, which takes place on the morning of Good Friday.'

Gripped by the significance of Good Friday and by the concepts of suffering, sacrifice and redemption, and fascinated at the same time by the demonic figure of Kundry, seductress of Amfortas and herald of the Grail, Wagner wrote a lengthy prose draft of his version of the story in August 1865 (it differs considerably, particularly in motivation and psychology, from Wolfram's epic). In March and April 1877 he worked at the poem – an archaic, sometimes contorted, symbolic assemblage of rhymed and unrhymed lines – handing it to Cosima in its complete form on April 20. Modifying the German form of the name Parzival, itself taken from the French Perceval, with the connotation of 'pierce', 'penetrate', he now called his work *Parsifal*, adopting a totally fictitious Persian derivation from *parsi* – 'pure' and *fal* – 'foolish, simpleminded'. This fanciful derivation symbolized the character of his hero, 'the guileless fool', who was to become the agent of forgiveness and salvation. The compositional and orchestral sketches occupied him from September 1877 to April 1879, but the finished score was not ready until January 1882. A short time after its completion the publisher Schott paid him a fee of 100,000 marks for it.

The all-informing central principle of *Parsifal* is the concept of salvation, and a predestined salvation governs the movement of the characters. Kundry, the temptress, a Magdalena figure, and Amfortas, King of the Grail, suffering under the curse of a wound that will not heal, achieve redemption through Parsifal, who has found his own self and his true vocation by resisting temptation and choosing spiritual peace, the peace that passes all understanding.

Amfortas harks back to Tannhäuser and to Tristan ('my Tristan of the third act to the *n*th power', Wagner had called him back in 1859). In one side of her being, Kundry is Venus, in the other, Elisabeth. Parsifal, confronted, like Tannhäuser, with the choice between sacred and profane love, and seeking, like Lohengrin, to avoid contamination through earthly attachments, is a Siegfried figure, sustained by a dimly perceived inner purpose and a romantic idealism, and at the same time a man of action. Out of the twenty years during which the subject lay in Wagner's mind there now emerges a text that synthesizes almost all the vital motifs that run through his life and art, a summary of his characteristic values and conflicts, and thus a statement of the intellectual and spiritual continuity of his *oeuvre*.

Dominating the scene in which this drama of salvation unfolds is the Holy Grail, the chalice from which Christ drank at the Last Supper and in which Joseph of Arimathea caught the blood that flowed from Christ's side as he hung on the cross. The Grail legend as such is a basic human myth, the prototype of a human situation and a human urge. In the various forms in which we have it, it consists of a mass of elements from both pagan, folkloristic traditions and from Christian legend, which at first sight appear almost totally incongruous. Like all myths, moreover, it has absorbed over the years numerous additional motifs and symbols which have their own special meaning in their own special contexts. In its Christian form the hero is the agent of redemption: in

Wagner as in Wolfram von Eschenbach, he embarks on a quest, not for adventure but for meaning, for the understanding that he must acquire, and the spiritual condition to which he must attain, before he can retrieve the holy lance that the magician Klingsor stole from Amfortas, and thus fulfil his purpose. Amfortas's wound is healed; Parsifal becomes King of the Grail, displays the holy vessel and releases the Knights, the community of the Grail, from their introverted and barren isolation. The framework is set, God's design pre-ordained. Hence the serene, static quality of the work, a far cry from the passion of *Tristan und Isolde*, the open good humour of *Die Meistersinger*, the tragic epic grandeur of *Der Ring des Nibelungen*.

Because *Parsifal* is a drama of situation and fulfilment, not of character, Parsifal himself is the most pallid of the main characters, while Kundry – like the Dutchman, the passionate bearer of a curse – is the most fascinating. Indeed, although the opera was born of Wagner's meditations on the significance of Good Friday, his attention turned increasingly towards this intense, unhappy, almost pathological figure, torn between good and evil, seeking her own salvation.

Klingsor, once an aspirant to the brotherhood of the Knights of the Grail, but now a black magician, raging against his powerlessness in the grip of sin, suffers a spiritual anguish whose intensity led Thomas Mann to find its equal in the tormented world of Dostoyevsky. The chromaticism of the extraordinary music in Act Two to Klingsor's Magic Castle and Magic Garden, as in the following seduction scene – a kind of intensification of the Venusberg in *Tannhäuser* – conveys these tortured emotions in a shattering form. Kundry's agonized memory of her one glimpse of her redeemer provokes a convulsive shriek of which Edvard Munch's frightening painting, 'The Scream', prototype of the savage expressionist protest of the early twentieth century, is the visual equivalent:

Set against the restless, jagged chromatic idiom of the
Klingsor-Kundry music of Act Two is the serene, deliberate, basically diatonic material of Acts One and Three –
the Grail motif, the solemn procession of the Knights of
the Grail and so on – though here too there is much

chromatic harmony, albeit less tense and less agitated. The liturgical nature of *Parsifal*, also reflected in certain details of the musical technique, and the static, devotional atmosphere that hangs over much of the opera, inevitably concentrate attention on the discursive musical experience, the experience of some of the most beautiful music that Wagner wrote. There have been some superbly imaginative productions of *Parsifal* at Bayreuth and elsewhere, but of all Wagner's operas it is the one that least needs to be actually seen.

The financial success of the Festival surprised everybody. The sale of tickets brought in 240,000 marks, and Wagner at once proposed a further Festival for 1883, again to be devoted solely to *Parsifal*. It took place as he had planned.

Preparations for *Parsifal* had taken a heavy toll of Wagner's fading strength. He passed many restless nights and had a severe heart spasm in the course of the Festival itself, which made him purple in the face as he gesticulated wildly with his arms and fought for breath. The many different pills and tinctures that he took seem to have done little to ease his suffering.

After the excitement of the final performance he, Cosima and the children drove back to Wahnfried in grave silence. 'We can, I think, give thanks,' wrote Cosima in her diary that night, 'though the achievement has been bought at high cost, and almost all our well-being and health have been sacrificed to it. Yet such activity is assuredly a necessity to R., and in spite of all the worries it brings, the only mode of life befitting to him.' She had faced his death many times before it finally came.

So had he. In a strange memoir on his 'Devotional Stage Play', written two months later, he sets *Parsifal* itself in the shadow of resignation and death – his own resignation and death:

The effect of the visual and acoustical atmosphere in the theatre on our whole emotional receptivity was to lift us out of the everyday world, and our awareness of this emerged clearly when we felt ourselves being told to return to this world. In truth, *Parsifal* itself owes its conception and its execution to my flight from this very world. Can anyone look with open heart and mind at the deception, the hypocrisy, the organized, legalized theft and murder around us without sometimes being forced to avert one's gaze from the world in horror and disgust? And where then can one look? So often into the abyss of death.

On September 14, two weeks after the end of his second Festival, Wagner left Bayreuth for his now customary winter sojourn in Italy. With him went Cosima, Daniela von Bülow, Isolde, Eva and Siegfried Wagner, together with a tutor for Siegfried, a governess for the Wagner daughters, now aged seventeen and fifteen, and three servants. (Cosima's eldest daughter, Blandine, had married Biagio Gravina, a Sicilian Count, just a few weeks earlier; Liszt came from Weimar to Bayreuth for the wedding but Bülow, who had remarried in July, did not.) Their destination was Venice, where they occupied a floor of the large sixteenth-century Palazzo Vendramin-Calergi, on the Grand Canal, which Wagner had reserved for himself when passing through Venice on his way back from Sicily the previous April.

The Bayreuth faithful visited him here from time to time – Hermann Levi, Joukovsky, Siegfried's former tutor Heinrich von Stein, the Countess Schleinitz and her husband, Joseph Rubinstein, Humperdinck. Liszt came to Venice in November and stayed until January. For all the sincerity and revived warmth of their relationship the two men generated a certain disharmony when they were together during these months. Liszt still looked for large gatherings, with himself at the piano, the centre of attraction, but Wagner, often irritable and under strain from his chest pains, desired only a small group of intimate friends before whom to expound his ideas. 'In conversation together,' wrote Joukovsky in his memoirs, 'neither paid attention to what the other was saying. They would both speak at the same time and this often led to the oddest exchanges. Each was so accustomed to being the sole focus of attention that there was always a certain amount of awkwardness when they were together.'

Wagner continued to plan the consolidation of his achievement. In November he announced to Ludwig his intention to mount all his works, one by one, in 'our' Festival Theatre, 'so that these productions can be bequeathed to my successors as models of perfection'. The King's reply from Hohenschwangau, 26 November 1882, his last letter to Wagner, expresses delight at the idea, promises him the Munich orchestra as before, hopes that his stay in Italy will be beneficial to his health, and enquires after young Siegfried: 'Is your idea of educating him according to Goethe's *Wilhelm Meister* proving a success?' He concludes:

In the deepest love and never faltering loyalty to the divine light which, I trust, may yet shine for a long, long time, a sun to refresh and quicken the world with its celestial rays.
Your truest friend and most zealous admirer,
Ludwig

With Liszt Wagner discussed the possibility of developing a new form of symphony in one movement – a kind of extension into absolute music of Liszt's symphonic poems, or a conversion into orchestral terms of the formal principle of his piano Sonata in B minor; he also talked of revising *Tannhäuser* yet again, this time definitively. He made frequent outings with the children to St Mark's Square, riding across to the Piazzetta in the gondola that was at the family's disposal. Yet he was as quick as ever to take offence if, for example, without his knowledge, Liszt happened to spend some time alone with one of his granddaughters. He continued to read in Gobineau's *Essai sur l'inégalité des races humaines* – virtually his cultural Bible during his last years – together with Nietzsche's *The Gay Science* and Hermann Oldenberg's book on Buddha. On evenings free of visitors, he would play and read aloud to the family – Shakespeare, Schiller, Goethe and other classics, almost invariably dramas. He had little taste for lyric poetry; novels, on the other hand – Balzac, Turgenev, Goethe's *Werther*, above all Sir Walter Scott – gave him considerable pleasure.

Family birthdays occupied a very particular place in the life of the Wagner household, and as on that wonderful day at Tribschen twelve years ago, when he had serenaded Cosima with the *Siegfried Idyll*, so now Wagner was secretly preparing a special moment for her forty-fifth birthday. This was a performance of his Symphony in C, written half a century ago, the orchestral parts of which had turned up in Dresden a few years earlier. Anton Seidl had reconstructed the score from these parts, and on Christmas Eve, to an audience consisting of Cosima, Liszt, Joukovsky, Humperdinck and Count Giuseppe Contini, president of the Venice conservatoire, Wagner performed the work in the Teatro la Fenice with a students' orchestra. 'We went home shortly before eleven,' Cosima recorded. 'Venice seemed covered in a blue shroud. The children were thrilled with the evening, and R. was deeply satisfied.'

Wagner's spasms were becoming more violent and more frequent. A German physician resident in Venice, Dr Friedrich Keppler, who had Wagner in his care, subsequently described him as suffering from advanced hypertrophy of the heart, with dilation of the stomach and an inguinal hernia; stomach and bowel disorders were responsible for much of his pain and disturbed the action of the heart, eventually leading to a rupture of the right ventricle. He received abdominal massage, which relieved the pain to some extent, and was later given valerian and opium. Dr Keppler also pointed out that Wagner's temperament, above all his fits of sudden irritation and anger when confronted with things not to his liking, only aggravated his condition.

Between January and February Wagner made plans for an essay, left unfinished when he died, called *Über das Weibliche im Menschen (On the Feminine Principle in Mankind)* a final appendix to *Religion and Art.* This emerges as a confused bundle of thoughts on the degeneration of the human race; on the mating of animals as serving merely the perpetuation of the species, whereas human beings were motivated by love, with its attendant principles of monogamy and faithfulness; and on the evolution towards these principles in the polygamous societies of the East. It seems as though his thoughts were returning to Buddhist legend, to the notion of reincarnation, and to the subject matter of his unfulfilled plan for *Die Sieger*.

Hermann Levi arrived in Venice from Munich on 4 February, an always welcome guest. The sirocco was blowing, and Wagner did not go out that day. During conversation in the evening Levi produced the amusing information that Nietzsche had approached him with the compositions of a new genius, a 'young Mozart', who turned out to be Nietzsche's protégé, Peter Gast, 'a totally insignificant musician', as Cosima unkindly called him. Provoked by the portrayal of his music in Nietzsche's latest book, *The Gay Science*, as the product of a mind steeped in suffering, sickness and decay, Wagner had become particularly spiteful about Nietzsche in recent months. Earlier on this same day Cosima wrote in her diary: 'R. said that a single photograph was enough to show what a conceited driveller Nietzsche was, and called him an absolute nonentity, a perfect example of the inability to see.' In the evening, after Levi had told his story, Wagner burst out: 'Nietzsche had not a single original thought in his head, no substance of his own! All the substance he had came from outside, put into his mind by others.'

The sixth of February was Shrove Tuesday. The children could not be denied the excitement of the carnival celebrations, and at nine o'clock in the evening the family went out among the crowds in St Mark's Square. At midnight the church bells rang out, the flames of the torches were doused and the carnival was 'buried'. It was one o'clock before they arrived home. 'He asked me whether I loved him,' Cosima wrote, 'and said: "I am so difficult."' Before he fell asleep he murmured: 'I feel like Othello – "Here is my journey's end . . ."'

The strain of the carnival left him exhausted and with a chill, and he stayed indoors during the following two days. On the 9th Levi also fell ill and went back to Munich three days later, leaving only Joukovsky, of Wagner's circle of close friends, still in Venice. Wagner felt despondent, almost cynical. He charged his supporters, even Wolzogen and the *Bayreuther Blätter*, with misrepresenting his ideas and exposing him to ridicule; he also rounded on the Jews, his invariable scapegoat in moments of strain, accusing them of laying a curse on the human race. He had a strange assortment of dreams – of a meeting with Schopenhauer, of his mother as a charming, elegant young woman, far younger than he could ever have known her, of the great soprano Wilhelmine Schröder-Devrient, idol of his younger days, and of receiving letters from some of the women in his life, among them Mathilde Wesendonk. 'All my affaires now leave me quite cold,' he commented.

His depression continued on the 10th, with severe chest pains. 'I hate myself for being such a burden to you,' he said to Cosima. Levi's indisposition, however, far from arousing his sympathy, only provoked another tirade against consorting with Jews. The following morning he started to write the essay *On the Feminine Principle*; in the evening he and Cosima were alone and read Fouqué's romantic fairy-tale *Undine* together.

The sirocco was blowing again on 12 February. Levi, far from well, came to say goodbye; Wagner worked at his essay in the morning and after lunch went across in the gondola to the Piazetta with Eva to sit in St Mark's Square. In the evening he read from *Undine* again. Cosima had already gone to bed when she heard him talking loudly in his room next door. 'I was talking to *you*,' he explained, embracing her tenderly as she went in to him. Then, enigmatically: 'Fortune comes every 5,000 years.' Walking across to the piano, he played the Rhine Maidens' song from the end of *Das Rheingold*, with its final words:

> Traulich und treu
> ist's nur in der Tiefe;
> falsch und feig
> ist, was dort oben sich freut.
>
> (Truth and peace lie only in the depths;
> those who dwell above are base and cowardly.)

The following morning, Tuesday 13 February 1883, Wagner breakfasted, went into his study as usual and worked on his essay until midday. Shortly before two o'clock Joukovsky arrived to join the family for lunch. As they were sitting at the table, waiting for Wagner, his valet, Georg, came in to say that the Master was not feeling well, and that they should start without him; he had already sent for the doctor. At about half-past two he sent the maid, Betty, to tell Cosima that he wanted her. Joukovsky wrote to Malwida von Meysenbug:

At three o'clock the doctor arrived, which set our minds at rest, but by about four we became anxious, because nobody had come out of his room. Suddenly Georg entered. He said simply that everything was over. Wagner had died at about three o'clock, lying on the couch in his wife's arms. He suffered no pain but passed away with an expression of sublime peace on his face, which I shall never forget. She stayed alone with him the whole day and the whole of the following night.

The final spasm had ruptured a blood vessel in his heart. Not until the afternoon of the next day could Dr Keppler persuade Cosima, silent and broken, to leave the body. Daniela sent telegrams to Liszt, to King Ludwig, to Adolf Gross, Feustel's son-in-law, who made the arrangements for Wagner's body to be taken back to Bayreuth and became one of Cosima's closest advisers, to Hans Richter and others, and soon the whole world knew.

Liszt, who heard the news in Budapest, at first refused to believe it. He then asked Cosima whether he should come to Venice and travel back with her to Bayreuth, but to his secret relief she did not accept his offer. Stronger, apparently, than the urge to pay his last respects to his great friend was his abhorrence of all the stereotyped customs and formalities inseparable from such occasions.

Nietzsche, working in Rapallo on *Thus Spake Zarathustra*, had his own dichotomy to face. After almost two weeks of tortured silence he finally wrote a letter of sympathy to Cosima. But to his friend Franz Overbeck he had already said: 'Although Wagner was by far the most complete man I have ever known, and although in this respect I have felt a deep sense of deprivation over the last six years, there was a kind of destructive grievance between us, and the situation could have become terrible if he had lived longer.'

King Ludwig, by contrast, could hardly control his emotion. 'Wagner's body belongs to me!' he cried, when his secretary Bürkel broke the news to him. 'Nothing must be done about bringing him from Venice without my orders!' By the time Bürkel returned from Bayreuth a few days later, the King had regained his composure and was able to recall with pride his share in his hero's achievement: 'This artist, whom the whole world now mourns – it was I who first understood him, I who saved him for the world.'

The same overwhelming sense of loss was felt by the sick Hans von Bülow, now Kapellmeister to the court of Meiningen, with whom, as it happened, Brahms was staying at the time. Since parting company from Wagner, Bülow had devoted himself more and more to the music of Brahms, both as pianist and conductor, but he could never cast off the weight of Wagner's memory. 'In his own words, which he brought out with great difficulty,' wrote his wife, 'he felt as though his own soul had perished with this fiery spirit, and only part of his body were still walking the earth.'

When Verdi read of Wagner's death in the newspaper, he wrote to his publisher Ricordi: 'A great personality has departed, a name that will leave a powerful (*potente*) impression upon the history of art.' He then re-read what he had written, crossed out *potente* and put instead *potentissima*. The two greatest operatic composers of the nineteenth century were born in the same year, within five months of each other. They never met.

Wagner's bitterest opponent, too, knew what the world had lost. 'He had no enemies, in the sense of a total and unconditional hostility,' wrote Hanslick in his obituary. 'I know of no musician, however incompetent or contentious, who fails to recognize Wagner's brilliant and extraordinary talent, or underestimates his immense influence, or refuses, whatever antipathy he may feel, to admit the grandeur and the inspiration of his works. People have opposed Wagner – but they have never denied him.'

On 14 February – against the wishes of Cosima, who could hardly be separated from the body long enough for the purpose – the sculptor Augusto Benvenuti made a death mask. The corpse was embalmed and laid in a coffin that had been ordered from Vienna. Before it was sealed, Cosima cut off her beautiful long hair and laid it on the body, staying by the coffin the entire five hours that the process of sealing lasted. As he left the room, the Venetian doctor who had signed the death certificate and supervised the sealing of the coffin said to Gross: 'I do not know these people, but I do know that no man was ever so loved by his wife.'

Finally, at about midday on 16 February, gondolas bore the coffin and the mourners – Cosima, the four children, Joukovsky, Richter and Gross – from the Villa Vendramin down the Grand Canal to the railway station, and at two o'clock the long journey northwards to Bayreuth began. On the afternoon of the 17th they arrived in Munich, where the station was filled with crowds bringing flowers. Shortly before midnight the train at last reached Bayreuth. Cosima and the children were taken to Wahnfried but, once more against her desire, the coffin remained at the station, surrounded by a guard of honour.

The eighteenth of February – a cold Sunday, with snow in the air. At four in the afternoon the cortège assembled at the railway station for the last stage of Wagner's final return to Wahnfried. Muncker and Feustel gave brief orations, a regimental band played Siegfried's Funeral March from *Götterdämmerung*, and a male voice choir sang the unaccompanied chorus composed by Wagner in 1844 for the reinterment of Weber's ashes in Dresden. A wreath was laid on the coffin in the name of the King. As he had always wanted to watch Wagner's operas in solitude, undisturbed by the intrusive public, so now too Ludwig could not let his grief be seen or share his homage with the masses. A few days after the burial he went secretly to Bayreuth, alone, and stood at night by the freshly-made grave of the man, thirty years his senior, who had given his life its meaning and whom he was to outlive by a mere three years.

The hearse, drawn by four horses, moved off on its mile-long journey down into the centre of the town, up past the old Margraves' Opera House and on to the Villa Wahnfried. By the side of the carriage walked the twelve men who were to bear the body to its last resting-place – Feustel, Muncker, Adolf Gross, Wolzogen, Joukovsky, Anton Seidl, August Wilhelmj, leader of the Bayreuth orchestra, Heinrich Porges, Hermann Levi, Hans Richter, Dr Josef Standhartner from Vienna, and the singer Albert Niemann (the Berlin Tristan of 1876 and the first Siegmund at Bayreuth). Crowds lined the route – men, women, even children. Few of them could have understood the genius who had come to build his own theatre on the Bürgerreuth hill, and whose body was now passing in front of their houses, but they all honoured the man who had made their little town famous throughout the world.

At five o'clock the procession reached the gates of Wahnfried. The cortège dispersed, leaving the coffin to be carried through the garden by the twelve pall bearers to the spot, surrounded by trees, that Wagner had chosen for himself. Daniela, Isolde, Eva and Siegfried held the corners of the pall. Leaving the coffin above the vault, the pall bearers quietly went away. Gross went into the house to fetch Cosima, who came out, leaning on his arm, to join her children as the coffin was lowered into the ground. Later the stone slab that Wagner had also chosen was set on top of the mound. Forty-seven years later, in April 1930, Cosima was laid to rest at her husband's side.

The stone bears no inscription. It does not need one.

POSTSCRIPT

Wagner: For and Against

Although the issues have been hinted at here and there in this book, the primary concern with the narrative of Wagner's life and work has left little room to discuss the arguments, philosophical, psychological and musical, that have raged to and fro over his music. The reader may, however, be interested to see how the terms of the controversy have been stated by some of the most prominent men who have responded to the challenge of his art. The following passages, from Wagner's own age and later, have been selected to show how irreconcilable, how passionate, often violent, these responses have been.

HANSLICK

Bayreuth, 18 August 1876

Yesterday we had *Götterdämmerung* as the finale of the whole cycle. With the Bayreuth programme now completed, the music of the future has become a force of the present – outwardly, at least, and for the moment. The critic indulges in prophecies about art with as little eagerness as the serious astronomer in prophecies about the weather. But this much is highly probable: the style of Wagner's *Ring* will not be the music of the future; it will be, at best, one style among many, possibly only a yeast for the fermentation of new developments harking back to the old. Wagner's most recent reform does not represent an enrichment, an extension, a renewal of music in the sense that the art of Mozart, Beethoven, Weber and

Schumann did; it is, on the contrary, a distortion, a perversion of basic musical laws, a style contrary to the nature of human hearing and feeling. One could say of this tone poetry: There is music in it, but it is not music . . .

Since, in the 'music drama', the people involved are not distinguished from one another by the character of the vocal melodies assigned them, as in the old-fashioned 'opera' (Don Giovanni and Leporello, Donna Anna and Zerlina, Max and Caspar*), but are identical in the physiognomy of their _Sprechton_, Wagner has sought to fill the gap with the so-called leitmotives in the orchestra. He had already employed this musico-psychological aid rather extensively in _Tannhäuser_ and _Lohengrin_; he overdid it in _Die Meistersinger_. In _The Ring_ he has carried it to the point where it becomes an actual arithmetical problem. It is easy to retain the few melodically and rhythmically pregnant leitmotives of _Tannhäuser_ or _Lohengrin_. But how does Wagner proceed in _The Ring_? The answer is given in a brochure by Hans von Wolzogen, _Thematic Guide,_ a musical Baedeker without which no respectable tourist here dares to be seen and which is on sale everywhere in Bayreuth. Anywhere but in Bayreuth one might well find such a book funny. The serious and sad thing about it is simply that it is necessary. Wolzogen cites no fewer than ninety separate and distinct leitmotives which the hapless festival visitor should impress upon his memory and recognize wherever they turn up in the tonal mass of four evenings.

The leitmotives are, with few exceptions (the 'Ride of the Valkyries', the 'Valhalla' motive, the 'arrival' motive, Siegfried's horn call), of meagre melodic and rhythmic substance, made up of only a few notes, and often very much alike. Only an extraordinary ear and memory can

*In Weber's _Der Freischütz._

retain them all. And supposing that one has actually accomplished it and has recognized that the orchestra is alluding here to the giants, there to the gods, and somewhere else to the giants and gods together, has anything really great been achieved? It is simply a matter of comprehension, a conscious process of comparison and association. Full enjoyment and reception are impossible when understanding and memory must be ever on the alert to catch the wary allusion . . .

On top of that is the incredible and iniquitous length of the individual scenes and conversations. I do not overlook the new element of greatness and exaltation which Wagner gives to his work by limiting each act to only two or three episodes, each unfolding in serene breadth, often appearing, like plastic pictures, to stand still. *The Ring* is most advantageously distinguished from the restless change of scene and surplus action in our 'grand opera' precisely through this simplicity. But an epic breadth must not be permitted to jeopardize the whole drama . . .

An eloquent and imaginative critic of Wagner's, Ludwig Ehlert, suggests in his critique of *Tristan and Isolde* that in order to ensure the opera's survival every episode might be considerably shortened. Now one may well ask: Where has there ever been a real dramatic composer in whose operas any piece might be cut at will without damage? But in listening to *The Ring* I felt that every scene could stand not only the most extensive cuts but also the most extensive expansion. The new method of 'dialogue music drama' does, indeed, reject every thought of musical proportion. It is the formless infinite.

'Richard Wagner's Stage Festival in Bayreuth', 1876

NIETZSCHE

The characters that an artist creates are not the artist himself, but the range of the characters on which he is seen to have lavished his affection does tell us something about him. Consider Rienzi, the Flying Dutchman and Senta, Tannhäuser and Elisabeth, Lohengrin and Elsa, Tristan and Mark, Hans Sachs, Wotan and Brünnhilde: they are all united by a continuous, hidden current of greatness and ethical nobility which becomes ever brighter, ever purer, exposing to us, as we watch discreetly and respectfully, the innermost development of Wagner's own soul. Where can we see something of comparable grandeur in any other artist? Schiller's characters, from *The Robbers* to *Wallenstein* and *William Tell*, show a similar progress of ennoblement and tell us something about their creator's development, but in Wagner everything is on a larger scale, the path of discovery longer. Everything is involved in this purification and gives expression to it, not only the myth but also the music. *The Ring of the Nibelung* contains the most highly moral music I know – as when, for example, Brünnhilde is awakened by Siegfried. At such moments Wagner reaches divine heights of achievement which make one imagine that the snow-covered peaks of the Alps are aglow: Nature emerges in all her purity, all her loneliness, all her unapproachability, bathed in the glow of love, leaving wind and storm below, and even all sublime beauties. Looking back from this point at the Dutchman and Tannhäuser, we can feel how Wagner the man evolved, starting in restless uncertainty, fighting to reach satisfaction, striving after power and the intoxication of pleasure, often fleeing in revulsion as he sought to rid himself of the burden and forget, reject, renounce – the current of his life carried him now into one valley, now into another, plunging him into deep, dark chasms. Then, high above the darkness of these depths, there appeared a star, a dim star. He called it Loyalty, Selfless Devotion. Why did it come to shine with a greater brilliance and a greater purity than anything else? What is its secret meaning for his personality? The image and the problem of Devotion has left its mark on everything he thought and wrote, and his works contain an almost unbroken pattern of all possible kinds of Devotion, among them the most glorious and the least suspected – the devotion of brother and sister, of friend to friend, of servant to master, Elisabeth to Tannhäuser, Senta to the Dutchman, Elsa to Lohengrin, Isolde, Kurvenal and Mark to Tristan, Brünnhilde to Wotan's deepest desire and so on. It is the profoundest and most vital of Wagner's own experiences, an experience that he revered like a religious mystery.

Richard Wagner in Bayreuth, 1876

The dramatic style in music, as Wagner understands it, is the renunciation of style altogether, on the assumption that something else is a hundred times more important than Music, namely Drama. Wagner can depict – he does not use music for the sake of music; he strikes poses – he is a poet. And then, like all artists of the theatre, he appeals to 'beautiful feelings' and 'noble emotions', winning over the women and even those in search of education. But what has music to do with women and those in search of education? What is the value of extending the means of expression, if that which is doing the expressing, *viz.* Art itself, has lost the principle that governs its very existence? Power and glory of depiction in sound, the symbolism of the harmony, of the rhythm, of the colours of concord and discord, the power of music on the mind, the whole sensuousness of music, which he brought to its culmination – Wagner saw that all this was in music, extracted it, developed it. Victor Hugo did something similar for language, but people are already wondering in France whether he did not thereby ruin the language, intensifying its sensuousness but demeaning its rational and intellectual qualities, the profound laws that underlie its nature. Poets in France have become sculptors, musicians in Germany have become actors and culturemongers – are these not signs of decadence?

The Will to Power, 1888

If it is my aim to sustain in this work the claim that Wagner is harmful, I wish equally to demonstrate to whom he is indispensable – the philosopher. Others might well survive without Wagner, but the philosopher is not free to dispense with him. It is the lot of the philosopher to be the bad conscience of his age – for this he must possess supreme knowledge of his age. Where could he find a more experienced guide through the labyrinth of the modern soul, a more eloquent, more consummate spiritual leader, than Wagner? It is through Wagner that the modern age speaks its most intimate language, concealing neither its good nor its bad side, utterly free from shame or embarrassment. Put the other way round: if one is clear in one's own mind about the good and the bad in Wagner, one finds that one has virtually drawn up a balance sheet for the *quality*, the *value* of the modern age. I understand perfectly when a musician says today: 'I hate Wagner, but I cannot stand any other music.' I would also understand a philosopher who said: 'Wagner summarizes the modern age. There is nothing for it – one has got to be a Wagnerian.'

The Case of Wagner, 1888

The last thing I am prepared to do is to look on innocently while this *décadent* ruins our health – and music as well. Is Wagner a person at all – or a disease? Everything he touches becomes infected – he has made music sick. A typical *décadent*, with the feeling that he and his perverted taste are necessary, claiming this taste to be in fact a superior taste, and giving his perversion the status of law, of progress, of fulfilment. And people make no move to defend themselves. His seductive power reaches massive proportions; clouds of incense swirl round his head, and the errors about him become known as the Gospel – for it is far from being merely the poor in spirit who are converted.

I am not surprised that the Germans are deceived by Wagner; in fact, the opposite would surprise me. The Germans have set up an image of Wagner which they can worship: they never possessed psychological insight, and are therefore happy to be in error. But that people in Paris are deceived too, where psychological perception is more highly developed than almost any other faculty! Or in St Petersburg, where people sense things not sensed even in Paris! How close Wagner must be to the *décadents* of the whole of Europe for them not to feel him as decadent himself! He is part of European decadence – its protagonist, its great name . . .

Because there is nothing more modern than this total sickness of Wagner's, its late arrival and the excessive nervous sensitivity that accompanies it, Wagner is the modern artist *par excellence*, the Cagliostro of today. His art is an intoxicating mixture of the things that the whole present-day world needs most, the three great vitalizers of the jaded and the exhausted – Brutality, Unnaturalness and Innocence (Simplemindedness).

Wagner has corrupted music. He has discovered in it how to stimulate tired nerves – and has thereby made music sick. His power to goad the weary into action, to rejuvenate the half-dead, is great; he is a master of hypnotic gestures; he can trample on the strongest of men, like a bull. Wagner's success – his effect on the nerves, and thus on women – has made all ambitious young musicians apprentices to his sorcery. Indeed, not only ambitious young musicians but wise, understanding ones also . . . Nowadays one can make money only with sick music: our great opera houses are living on Wagner.

The Case of Wagner, 1888

TOLSTOY

To what an extent people of our circle and time have lost the capacity to receive real art, and have become accustomed to accept as art things that have nothing in common with it, is best seen from the works of Richard Wagner, which have latterly come to be more and more esteemed not only by the Germans but also by the French and the English as the very highest art, revealing new horizons to us.

The peculiarity of Wagner's music, as is known, consists in this, that he considered that music should serve poetry, expressing all the shades of a poetical work.

The union of the drama with music, devised in the sixteenth century in Italy for the revival of what they imagined to have been the ancient Greek music-drama, is an artificial form which had, and has, success only among the upper classes, and among them only when gifted composers such as Mozart, Weber, Rossini and others, drawing inspiration from a dramatic subject, yielded freely to the inspiration and subordinated the text to the music, so that in their operas the important thing to the audience is merely the music on a certain text, and not the text at all, which latter, even when it was utterly absurd, as for instance in *The Magic Flute*, still does not prevent the music from producing an artistic impression.

Wagner wishes to correct the opera by letting music submit to the demands of poetry and unite with it. But each art has its own definite realm, which is not identical with the realm of other arts but merely comes into contact with them; and therefore if the manifestations, I will not say of several but even of two arts – the dramatic and the musical – be united in one complete production, then the demands of the one art will make it impossible to fulfil the demands of the other, as has always occurred in ordinary operas, where the dramatic art has submitted to, or rather yielded place to, the musical. Wagner wishes that musical art should submit to dramatic art and that both should appear at full strength. But this is impossible, for every work of art, if it be a true one, is an expression of the intimate feelings of the artist, which are quite peculiar to him and not like anything else. Such is a musical production and such is a dramatic work, if they be true art. And therefore, in order that a production in the one branch of art should coincide with a production in the other branch, it is necessary that the impossible should happen: that two works from different realms of art should be absolutely exceptional, unlike anything that existed before, and yet should coincide and be exactly alike.

And this cannot be, just as there cannot be two men, or even two leaves on a tree, exactly alike. Still less can two works from different realms of art, the musical and the literary, be absolutely alike. If they coincide, then either one is a work of art and the other a counterfeit, or both are counterfeits. Two live leaves cannot be exactly alike but two artificial leaves may be. And so it is with works of art. They can only coincide completely when neither the one nor the other is art, but both are only cunningly devised semblances of it . . .

And such Wagner's productions are. A confirmation of

this is to be seen in the fact that Wagner's new music lacks the chief characteristic of every true work of art, namely, such entirety and completeness that the smallest alteration in its form would disturb the meaning of the whole work. In a true work of art – poem, drama, picture, song or symphony – it is impossible to extract one line, one scene, one figure or one bar from its place and put it in another, without infringing the life of an organic being to extract an organ from one place and insert it somewhere else. But in the music of Wagner's last period, with the exception of certain parts of little importance which have an independent musical meaning, it is possible to make all kinds of transposition, putting what was in front behind and *vice versa*, without altering the musical sense. And the reason why these transpositions do not alter the sense of Wagner's music is because the sense lies in the words and not in the music . . .

Wagner is not only a musician, he is also a poet, or both together; and therefore, to judge of Wagner one must know his poetry also – that same poetry which the music has to subserve. The chief poetical production of Wagner is *The Ring of the Nibelung* . . . It is a model work of counterfeit art so gross as to be even ridiculous.

What is Art?, 1898

GEORGE BERNARD SHAW

First *The Ring*, with all its gods and giants and dwarfs, its water-maidens and Valkyries, its wishing-cap, enchanted sword and miraculous treasure, is a drama of today, and not of a remote and fabulous antiquity. It could not have been written before the second half of the nineteenth century, because it deals with events which were only then consummating themselves. Unless the spectator recognizes in it an image of the life he is himself fighting his way through, it must needs appear to him a monstrous development of the Christmas pantomimes, spun out here and there into intolerable lengths of dull conversation by the principal baritone. *The Ring* is full of extraordinarily attractive episodes, both orchestral and dramatic. The nature music alone – music of river and rainbow, fire and forest – is enough to bribe people with any love of the country in them to endure the passages of political philosophy in the sure hope of a prettier page to come. Everybody, too, can enjoy the love music, the hammer and anvil music, the clumping of the giants, the tune of the young woodsman's horn, the trilling of the bird, the dragon music and nightmare music and thunder and lightning music, the profusion of simple melody, the sensuous charm of the orchestration: in short, the vast extent of common ground between *The Ring* and the ordinary music we use for play and pleasure. Hence it is that the four separate music-plays of which it is built have become popular throughout Europe as operas. We shall presently see that one of them, *Night Falls on the Gods*, actually is an opera . . .

My second encouragement is addressed to modest citizens who may suppose themselves to be disqualified from enjoying *The Ring* by their technical ignorance of music. They may dismiss all such misgivings speedily and confidently. If the sound of music has any power to move them, then they will find that Wagner exacts nothing further. There is not a single bar of 'classical music' in *The Ring* – not a note in it that has any other point than the single direct point of giving musical expression to the drama. In classical music there are, as the analytical programs tell us, first subjects and second subjects, free fantasias, recapitulations and codas; there are fugues, with counter-subjects, strettos and pedal-points; there are passacaglias on ground-basses, canons ad hypodiapente

and other ingenuities, which have, after all, stood or fallen
by their prettiness as much as the simplest folk-tune.
Wagner is never driving at anything of this sort any more
than Shakespeare in his plays is driving at such ingenuities
of verse-making as sonnets, triolets and the like. And this
is why he is so easy for the natural musician who has had
no academic teaching . . . The layman neither knows nor
cares about any of these things. If Wagner were to turn
aside from his straightforward dramatic purpose to prop-
itiate the professors with correct exercises in sonata form,
his music would at once become unintelligible to the
unsophisticated spectator, upon whom the familiar and
dreaded 'classical' sensation would descend like the in-
fluenza. Nothing of the kind need be dreaded. The
unskilled, untaught musician may approach Wagner
boldly; for there is no possibility of a misunderstanding
between them: the *Ring* music is perfectly single and
simple. It is the adept musician of the old school who has
everything to unlearn; and him I leave, unpitied, to his
fate.

'Preliminary Encouragements', from *The Perfect Wagnerite*, 1898

DEBUSSY

Wagner has set a number of precedents in how to write
music for the theatre. One day we shall see how useless
they all are. He evolved, for his own benefit, a 'leitmotif
guide' to help those who are unable to read a score. It is a
perfect idea and makes it possible for the listener to make
his way through the music more quickly. But, more
seriously, he has made us accustomed to regard the music
as serving the function of character-development. I think I
should try to explain this, because it strikes me as the main

problem in modern opera. The inner rhythm of music has a mysterious power which determines the development of the work. But the rhythm of the soul – more instinctive, more general, subject to the pressure of many events. As a result of the incompatibility of these two rhythms, there is a permanent state of conflict, since they do not move at the same speed. Either the music runs out of breath chasing after a character, or the character has to rest on a note so that the music can catch up with him. Yet there are wonderful moments in opera when the two are in harmony, and Wagner bears the credit for having achieved some such moments. But for the most part they are fortuitous, and in addition they are misleading and awkward more often than not. In sum, the superimposition of symphonic form on to dramatic action succeeds in killing opera rather than rescuing it, as it was claimed Wagner had done when he was crowned King of opera.

in *La revue blanche*, 1901

Wagner was a beautiful sunset that has been mistaken for a sunrise.

in *Mercure de France*, 1903

ROMAIN ROLLAND

The quality that touches me most deeply in *Tristan* is the evidence of honesty and sincerity in a man who was treated by his enemies as a charlatan who used superficial and grossly material means to arrest and amaze the public eye. What drama is more sober or more disdainful of exterior effect than *Tristan*? Its restraint is carried almost to excess. Wagner rejected any picturesque episode in it that was irrelevant to his subject. The man who carried all Nature in his imagination, who at his will made the storms of the *Walküre* rage, or the soft light of Good Friday shine, would not even depict a bit of the sea round the vessel in the first act. Believe me, that must have been a sacrifice, though he wished it so. It pleased him to enclose this terrible drama within the four walls of a chamber of tragedy. There are hardly any choruses; there is nothing to distract one's attention from the mystery of human souls; there are only two real parts – those of the lovers; and if there is a third, it belongs to Destiny, into whose hands the victims are delivered. What a fine seriousness there is in this love play! Its passion remains sombre and stern; there is no laughter in it, only a belief which is almost religious, more religious perhaps in its sincerity than that of *Parsifal*.

It is a lesson for dramatists to see a man suppressing all frivolous, trifling and empty episodes in order to concentrate his subject entirely on the inner life of two living souls. In that Wagner is our master, a better, stronger and more profitable master to follow, in spite of his mistakes, than all the other literary and dramatic authors of his time.

'Wagner: a Note on *Siegfried* and *Tristan*', 1915

ERNEST NEWMAN

In a long article on program music in my *Musical Studies* (1905), I have argued that the strictly logical conclusion of Wagner's own theory is not the music drama but the symphonic poem. He himself admitted that the more we can refine away from the music drama all the non-musical matter – the matter that is required merely to make the nature of the characters and the thread of the story intelligible to an audience sitting on the other side of the footlights – the nearer we shall approach to ideal. It was for this reason that he was dissatisfied with his earlier works, and so proud – justifiably proud – of *Tristan*, where, as he said, he 'immersed himself in the depths of the spiritual events pure and simple, and from out of this innermost centre of the world fearlessly fashioned its outward form.' . . . *Tristan* comes nearer to being *all music and nothing else but music* than any other work of Wagner. I suggested that in the symphonic poem, rightly planned and rightly worked out, we had the nearest possible approach to this ideal . . .

It is true that Wagner tried to demonstrate that the symphonic poem was a less perfect art form than the music drama, inasmuch as it left it to the imagination to supply the characters, the events, or the pictures upon which the music is founded, whereas these really ought to be shown to the eye upon the stage. But a twofold answer can be given to Wagner. In the first place, there are dozens of passages in his own works which depend for their effect upon precisely that visualizing power of the imagination the legitimacy of which he denied in the case of the symphonic poem. Is Siegfried's Rhine Journey, for example, intelligible on any other supposition than that with each change of theme in the music the hearer's imagination visualizes a fresh episode in the hero's course? How do we listen to the *Meistersinger* overture except just in the way we listen to a symphonic poem – the imagination calling up before it the bodily presence of each of the characters in turn? In the second place, the evidence is overwhelming that Wagner's own imagination was much more restricted in this respect than that of other people; and it was precisely this inability to trust very much to the visualizing power of the imagination which made him fall into so many crude errors of realism. All his life he was unable to see that the imagination has a much wider scope than the eye because, not being tied down to the mere spatial dimensions of an object, it can add enormously to it out of its own store of memory and vision. Vastness is a quality inseparable from any concept of a god; but can the grandest creation of sculpture or the most heroic of stage figures ever hope to give us such a sense of the illimitable power and beauty of godhead as the imagination can supply? Whose god comes nearest to filling the earth with his presence – the invisible one of Milton or Spinoza, or the visible Wotan of Wagner? Does not the least analytical spectator of a Wagnerian opera often feel that it would have been better if the composer had insisted less on material facts upon the stage and left our imagination a freer wing? . . .

It is the music that accounts for ninety-five per cent of our enjoyment of a Wagner opera. The 'philosophy' of *The Ring* may be something to read or write about in the study, but in the theatre it really goes for very little. It is interesting to talk about the Schopenhauerian or Hindu significance of the discourse of the lovers, in the second act of *Tristan*, upon Love and Death, and Night and Day; but again – for how much does this count in the theatre? Has there ever been a single spectator, since *Tristan* was first given, who could make out from the performance alone what philosophy it was the lovers were talking, or whether they were talking philosophy at all? And how many people who *do* know the text at this point – because they have read it – feel in the theatre that very much of the essential emotion of the work would be lost if the characters sang Chinese words, or Choctaw words, or no words at all, so long as the music was left to tell its own tale?

Wagner as Man and Artist, 1914

THOMAS MANN

Suffering and great as that nineteenth century whose complete expression he is, the mental image of Richard Wagner stands before my eyes. Scored through and through with all his century's unmistakable traits, surcharged with all its driving forces, so I see his image; and scarcely can I distinguish between my two loves: love of his work, as magnificently equivocal, suspect and compelling a phenomenon as any in the world of art, and love of the century during most of which he lived his restless, harassed, tormented, possessed, miscomprehended life, and in which, in a blaze of glory, he died . . .

What is it that raises the works of Wagner to a plane so high, intellectually speaking, above all older musical drama? Two forces contribute, forces and gifts of genius, which one thinks of in general as opposed; indeed, the present day takes pleasure in asserting their essential incompatibility. I mean psychology and the myth. Indeed, psychology does seem too much a matter of reason to admit of our seeing in it no obstacle at all on the path into the land of myth. And it passes as the antithesis of the mythical as of the musical – yet precisely this complex, of psychology, myth, and music, is what confronts us, an organic reality, in two great cases, Nietzsche and Wagner. A book might be written on Wagner the psychologist, on the psychology of his art as musician not less than as poet – in so far as the two are to be separated in him.

Our second phenomenon is Wagner as mythologist, as discoverer of the myth for purposes of the opera, as saviour of the opera through the myth. And truly he has not his like for soul-affinity with this world of thought and image, nor his equal in the power of invoking and reanimating the myth. When he forsook the historical opera for the myth he found himself; and listening to him one is fain to believe that music was made for nothing else, nor could have any other mission but to serve mythology . . .

What I did take exception to, always – or rather, what left me cold – was Wagner's theory. It is hard for me to believe that anyone ever took it seriously. This combination of music, speech, painting, gesture, that gave itself out to be the only true art and the fulfilment of all artistic yearning – what had I to do with this? A theory of art that would make *Tasso* give way to *Siegfried*? I found it hard to swallow, this derivation of the single arts from the disintegration of an original theatrical unity, to which they should all happily find their way back. Art is entire and complete in each of its forms and manifestations; we do not need to add up the different kinds to make a whole . . . Wagner's genius lies in a dramatic synthesis of the arts, which only as a whole, precisely as a synthesis, answers to our conception of a genuine and legitimate work of art. The component parts – even to the music, in itself, not considered as part of a whole – breathe something rank and lawless, that only disappears when they blend into the noble whole . . .

Yes, Wagner is German, he is national, in the most exemplary, perhaps too exemplary, way. For besides being an eruptive revelation of the German nature, his work is likewise a dramatic depiction of the same; a depiction the intellectualism and the poster-like effectiveness of which is positively grotesque, positively burlesque; it seems calculated to move an eager and palpitating world-public to the cry: '*Ah, c'est bien allemand, par exemple!*' Well, then, this Germanness, true and mighty as it is, is very modern – it is broken down and disintegrating, it is decorative, analytical, intellectual; and hence its fascination, its inborn capacity for cosmopolitan, for world-wide effectiveness. Wagner's art is the most sensational self-portrayal and self-critique of the German nature that it is possible to conceive; it is calculated to make Germany interesting to a foreigner even of the meanest intelligence; and passionate preoccupation with it is at the same time passionate preoccupation with the German nature which it so decoratively criticizes and glorifies . . .

A last word upon Wagner's relation to the past and to the future. For here too there reigns a duality, an inter-weaving of apparent contradictions, similar to the antithesis of Germanness and Europeanism which I have just analysed. There are reactionary traits in Wagner, traces of reversion and cult of the dark past; we might interpret in this sense his love of the mystical and mythological; the Protestant nationalism in the *Meistersinger* as well as the Catholic spirit in *Parsifal*; his general fondness for the Middle Ages, for the life of knights and princes, for miracles and perfervid faith.

How would Richard Wagner stand toward our problems, our needs and the tasks before us? That 'would' has a hollow sound, the position is unthinkable. Views are of secondary importance, even in their own present; how much more so when that has become past! What is left is the man, and his work, the product of his efforts. Let us be content to reverence Wagner's work as a mighty and manifold phenomenon of German and Western culture, which will always act as the profoundest stimulus to art and knowledge.

Sufferings and Greatness of Richard Wagner, 1933

VIRGIL THOMSON

Many persons, of course, consider Wagner the *most* satisfactory of the larger musical phenomena. But that he *is* one of the larger musical phenomena is not disputed. What has long been argued about is the nature of the phenomenon and its value to civilization. Its value to individual persons is a private matter, and the voting or ticket-buying power of those persons is a statistical fact. Neither private pleasures, however, nor public devotions prove anything in art. Unless there is unanimous acceptance of a man's work, which is rare, it is the people who don't like it that have the last word in its evaluation.

There is no sounder proof of Shakespeare's central position in English literature, or of Dante's in Italian, than the fact that nobody objects to it. Such a position in music is occupied, through common consent, by a triumvirate – Bach, Beethoven and Mozart. Wagner's pretensions to universal authority are inadmissible from the very fact that the music world is not unanimous about admitting them. Mozart is a great composer, a clear value to humanity, because no responsible musician denies that he is. But Wagner is not an absolute value from the very fact that Rossini denied it and Nietzsche denied it and Brahms denied it and, in our own time, Debussy and Stravinsky have denied it. This does not mean that, with the exception of Rossini, all these composers (including Nietzsche) have not stolen a trick or two from Wagner or accepted him as a major influence on their style. They have. But the fact that they have accepted his work with reservations is what proves my thesis.

. . . the music of Richard Wagner is an achievement somewhat less remarkable than that of the undisputed major masters of our tradition. The argument for this thesis is the simple syllogism that the canonization of a major master in any art requires a virtually unanimous vote of the initiates and that Wagner has never got anything approaching such a vote. He hoped, and many of his friends believed, that he would get it eventually, that the hesitant of spirit would come round. In the decade succeeding his death they seemed to be about to. The peak of his music's prestige within the profession occurred around 1890. The decline of this has been continuous ever since, though there was a notable rise in its popular acceptance between the two world wars. It seems now most unlikely that any thorough or intellectual rehabilitation of Wagner will take place until the wave of his box-office popularity shall have subsided.

Dissent from Wagner, 1943

BRUNO WALTER

There was a deep-seated antagonism to Wagner at the Conservatoire [the Stern Conservatoire in Berlin, 1889], at my parents' house, and among the people with whom I associated. They were all 'classically' minded. Brahms was considered the man to carry on the traditions of great music, and Wagner was the destroyer and corrupter from whom to guard the ear and the soul. To be sure, *Lohengrin* and *Tannhäuser* were beautiful. That was admitted not only by my relatives and acquaintances but also at the Conservatoire, while the true Wagnerites were already beginning to speak of these early works somewhat condescendingly. But the *unisono* of the chorus was to the effect that after *Lohengrin* Wagner had gone astray . . . When I said uncertainly that it was impossible that a composer who had written two operas of such beauty could all at once utterly lose his power, I had to listen to scornful references to '*Wagalaweia*' and '*Hojotoho*'. Besides, the corrupter of the language had also corrupted the music, had abandoned all moderation and form, and had vitiated the sound of the orchestra by the augmentation of brass and percussion instruments. Such noise could not be borne by any cultivated ear, and, more than that – it was added in a low voice – there was another wicked and impure element in Wagner's music. one that was still beyond me. I knew quite well that they were referring to sensuality, which I found rather interesting and by no means wicked. My position in regard to Wagner's tendency to coin new words was weak, for I actually rather disliked it. But my interest in him had mounted mightily. I longed to hear his orchestral sound and found his lack of moderation most attractive . . .

So there I sat in the topmost gallery of the Berlin Opera House, and from the first sound of the cellos my heart contracted spasmodically. The magic, like the terrible potion that the mortally sick Tristan curses in the third act, 'burst raging forth from heart to brain.' Never before had my soul been so deluged with floods of sound and passion, never had my heart been consumed by such yearning and sublime bliss, never had I been transported from reality by such heavenly glory. I was no longer in this world. After the performance I roamed the streets aimlessly. When I got home, I did not say anything and begged not to be questioned. My ecstasy kept singing within me through half the night, and when I awoke on the following morning, I knew that my life was changed. A new epoch had begun: Wagner was my god, and I wanted to become his prophet.

Theme and Variations, 1947

STRAVINSKY

Are Wagner's writings – were they ever – helpful to an understanding of his musico-dramatic art? Can lovers of *Tristan and Isolde* glean any advantage from his clumsy apologetics? I doubt it (though I would not be surprised to hear an academic barrel-scraping 'yes' contradicting me). As I see them, the writings would be most useful simply as Exhibit A in a demonstration of the split between a man's genius and the accessory parts of his mind.

Wagner had little talent for theoretical exposition. He is better with cases, is in fact an acute, if injudicious, critic both of the theatre of his time and of other composers. But he seems to prefer those theoretical rambles. His criticism is remarkable above all, however, because it is governed by a consistent historical point of view. He appears to have been the first great composer to begin from the outside, so to speak, with an analysis of music history, and to have determined his own place in its future from a historical perspective. His view of this role, moreover, seems to have occurred to him almost as early as the awakening of his musical talent; and thereafter it was to remain the 'drive', 'Bayreuth or bust', behind everything he wrote. History pointed straight home to the Fatherland, of course, and, as unerringly as a compass needle, from there to the Wagner front door. Besides that, it directed him away from 'absolute' music (though his own discussions of the term leave one with no clear idea of what he really meant by it) toward the 'unification of the arts' in a new form of 'dramatic expression'. Which may only be a long way of saying that he had the knowledge of his own gifts. And, finally, the accuracy of the historical diagnosis matters only because the prognosis was *Tristan* and *The Ring*.

'Wagner's Prose', 1965

I am not without motive in provoking a quarrel with the notorious Synthesis of the Arts. I do not merely condemn it for its lack of tradition, its *nouveau riche* smugness. What makes its case much worse is the fact that the application of its theories has inflicted a terrible blow on music itself. In every period of spiritual anarchy wherein man, having lost his feeling and taste for ontology, takes fright at himself and at his destiny, there always appears one of these gnosticisms which serve as a religion for those who no longer have a religion, just as in periods of international crisis an army of soothsayers, fakirs and clairvoyants monopolize journalistic publicity. We can speak of these things all the more freely in view of the fact that the halcyon days of Wagnerism are past and that the distance which separates us from them permits us to set matters straight again. Sound minds, moreover, never believed in the paradise of the Synthesis of the Arts and have always recognized its enchantments at their true worth.

I have said that I never saw any necessity for music to adopt such a dramatic system. I shall add something more: I hold that this system, far from having raised the level of musical culture, has never ceased to undermine it and finally to debase it in the most paradoxical fashion. In the past one went to the opera for the diversion offered by facile musical works. Later on one returned to it in order to yawn at dramas in which music, arbitrarily paralyzed by constraints foreign to its own laws, could not help tiring out the most attentive audience in spite of the great talent displayed by Wagner.

So, from music shamelessly considered as a purely sensual delight, we passed without transition to the murky inanities of the Art-Religion, with its heroic hardware, its arsenal of warrior-mysticism and its vocabulary seasoned with an adulterated religiosity. So that as soon as music ceased to be scorned, it was only to find itself smothered under literary flowers. It succeeded in getting a hearing from the cultured public thanks only to a misunderstanding which tended to turn drama into a hodgepodge of symbols, and music itself into an object of philosophical speculation. That is how the speculative spirit came to lose its course and how it came to betray music while ostensibly trying to serve it the better . . .

Wagner's work corresponds to a tendency that is not,

properly speaking, a disorder but one which tries to compensate for a lack of order. The principle of endless melody perfectly illustrates this tendency. It is the perpetual becoming of a music that never had any reason for starting, any more than it has any reason for ending. Endless melody thus appears as an insult to the dignity and to the very function of melody which, as we have said, is the musical intonation of a cadenced phrase. Under the influence of Wagner the laws that secure the life of song found themselves violated, and music lost its melodic smile. Perhaps his method of doing things answered a need; but this need was not compatible with the possibilities of musical art, for musical art is limited in its expression in a measure corresponding exactly to the limitations of the organ that perceives it. A mode of composition that does not assign itself limits becomes pure fantasy. The effects it produces may accidentally amuse but are not capable of being repeated.

Poetics of Music, 1947

ADORNO

Wagner's work bears witness to the early stage of the decay of the bourgeoisie. His urge to destruction is a kind of anticipation of society's urge to destruction; it is in this sense that Nietzsche's critique of Wagner's decadence is valid, not, of course, in a biological sense. But if a decaying society develops in itself the potentialities of the society that may one day take its place, then Nietzsche, like the twentieth-century Russian despotism that came later, failed to comprehend the forces released in the early stage of bourgeois decline. There is no element of decay in Wagner's works from which elements of growth and development could not have been creatively extracted.

The weakening of the monad that is no longer equal to its situation, and thus passively abandons itself to the pressure of the totality, not only has representative validity for a doomed society but at the same time releases what had rigidified in the monad, thus making it the mere 'phenomenon' that it is in Schopenhauer. More of the process of social development finds its way into Wagner's work, weakened by its isolatedness, than into aesthetic subjects, which have shown themselves better able to stand up to society and have thus presented a more solid front against it. Also, the masochistic surrender of the ego is more than just masochistic. To be sure, subjectivity abandons its happiness to death, but in so doing, it realizes that it is not entirely its own master. The monad is 'sick', too feeble to endure. So it surrenders. Its surrender, however, not only helps a rotten society to defeat its protest but ultimately undermines the basis of the monad's own independence. To die in love means among other things, becoming aware, in human terms, of the limits of ownership and possession; it also means learning that, if they were ever thought through to the end, the claims of pleasure and desire would destroy any responsible individual who believed, in his illusion, that he would find pleasure in the possession of his own self; in fact, possession takes this pleasure away from him. To be sure, the mean Siegfried withholds the ring from the Rhine Maidens. But by completing the circle of delusion, he puts behind him the life which, once it has redeemed its promise to him, he no longer needs to retain.

Wagner's work is thus not only the eager prophet and zealous herald of imperialism and neo-bourgeois terror; it also possesses the power, the nervous power, to face its own decay and to transcend this decay through rich, strong images. One may well wonder whether Nietzsche's demand for health is of greater value than the critical consciousness that the grandeur of Wagner's sickness derives from its association with the unconscious forces of its own decay. As he falls, he gains power over himself. His consciousness is forged in the darkness which threatens to engulf consciousness itself. The imperialist dreams the dream of the catastrophe of imperialism, and the bourgeois nihilist grasps the nihilism of the epoch that will succeed him.

Essay on Wagner, 1952

PIERRE BOULEZ

Perhaps Wagner himself provides the best analysis of his own personality. The 'projection' is imprinted like a watermark on many of his writings. Being adventurous – even irrational – and extremely analytical by nature, Wagner reveals to us in his correspondence and his writings an extraordinary perception of his own development and importance, of his impact, as well as of the mechanics of his creative process. Such introspection furnishes us with incredibly perspicacious views on the salient points of his inventiveness, on the cardinal aims of his quest. Indeed, in *Tristan* he describes what we find most obvious in this work, but in addition, and most precisely, he sees the quality that makes it unique in history: a music of transition and not of repetition and retrospection. These thoughts on continuity and transition as indelible stamps of the music of the future are seen again many years later in an arresting conversation with Liszt, in which he states his desire to regenerate the symphony in accordance with the following principle: as Beethoven had exhausted the possibilities of antagonism, of the opposing of themes, so the future would belong to their fusion and their transformation. Such analytical

ability and inventiveness based on analysis are truly
fascinating. Especially with regard to Beethoven, to
whom he felt a particularly close affinity by inheritance,
his private conversations are revelations of the manner in
which he accepted his inheritance. Alongside this 'Germanic orthodoxy' we note on many occasions a mixture of
fascination and amusement vis-à-vis Italian opera – not
the works of his contemporary Verdi but those of popular
composers at the beginning of the nineteenth century.
Although well aware of the superficiality of their musical
content, he was none the less envious of their melodic
invention and expressive power; we note his resolve to
reconcile the two approaches – the German symphonic
tradition and the expressiveness of Italian *bel canto*.
Speaking more generally, he refused to sacrifice expression to polyphony but endowed each voice forming this
polyphony with great expressive power, to the point
where there is almost a conflict of interest: everything is
melody, unending melody. The sensuality and density of
his writing, as well as its continuity on such a wide scale,
were the characteristic qualities which most disturbed his
contemporaries – especially in opera, a field in which the
listener was not particularly discerning. And what of his
harmonic invention, resulting equally from his need for
continuity and his striving for endless transition? The
more he advances, the more often he reaches towards
areas in which certainty of language is lost for long
periods: the uncertainty of development, the fickleness of
the transient solution, the discovery of twilight zones in
which outlines dissolve – these become more and more his
fundamental preoccupations. He abandons the known
absolute of the musical language only to discover a much
wider, more gripping absolute. He abandons established
forms in order to create the fundamental unity of the work
in which each successive moment blends into the next,
thanks to our recollection of individual motifs, each with

an unmistakable identity, which are repeated and metamorphosed to suit the occasion.

Preface to *Wagner – A Documentary Study*, compiled and edited by Herbert Barth, Dietrich Mack and Egon Voss, 1975

Sources

A selection of biographies of Wagner, books on his operas and other secondary works is given in the Bibliography. The following chapter-by-chapter summaries contain information on the main primary sources used and quoted in the text.

There are three autobiographical works that form the basis of any account of Wagner's life: i) the brief *Autobiographical Sketch* of 1842; ii) the longer *Communication to my Friends* of 1851; and iii) the full-length autobiography *Mein Leben* (complete edition by Martin Gregor-Dellin, Munich 1963; the same with a commentary by the same editor, Munich 1976), which covers the years 1813 to 1864. Wagner's diary jottings known as the *Annals* (included in the edition of *Mein Leben* above) carry the story on another four years, to the end of 1868, and the sporadic notes in the so-called 'Brown Book' (Richard Wagner, *Das Braune Buch, Tagebuchaufzeichnungen 1865 bis 1882*, ed. Joachim Bergfeld, Zurich/Freiburg i.Br. 1975) take us to 1882. From 1 January 1869 to 12 February 1883, the day before he died, Cosima Wagner kept a diary (*Die Tagebücher I*, 1869-1877, Munich 1976; *Die Tagebücher II*, 1878-1883, Munich 1977) in which she recorded his activities, his physical and psychological condition, his utterances, the progress of his works and the circumstances of his family life. We thus have a complete record of his life, from birth to death, either in his own words or in Cosima's. And since he dictated the whole of *Mein Leben* to Cosima between 1865 and 1880, her diary and his autobiography ran side by side for eleven years, and the entire story is in her handwriting. The so-called *Lebensbericht*, which appeared in 1884 as a German translation of Richard Wagner, *The Work and Mission of my Life*, published in America in 1879, is the work of Wolzogen.

CHAPTER 1: CHILD, SCHOOLBOY AND STUDENT

Sämtliche Briefe, ed. Gertrud Strobel and Werner Wolf, Vol. I (1830-1842), Leipzig 1967: this first complete edition of Wagner's letters is planned to cover some fifteen volumes, of which three have so far appeared; Vol. I contains details of earlier collections of Wagner's letters. *Letters of Richard Wagner. The Burrell Collection*, ed. John N. Burk, New York 1950: a fascinating catalogue, with biographical editorial material, of letters to and from Wagner, his relatives and friends, pictures, musical scores, newspaper clippings and other documents, most of it from the pre-Cosima period. Mary Burrell, *Richard Wagner. His Life and His Works from 1813 to 1834*, London 1898: a huge (c. 28in. X 22in.) tome, weighing 37 pounds, with 129 pages, printed on handmade paper, the text in hand-engraved script characters, of which only one hundred copies were made and privately presented; a closely documented biography with numerous illustrative prints, facsimiles and copies of letters, broken off by the death of the remarkable Mrs Mary Burrell in 1898. Ferdinand Avenarius, 'Richard Wagner als Kind. Nach Erinnerungen seiner Schwester Cäcilie Avenarius und anderer Jugendgenossen' (*Allgemeine Zeitung*, Munich, 15 March 1883): the author was the son of Cäcilie Avenarius *née* Geyer, Wagner's half-sister.

CHAPTER 2: THE YOUNG PROFESSIONAL

Sämtliche Briefe, ed.cit. Vol.I. *The Burrell Collection, ed.cit. Richard Wagner an Minna Wagner*, 2 vols, Berlin/Leipzig 1908. *Richard Wagners Briefwechsel mit seinen Verlegern*, 2 vols, Leipzig Mainz 1911: Vol.I contains his correspondence with Breitkopf and Härtel, Vol.II that with Schott, from various periods of his life. Sir Charles Hallé, *Autobiography* 1896; new edition edited by Michael Kennedy, London 1972: Hallé met Wagner in Paris in 1840 and again at the Bayreuth Festival in 1876. Berthold Litzmann, *Clara Schumann* Vol.I, Leipzig 1902: personal experiences of Wagner. Friedrich Pecht, 'Aus Richard Wagners Pariser Zeit' (*Allgemeine Zeitung*, Munich, 22 March 1883): reminiscences by a friend of Wagner's, a painter, in Paris in 1840. Hector Berlioz, *Mémoires*, Paris 1870: accounts of meetings with Wagner in Paris and of *Rienzi* and *Der fliegende Holländer* in Dresden in 1843.

CHAPTER 3: ART AND REVOLUTION

Sämtliche Briefe, ed.cit. Vol.II (1842-1849), Leipzig 1970. Ernst Benedikt Kietz, *Richard Wagner in den Jahren 1842-1849 und 1873-1875*, Dresden 1905: recollections of the friend and painter who knew Wagner in Paris and with whom Wagner kept up a regular correspondence. Friedrich Pecht, *Aus meiner Zeit*, Munich 1894: reminiscences from Wagner's years in Dresden. Robert Schumann, *Briefe*, New Series, ed. F. Gustav Jansen, Leipzig 1904: Wagner in Dresden, together with accounts of *Tannhäuser* and *Lohengrin*. Berthold Litzmann, *Clara Schumann*, Vol.I, Leipzig 1907: Clara Schumann's diary of the revolt in Dresden in 1849. Karl Gutzkow, *Lebenserinnerungen* (Gesammelte Werke, Leipzig, 1910): the Young

German writer Gutzkow became dramaturge at the Dresden theatre in 1844 and had a stormy relationship with Wagner there. August Röckel, *Sachsens Erhebung und Die Zuchthaus zu Waldheim*, Frankfurt 1865: an eyewitness account of the 1849 revolt by a leading participant, a comrade-in-arms of Wagner's. *The Letters of Richard Wagner to Anton Pusinelli*, translated and edited by Elbert Lenrow, New York 1932: some 75 letters written between 1843 and 1878, when Pusinelli – family physician to Minna and Richard Wagner for many years – died.

CHAPTER 4: EXILE

Sämtliche Briefe, ed. cit. Vol.III (1849-1851), Leipzig 1975. The Burrell Collection, ed. cit. *Briefwechsel zwischen Wagner und Liszt*, 4th edition ed. Erich Klass, Leipzig 1919: the text of 330 letters written between 1841 and 1882, all but the last ten concentrated in the twenty years 1841-1861, i.e. the years of Wagner's struggle to establish himself. *Briefe an August Röckel*, Leipzig 1912: the Dresden musician and revolutionary who was close to Wagner at the time; many of Wagner's letters were sent to him during his imprisonment between 1849 and 1862. *Briefe an Theodor Uhlig, Wilhelm Fischer, Ferdinand Heine*, Leipzig 1888: friends and colleagues at the Dresden theatre. *Briefe an Mathilde Wesendonk*, ed. Wolfgang Golther, Leipzig 1912. *Briefe Richard Wagners an Otto Wesendonk*, Berlin 1905. *Richard Wagner an Mathilde und Otto Wesendonk. Tagebuchblätter und Briefe*, ed. Julius Kapp, Leipzig 1915. Hans von Bülow, *Briefe und Schriften*, 8 vols, Leipzig 1895-1908; the same, *Neue Briefe*, Munich 1927: Bülow's intimate association with Wagner dates from Wagner's period in exile; there are letters to Wagner and Cosima (see also Wagner, *Briefe an Hans von Bülow*, Jena 1916) and references to family matters in letters to others. *Richard Wagners Briefe an Frau Julie Ritter*, ed. Siegmund von Hausegger, Munich 1920: the mother of Wagner's young admirer Karl Ritter and one of his most generous patrons over the years. Eliza Wille, *Fünfzehn Briefe von Richard Wagner*, Berlin 1894; the same, *Erinnerungen an Richard Wagner*, Munich/ Berlin/Zurich 1935: an authoress who, with her husband François, befriended Wagner in Zurich. Carl Schurz, *Denkwürdigkeiten*, Berlin 1906: memoirs of the German-American politician, only twenty at the time, who was a fellow-exile of Wagner's in Zurich in 1849. Malwida von Meysenbug, *Memoiren einer Idealistin*, 2 vols, Berlin 1917: the revolutionary aristocrat and exile who first met Wagner in London in 1855 and remained a close friend and supporter throughout his life. Peter Cornelius, *Ausgewählte Briefe, nebst Tagebuchblättern und Gelegenheitsgedichten*, 2 vols, Leipzig 1904-5: the composer of the opera *The Barber of Baghdad*, who first met Wagner in 1853 and maintained a close, though not uncritical friendship with him until his death in 1874.

CHAPTER 5: CAREER WITHOUT A CENTRE

The Burrell Collection, ed. cit. *Richard Wagners Brief-wechsel mit seinen Verlegern*, ed. cit. *Richard Wagner an Mathilde und Otto Wesendonk*, ed. cit. *Richard Wagner an Mathilde Maier 1862-1878*, ed. Hans Scholz, Leipzig 1930: Wagner's affair with Mathilde Maier was short-lived but she continued to see both him and Cosima right down to the Bayreuth Festival of 1876 and beyond. *Briefe an eine Putzmacherin*, Vienna 1906: the famous little group of letters written by Wagner between 1864 and 1868 to his milliner in Vienna, showing the extent of his lavish taste in furnishings and materials, and also his chronic lack of funds. Malwida von Meysenbug, op. cit. Hector Berlioz,

A travers chants, Paris 1862: accounts of Wagner's concerts in Paris in 1860. Charles Baudelaire, *Richard Wagner et Tannhäuser à Paris*, Paris 1861: an essay prompted by the fiasco of the 1861 *Tannhäuser* in Paris; this was preceded by a letter of 17 February 1860 to Wagner from Baudelaire, who also attended the Wagner concerts of that year (*Correspondence générale de Charles Baudelaire*, Paris 1963). Wendelin Weissheimer, *Erlebnisse mit Richard Wagner, Franz Liszt und vielen anderen Zeitgenossen*, Stuttgart/Leipzig 1898: a rich young musician who mingled with the great; he first met Wagner at Biebrich in 1862 and remained in contact with him until the end. Eliza Wille, op. cit. Edgar Istel, 'Richard Wagner im Lichte eines zeitgenössischen Briefwechsels' (*Die Musik* I, Berlin 1902): letters by the Viennese conductor Heinrich Esser describing Wagner as man and musician in 1863.

CHAPTER 6: THE ROYAL MIRACLE

The Letters of Richard Wagner to Anton Pusinelli, ed. cit. Richard Wagner, *Briefe an Hans Richter*, Berlin/Vienna/Leipzig 1924: a hundred letters, written between 1868 and 1883 to the horn-player who came to Tribschen as Wagner's secretary, was one of the witnesses at the wedding of Wagner and Cosima in 1870 and conducted *The Ring* at the first Bayreuth Festival in 1876. Cosima Wagner, *Die Tagebücher I*, 1869-1877, Munich 1976: Cosima's record of every day in her and Wagner's life from 1 January 1869 until his death. Carl Friedrich Glasenapp, *Bayreuther Briefe*, Berlin/Leipzig 1907: some 200 letters (1871-1883) from Wagner to Feustel, Muncker and Carl Brandt on the establishment and conduct of the Bayreuth Festival. *König Ludwig II. und Richard Wagner, Briefwechsel*, 5 vols, Karlsruhe 1936-1939: the complete correspondence between Wagner and the King from 1864 to 1883, together with other documents relating to the last eight years of Wagner's life. Eliza Wille, op. cit. Friedrich Pecht, *Aus meiner Zeit*, Munich 1894: later recollections of Wagner by his old painter friend of Paris days who had been in Munich since 1855 and observed the friendship between Wagner and the King. Peter Cornelius, op. cit. Sebastian Röckl, 'Von der Pfordten und Richard Wagner' (*Süddeutsche Monatshefte*, XXV, 1928): Baron Ludwig von der Pfordten was Prime Minister of Bavaria when Ludwig II came to the throne, and thus saw the relationship between his monarch and Wagner from close quarters. Eduard Hanslick, *Music Criticisms 1846-1899*, trans. Henry Pleasants, Harmondworth, 1963; the same, *Aus Meinem Leben*, 2 vols, Berlin, 1894: one of the leading music critics of the day and a bitter opponent of Wagner's music. Friedrich Nietzsche, *Briefe*, Vol. II, Munich 1938: letters to his mother, to Erwin Rohde and to others about his frequent visits to Tribschen between 1868 and 1872. *The Nietzsche-Wagner Correspondence*, ed. Elisabeth Förster-Nietzsche, trans. C. V. Kerr, London, 1922. E. Istel, op. cit.

CHAPTER 7: BAYREUTH

The Burrell Collection, ed. cit., in particular for the account of the diary kept by Susanne Weinert, governess at Wahnfried between 1875 and 1876. *Briefe an Hans Richter*, ed. cit. *Bayreuther Briefe*, ed. cit. *Die Briefe Richard Wagners an Judith Gautier*, ed. Willi Schuh, Zurich/Leipzig 1936: the record of Wagner's last emotional involvement. Carl Friedrich Glasenapp, *Bayreuther Briefe*, ed. cit. *Richard Wagner an Mathilde Maier*, ed. cit. Cosima Wagner, *Die Tagebücher I*, ed. cit.; *II*, 1878-1883, Munich 1977. Gustav Adolf Kietz, *Richard Wagner in den*

Jahren 1842–1849 und 1873–1875, ed. cit. Paul Lindau,
Nüchterne Briefe aus Bayreuth, Breslau/Leipzig 1876: a
Berlin critic's view of the Bayreuth scene at the time of the
first Festival. Siegfried Wagner, *Erinnerungen*, Stuttgart
1923: memoirs of Wagner's and Cosima's son, who was
thirteen when his father died. Franz Liszt, *Briefe*, ed. La
Mara, 2 vols, Leipzig 1909: many references to Bayreuth,
in particular to *Parsifal*. Sir Charles Hallé, op. cit. Judith
Gautier, *Le troisième rang due collier*, Paris 1909: her
memories of Wagner from Tribschen in 1869 to Wahnfried. Malwida von Meysenbug, op. cit. Berthold Kellermann, *Erinnerungen*, Stuttgart, 1932: a young musician
who became a copyist and piano tutor at Wahnfried in
1878. Eduard Hanslick, op. cit. Richard Fricke, *Bayreuth
vor dreissig Jahren: Erinnerungen an Wahnfried und aus
dem Festspielhause*, Dresden 1906: the reminiscences of
the choreographer whom Wagner brought to Bayreuth for
the Festival of 1876. Tchaikovsky's account of his visit to
Bayreuth in 1776 was published posthumously (*Musikalische Erinnerungen und Feuilletons*, Berlin 1899). The
quotation from Hans Keller is taken from his review of
Cosima Wagner's Diary in *Wagner*, 61, London 1977.

Bibliography

Adorno, Theodor W., *Versuch über Wagner*, Frankfurt, 1952

Bainville, Jacques, *Louis II de Bavière, Paris, 1964*

Barth, Herbert, *Bayreuth in der Karikatur*, Bayreuth 1957

Barzun, Jacques, *Darwin, Marx, Wagner*, 2nd ed., New York, 1958

Bekker, Paul, *Richard Wagner, Das Leben im Werke*, Stuttgart, 1924

Bélart, Hans, *Richard Wagner in Zürich 1849–1858*, 2 vols, Leipzig, 1900-1

Böhm, Gottfried von, *Ludwig II, König von Bayern, Sein Leben und seine Zeit*, Berlin, 1922

Bory, Robert, *La vie et l'oeuvre de Richard Wagner par l'image*, Paris, 1938

Boucher, Maurice, *The Political Concepts of Richard Wagner*, trans. Marcel Honoré, London/New York, 1950

Bülow, Hans von, *Letters of Hans von Bülow*, trans. Hannah Waller, London/New York, 1931

—*Briefe und Schriften*, 8 vols, Leipzig, 1895-1908

—*Neue Briefe*, ed. Richard Graf du Moulin Eckart, Munich, 1927

The Burrell Collection ed. John N. Burk, New York, 1950

Burrell, Mary, *Richard Wagner, His Life and his Works from 1813 to 34*, London, 1898

Chamberlain, Houston Stewart, *Richard Wagner*, Munich, 1896

—*Richard Wagner*, trans. G. Ainslie Hight, London/Philadelphia, 1897

Conrad, Peter, *Romantic Opera and Literary Form*, Berkeley, Calif., 1978

Cornelius, Peter, *Ausgewählte Briefe, nebst Tagebuch-blättern und Gelegenheitsgedichten*, 2 vols, Leipzig, 1904-5

Culshaw, John, *Reflections on Wagner's 'Ring'*, London/New York, 1976

Curzon, Henri de, *L'oeuvre de Richard Wagner à Paris et ses interprètes (1850-1914)*, Paris, 1920

Donington, Robert, *Wagner's 'Ring' and its Symbols*, London/New York, 1963

Dorn, Heinrich, *Aus meinem Leben*, 3 vols, Berlin, 1870-2

Eckart, Richard Graf du Moulin, *Cosima Wagner*, 2 vols, Munich, 1929, 1931

—*Cosima Wagner* trans. Catherine Alison Phillips, 2 vols, New York, 1931

Einstein, Alfred, *Music in the Romantic Era*, London/New York, 1954

Ellis, William Ashton, *Life of Richard Wagner*, 6 vols, London, 1900-8

Engel, Erich W., *Richard Wagners Leben und Werke im Bilde*, 2nd ed., Leipzig, 1922

Fehr, Max, *Richard Wagners Schweizer Zeit*, 2 vols, Aarau/Leipzig, 1934, 1953

Der Festspielhügel, Richard Wagners Werk in Bayreuth 1876-1976, Munich, 1976

Finck, Henry T., *Wagner and his Works*, 2 vols, 7th ed., New York/London, 1904

Fischer-Dieskau, Dietrich, *Wagner und Nietzsche*, Stuttgart, 1974, trans. Joachim Neugroschel, New York, 1976

Förster-Nietzsche, Elisabeth, *Wagner und Nietzsche zur Zeit ihrer Freundschaft*, Munich, 1915

—*The Nietzsche-Wagner Correspondence*, trans. Caroline V. Kerr, London/New York, 1921

Fricke, Richard, *Bayreuth vor dreissig Jahren*, Dresden, 1906

Gal, Hans, *Richard Wagner*, trans. Hans-Hubert Schönzeler, London/New York, 1976

Ganzer, Karl Richard, *Richard Wagner, der Revolutionär gegen das 19. Jahrhundert*, Munich, 1934

Garten, H. F., *Wagner the Dramatist*, London, 1977

Gautier, Judith, *Le troisième rang du collier*, Paris, 1909

—*Wagner at Home*, trans. Effie Dunreith Massie, London, 1910

Geck, Martin, *Die Bildnisse Richard Wagners*, Munich, 1976

Glasenapp, Carl Friedrich, *Das Leben Richard Wagners*, 6 vols, Leipzig, 1894-1911

Gregor-Dellin, Martin, *Richard Wagner – die Revolution als Oper*, Munich, 1973

—*Wagner-Chronik*, Munich, 1972

Grout, Donald Jay, *A Short History of Opera*, New York/London, 1947

Gutman, Robert W., *Richard Wagner, The Man, His Mind and His Music*, London/New York, 1968

Hanslick, Eduard, *Vienna's Golden Years of Music 1850-1900*, trans. Henry Pleasants III, London/New York, 1950

Herzfeld, Friedrich, *Königsfreundschaft, Ludwig II und Richard Wagner*, Leipzig, 1939

—*Minna Planer und ihre Ehe mit Richard Wagner*, Leipzig, 1938

Hildebrandt, Kurt, *Wagner und Nietzsche, ihr Kampf gegen das 19. Jahrhundert*, Breslau, 1924

Hohenlohe, Marie von, *Erinnerungen an Richard Wagner*, Weimar, 1938

Hollingdale, R. J., *Nietzsche, The Man and his Philosophy*, London, 1965

Hutcheson, Ernest, *A Musical Guide to the 'Ring of the Nibelung'*, New York/Toronto, 1940

Jacobs, Robert L., *Wagner*, London 1947/New York, 1949

Kapp, Julius, *Wagner und Liszt, Eine Freundschaft*, Berlin, 1908

—*Wagner und die Frauen*, Berlin, 1912

—*The Women in Wagner's Life*, trans. Hannah Waller, London, 1932

Karbaum, Michael, *Studien zur Geschichte der Bayreuther Festspiele*, Regensburg, 1976

Kaufmann, Walter, *Nietzsche: Philosopher, Psychologist, Antichrist*, Cleveland/New York, 1962

Kellermann, Berthold, *Erinnerungen*, Zurich/Leipzig, 1932

Kerman, Joseph, *Opera as Drama*, New York/Oxford, 1956

Kietz, Ernst Benedikt, *Richard Wagner in den Jahren 1842-1849 und 1873-1875*, Dresden, 1905

Kohn, Hans, *The Mind of Germany*, New York/London, 1960

Kreowski, Ernst and Fuchs, Eduard, *Richard Wagner in der Karikatur*, Berlin, 1907

Lippert, Woldemar, *Richard Wagners Verbannung und Rückkehr 1849-1862*, Dresden, 1927

—*Wagner in Exile*, trans. Paul England, London, 1930

Loos, Paul Arthur, *Richard Wagner, Vollendung und Tragik der deutschen Romantik*, Bern/Munich, 1952

Magee, Bryan, *Aspects of Wagner*, London, 1968/New York, 1969

Mann, Thomas, *Essays of Three Decades*, trans. H. T. Lowe-Porter, London/New York, 1947

Mayer, Hans, *Richard Wagner in Selbstzeugnissen und Bilddokumenten*, Reinbek, 1959

—*Richard Wagner in Bayreuth 1876-1976*, London/New York, 1976

Mendès, Catulle, *Richard Wagner*, Paris, 1886

Meysenbug, Malwida von, *Memoiren einer Idealistin*, 2 vols, Stuttgart/Berlin/Leipzig, 1927

Millenkovich-Morold, Max, *Cosima Wagner: Ein Lebensbild*, Leipzig, 1937

—*Richard Wagner in Wein*, Leipzig, 1938

Neumann, Angelo, *Erinnerungen an Richard Wagner*, Leipzig, 1907

—*Personal Recollections of Wagner*, trans. Edith Livermore, New York, 1908

Newman, Ernest, *The Life of Richard Wagner*, 4 vols, London/New York, 1933-46

—*Wagner as Man and Artist*, London/New York, 1914

—*The Wagner Operas*, New York/Glasgow, 1949

—*Wagner Nights*, London/New York, 1949

Osborne, Charles, *Wagner and His World*, London/New York, 1977

Panofsky, Walter, *Wagner – A Pictorial Biography*, London/Ontario, 1963

Petzet, Detta and Michael, *Die Richard-Wagner-Bühne König Ludwigs II.*, Munich, 1976

Scheffler, Siegfried, *Richard Wagner, Sein Leben, seine Persönlichkeit und seine Werke*, 2 vols, Hamburg, 1928

Schemann, Ludwig, *Meine Erinnerungen an Richard Wagner*, Stuttgart, 1902

Shaw, George Bernard, *The Perfect Wagnerite*, London/New York, 1898

Sitwell, Sacheverell, *Liszt*, London/New York, 1955

Skelton, Geoffrey, *Wagner at Bayreuth*, London/New York, 1965

Stein, Herbert von, *Dichtung und Musik im Werk Richard Wagners*, Berlin, 1962

Stein, Jack M., *Richard Wagner and the Synthesis of the Arts*, Detroit, 1960

Stein, Leon, *The Racial Thinking of Richard Wagner*, New York, 1950

Stempflinger, Eduard, *Richard Wagner in München 1864-70*, Munich, 1933

Strobel, Otto, *Richard Wagner über sein Schaffen*, Munich, 1924

Tappert, Wilhelm, *Richard Wagner im Spiegel der Kritik*, Leipzig, 1903

—*Wörterbuch der Unhöflichkeit Richard Wagners im Spiegel der zeitgenössischen Kritik*, Munich, 1976

Taylor, Ronald, *The Romantic Tradition in Germany*, London, 1970

—*The Intellectual Tradition of Modern Germany*, London, 1973

Viereck, Peter, *Metapolitics: The Roots of the Nazi Mind*, New York/Toronto, 1961

Wagner, Cosima, *Briefe an Ludwig Schemann*, Regensburg, 1937

—*Briefe an ihre Tochter Daniela von Bülow 1866–85*, Stuttgart/Berlin, 1933

—*Die Briefe Cosima Wagners an Friedrich Nietzsche*, 2 vols, Weimar, 1938, 1940

—*Die Tagebücher*, 2 vols, Munich, 1976, 1977

Wagner, Richard, *Gesammelte Schriften und Dichtungen*, 10 vols, ed. Wolfgang Golther, Berlin, 1914

—*Gesammelte Schriften*, 14 vols, ed. Julius Kapp, Leipzig, 1914

Richard Wagner's Prose Works, trans. William Ashton Ellis, 8 vols, London, 1892-99

—*Stories and Essays*, ed. Charles Osborne, New York, 1973

—*Wagner on Music and Drama*, arr. Albert Goldman and Evert Sprinchorn, London, 1970

—*The Ring of the Nibelung*, German text with English translation by Andrew Porter, London/New York, 1976

—*Mein Leben (Vollständiger Text)*, ed. Martin Gregor-Dellin, Munich, 1963

—*My Life*, 2 vols, London, 1963

—*Sämtliche Werke (In Zusammenarbeit mit der Bayeris-*

chen Akademie der Schönen Künste), ed. Carl Dahlhaus, Munich, 1970-

—*Sämtliche Briefe*, ed. Gertrud Strobel and Werner Wolf, Leipzig, 1967-

—*Letters of Richard Wagner*, trans. M. M. Bozman, 2 vols, London, 1927

—*Letters of Richard Wagner: The Burrell Collection*, ed. John N. Burk, New York, 1950

—*Briefe in Originalausgaben*, 17 vols, Leipzig, 1912

—*Bayreuther Briefe*, ed. C. Glasenapp, Berlin/Leipzig, 1907

—*The Story of Bayreuth as told in the Bayreuth Letters of Richard Wagner*, trans. Caroline V. Kerr, London/Boston, Mass., 1912

—*Briefe an Hans Richter*, ed. Ludwig Karpath, Berlin/Vienna/Leipzig, 1924

—*Briefe an Hans von Bülow*, Jena, 1916

—*Briefe Richard Wagners an eine Putzmacherin*, ed. Daniel Spitzer, Vienna, 1906

—*Richard Wagner and the Seamstress*, trans. Sophie Prombaum, New York, 1941

—*Die Briefe Richard Wagners an Judith Gautier*, ed. Willi Schuh, Zürich/Leipzig, 1936

—*Briefe Richard Wagners an Otto Wesendonk*, Berlin, 1905

—*Briefe an Mathilde Wesendonk*, ed. Wolfgang Golther, Leipzig, 1912

—*Richard Wagner an Mathilde und Otto Wesendonk, Tagebuchblätter und Briefe*, ed. Julius Kapp, Leipzig, 1915

—*Richard Wagner: Letters to Wesendonk et al.*, trans. William Ashton Ellis, London, 1899

—*Richard Wagner to Mathilde Wesendonk*, trans. William Ashton Ellis, New York, 1905

—*Briefwechsel zwischen Wagner und Liszt*, 2 vols, Leipzig, 1910

—*Correspondence of Wagner and Liszt*, trans. Francis Hueffer, 2 vols, London, 1888

—*Familienbriefe von Richard Wagner 1832–1874*, Berlin, 1907

—*Family Letters of Richard Wagner*, trans. William Ashton Ellis, London, 1911

—*König Ludwig II. und Richard Wagner, Briefwechsel*, ed. Otto Strobel, 5 vols, Karlsruhe, 1936-9

—*The Letters of Richard Wagner to Anton Pusinelli*, trans. Elbert Lenrow, New York, 1932

—*Lettres françaises*, ed. Julien Tiersot, Paris, 1935

—*Richard Wagner an August Röckel*, Leipzig, 1912

—*Richard Wagner's Letters to August Röckel*, trans. Eleanor C. Sellar, London, 1897

—*Richard Wagner an Ferdinand Praeger*, ed. Houston Stewart Chamberlain, Berlin/Leipzig, 1908

—*Richard Wagner an Freunde und Zeitgenossen*, ed. Erich Kloss, Berlin/Leipzig, 1908

—*Richard Wagner an Mathilde Maier*, 1862–1878, ed. Hans Scholz, Leipzig, 1930

—*Richard Wagner an Minna Wagner*, 2 vols, Berlin/Leipzig, 1908

—*Richard to Minna Wagner: Letters to his First Wife*, trans. William Ashton Ellis, London/New York, 1909

—*Richard Wagner an seine Künstler*, ed. Erich Kloss, Berlin/Leipzig, 1908

—*Richard Wagner an Theodor Apel*, Leipzig, 1910

—*Briefe an Frau Julie Ritter*, ed. Siegmund von Hausegger, Munich, 1920

—*Briefe an Theodor Uhlig, Wilhelm Fischer, Ferdinand Heine*, Leipzig, 1888

—*Richard Wagner's Letters to his Dresden Friends Theodor Uhlig, Wilhelm Fischer and Ferdinand Heine*, trans. J. S. Shedlock, London/New York, 1890

—*Richard Wagners Briefe nach Zeitfolge und Inhalt*, ed. Wilhelm Altmann, Leipzig, 1905

—*Richard Wagners Briefwechsel mit seinen Verlegern*, ed. Wilhelm Altmann, 2 vols, Leipzig/Mainz, 1911

—*Richard Wagner und Albert Niemann*, ed. Wilhelm Altmann, Berlin, 1924

—and Wagner, Cosima, *Lettres à Judith Gautier*, ed. Lon Guichard, Paris, 1964

Wagner. A Documentary Study, ed. Herbert Barth, Dietrich Mack and Egon Voss, London/New York, 1975

Wagner 1976. A Celebration of the Bayreuth Festival, Wagner Society, London, 1976

Richard Wagners photographische Bildnisse, ed. A. Vanselow, Munich, 1908

Wagner, Siegfried, *Erinnerungen*, Stuttgart, 1923

Wagner, Wieland, *Richard Wagner und das neue Bayreuth*, Munich, 1962

Walzel, Oscar, *Richard Wagner in seiner Zeit und nach seiner Zeit*, Munich, 1913

Weingartner, Felix, *Erinnerungen*, Stuttgart, 1913

—*Buffets and Rewards: A Musician's Reminiscences*, trans. Marguerite Wolff, London, 1937

Weissheimer, Wendelin, *Erlebnisse mit Richard Wagner, Franz Liszt und vielen anderen Zeitgenossen nebst deren Briefen*, Stuttgart/Leipzig, 1898

Westernhagen, Curt von, *Richard Wagner: Sein Welt, sein Wesen, seine Welt*, Zurich, 1956

—*Wagner*, Zurich, 1968

—*The Forging of the 'Ring': Richard Wagner's Composition Sketches for 'Der Ring des Nibelungen'*, trans. Arnold and Mary Whittall, Cambridge, 1976

Wille, Eliza, *Erinnerungen an Richard Wagner*, Munich/Berlin/Zurich, 1935

—*Fünfzehn Briefe von Richard Wagner nebst Erinnerungen und Erläuterungen*, Berlin, 1894

Wolzogen, Hans von, *Erinnerungen an Richard Wagner*, Leipzig, 1892

Zarek, Otto, *The Tragic Idealist, Ludwig II of Bavaria*,

trans. Ella Goodman and Paul Sudley, London/New York, 1939

Zeh, Gisela, *Das Bayreuther Bühnenkostüm*, Munich, 1976

Zuckerman, Elliott, *The First Hundred Years of Wagner's Tristan*, New York, 1964

Index